THE LIBERATION
OF AMERICAN LITERATURE

THE LIBERATION
OF
AMERICAN LITERATURE

BY

V. F. CALVERTON

OCTAGON BOOKS

A DIVISION OF FARRAR. STRAUS AND GIROUX

New York   1973

Copyright, 1932, by Charles Scribner's Sons

Copyright renewed 1960 by Nina Melville Berdeshevsky

Reprinted 1973
by special arrangement with Mrs. Margo Ann Solin

OCTAGON BOOKS
A DIVISION OF FARRAR, STRAUS & GIROUX, INC.
19 Union Square West
New York, N. Y. 10003

Library of Congress Cataloging in Publication Data

Calverton, Victor Francis, 1900-1940.
  The liberation of American literature.

    1. American literature—History and criticism.   I. Title.

[PS88.C26   1973]   810'.9   73-404
ISBN 0-374-91245-9

Printed in USA by
Thomson-Shore, Inc.
Dexter, Michigan

CONTENTS

PREFACE

In a sense, this book is as much a study of American culture as it is of American literature, for its aim is to interpret American literature in terms of American culture. The American cultural pattern, shaped as it has been by the conflicting class interests in American society, has revealed a number of new and contradictory characteristics, distinguishing it from the cultural patterns of various European countries. These differentiating characteristics have reflected themselves in manifest form in the spirit of American literature. It is the relationship between that cultural pattern and the character of our literature which I have tried to trace in this study.

To have dealt with that relationship in all its varied implications would have required a study far more extensive than this one, indeed, one which would have filled several volumes instead of one. My aim obviously was not so ambitious. What I have attempted to do is to point out general tendencies rather than deal with specific details. At best I have tried to get at the root-factors in American culture which have determined the nature of our literature. It is only by an appreciation of the class psychologies dominant at the time, as Marx has shown, that we can understand the nature of a culture or the direction and trend of a literature. While literature is possessed of an imaginative element which makes it assume forms which are more elusive than economic charts and political programmes, the roots of that imagination lie as close to the culture from which they have arisen as do the less imaginative materials of economics and politics. The point of difficulty, of course, is to trace those imaginative elements to their roots, and discover the kind of soil from which they have sprung. In the case of economics and politics the task is somewhat easier because the evidence is more obvious and tangible. In the field of literature, on the other hand, the task is rendered more difficult by the intrusion of emotional factors and individual eccentricities and deviations which complicate both the nature of the analysis and the problem of evaluation. In addition to the matter of content, there is also the element of form which must be considered. In a fundamental sense, to be sure, content and form are inseparable, and constitute indisseverable parts of the same synthesis, and it is the object of literary criticism per se to analyze and evaluate literary creations in terms of that synthesis. Considered from that view point, this study does not fall as closely into the category of literary criticism as into that of social history. Aside from the inevitable use of adjectives here and there, indicating the quality of an author's work, I have intentionally avoided the problem of æsthetic analysis and evaluation. In short, as an expedient, I have taken the æsthetic element for granted, and in almost all cases have immediately proceeded to an analysis of the philosophy, or ideology if you will, that underlay the individual author's work. From the point of view of literary criticism such an expedient would prove disastrous, but, as I said above, in this book I have not been interested in that problem at all, or at least not in its specific applications to the work of individual authors. Instead I have been concerned with the nature of the culture, its class-roots, and the degree to which that culture expressed itself in the work of American writers.

I should not want the reader, however, to think that I consider the matter of æsthetic evaluation of little consequence. On the contrary, I should say that literary criticism is futile without it. Nevertheless, I believe that æsthetic criticism is fundamentally social in character, and can only be significant when derived from a sound social philosophy. What I have endeavored to do in this study, then, has been to trace the development of American literature in relationship with those social forces, expressed in the form of class content, which it is necessary for us to understand first if we are to work out a sound critical method. Without such an understanding, criticism cannot found itself upon a secure social basis, and all analysis of the æsthetic element can amount to nothing more than subjective caprice.

I have not tried to include the whole of American literature within my scope, but, as I shall point out later on in this preface, I have definitely omitted certain sections of it and certain writers from my consideration. I have limited myself to the task of clearing away, as far as I can, those confusions of background which have arisen in the past from our failure to consider the class forces active in the creation of American literature—and American culture. That task alone is a huge one, and I lay no claim to have done more than begin what I am certain many others will do much more to clarify and complete within the next few years. Unfortunately, due to the nature of the American environment which has made American thinkers adopt a different outlook, few American writers have been interested in the influence of class factors in our cultural life. As a result much spade work remains to be done, and until that spade work is completed no final synthesis of American culture can be effected. While I have attempted to do a small part of that spade work, it should be obvious at once to any one intimate with the field that such spade work must be carried out by many hands for more than a few years before materials adequate to the Marxian approach will be at our disposal. Happily enough, there are at this very time more than a few of the younger critics who are beginning to dig away at those materials, unearthing significant parts of them that hitherto have been obscured or neglected, and revaluating those that already have been unearthed. Within a few years, we should have enough materials at hand to begin a more extensive and exhaustive reinterpretation and revaluation of American literature and culture.

In another book which is to follow this, almost a sequel to it in a sense, I plan making a study of eight American writers, Cotton Mather, Jonathan Edwards, Ralph Waldo Emerson, John Greenleaf Whittier, Walt Whitman, Henry James,

Theodore Dreiser, and Sinclair Lewis, tracing in that study the fusion of background with personality, and considering in detail the nature of the æsthetic elements embodied in their works. In that study I also hope to complete that synthesis which is not attempted in this volume, devoted as it is to tendencies rather than to individuals, but which, as I suggested above, is the *sine qua non* of literary criticism.

Obviously in a volume which makes no pretense at completeness, there are many omissions which I found it necessary to make in order to keep it within the scope of my design. The Abolitionist movement, for example, I have treated with undeserving brevity because it falls somewhat without the radius of my immediate concern, and because, in its way, it represents a derivative outgrowth of a more fundamental force which I have dealt with in ample detail in several chapters of this volume. In the study which I plan to make of Whittier, which will appear in the book noted above, I shall give the Abolitionist movement that consideration which it undoubtedly merits. I have also avoided discussion of the Expatriates because it does not bear immediately upon the tendencies which I have discussed in this volume, and likewise because I intend taking up their problem in my chapter on Henry James in the volume which will complement this one.

Another omission, or rather shift in emphasis, which I should note in order to avoid misunderstanding on the part of the reader, is the fact that I have purposely devoted little space to the consideration of French and German influences upon American literature. On the other hand, I have treated in detail the prevalence of the English influence which was the dominant one, and which, expressing itself in the form of the *colonial complex*, continued to shape the character of American literature until near the close of the nineteenth century. While French and German influences were unquestionably potent at various periods, their impact was felt much less keenly in literature than in the other arts, in particular music and the opera. In addition, for years now academic critics have discussed and rediscussed the matter of European influences, and in many cases without ever examining the American facts in the case, or attempting to come to grips with the forces in the American environment which made it so receptive to those influences. (Fortunately, Howard Mumford Jones, in his admirable study, *America and French Culture,* which deals with French influences upon American life, has escaped that fallacy.) If I have thus shifted the emphasis somewhat, it has not been because I deny in any way the presence of those influences, or even the wisdom of tracing them, but because I believe the more important problem is to understand the nature of the American environment which in the past was so prone to absorb them. No foreign influence, as, for instance, the Transcendentalist movement, could make headway in the American environment, it is my contention, unless the conditions of American culture were receptive to it. Individual thinkers or writers might adopt European ideas or tendencies, but the test of their success or failure was ultimately determined by the character of the native cultural environment at the time. Important as it is to know the European source of such ideas, then, it is even more important, in my opinion, to know what were the conditions in the American environment which made it absorb certain of those ideas and reject others. If in places, therefore, I have done little more than note in brief fashion the European source of certain American ideas, and have dealt in extensive detail with the American form which those ideas took, it has been simply because I believe it is more significant for us to analyze the American side of the case, which has been altogether too much neglected, if we are to understand the social forces in our life that have determined the development of American literature—and culture.

V. F. CALVERTON.

NEW YORK,
February 6, 1932.

THE LIBERATION
OF AMERICAN LITERATURE

THE LIBERATION OF AMERICAN
LITERATURE

CHAPTER I

THE COLONIAL COMPLEX

FROM its very beginnings American literature derived
its inspiration from English soil. It carried over with
it the seeds of English culture, in language, in spirit,
in tradition. For a long time the colonists thought of themselves as Englishmen and viewed their work as belonging
more to England than to America. Almost every American
writer in those days was in close touch with the English authors of his time, seeking thus to preserve that cultural continuity which he considered most precious.

It was as a colonial literature, then, that American literature began, and it was as a result of its colonial heritage that
it took on its early forms and convictions. Like every colonial literature, American literature inevitably suffered from
all the handicaps of such a heritage: intellectual inferiority,
artistic imitativeness, and cultural retardation. In its attempt
to express itself it was more devoted to its maternal background than to its immediate environment. While its poets
and preachers—as well as its merchants and workers—were
occupied with the inescapable tasks of taming a hostile environment, their literary effusions, in poem and sermon,
might have been written or spoken almost as easily in England as in America, so obviously did they stem from the
English tradition.

As is the case with all colonies, the colonial environment
becomes first a place upon which old traditions are fastened

and not a setting in which new traditions are conceived. It is only as the colony grows away from its maternal matrix that a new tradition can arise. By that time, however, the old tradition, in language as well as in spirit, has rooted itself so deeply into the colonial culture that even that which aspires to be new is inevitably burdened with much that is old. Every colonial literature, we can say, therefore, goes through several stages of development; first, the stage of determined adaptation, in which the colonials attempt to adapt their original culture to the new environment, stressing continuity between the old and the new; second, the stage in which the colonials begin to become conscious of themselves, national-minded, as it were, and in which the new conditions have already begun to modify the old traditions to such an extent that differences become more important than resemblances; at this point, inaugurating the third stage in the process, the struggle for freedom from the mother culture becomes apparent and revolt in favor of a national culture takes on a definite turn; in the fourth and final stage the colonial literature, if the colony grows of itself and the environment provides it with sufficient strength definitely to sever its umbilical connections with the mother country, manages to create a national literature of its own.[1] In a fundamental

---

[1] Canadian, South African, and Australian literatures have all gone through certain of these stages, in accordance with the different economic and political factors involved. Even Norse literature, which at one time was dominated by the culture of Denmark, went through several aspects of the same process. In early Canadian literature, for example, we find Canadian authors sycophantically emulative of their English predecessors and contemporaries. As late as July, 1823, in the *Canadian Magazine and Literary Repository* we discover the editor stating that the aim of the magazine is to aid "in keeping alive the heroic and energetic sentiments of our (English) ancestors." The literature itself, to be sure, bore out this influence in irrefragable detail. (Cf. Ray Palmer Baker: *History of English-Canadian Literature to the Confederation . . . Its Relation to the Literature of Great Britain and the United States:* p. 65.) Later on in the nineteenth century, in the stage in which the colonials begin to become conscious of themselves, we find such Canadian writers as Roberts, Johnson, Saunders, and Carmen becoming national-minded, and showing more concern for their own environment than for that of the mother culture. They found their inspiration, as Doctor Logan has indicated, "in the natural beauty and sublimity of their country and the lives of their com-

sense, however, it must be remembered that no colonial literature ever succeeds in completely separating itself from its maternal origins. Its linguistic kinship alone links it in a most intimate way with the mother culture. For that reason one still can observe in American literature, which is the only colonial literature to reach the fourth stage in the colonial process, evidences of the fact that in certain respects it is still a colonial literature, although, in the main, in recent years, it has undoubtedly begun to develop an American tradition.

American literature reflects all these stages of change and conflict in striking detail. Indeed, one can say at the very outset that it is these changes and conflicts, occasioned by its colonial heritage, that have determined in large degree the

patriots. . . . In short, their literary conspectus is thoroughly Canadian; and their inspiration and ideals too are Canadian." (Cf. J. D. Logan: *Highways of Canadian Literature:* Toronto, 1924: p. 106.) With the coming of the Confederation, Canadian literature entered the third stage in the colonial process, in which revolt in favor of a native literature became insistent. It was at that time that the slogan "Canada first" became popular. "People begin to see from the Canadian view point," as Bernard Muddemain noted. . . . "Something indefinable has now arisen which is absolutely unexplainable as a purely literary factor. It is the Canadian spirit as begotten in the political contests and struggles that were to culminate in the Confederation. . . . It is Canada for the Canadians, and the immigrant as a literary force is past. A native literature is arising." (Cf. Bernard Muddemain: *Queens Quarterly*, Vol. XX, July, 1912—April, 1913: Kingston article, *The Immigrant Element in Canadian Literature:* p. 415.) Despite this protest, and the many evidences of change that went with it, Canadian literature has not escaped the influence of the colonial complex any more than Australian literature—or than American literature had prior to the twentieth century. It is only in the fourth stage, which Canadian, South African, and Australian literatures have not yet reached, that the effects of the colonial complex can be considerably diminished if not altogether eradicated.

Australian literature has gone through practically the same stages as the Canadian and the American. The early writers in Australia were as imitative of British writers as were the early writers in Canada and the United States. In fact, as H. M. Green has shown, they "neither learned to live in their new country nor to see it with their own eyes." (Cf. H. M: Green: *An Outline of Australian Literature:* Sydney and Melbourne, 1930: p. 22.) Since 1845 Australian literature has gone through the second and now is in the third stage of the process—the stage in which Australian writers are striving as hard as they can to be Australian first of all. As is pointed out in a later part of this chapter, in which the changing aspects of the American colonial complex are dealt with in more definite detail, this attempt to be native, this straining after the indigenous, is more of character and tendency of American literature throughout the seventeenth, eighteenth, and most of the nineteenth centuries. Our writers have been either openly imitative of their English contemporaries and predecessors, and obsequious of their approval, or they have been in definite revolt against them in an attempt to escape their dominancy. This very struggle toward imitation, on the one hand, and toward revolt against imitation on the other, exercised a most disastrous influence upon our literary life. It throttled our creative energies, warped their expression, and, by setting them at cross purposes to one another, divided their strength and

an evidence of the continuance of the complex than of its disappearance. It marks rather a change in the nature of the complex itself than an escape from it. Even to-day, for instance, notwithstanding their emphasis upon Australianness, it is still to England, as C. Hartley Grattan soundly remarks, that Australian "writers of poetry, fiction and drama have looked and do look." (Hartley Grattan: *Australian Literature: University of Washington Chapbooks:* p. 13.) Melbourne at this very time, as a writer in the London *Times Literary Supplement* just recently stated, is "a mere Pacific outpost of London." (*The Times Literary Supplement*, No. 1,548, article entitled *Literature in Australia:* London, October 1, 1931: p. 738.) Despite all the teapot tempest about Australian writers going native, practically all its leading poets and novelists have been caught in the web of the colonial complex. Christopher Brennan's poetry revealed "echoes of rhythms from Henley; Henry Kendall's and Adam Lindsay Gordon's verses were no more natively Australian than Anne Bradstreet's were natively American; Katherine Susannah Pritchard, "who began as a disciple of D. H. Lawrence . . . is moulding herself nowadays on Sheila Kaye Smith." (*The Times Literary Supplement*, No. 1,548, article entitled *Literature in Australia:* London, October 1, 1931: p. 738.)

While South African literature has not advanced as far as these other colonial literatures, it has evidenced in every way all the same signs of literary evolution. The difficulties of the author have been similar. Caught still between the first and second stages of the colonial process, the native author even to-day "has to struggle in the teeth of a constant prejudice against 'the local article.'" (Manfred Nathan: *South African Literature:* Capetown and Johannesburg, 1925: p. 15.)

Norway's struggle for a national literature, dominated as it was by the culture of Denmark for more than a brief period, reveals a number of the same characteristics which we have noted in these other colonial literatures. The same nationalistic assertiveness is there, with the poet Wergeland playing something of the part of a Norwegian Emerson. (Cf. Frederick W. Horn: *Literature of the Scandinavian North:* Chap. VII, p. 295: 1884.) After Norwegian independence was won, we find again a similar flood of change, with the ensuing patriotism undergoing the various mutations characteristic of such a period. (Cf. C. B. Curchardt: *Norwegian Life and Literature:* 1920.)

confused their aim. Like a youth who is ever seeking to emulate his father's attainments, but who is without his father's original advantages of age and strength, American literature failed to be itself not because of its youth, as many have said, but because it tried to be old before it was young. Its maturity, therefore, was an artificial product; it did not spring up spontaneously of itself, as a mellowed part of its environment, but developed like an unnaturally precocious child who, under the tyrannous tutelage of his father, memorizes dates without understanding their significance.

It was not until a short while before the Revolutionary War that our authors became aware of the need to be American. The war itself, effecting the political separation of the colony from the mother country, created this need as part of the rising national consciousness. The need for political and economic separation, however, did not necessitate the need for cultural separation, for the American Revolution was not a cultural revolution at all. The same traditions which prevailed before the Revolution persisted after it, with the exception that protest against their English origins grew more manifest. In time this protest became vociferous. Nevertheless, its whole expression was futile. The conditions of American life, the status of the American nation, were in conspiracy against its success. Political emancipation alone is not sufficient to establish cultural independence, for culture has its roots in ways of life that are deeper than politics. That England continued to dominate American culture long after its political hegemony had been overthrown is not surprising, therefore, when we realize that however strenuously a colony may struggle to free itself of its maternal influence, its earlier attitude of inferiority is bound to linger until it is the economic equal of the mother country. And it was this domination which forced American literature to remain a colonial literature until practically the beginning of the twentieth century.

It is doubtful whether the psychological influence of this condition of cultural inferiority, its effect upon the mind of

the American writers, its impact upon the artistic consciousness of the people, readers as well as writers, has ever been
adequately appreciated. The inhibition of reaction and response which it created has been discussed with sufficient frequency but seldom with sufficient realization of its consequences.[2] Yet the history of our literature can only be understood by an apprehension of that factor. The stunted talents
of our authors, their failure to advance beyond the point of
adolescent vision, find part of their early origin in this handicap—and, of course, in that greater handicap which is discussed in the second chapter, namely, the dominance of a
petty bourgeois ideology which considered art a demoralizing
luxury born of aristocratic vice.

The inspiration necessary to creative art was thus defeated by the unhappy contradiction of the presence of an
old tradition upon a new soil. The new artists, intellectual
pioneers upon the new land, were forced thus, however imperceptibly, to translate their fresh experiences in terms of
an old environment. A whole world of native experiences in
this way was denied expression save in form adapted to the
spirit of an old civilization.

The work of few writers bears out this contradiction so
well as that of Samuel Sewall. His *Diary* is filled with any
number of prosaic observations upon his own environment,
with witty comments interspersed ever so often as a form of
literary condiment. His reflection upon periwigs and even
his concern over his finding a Maid, are all described in a
terse, unaffected style, characteristic of the simplicity of his
surroundings. The moment he turns to poetry, however, or
to anything that is supposed to be artistic, his pen is no longer
free to move in the same manner. At such times he reverts
immediately to the stilted style of his English predecessors.
When he wants to tell us, for example, that the Indians have

[2]"American authors," as Henry Seidel Canby excellently pointed out,
"have been urged toward an artificial refinement as much out of place in
American communities as chaps in London, and have been most heartily
praised when they were most imitative." (Henry Seidel Canby: *Classic
Americans*: New York, 1931: p. xii.)

made an attack and escaped with three colonists, he writes as follows:

Three men are carried away from Lancaster from Mr. Sawyer's saw mill.

But when a second later, in his next item, his mood becomes literary and his spirit begins to soar even English is not good enough for him, and, turning to Latin, he scribbles this distich:

Roma inhonesta jacet. Sanctae guadate puellae Vindicis et vivi vivitis Urbe Dei.

Vast wildernesses, a far-stretching sky-line ridged against a hostile sea, frontier fights with the strange warriors of an unchristian race, are nothing but matter-of-fact realities to Sewall, without poetry, without a beauty in their own right.

Only when the American writer descanted upon American things was he able to be natural and forthright and sincere in his utterance. When Anne Bradstreet, the first of the American poets, described America in letters to her friends she was able to be herself and set up a contact between her own personality and the new world in which she lived. When she ventured into literature, on the other hand, she forgot this world entirely and hopelessly tried to emulate the style of the English masters whose tradition had had a very different setting. Nature to her did not come direct, as a bird in flight, but as something which had to be translated into the regular rhythms and rhetorical exaggerations of the English school of the time. In *Contemplations* a sunset becomes a more tortured event than a Popian simile:

> "Some time now past in the Autumnal Tide,
> When *Phœbus* wanted but one hour to bed,
> The trees all richly clad, yet void of pride,
> Were gilded o'er by his rich golden head."

When she writes a letter to her husband in prose it is human and natural; when she turns to poetry and does the same thing, as in *A Letter to Her Husband*, she becomes as unhuman as a verbal mannikin and as unnatural as a sophomore aspiring to be a Milton. But Anne Bradstreet is not at all singular in this respect. The poetry of Thomas Godfry is just as imitative in character as hers. All the vast differences between the American environment and the English are as nothing to him. Spring comes the same for him across English downs as it does upon the far-flung line of the frontier. In his poem *The Invitation* "Spring in livery gay appears" and, in characteristic fashion, "each grove its leafy honours rears"—and so the poem proceeds without a single touch of anything, suggestion or allusion, that might not have been written by any fifteenth-rate English poet of the day. Nothing of America breathes in his verse—or in the verse of any of his contemporaries. Only imitation is there, sick, spineless imitation, which is without clarity or conviction.

When we turn to the American newspapers and magazines in the next century we can readily see just why this imitativeness was so ubiquitous. The observation of Peter Peckpenny in *The American Magazine* affords us with ready clue as to one of the immediate causes of this tendency:

> Another thing which is necessary to give reputation to a literary work is that it should *cross the ocean*. It is therefore recommended to all authors to send their manuscripts to England, and on their return they may be sold for British manufacture and pass with great reputation. No work, however good, will be esteemed at home.[3]

The influence of this factor, as a basis for reputation, naturally made American authors tend to scorn the idea of American publication and to seek out English publishers as their sponsors. At the same time, in order to win the approval of the English audience, American authors necessarily exalted English attitudes as civilized and dismissed American materials as crude and barbarous. As one writer had expressed it in *The American Magazine*, it was better to "inculcate a desire on the part of the American authors to excel the English

[3]*The American Magazine*, January 17, 1788: New York: p. 105.

masters than to encourage them to strike out new paths."[4] It should be a source of no surprise, therefore, to note that the first literary newspaper in America, *The New England Courant,* set out as its main purpose to imitate the English *Spectator.*[5]

An important force in handicapping the advance of American literature, and which tended to intensify our dependence upon English books and periodicals, was the unhappy character of the copyright situation. The existence of what was known as International Copyright, which made it possible for English authors to be secured for nothing, militated against the development of our literature. American authors were rendered helpless by this condition. Publishers were not eager to encourage them since they could pirate English authors for greater profit. Not until American books and American magazines, though more expensive than reprints, sold better than English literary merchandise did the American authors receive any real encouragement from American publishers. During the period when American authors were handicapped at every point in the literary market, the tendency toward cultural imitativeness, as a sheer defensive, rooted itself deeper than ever into our literary practice. It is illuminating to note that during the entire time when International Copyright exercised such a devastating influence upon our literature, there was not a single statesman in the country "who had the courage," to quote Nathaniel P. Willis, "to take the chance of making or marring his career by exposing the question."[6] In short, few Americans were willing to put up a fight for a native literature—especially when that fight meant favoring our creative interests instead of our commercial ones.

Another way in which this cultural subservience was deep-

[4]*The American Magazine,* January 10, 1745: *Upon Originals in Writing:* p. 65.

[5]In Chapter IV, where the colonial complex is treated in terms of that period, quotations from several English and American publications are set side by side, showing in what a slavish sense American writers copied English materials, even to the point of adjectival verisimilitude.

[6]Nathaniel P. Willis: *The New Literary Epoch:* Philadelphia, 1852: p. 701.

ened was through educational contact. English universities for a long time became the main intellectual resort of American youths who sought to study literature, law, medicine, or any of the various branches of higher learning. It was only after American universities became established as educational institutions of worth that the migration of American students to England was abated. American universities, however, were constructed so completely upon the English style, even to the point of modelling their curricula upon exactly the same pattern, that little influence of the mother country was lost in the change.[7] Literary instruction in the American universities as well as English discouraged American students from tackling American themes. As a result American writing in the seventeenth and eighteenth centuries was little concerned with being American, or being approved of in America, but was much concerned with being English and approved of in England. Even many of the American divines who published their sermons were more anxious to have them read in the mother country than in their own. American newspapers and magazines were replete with the writings of men who were anxious to become American Addisons in prose or American Popes in verse.[8]

When one turns to the political literature of the time, one is confronted at once with an array of statements and sentiments which show how deeply this cultural inferiority was rooted in the economic and the political situation of the colonies. In order to gain advantages from the crown many and devious forms of subservience had to be exploited. If such expressions of subservience were often no more than devices of strategy, they nevertheless left a lasting impression upon

[7]Michael Kraus: *Intercolonial Aspects of American Culture on Eve of the Revolution*: New York: p. 12.

[8]Another contributing factor in this link of cultural continuity was correspondence. Literary persons in America corresponded frequently with those in England. Cromwell, Milton, Marvell, and Defoe were all constant recipients of letters from their American friends, and the passage of these letters back and forth undoubtedly increased the dependence of American writers upon English contemporaries. (Cf. Thomas Goddard Wright: *Literary Culture in Early New England*.)

the attitude of the country as a whole. Until the outbreak of the Revolution, American economic life was controlled by the crown through land grants and taxation and American political life was similarly controlled by royal governors or by special regulations of Parliament.[9] These conditions of economic and political inferiority could not but communicate themselves into the culture of the country as a whole. It was just as impossible for the literary artist to escape this influence as it was for the politician, and if American poets did not become as obviously sycophantic in their verse as the politicians in their addresses, it was only because their form of obeisance was in the sphere of intellectual imitation instead of moral humiliation.

It was during the several decades of crisis which preceded the Revolutionary War that the American literati first became intelligently conscious of their cultural servitude. With the political emancipation of the American colonies the desire for cultural independence arose in earnest. Where before the desire to be English had been extolled, the desire to be American now took its place. At last American newspapers and magazines became aware of the plight which the American author had previously endured, and, as if borne on the wings of a dazzling intuition, American critics suddenly realized the appearance of a new necessity—the creation of a native literature. Articles sprang up everywhere challenging the American author to answer this necessity. "For many years subsequent to the establishment of our independence," a critic wrote in *The American Quarterly*,[10] "an American writer labored under the worst species of discouragement to an inspiring mind. There were but comparatively few readers and those were so accustomed to the productions of their

[9]Of course, as Pitt and Burke pointed out, the colonies, despite the legal tie which insured their subservience, possessed a kind of half-way economic autonomy between 1700 and 1765. But that partial autonomy, dependent always in the last analysis upon the whim of the Crown, was too insecure a reality to inspire independence of outlook.

[10]*American Quarterly*, No. 11, June, 1827: *American Drama*: p. 340.

mother country, that they viewed the appearance of an American work pretty much in the light a Parisian coterie would the intrusion of a half-civilized Indian. A gentleman of that day," the critic continued, "could as soon have thought of wearing a home-spun coat as of reading a book of home manufacture." "The sense of inferiority in consequence," he added, "kept down and discouraged the restless aspirations of actual or imagined genius: and if by chance a daring adventurer desperately invaded the barren regions of Parnassus it was in the disguise of a foreigner or behind the leaden shield of abject imitation. He dared not attempt originality, for fear of being stigmatized as a barbarian, or select a purely native subject lest he should be laughed at by those who presided over the public taste, as a dabbler in 'Indian poetry,' the favorite phrase of the day." If in Europe, on the other hand, there was an interest in American things, testified to by the interest shown in the writings of Bartram, Woolman, Franklin, Crevecœur, it was more of an interest in the curious than in the excellent. But even so Europeans often showed more interest in American things than did Americans. Burke, for example, had more respect for American political literature than did most of the Americans themselves.

The struggle against imitation and the fight for originality in American literature—for an American literature in its own right—developed in real earnest after the political independence of the country was finally established. As early as 1786 we find the Reverend T. Dwight contending that life as portrayed in English literature is so different from life as it is lived in America, that the American writer must now turn to his own country for inspiration.[11] In a later issue of the same magazine in which Dwight's observations appeared, *The American Museum*, we find another author, signing himself as a *Sentimental Traveller*, stating that "as a nation we ought to form some national customs and not be eternally

[11]*The American Museum*, January, 1789: p. 70. The essay referred to and included therein was written on March 23, 1786.

subservient to those which prevail abroad."[12] In 1804 *The Boston Weekly Magazine* presented an even more direct challenge. While in the past this country was "the offspring of Great Britain and appeared rather as a branch than a distinct nation," *The Boston Weekly* writer went on to state that no longer did America need "the support of its parent, [for] by its rapid progress in some acquirements [it] bids fair one day to be her rival."[13] Despite the political and economic advance of the country, however, in which all the promise of a rich future inhered, the author was forced to admit that "literature makes but little advancement," and, failing to find itself, and orient itself about a new national orbit, it continued to do nothing more than "pervert the public taste."

Peter S. Du Ponceau was even more emphatic in claiming that American literature will never be able to advance until it outgrows its colonial spirit:

Literature has never flourished anywhere under a colonial system of government. . . . Nothing can be more certain than if we confine ourselves to any one school (excellent as it may be) we shall never be able to have a school of our own. Imitation destroys genius; it narrows the range of our imaginations. That we follow too closely British models and that our compositions are not sufficiently stamped with originality is what I am not prepared to deny and we cannot blame too much the satirist for giving it the name of mental dependence.[14]

An author in *The American Quarterly Review* became even belligerent in his criticisms of the imitativeness of our literature and its need of becoming natively American in theme and technique:

[12]Ibid., issue February, 1789: *Miscellaneous Observations on Certain National Customs and Prejudices*, by a Sentimental Traveller, November 15, 1788.

[13]*Boston Weekly Magazine*, Vol. II, No. 25, Saturday evening, April 14, 1804: essay by "Atticus."

[14]Peter S. Du Ponceau: *A Discourse on the Necessity and Means of Making Our National Literature Independent of that of Great Britain:* February 15, 1834: pp. 15 and 23.

We have almost exclusively borrowed our books and our opinions, as well as our fashions from England; adopted our national prejudices and antipathies and condemned the world by wholesale, and just as her caprices, fashions or interest dictated. . . . It generates and perpetuates ideas of a natural and irremediable inferiority . . . every nation ought to have a literature of its own, adapted to its peculiar situation. To no people now existing does this assertion apply more forcibly than to those of the United States.[15]

In the nineteenth century this conflict between the cultural tug and pull of the English tradition and the rising desire on the part of our authors to create an American resulted in a kind of oratorical independence without an accompanying intellectual emancipation. Our creative as well as critical writers became vociferous in their demand for Americanness, exaggerating differences and obscuring resemblances in an ardent attempt to cultivate an indigenous literature, disengaged from its British origins. In his introduction to the English edition of Bryant's poems in 1832, Washington Irving[16] insisted upon the fact that "the descriptive writings of Mr. Bryant are essentially American"—for after all, such poems as *A Meditation on Rhode Island Coal, The Planting* and *To A Water Fowl* had a background that was native enough to appeal to the most fiery of the literary nationalists of the period. Mr. Bryant was equally anxious to encourage Americanness in others as well as in himself, and in his criticisms he attacked the state of mind which allowed American literature to be divorced from American soil:

"With respect to the style of poetry prevailing at the present day in our country, we apprehend that it will be found in too *many instances tinged with a sickly and affected emulation of the peculiar manner of some of the late popular poets of England . . . we desire to set a mark on that servile habit of copying . . . this way of writing has an air of poverty and meanness.*"[17] . . . all the mate-

[15]*American Quarterly Review*, No. 2, September, 1827: *Yorktown: A Historical Romance.*
[16]Irving's failure to become American, in fact his complete subservience to the colonial complex, is discussed at length in the third chapter.
[17]*William Cullen Bryant . . . Prose Writings of William Cullen Bryant. Early American Verse*, from *The North American Review*, July, 1818.

rials of poetry exist in our own country, with all the ordinary encouragements and opportunities of making successful use of them. The elements of beauty and grandeur, intellectual greatness and moral truth, the stormy and the gentle shed upon man's nature by the story of past times and a knowledge of foreign manners have not made their sole abode in the old world beyond the waters.[18]

Even Poe, whose own creative writings were as far removed from the familiar chauvinisms of the day as lyric poetry is from political propaganda, stressed "the need of *that* nationality which defends our own literature, sustains our own men of letters, upholds our own dignity, and depends upon our own resources," for, as he added, "in letters as in government we require a Declaration of Independence."[19] Nathaniel Willis, who was the witty fop of the forties, and the critic who later was to become Poe's unflinching advocate in the controversy with Griswold after the former's death, was a still more vehement Americanophile:

It is the most natural thing that America should grow American at last! What more natural than that we should tire of having our thinking done for us in London, our imaginations fed only with food that is Londonish and our matters of feeling illustrated and described only by London associations, tropes and similitudes. The country is tired of being Be Britished.[20]

Even before the Civil War this fervor for literary independence was active in the South as well as the North, and in the writings of William Gillmore Simms, the well-known South Carolinian writer, the attitude of the Southern states found a direct echo:

Europe must cease to taunt us because of our prolonged servility to the imperious genius of the Old World. We must set ourselves

[18]*Prose Writings of William Cullen Bryant:* New York, D. Appleton & Co., 1884. *On Poetry, Its Relation to Our Age and Country*, April, 1825: p. 33.
[19]Edgar Allan Poe . . . *Marginalia CLVIII.*
[20]Nathaniel P. Willis: Prose Works, *Ephemera*, New Literary Epoch, p. 701.

free from the tyranny of this genius and the time has come when we must do so. We have our own national mission to perform—a mission commensurate to the extent of our country—its resources and possessions. . . . The inferior necessities of our condition have been overcome. The national mind is now free to rise to the consideration of its superior wants and more elevated aims.[21]

The early patriotism which had moved Joseph Hopkinson in 1789 to write his popular poem *Hail Columbia*, and which inspired Francis Scott Key to compose *The Star-Spangled Banner*, and Joseph Rodman Drake to pen *The American Flag* was succeeded, then, by a national consciousness, which aimed to be American by instinct rather than by design.[22] Cooper plunged into American themes in order to escape the influence of the English novel.[23] Edwin Forrest tried to found an American theatre and over a considerable period of years expended more than twenty thousand dollars in prizes in an endeavor to encourage native playwrights.[24] In response to Forrest's desire for native plays American dramatists arose in every direction and flooded him with over two hundred dramas, many of them upon themes as autochthonous in background as John Augustus Stone's Indian drama *Metamora*.[25] Henry Wadsworth Longfellow, ambitiously American also, turned toward the Indian for his native materials and in *Hiawatha* and *Minnehaha* sought to create genuinely American characters—for who could be more genuinely American than the Indian?—in a primeval American environment. John Greenleaf Whittier gave New

[21]William Gillmore Simms: *Views and Reviews in American Literature*. Subject: *Americanism in Literature:* an Oration before the Phi Beta Kappa and Demosthenean Societies of the University of Georgia, August 8, 1844.

[22]Miss Sedgwick: *North American:* Vol XX, p. 243.

[23]In connection with his work, *Bravo*, Cooper himself wrote: "The book was thoroughly American in all that belonged to it." (A Letter to His Countryman, New York, 1834.)

[24]Of course, following Royal Tyler's play, *The Contrast*, there were many patriotic plays which usurped the American stage directly preceding and immediately following the Revolutionary War, but despite the nativity of their themes they were exceedingly imitative in concept and design.

[25]Walter Long: *The Modern Quarterly*, Vol. II, No. 4, p. 269.

England farm life a poetic setting, and Nathaniel Hawthorne revivified the wraithlike spirits of the Puritans. But it was Ralph Waldo Emerson, the American Carlyle, who, with all the fury and fanfare of a prophet, gave what has often been called the final signature to our literary Declaration of Independence:

Our day of dependence, our long apprenticeship to the learning of other lands, draws to a close. The millions that around us are rushing into life cannot always be fed on the mere remains of foreign harvests. . . .[26]

The development of our American internal resources, the extension to the utmost of the commercial system and the appearance of new moral causes which are to modify the state, *are giving an aspect of greatness to the future, which the imagination* fears to open. One thing is plain for all men of common sense and common conscience *that here, here in America is the home of man.*[27]

Despite these assertions of independence, and despite these valiant efforts to abandon English materials and exploit American, the influence of the mother country was not destroyed. In point of fact the colonial complex continued to function throughout the greater part of the nineteenth century. Indeed these very assertions of independence, with their attendant excess of desire to dwell upon American things and American things only, which amounted almost to an intellectual obsession, were attestations of inferiority rather than of confidence. When writers are certain of themselves, convinced of their national independence, as is the case of the American writers of to-day, they approach their work in a different spirit. They do not stress their independence, nor become verbally obstreperous about its achievement; they accept it as a reality and proceed with their work without giving it further consideration. In colonies, however, as we noted before, where in the early stages of development the inferiority of the colonial culture to that

[26]Ralph Waldo Emerson: *The American Scholar*, an oration delivered before the Phi Beta Kappa Society, Cambridge, August 31, 1837.
[27]Ralph Waldo Emerson: *The Young American.*

of the mother country is accepted as naturally as the inferiority of the colonial government to that of the mother nation, the intellectual subservience resulting therefrom creates a *colonial complex*—that is an inferiority complex of a social order—which clings to the culture long after its original causation has disappeared. In no colonial literature is this fact manifested more clearly than in American. In fact the first clue to an understanding of the nature and the making of American literature is to be found in an appreciation of the importance of this colonial complex in shaping the American literary mind.

It is only fair, of course, to warn the reader against the danger of trying to extend this interpretation to an extreme where its meaning is lost in exaggeration. A social tendency or compulsive such as the colonial complex, which we have been concerned with in this chapter, can only be compared roughly to the psychological complex which is characteristic of individual behavior. Nevertheless, rough as the analogy may be, it is of distinct service here, since the social factor involved can be accounted for best in terms of this psychological nomenclature. Wherever we have a form of behavior, social or individual, which contradicts its objective without being aware of the contradiction, we can be reasonably certain that a complex is at work in the process. Once an attitude of mind has been created and continued for a period, it has an inevitable tendency to persist even after its cause has disappeared. The colonial complex is a striking illustration of this in psycho-sociological form. The very assertiveness of the attitude, as we showed before, betrayed the feeling of inferiority that underlay it. The fact that long after our political independence was won, our literati continued to demand our cultural independence was sufficient evidence to prove that the state of mind at work was one which was bound up with the present as well as the past, a carry-over, as it were, a vestigial lag in intellectual development, affecting our existence in every form, philosophic as well as literary, investing itself even deeper in our creative life, however, than in our critical. If we had escaped the overshadowing influence of the mother-country as soon as we had politically escaped her control, the colonial complex would have been of importance only as a pre-revolutionary consideration. The fact that we did not escape it—a fact attested by the admissions of our own writers and by the even more patent evidence of our literature itself—is proof that its basis was deeper than politics. Arising out of our original status as a colony, inferior to the mother country, subjected thus to all experiences of a people whose economic life is dependent upon the dictation of another, our culture early became afflicted with this colonial complex which soon became an inalienable part of our psychological heritage. This has been as true in point of fact, of the culture of other colonial peoples,[28] as we have seen, as of the culture of the American. Undoubtedly, the fact that we took over the language of the mother country was one of the most decisive factors in rooting this complex as deeply in our culture as in the cultures of Canada, Australia, and South Africa. Developing thus into a way of thought, a mind-set, this state of *colonialness* gathered about itself all the attributes of a complex, a cultural complex with an *inferiority* motivation.

It would be a mistake, however, to infer that the colonial complex was fundamentally psychological in origin. On the contrary, its origin was entirely economic. It was the economic inferiority of the colonies to England, an inevitable corollary of the colonial status wherever it occurs, that established its existence. Once established, however, its manifestations at once took on a psychological cast, and, deep-rooted as they became, maintained an existence of their own, as we have pointed out, even after the original political and

---

[28]A distinction should be made here, of course, between colonies which are founded by a mother country, such as the American, the Canadian, the Australian, and countries which are conquered by an aggressive power, and made into colonies, as is the case of Ireland and India. In the latter case, of course, the colonial complex has little chance to intrude, especially if, as in Ireland, the conquered country has a well-founded culture of its own. When such is the case, the culture of the conquering nation is more often rejected than respected.

economic conditions had altered. Only at the close of the nineteenth century, when the whole psychology of the nation changed with its newly growing economic superiority, did its hold weaken. To study the colonial complex, therefore, as an economic outgrowth alone, or a psychological force alone, would be to misunderstand its nature and influence. It is an evolution of both—a psychological outgrowth of the economic basis of the culture.

A considerable part of the literary energy of the American writers in the nineteenth century was consumed in the struggle to escape this colonial complex. The repressions of spirit which inevitably accompany the intellectual practice of imitation were only intensified by this third stage in the colonial process. The cultural conditions of the country were not of such a character as would actually encourage the nationalistic originality which the American literati began to demand. Although the American nation had established its political independence, its economic life was lacking in unity until after the Civil War, and its place among the countries of the world, despite the contention of its inhabitants, was minor instead of major. At the same time that its writers advocated independence from English influence they continued to turn with eagerness to English critics for approval. As Poe regretfully noted, "even when publishers at their own obvious risks do publish an American book, we turn up our noses at it with supreme contempt until it has been dubbed 'readable' by some illiterate cockney critic." Cooper's observation was similar. "The American who wishes to illustrate and enforce the peculiar principles of his own country by the agency of polite literature," Cooper wrote, "will, for a long time, come to find that his constituency is still too much under the influence of foreign theories to receive them with favor." As late as 1869, James Russell Lowell took up the cudgels in defense of Americanism. "We are worth nothing," Lowell exhorted, "except so far as we have disinfected ourselves of Anglicism."[29] Always on the

[29]James Russell Lowell: *Prose Works*, Vol. III—Riverside Edition, 1870—from essay *On a Certain Condescension in Foreigners:* 1869: p. 272.

defensive, an attitude of mind which was a direct outgrowth of the sense of inferiority out of which our colonial complex was devised, we were ever anxious not to be treated as "inferior and deported Englishmen,"[30] and it was against such treatment that Lowell directed his salvos. The dominancy of the mother culture persisted, then, long after its political and economic tentacles had been severed, and our literature consequently continued to be a colonial one in both character and conception.[31]

Even the boldest attempts to build up an American culture accomplished little in the battle for literary freedom. The colonial complex, strengthened by the economic inferiority of the country to that of England and other European nations, and the resulting intellectual immaturity which went with such a condition, could not be shaken off by a mere verbal gesture. Bryant and Cooper, notwithstanding their avowed determination to be American at all costs, were no more successful than Trumbull and Barlow, the Hartford Wits, in achieving such emancipation. When Trumbull set forth, in his epic *M'Fingal,* upon the patriotic task of satirizing the Tories, he expressed his most rebellious sentiments in a style that was immediately imitative of the poetry of Samuel Butler. His anxiety to be American, however, inclined him at no point to develop anything peculiarly American in spirit or design. M'Fingal himself is no more American than are the classical allusions which encumber the style of the poem at every point with their irrelevancy and inappropriateness. But Bryant succeeded no better in approximating a national identity. Although his mind reverted more often to the American scene, and he found Oregon a more

[30]Ibid., p. 252.
[31]Even in the twentieth century, for that matter, D. H. Lawrence, during his stay in America, complained about the continuance of the American feeling of inferiority concerning its own culture. "Why aren't Americans more interested in their own things?" he asked. "They come over to Europe and look at our castles and ignore their own old culture." Quoted from article in *New York Herald Tribune,* May 20, 1931. Article appeared after Lawrence's death. Lawrence's words, above quoted, were ascribed to him by his wife.

haunting form of remoteness than Timbuctu, his resemblance to Wordsworth "in the temper of his thought," as Bayard Taylor noted,[32] was so marked that any assertion as to his Americanness is without conviction.[33] Cooper made no greater advance. While he undoubtedly turned to American themes, particularly in his *Leatherstocking Tales,* with more frequency and consistency than any other writer of his day, his characters are scarcely more American than M'Fingal. His Indians, for example, as Mark Twain showed, were anything but Indians as they really were. In fact, they were no more realistic than are the cowboys to-day in the American cinema. His Natty Bumppo was nothing more than an Anglicized red man.[34] Longfellow was even less native than Cooper. His Americanisms were of that sentimental school which derived its impetus from the philosophy of sweetness and light. Hiawatha and Minnehaha were embodiments of that Sunday-school conception of the Indian which made him as sweet and pure and moonsick as the ideal Victorian gentleman. Longfellow studied Indian life and legend, studied it even conscientiously, and yet studied it like a missionary seeking to find the Indian a good moral Christian at heart. While Longfellow lived in America most of his life, and Chateaubriand spent less than a few months in America, and spent it swiftly at that, the former's creation of the Indian character Hiawatha was no more real, no more actually American, than the latter's creation of *Atala*. Even Thoreau, who has been called by many the most American of Ameri-

[32]Bayard Taylor: *Essays and Notes:* p. 264.

[33]"When Bryant's *Thanatopsis* appeared, people were carried away by the poem—because they were reminded of Wordsworth, Keats, and Shelley. In fact, the Greek word itself—an arbitrary coinage of Bryant's as Epipsychidion was a coinage of Shelley's—indicates an English model, and the rhythm of English blank verse was ringing in the ears of the American." (Leon Kellner: *American Literature:* New York, 1915: p. 9.)

[34]Even before Mark Twain, readers on the frontier sensed the lack of native genuineness in Cooper's Indian fiction. Although it is true that there were frontier writers such as M'Clurg who aspired to "wing a flight a little below Cooper," Cooper's novels, especially *The Prairie*, were sharply attacked for failing "lamentably to catch the true spirit of the West." (Rusk: *Literature of the Middle Western Frontier:* New York, 1926.)

cans, withdrew from American life in order to build himself a forest hermitage, removed from the American people and the culture that he had known. Even Hawthorne, who strongly emphasized American themes, created shadow figures and puppets instead of real beings in fleshly form. His *Scarlet Letter,* concerned as it was with a purely American situation and background, reads more like a romantic legend than a realistic fiction, so ghostlike are its characters and so weird is its conception. Poe for all his insistence upon a naturalistic culture was less American still. His pen, except when devoted to criticism, went far afield in search of the strange—a strangeness which derived its main inspiration from the European romanticism of the time, especially from the German school, and had nothing more American about it than Hoffman's tales of terror.[35]

One of the most revealing expressions of our feeling of inferiority, continuing throughout this third stage in the colonial process, and lingering on slightly even to-day, was our constant habit of referring to American authors in terms of their English prototypes. By such form of identification *our critics unconsciously sought to justify the work* of our native authors. Emerson was repeatedly referred to as the American Carlyle, Fitz-Greene Halleck was described as the "American town brother of Campbell,"[36] Bryant as the American Wordsworth, Poe as a scion of Coleridge, and even as shallow a poet as Mrs. Sigourney was spoken of constantly as the American Mrs. Hemans.[37] Hawthorne's creations "are statuesquely molded like Goethe's";[38] Richard Henry Dana's are "colored by that of Crabbe, of Wordsworth, and of Coleridge";[39] even Cooper is seen to embody "some of the mental and physical characteristics of Byron"; and Irving is alluded to as the 'American Gulliver. But this form of

[35]This point will be discussed in detail in a later chapter.
[36]Bayard Taylor: *Essays and Notes:* New York, 1886.
[37]Gordon Haight: *Mrs. Sigourney:* New Haven, 1930: p. 101.
[38]Geo. Parsons Lathrop: *A Study of Hawthorne:* Boston, 1876: p. 331.
[39]Wm. Gillmore Simms: *Views and Review in American Literature: The Writings of J. F. Cooper:* 1845: pp. 223–224.

English identification did not stop there. So completely did English influence monopolize our life that such poets as Scott and Byron became a more intimate part of our culture than any American poets of the period. Steam boats were named the "Lady of the Lake," Ellen Douglas, Marmion, the Corsair, and the Mazeppa.[40] In a single travel book written by Edmond Flagg in 1838 there were "more than score of quotations or allusions which testify to Byron's fame."[41] Indeed during the early days on the frontier, before the revolt against the East began, frontier writers such as Flint and Pierce urged their literary compatriots to emulate the verses of the "unequal Felicia Hemans," and the exalted traditions of Pope, Thomson, and Byron. In prose the ambition was to create American Scotts and it was this appellation which Flint and M'Clurg soon won with their novels: *Francis Berrion*, and *Camden*. It was on the frontier, of course, that these obvious forms of limitation were later on to be first abandoned.

The only definite advance which American literature made at this time in the way of its emancipation was in the nature of its setting. If Longfellow and Cooper did not break away from the mother culture in the spirit of their works, they did not turn to the maternal environment for the settings which they adopted. American soil and American things were their constant emphasis. It was the physical fact which changed at this period but not the psychological. The change in physical background, however, gave the illusion of change in psychological outlook. This change in physical setting, nevertheless, unassociated though it was with a corresponding psychological shift, prepared the way for the early development of a genuinely American psychology in the literature of the frontier. Aided by conditions favorable to the development of native originality, literature that grew up on the frontier, or in response to its stimulus, extended the change in literary emphasis to the psychological plane. It

[40]Rusk: *Literature of the Middle-Western Frontier:* New York, 1926: p. 15.
[41]Ibid., p. 17.

was the frontier, in fact, as we shall show in more detail in the fifth chapter, which first made it possible for physical independence to be conjoined with psychological.

One of the most striking ways in which the colonial complex rooted itself into our culture was through the medium of language. While the American people spoke a language which became an articulate part of their environment, American writers refused to employ that language, but insisted upon using the literary English of the old country as their form of style. This tendency alone prevented them from coming close to the country in which they lived and the people who surrounded them. It was impossible for them to describe America or Americans in the style of the English masters. Yet that is what Hawthorne, what Cooper, what most nineteenth-century writers, tried to do. A native literature can only spring out of the living language of the people. Languages are not made by linguists. And when authors try to write about a people in the language of another tradition, no matter how excellent that tradition, they will not be able to describe that people. Van Wyck Brooks saw that contradiction, and pointed out its pathos in *America's Coming of Age:*

Consider, for example, our use of the English language. Literary English in England is naturally a living speech, which occupies the middle of the field and expresses the flesh and blood of an evolving race. Literary English with us is a tradition just as Anglo-Saxon law with us is a tradition. They persist not as the normal expressions of a race, the essential fibre of which is permanently Anglo-Saxon, but through prestige and precedent and the will and habit of a dominating class largely out of touch with a national fabric unconsciously taking form "out of school." No wonder that our literary style is "pure," that our literary tradition, our tradition especially in oratory and political prose, retains the spirit of the eighteenth century. But at what cost! At the cost of expressing a popular life which bubbles with energy and spreads and grows and slips away ever more and more from the control of tested ideas, a popular life "with the lid off," which demands an intellectual outlet and finds one in slang, journalism, and unmannerly fiction.[42]

[42]Van Wyck Brooks: *America's Coming of Age:* New York, 1915: p. 15.

It was only in the west, in the frontier regions, as we shall
see, that American writers learned to write the language of
the American people—a language that took form as the
environment demanded, acquiring a spontaneity and elasticity
of expression which was creative and not imitative.[43]

II

The economic conflict between the rising industrial power
in the East and the life on the frontier swiftly brought into
being those antagonisms of spirit which later were to exercise
such a salutary influence upon our literary development. But
the frontier did not assert its psychological independence at
once. It too, as we showed before, had its era of imitation.
The stiff and pompous diction of the eighteenth-century
Johnsonians, the heroic grandiloquence of the Byronic school,
seized their untutored imagination and infected their early
literature with the same artificial imitativeness which marred
the literature of the West. Indeed their imitativeness at that
time exceeded that of the writers of the East.[44] It was only
when the cleavage between the frontier and the East became
sharp, and crystallized into a definite opposition, that a contempt for the culture of New England became pronounced.
Book learning was scorned and bad grammar and misspelling
were encouraged. It was in this way that the frontier could
sneer at the East, and free itself from its hold. America for
the Americans thus became a cry which had far more meaning in the ever shifting frontier regions than in the Eastern
coastal states. The people along the frontier, by the very
nature of their life, were more readily able to think in terms
of their immediate environment, and disregard the dictates
of London. Foreign influences quickly became taboo, and
New England as an American embodiment of English cul-

[43]Cf. Henry L. Mencken's excellent study: *The American Language.*
In Chapter IV Mr. Mencken's contribution to the theme is treated in
more detail.

[44]See the excellent observations upon this literature in Howard Mumford Jones's *America and French Culture*: Chapel Hill, N. C., 1927: Chap.
III.

ture was despised by this new army of frontiersmen who were convinced that they "were the possessors of a new and vast country destined to become the commercial, political and cultural centre of the world."[45]

The frontier thus was the most decisive force in breaking down our colonial complex. While the literary traditions of both the North and South, as we have seen, were imitative in character, the tradition of the frontier, emerging out of a more removed geographic and economic matrix, was able to acquire a native originality of its own. Bret Harte,[46] Artemus Ward, Walt Whitman, Joaquin Miller, and Mark Twain, all products of this frontier tradition, were the first American writers to reveal any signs of native Americanness in their works. The annihilating scorn for European culture which was embodied in Mark Twain's *Innocents Abroad* found its positive manifestation in the iconoclastic poetry of Joaquin Miller and Walt Whitman. It was just these frontier writers who immediately became representative of American litera-ture abroad although they were held in contempt at home. The very fact that Whitman was practically refused recog-nition in America until the twentieth century was a very clear indication of the tendency of American authors to scorn Americanness and exalt Englishness, evincing thus their preference for imitation rather than for originality. Although here and there individual critics arose in praise of Whitman, it was not until then that the Whitman society was first organized, and Whitman became an accepted American poet of important rank. American criticism, monopolized by the East until almost the end of the century, was dominated too obviously by the colonial complex to treat hospitably the rebellious Americanness which soon became characteristic of the literature of the frontier. To such critics the American-

[45]Rusk: *Literature of the Middle-Western Frontier:* New York, 1926: Vol. I, p. 205.
[46]Bret Harte, to be sure, was influenced as much by the Dickensian tradition as by the force of the frontier. In a sense, he was scarcely more than the Cooper of the far West, although in another way he did embody something of the new region which he described.

nesses of Walt Whitman, Joaquin Miller and Mark Twain were evidences of backwardness and not of advance.[47] Mark Twain won the populace to his side long before the critics. Whitman's revolt against the prevailing poetic forms, embodying his complete disregard for the artistic convention and tradition of English practice, was attacked as an expression of the intellectual immaturity of a western parvenu. Nevertheless, it was these men, with their artistic revolt in defense of a native tradition, who foreshadowed the coming of an authentic American literature. It was their own freedom from the more obvious oppressions of the colonial complex, which weighed down so heavily upon the state of mind of the Eastern states, that made it possible for them to become the precursors of that native literature which reached a point of maturity, if not of total independence, in the twentieth century.

Nationalistic consciousness, in its modern form, has arisen out of the philosophy of individualism and its application to political life. The rise of modern nations occurred as a result of the development of individualistic enterprise, and the psychological growth of nationalism was closely connected with the individualistic way of existence. It is not surprising, therefore, that the first signs of real Americanness in our literature sprang up on the frontier where individualism secured its most wide-spread lease of life. Of course, an individual such as Franklin revealed early signs of what may be called embryonic Americanness in his literary work, but Franklin's work in the main fell more within the critical field than the creative. Individualism in the East was far more of a class philosophy than a mass philosophy. Bound by the same ideals of its middle-class forebears in England, and other European countries, the East found greater difficulty in escaping the colonial complex than the West which repre-

[47]"*The North American* and *The Knickerbocker* and *The Southern Literary* and *Harpers* and *The Atlantic* and *Russell's* and *The Galaxy* . . . none of them printed Walt Whitman. Whitman, the native product whom nobody read . . . had to wait for posthumous critical recognition." (Percy H. Boynton: *The Rediscovery of the Frontier*: Chicago, 1931: p. 31.)

sented an environment unknown to any European country. The frontier changed individualism from a class doctrine into a mass phenomenon—a petty bourgeois mass phenomenon, it is true, as is shown in the fifth chapter, but a mass phenomenon none the less. It gave democracy a mass meaning which the European tradition had never communicated to it, and which the East, above as well as below the Mason and Dixon line, had fought rather than encouraged in action. The frontiersman believed in democracy as a fact and not a fiction. His individualism was a fighting faith which burned in him with religious force. His political heroes, Jackson, Harrison, Lincoln, were the embodiment of the pristine nature of his life. Simple men, straightforward, violently individualistic, contemptuous of culture in its European aspects, these heroes were idolized by the Western masses, because they represented revolt against the cultural hegemony of the East which in its economic forms had constantly threatened to throttle their growth. After the Civil War, which had been preceded by the election of the frontiersman, Lincoln, this frontier force broke like an enormous flood upon the face of the country. "The eight years in America from 1860 to 1868," wrote Mark Twain, "uprooted institutions which were centuries old, changed the politics of the people, transformed the social life of half the country, and wrought so profoundly upon the entire national character that the influence cannot be measured short of two or three generations."[48] The influence of this force is with us yet.

It was the West, then, with its frontier philosophy, which shot America agog with a quickened sense of nationalism after the Civil War. Before the Civil War, the frontier was gathering up force; with the election of Lincoln, it had usurped political control from the Atlantic seaboard, and after the Civil War, its momentum having been acquired, its philosophy was able to make its inroads upon the American mind. No other influence has been so decisive in shaping what to-day has become known as the philosophy of Ameri-

[48]Mark Twain: *The Gilded Age:* p. 200.

canism as this frontier tradition.[49] The nationalistic insurgency of the frontier after the Civil War demanded a native literature instead of the sick imitations of Scott and Byron which had preceded. The day when Thomas Pierce, the frontier critic, had exalted Milton, Thomson, and Pope as poets to emulate was ended.[50] Even the influence of New England critics who, as Rusk points out,[51] had formerly "furnished the mould in which Western literary estimates were formed" weakened rapidly in the face of this change. Walt Whitman, Mark Twain, Artemus Ward, Joaquin Miller, the avatars of that change, can very well be said to be our first nationalistic sansculottes. If Bryant in *Thanatopsis* composed a poem which was American in background, it certainly was not American in motivation. It stemmed as definitely from the English tradition in spirit and temper, and in the nature of its style and conception, as did the American poetry of the eighteenth century. The frontier added psychological independence to geographic. What Whitman and Twain did was to combine in their works native settings with a truly nationalistic outlook. Whitman's poetry, therefore, as we have learned from his memoirs, was refused constantly by American magazine editors, because it was so violently unrefined and untraditional—which was but another way of saying that it did not follow the English tradition. While there were exceptions, it can be said that in general frontier writers were inhospitably criticised by the New England and mid-Atlantic literati, and very often by those very literati who were most aggressive in their demand for our cultural independence.

But it was not the frontier force in itself which created an

[49]The familiar tendency to deride book learning and exalt practical knowledge and experience, which is common throughout America to-day, can be traced directly to this source. The attitude of mind which condemned Woodrow Wilson, for example, because he was a professor and a scholar and extolled Al Smith in the last election because he had no interest in books except the Bible is a distinct illustration of the frontier philosophy in twentieth-century thought.

[50]Thomas Pierce: *The Muse of Hesperice*, 1823: p. 43.

[51]Ralph Leslie Rusk: *Literature of the Middle-Western Frontier*: New York, 1926: p. 17.

American tradition. The frontier began the revolt in favor of Americanness, but it did not crystallize that revolt into a tradition. American life on the frontier was constantly in a stage of break-up, the new becoming old before it had time to be appreciated, so that little had a chance to exist long enough to become mellow. Instability there was a constant. All the many and devious centrifugal forces of the frontier tended to upset any movement in the direction of that equilibrium which is necessary for the ripening of a tradition. Wherever social organization is so fluid, so somersaulting in time and place, it is difficult for traditions to grow and deepen. The frontier, thus, might provide stirring writers, as it did, but without developing a tradition from which they could continue to derive inspiration. Important as the frontier was, therefore, in breaking ground for the rise of an American tradition, it is doubtful that it would have succeeded in creating a definite native tradition had it not been for the economic and political developments at the close of the century which made it possible for its spirit to sweep down like a conquering invader upon the East.[52]

While the frontier provided the first source of real Americanness in our literature, it was the accumulative growth of power of the nation as a whole which made it possible for these Americannesses to be capitalized into a nationalistic tradition. It was only when America arose to the position of a world power among the nations of our time, a rival in rank with its mother country, that it was able to release itself from its colonial complex and actually begin the development of a native literature of its own. It was as a result of the change of psychology which came with this new status, influencing the East as well as the West, and remaking the national mind of the country as a whole, that Whitman and Twain came to

---

[52]As is shown in the fifth and sixth chapters, it is when the petty bourgeois ideology of the frontier becomes allied with the petty bourgeois forces in the East, in mutual opposition to the dominancy of the upper bourgeoisie in the affairs of the nation, that Whitman becomes the inspiration of the East as well as the interpreter of the West.

be looked upon as native geniuses instead of as isolated eccentrics.

Although no specific date can be established as to precisely when this change occurred, we can conveniently say that at the close of the Spanish American War it attained a definite focus. Throughout the nineteenth century America had been a second-rate power. European ambassadors to America in the nineteenth century had looked upon their appointments as scarcely more significant than those they might have received to Paraguay or Brazil. After its victory over Spain in 1898, with its consequent acquisitions of foreign colonies and an imperialist psychology which went with such acquisition, America for the first time became a major power, ranking with the leading European nations in influence. The impact of that change was almost immediate. It gave form to what before had been so uncertain and chaotic. The psychology which in the nineteenth century had sought to become nationalistic by verbal assertion found itself so changed in the twentieth century that it could become nationalistic without justification or defense. Although American authors throughout the nineteenth century had argued for our cultural emancipation from England, the nation as a whole, particularly in its economic life, had never questioned British hegemony in the international scheme of control. Our earlier conflicts with England had always been the struggles of a small power against a greater. In the political sphere we had never ceased to look up to England as a guiding force in world affairs. Even our intellectuals, notwithstanding their literary chauvinism, had never learned to discount English opinion or feel themselves independent of English criticism. After all, however much our Bryants and Poes and Lowells argued for the need for a native literature, it could not be denied that England was the leading country in the world at the time, and that its literature had a standing of its own because of this dominating position as well as because of its excellence—and the American authors were more loath to disregard this advantage and influence than their words might often have indicated.[53] Until the end of the century one of the highest honors an American author could seek was to be praised in England.[54] Just as London tended to dictate the state of American finance, English papers and periodicals tended to dictate the American critical tastes and convictions of the day. An American author who was recognized in England became an international figure. An American author who was not recognized in England remained only a provincial.

Only when America arose into a world power was it able to escape this feeling of inferiority, this colonial complex. Once the American nation became a force in itself, equal to that of European nations, and respected as such an equal, it did not have to turn to England for its psychological identity. Its new imperialism gave it added release from its colonial psychology, for in becoming an empire itself with colonies of its own, its former inferiority was able to find ready compensation—and cancellation. It was not long after those changes that American authors came to realize that American literature could stand by itself, on its own legs, as it were, and literary success, critical as well as commercial, came to be thought of in connection with America alone. It was then

[53]In the fourth chapter, this aspect of the colonial complex is taken up in more detail. Its status during the Revolutionary War is analyzed, and its more specific influence upon nineteenth-century writers, particularly Irving and Bryant, is described.

[54]How deeply the sense of inferiority born of the colonial complex wrote itself into the minds of American intellectuals is illustrated interestingly as late as 1901 by William James, one of the leading American thinkers of the time, in his introductory words to his Gifford lectures which he delivered at Edinburgh:

"It is with no small amount of trepidation that I take my place behind this desk, and face this learned audience. To us Americans, the experience of receiving instruction from the living voice, as well as from the books, of European scholars, is very familiar. At my own University of Harvard, not a winter passes without its harvest, large or small, of lectures from Scottish, English, French, or German representatives of the science or literature of their respective countries whom we have either induced to cross the ocean to address us, or captured on the wing as they were visiting our land. It seems the natural thing for us to listen whilst the Europeans talk. The contrary habit, of talking whilst the Europeans listen, we have not yet acquired; and in him who first makes the adventure it begets a certain sense of apology being due for so presumptuous an act." (*The Varieties of Religious Experience*, p. 1.)

that Whitman and Twain came into their own, and received the recognition from artists and critics that they deserved.

The frontier, thus, became linked up in an intense and intimate way with the genuinely nationalistic developments in our literature in the twentieth century. As background and foreground it became a decisive factor in our literary life. The influence of Whitman upon our poetry was one of its most striking manifestations. Whatever else might be said of our poetry in the last generation, the influence of Whitman upon it cannot be gainsaid. Nor can its genuine Americanness, as contrasted with the lack of Americanness in the poetry of Halleck, Bryant, Longfellow, be denied either. Carl Sandburg, Vachel Lindsay, Edgar Lee Masters, Robert Frost, Robinson Jeffers, Hart Crane, are American poets first of all. They are unequivocally American.[55] No one would ever speak of them in terms of English prototypes. Even Amy Lowell, whose whole heritage was steeped in the English tradition and whose affections clung still to the memory of mandolins and the sight of twisted eglantine, breathed in enough of the spirit of her period to participate in something of this swift growth of Americanness in our verse. *The Spoon River Anthology* like the *Deserted Village* deals with the decay of village life, but the philosophies of the two poems are as disparate as their themes are similar. Masters' poem is as unmistakably American as Goldsmith's is incontrovertibly English. An American Masters of the nineteenth century would have described the inhabitants of Spoon River in a vein much closer to the tradition of Goldsmith, Crabbe and Clare than to that which actually found its expression in the *Spoon River Anthology* itself. Hart Crane's *The Bridge,* Stanley Kunitz's *On Intellectual Things,* and

[55]James Oppenheim, in manner more sentimental than scientific, has heralded this change in these words: "Something new, and also young, has appeared in the world—namely, the American race. . . . Just stand up in a line Graham McNamee, Edison, Ford, Hoover, Sinclair Lewis, Clarence Darrow, John Dewey, and H. L. Mencken. Could these men be anything but American?" (James Oppenheim: *American Types:* New York, 1931: pp. 3 and 17.)

MacLeisch's *New Foundland* all voice the same Americanness in even more daring form. Turning from poetry to
prose, Anderson's *Winesburg Ohio*[56] and Lewis' *Main Street*
are as authentically American as Sandburg's *Smoke and Steel*
and Lindsay's *Congo*. In the drama a national awareness
also reached a point of stirring fulfillment. Eugene O'Neill
represented that fulfillment in its most challenging form.
There is no return to English drama for inspiration in the
plays of O'Neill—any more than there is in that of the
younger contemporary school, circling about Paul Green,
Sydney Howard, Phillip Barry and Lynn Riggs.

Of course, it would be a childish exaggeration to say that
none of the writers along the Atlantic seaboard in the nineteenth century revealed any traces of Americanness in their
literature. The very fact that Bryant, Longfellow, Cooper
and Hawthorne focussed their attention in many of their
poems and novels upon the American scene unquestionably
marked a step in advance in the establishment of our literary
identity. But it was a short step and not a long one. The
differences between their work and that of English writers
were differences of degree and not of kind. Their work was
of the same order and followed the same patterns as that in
England. The qualitative differences which distinguish
French literature from English literature, German literature from Italian literature, Spanish literature from Russian
literature, did not develop in American literature as a result
of the work of the New England, Mid-Atlantic or Southern
school of writers. No one, of course, can describe in any precise way the actual constituents which make one literature
differ from another, although one can easily enough trace
the growth of those differences in terms of the cultural
process. It would be hard to state just what it is which makes
Anatole France's work French, and yet we know that it is

---

[56]In 1920 Ernest Boyd observed, in his introduction to the Modern
Library edition of *Winesburg Ohio*, that Sherwood Anderson was one of
those "names which now give contemporary American literature a quality and a significance that are truly national."

French and could be nothing else than French. Undoubtedly
the fact that it is modelled upon the same French tradition
which has inspired French prose since the days of Rabelais
explains more of the difference than anything else. It would
be just as difficult to define exactly what it is which makes
Thomas Mann's novels German or John Galsworthy's English. There are many adjectives, to be sure, which can be and
have been used to describe these national differences as they
express themselves in literature, and yet, when all is said,
few of these adjectives succeed in clearing up many of the
difficulties involved in the problem. To describe nineteenth-
century Russian literature as morbid and introspective means
little, for many other literatures have morbid and introspective writers strewn among them. It is the literature in its
totality, a qualitative and not a quantitative thing, which we
are forced to think of when we discuss the Frenchness of
Anatole France, the Germanness of Thomas Mann, the Englishness of John Galsworthy, the Russianness[57] (that is prior
to the Soviet revolution which has already produced a new
kind of Russianness) of Dostoyevsky. When we say therefore, that American literature in the nineteenth century
lacked Americanness, what we mean is that in its totality it
revealed little that was different, new, unique—little that
deviated from the English pattern. The new national
environment in short had not created a new pattern. Those
writers who began the creation of a new pattern were those

[57] The contradiction involved here, in this whole problem of the national
identity of literature, takes on a new resolution with the development
of literatures which revolve about a proletarian motivation. The implicit
aim of writers who dedicate their interest and energies to the proletariat
is in the final destruction of this national identity of literatures and in
the construction of literatures which revolve about the international proletariat. International unity and not national diversity is their ultimate
aim. For the time being, however, and until present-day national cultures
are superseded by an international one even authors allied to the proletariat will continue to write in terms of the national culture of which
they are a part. In other words, radical literatures the same as bourgeois
literatures will take on their caste from the national environment for
some time to come. John Dos Passos will write like an American radical,
Barbusse like a French radical, and Plivier like a German radical.

who were influenced by the frontier and were the first to abandon and even to contemn the English pattern. The New England, Mid-Atlantic, and Southern schools did little toward the creation of an American pattern, because, their protestations notwithstanding, they imitated the English. They did not even come close to the actual speech of the people with whom they lived. In truth, they even eschewed that speech as something crude and barbarous. Wherever fragments of Americanness appeared in their works it was due to the impact of the frontier force and not the pressure of their immediate environment. Whitman, as we pointed out, was the most important Easterner to respond to the influence of the frontier force and to begin the creation of an American pattern. In the twentieth century, as we have just stressed, that pattern has already begun to crystallize. No one any longer can confuse the majority of American writers with English ones. *In Our Time, Look Homeward Angel, Main Street, Winesburg Ohio, The Great Gatsby, An American Tragedy, The Company, Sanctuary* are fictions which are American and not English in spirit and conception. The environment and the people and the speech of America live as intimately within them as the environment and the people and the speech of England live in the fictions of Thomas Hardy, John Galsworthy, and Sheila Kaye Smith.

III

All this vast nationalistic coming-of-age, all this sudden insurgency of sentiment and invigorating independence of outlook, releasing us more completely from our colonial complex than ever before, reached a final climax of conviction in the World War. The World War ended with America instead of England as the leading world power.[58] One of the

---

[58]A factor which should not be disregarded in this connection, and which in its economic form underlay this whole political change long before it achieved this definite expression, was the difference in energy-production of the two countries which reached a common level at the beginning of this century. In 1870, as Doctor C. K. Leith has shown,

best illustrations of the effect of this shift in power, resulting in such an important mutation in the American temper, is to be found in the change of status of New York as a city. It was only after the War that New York really became a world-city. As Mr. Spingarn observed some time ago, when he left America to fight in Europe New York was just a big city; on his return, however, a year and a half later, it was transformed into a cosmopolitan centre, equal, as a great capital, to such European cities as London, Paris, and Berlin. The experience of many other minds has been very similar. This change of New York from a big city into a world city had its immediate effect upon our whole cultural consciousness. Not only did all the great European artists flock to the American metropolis—many of them even taking up permanent residence here—but American artists themselves became conscious of a new power. All this, however, was but a climax to the spirit of national confidence which had grown up in America after the Spanish American War.[59]

The selection of Sinclair Lewis as the Nobel prize winner in 1931 marked a further if not a final release from the last lingering traces of our colonial complex. At length Europe,

Great Britain was releasing about three times as much energy as the United States. Now the ratio is reversed, the United States producing three times that of Great Britain. The two curves of production crossed about the opening of the century, but the significance of the crossing was hardly realized at the time. (C. K. Leith: *World Minerals and World Politics:* New York, 1931: p. 49.)

[59]One of the most important forces in the expression of this new and genuine national consciousness was—and is still—to be discovered in the change in the nature of our periodical literature. Beginning with such little magazines as Harriet Monroe's *Poetry* and Margaret Anderson's *Little Review,* the conservatism of the older magazines, which were bound by the most obvious allegiance to the English tradition, was steadily undermined until in the decade of the twenties we even see such old periodicals as *Scribner's, Harpers,* and *The North American Review* changing their intellectual front. Even the weeklies revealed this change with amazing swiftness. *The New Republic* from the very beginning manifested an early expression of it, while *The Nation* had to change hands before it could become an embodiment of the same force. Thus it was that the task which *The North American Review* set out for itself early in the nineteenth century, namely, that of cultivating a truly national literature, did not find a realization finally in our periodical literature until almost a century later.

which had steadily sneered at American literature in the past, gave one of our writers international recognition. But the gesture was more than the recognition of an individual writer. It was also the recognition of a literature—for Sinclair Lewis, after all, is the most American of American writers. Lewis has revealed America as it had never been revealed in nineteenth-century literature. Babbitt is an American type, a "hundred per cent American." Zenith is and only could be an American town. Elmer Gantry could only be an American. Even the style of his satires could only be American. It was this very Americanness which in large part won the prize for Lewis.

The environment in which our colonial complex was born and nurtured is now dead. The attitude of inferiority which accompanied that complex has already begun to lose its grip upon the writers of this generation.[60] Although we still lack what Henry Seidel Canby has recently called "a confident intellectualism" in our literary life—it is not because we continue to look to a European country for emulation, but because we have not yet realized the full potentialities of growth that lie before us.[61]

[60] The revolt against the colonial complex in this century has taken on curious forms. In the words of Waldo Frank: "We are in revolt against the academies and institutions which would whittle America down to a few stale realities current fifty years ago when our land in all but the political surface of its life was yet a colony of Britain." (Waldo Frank: *Our America:* New York, 1919: p. 9.)

[61] It is an interesting and significant fact that, as a result of the factors which we have discussed in this chapter, music in America has begun to follow a path parallel to that of literature. American music is at last beginning to escape from the bondage of the colonial complex. "America is drawing toward the end of her long, necessary period of musical childhood and timid dependence on Europe," Daniel Gregory Mason has recently declared, "(and) she is even now in the somewhat awkward self-conscious stage of adolescence, and that before long she will be musically adult." Later on Mr. Mason states that "what we still need is for that American culture to get, so to speak, into our blood, to become a part of us, so that we may become musically natural, easy, free from the sense of inferiority—in short, no longer merely assimilative, but at length creative." (Daniel Gregory Mason: *Tune In, America:* New York, 1931: pp. viii and 4.) It is revealing also to observe that in keeping with our literary development, it has been the West rather than the East—"Eastern orchestras, more dominated by European traditions," Mr. Mason avers,

The problems that face our writers to-day are not American problems in a nationalistic sense, for American writers of to-day, in their rediscovery of America, are far from patriotic in their outlook. On the contrary, they are much more critical of the country in which they live than most of their predecessors ever were. They insist upon seeing America as it really is and not as they were taught to believe it is. Certainly no one could call *120 Million, Jews Without Money, Manhattan Transfer, 42nd Parallel, The Company, Look Homeward Angel, Daughter of Earth* or *Lumber* patriotic novels—and yet they are, all of them, American to the core. Little if anything of the English tradition lives in them. They have sprung out of the American environment as expressions of our life in its raw and naked form. The problems that these writers have to confront are problems connected with the class structure of our society, the economic set-up of our life; problems which spring out of the need to interpret a country which has never been interpreted genuinely and truthfully in the past. It is to the fulfillment of that end that the work of John Dos Passos, Michael Gold, Thomas Wolfe, Edwin Seaver, Charles Yale Harrison, Lester Cohen, Agnes Smedley, Louis Colman, Horace Gregory, and a score of younger writers is already dedicated.

"prove to be the ones that neglect our music"—which has encouraged American composers. In painting, the same desire for native independence has arisen. American painters "must enter emotionally into the strong native tendencies of their own land and kind," Thomas Craven has declared, and "have done with European traditions and alien cultural fetishes." (Thomas Craven: *American Painters: The Snob Spirit: Scribner's Magazine*, Vol. XCI, No. 2, February, 1932, pp. 81–87.) The American artist in the past, Mr. Craven contends, has been "taught by the snobs who dominate the art schools that Europe offers the standard of values." He has been "afflicted with submerged feelings of inferiority which explains his snobbish adoration of European manners," Mr. Craven insists, and then goes on to show that only when "American life develops in painters interests stronger than the interests aroused by canonized art, (can) we . . . hope for a native American school."

CHAPTER II

THE PURITAN MYTH

WHILE the colonial complex influenced the entire spirit of American literature, it was in New England that its manifestations were most conspicuous. The philosophy of Puritanism, with its contempt for art as a form of aristocratic extravagance, was peculiarly adapted to the state of mind in which such a complex could best survive. Moreover it was this specific state of mind which handicapped New England literature—and American literature as a whole—from the very outset. Where the incentive indispensable to art creation was discouraged, opportunity for originality was practically eliminated. This second force, then, the so-called puritanic attitude toward art, conjoined with the psychological encumbrance of the colonial complex, stunted our literature from its very beginnings.

Overwhelmed thus by an attitude toward art which was uncordial if not hostile, and hampered by the sense of inferiority nurtured by the colonial complex, New England talent addressed more of its energy in the direction of religion than in that of art. Literature and religion, for example, almost became synonymous. Much has been made of the fact that the Puritans were not so opposed to art as has often been claimed, that Cotton Mather advised both the reading and writing of poetry, and even worked out his own theory of prose style, and yet it cannot be denied that the Puritans never encouraged art with any whole-hearted vigor. Beneath Cotton Mather's entire attitude, there dwelt an obstinate religiosity. His interest in the religious always obscured his concern for the æsthetic. His observation on how to read history revealed the real nature of his interest: "In Reading of all History, every now and then make con-

venient Pause; to think What can I see of the Glorious God
in these occurrences?" Even in the most trifling and prosaic
of things this attitude found a religious extension. The mundane affairs of the household as well as the spiritual business
of the state deserved the attention of religion. Nothing, in
Mather's eyes, escaped the religious imprint. If the people
in the house happened to be brewing, he was wont to say
"Lord let us find in a Glorious Christ, a providence for our
thirsty souls." If baking was going on, his prayer was: "Lord,
let a Glorious Christ butter bread of life to us," and if it
was washing that was being undertaken, his words were: "O
wash us thoroughly from sin! O, take away our filthy garments from us!"[1] This obsession for things religious dominated the outlook of New England literature for over a
century.

The Puritan tradition, which was directly carried over
from England, naturally embodied many of the characteristics of its original setting. The English Puritans, it must
be remembered, were in large part members of the upper
and not the lower middle class. Contrary to the usual conception, the Puritan group in England combined in its ranks
members of the aristocracy as well as bona fide representatives of the bourgeoisie. The Earl of Essex, for instance, was
first commander in chief of the army of Parliament.[2] Pym,
the Puritan leader, rallied over thirty peers to his support.[3]
Many of the nobles, depending upon whether they lived in
those parts of the country where trading interests were on
the increase, shifted their activities from landed to commercial enterprise, and allied themselves, thus, more closely
with the merchant class than with the aristocratic. The upper
ranks of the English Puritan group, consequently, were filled
with many men whose inclinations and ideals were scarcely
very *puritanic* in their stress. Even Cromwell, a genuine

[1]Wm. B. Peabody: *Life of Cotton Mather:* Boston, 1836: p. 191.
[2]Samuel Rawson Gardner: *Puritan Revolution:* London, 1884: p. 132.
[3]Sir John Marriott: *The Crisis of English Liberty:* Oxford, 1930: pp.
140–146.

Puritan in spirit if there ever was one, was not so *puritanic* in his attitude as we have often been led to believe. A great lover of music, he was wont to entertain foreign ambassadors with all the fascinating devices of that art.[4] It was Cromwell also who insisted upon the nation's retaining possession of the cartoons of Raphael and the "Triumph of Cæsar" by Montegna, which later Charles II attempted to sell to the King of France.[5] Cromwell, then, was not so insensitive to the appeal of art as he has usually been represented. Nor was Colonel Hutchinson, who was, as we have learned from his wife's memoirs, a patron of art and learning, with an intense zest for living in forms that were very remote from the ascetic. A skilled musician himself, he maintained a lively interest in painting and literature as well as in music. Like Cromwell, he was fond of hunting and all the many attractions of the sportsman's life.[6] And so it was with many if not most of the leaders and members of the upper ranks of the English Puritan movement. In a certain sense they were closer, far closer, to the ideology of the ruling class, so powerful had they already become, than they were to the ideology of the lower ranks of their own party. While they were turbulently determined to exclude from their churches those forms of art which tended to strengthen Catholic superstition, they were not fanatically bent upon destroying art upon principle.[7] In point of fact, as we have observed, these upper and wealthier members of the Puritan party were more hospitable to art than hostile to it. Their aim was to purify the Anglican Church rather than to separate from it, and it was they, who, in quite reactionary manner, offered to compromise with Charles I, if he would make their Puritan Church into the Established Church of England. It was the army, which was inspired by the sentiments of the lower middle class, the Dissenters, instead of the upper middle

[4]John Brown: *The English Puritans*: Cambridge, 1910: p. 152.
[5]Ibid., p. 152.
[6]C. Sydney Carter: *Puritanism, Its History, Spirit and Influence*: London *Quarterly Review*, October, 1924.
[7]Ibid., p. 184.

class, that kidnapped Charles just as he was about to concede to the Puritan compromise. *The conflict which has been altogether too little considered by the scholar, between these upper and lower middle-class elements in the English religious movements of the day, has created so much of the confusion which exists as to what Puritanism is and what it is not.* One thing is certain; that is that Puritanism was not the same for both elements. It could not be. The harsh and unyielding antagonism to art which has been usually ascribed to Puritanism as a whole loses its meaning in the light of our earlier observations. Upper middle-class Puritanism, as exemplified by the attitudes and interests of Cromwell and Hutchinson, was not nihilistic in its reaction to art; the lower middle-class Dissenters, on the other hand,—certain of the lower middle-class elements in the Puritan movement in this respect shared the same sentiments as the Dissenters,—were devastatingly intense in their antipathy for art in every form.[8] This contrast and contradiction was as natural as it was inevitable. The upper middle-class elements had shared many of the advantages of culture with the aristocracy, and in closer touch with the aristocracy as they were, and having more to gain from it by way of compromise, they were bound to be

[8]As Thomas Cuming Hall shows, in illuminating detail, it was this lower middle class, with its Lollard tradition, which expressed that special type of asceticism which is usually thought of as the embodiment of the spirit of Puritanism. It was they who developed the "deep-seated antagonism to the amusements, the forms of worship, the spirit and drift of the ruling classes." The upper-class Puritans, the Cromwells, Hutchinsons, and Pyms, never took such a decisive attitude. It must be remembered that, bitter as was the attitude of the lower middle classes toward the amusements and arts of the aristocracy, it was never shared by the very lowest classes, the serfs and groundlings, who were directly dependent upon the aristocracy for their subsistence. *The lower classes, therefore, never adopted Lollardy as their tradition;* only "the serious-minded and upward-struggling," lower middle class adopted it. It was this rising, hard-working, lower middle class, then, with its dedication to a religion of asceticism, a dedication that was part of the inwrought consecration of its economic way of life, which saw nothing but futility in an existence of pleasure and, consequently, swiftly came to hate, with what soon was almost an instinctive venom, the art, religion, and manners of the aristocracy. (Thomas Cuming Hall: *Religious Background of American Culture*: Boston, 1930: p. 34.)

less hostile to many of its cultural tendencies.[9] The lower
middle class, however, which had shared practically nothing
of the advantages of aristocratic culture, and which, lacking
power itself, had nothing to gain from it, developed all the
hostilities to its way of life, in dress, in speech, in art, which
have become characteristically but erroneously associated
with the word Puritanism.[10]

The American colonists in the main were drawn from this
lower middle-class element,[11] and embodied its philosophy

[9]A striking analogy here can be made between the upper and lower
middle-class forces of that day and the upper and lower class elements
in the British labor movement at the present time. While the economic
objectives are very different, the psychological tendencies, as we shall
see, are remarkably similar. Ramsay MacDonald and Philip Snowden, for
instance, can conveniently be looked upon as the Cromwell and Pym of
to-day; for despite all their affection for labor, they are really much
closer in their inclinations to the ruling (capitalist) class than they are to
the spirit of the proletariat. Ramsay MacDonald can more easily don a
court costume and enter into sweet audience with the king than he can
mingle with the embittered and desperate workers in the English mines
and mills. Like Cromwell in his day, MacDonald has a warmer appreciation of the culture of the ruling class than he has contempt for it. The
communist elements in the working-class movement to-day, hating as
they do every aspect of the ruling-class ideology, are similar in their
psychology to the lower middle-class Dissenters, the Levellers and Inde-
pendents of the seventeenth century. Sharing nothing of the advantage
of the supremacy of the ruling class, advantages which MacDonald,
Snowden, and Webb have been able to share in so many ways, they have
nothing to lose in working for its complete destruction, ideologically or
economically. Hence the difference between the evolutionary emphasis
of the upper-class leaders and members of the labor movement—this is as
true in Germany and France as in England—and the revolutionary emphasis of the lower-class elements, the totally dispossessed proletariat.
(Since the time when this was written, the gestures of these gentlemen
of the Labor Party have borne out in even more conclusive detail the truth
of the foregoing observation. At the present time, for instance, Mr.
MacDonald has found it fitting to sever his connections with the Labor
Party "in order to save the nation" for the bourgeoisie.)

[10]The larger part of this lower middle class never associated itself with
the Puritan movement at all but, in keeping with traditions of the
Lollards, became Dissenters and Levellers, and in general scorned the
Puritans as "compromisers."

[11]Samuel Eliot Morison: *Builders of the Bay Colony*: p. 342. As Doctor
Morison shows, the "emigrants came mostly from the middle classes in
town and country . . . they came in small family and neighborhood
groups, often following some popular non-conformist preacher such as
Cotton or Shepard; or Ezekiel Rogers who brought a colony of Yorkshire
clothiers to Rowley, or Richard Mathew, who brought a Lancashire group

in thought and action. It was the morality and outlook of
that class which they expressed in their culture. The overwhelming concern for religion which literally obsessed their
pioneer minds, the fierce hatred of amusements, which made
them attack every form of festivity that was without sacred
connotation, were all forthright manifestations of this lower
middle-class logic of conviction. Inwoven here, as an intimate part of their social philosophy, was their detestation of
every form of art which had an aristocratic savor. Their predilection for plainness in every way, driving them to exclude
all evidence of art in their churches and to subdue any semblance of ornamentation in their dress, was a direct outgrowth of the petty bourgeois psychology which had first
revealed itself in the early protests of the English Lollards.
Nothing that smacked of aristocratic origin was tolerated.

The Bay Colony, to be sure, was not made up entirely of
members of the petty bourgeoisie. A number of the leaders in
that colonial enterprise, as Charles Beard has noted, were
"people of substance." The majority of them, however, were
of lower middle-class extraction, people of little substance,
if you will,[12] members of the English yeomanry, the poor
gentry, renters of farms, small merchants of sundry sort, descendants of butchers and grocers and other varieties of commercial life of undistinguished station. The official Puritanism, with its Calvinistic conceptions, which the leaders attempted to install in America, was far more upper middle
class than lower middle class in its stress, but the conditions
of the environment, the presence of the frontier factor, the
absence of sufficient wealth in the community, and the lower
middle-class character of the colonists as a whole, forced it
in time to forsake its upper middle-class attitude toward life.
Puritanism, in England, as we have noted, was primarily an
upper middle-class phenomenon. Indeed, as Thomas Cum-

to join the West Countrymen at Dorchester." Thomas Cuming Hall also
states that "the great body of those going out as colonists were of the
class from which Dissent drew its members." (P. 79.)

[12]James Truslow Adams: *The Founding of New England:* Boston, 1921:
p. 124.

ing Hall has shown, Puritanism can be accurately described
as "aristocratic and imperial in tone and temper."[13] It opposed rather than favored the principles of equality and
freedom. It conceived of democracy, to quote the words of
Winthrop, as "the meanest and worst of all forms of government." The lower middle classes could not very well sub-
scribe to such a creed, for it would have violated the very
essence of their existence. As we have seen, it was to the doctrines of Dissent, with their democratic conceptions, as exemplified in the organization of the Plymouth colony, that the
petty bourgeois elements were dedicated. Constituting the
vast majority of the population, and aided by the nature of
the environment which emphasized its virtues, it was not
long before the Dissenting elements in the population forced
this official Puritanism, in the Synod of Cambridge in 1648,
to capitulate.[14] This early victory of the Dissenters over the
Puritans prevented Puritan doctrine from establishing itself
as the prevailing cultural pattern.

Another point which deserves consideration here is the
fact that few of the leaders of the official Puritan group were
men of large possessions, or descended from families of extreme wealth. In general they belonged to the lower ranks
of the Puritan movement rather than to the upper. While
religion did bring to America persons like Winthrop who at
one time was a large landowner in England—it is interesting to observe that his estates had declined rapidly before he
departed for America—and other members of the wealthier
sections of the middle class, Robert Beverly was, nevertheless, almost as correct in connection with New England as
he was with Virginia when he said that "it is not likely that
any man of a plentiful (means) should voluntarily abandon

---

[13]Thomas Cuming Hall: *The Religious Background of American Culture*:
Boston, 1930: p. 174. V. L. Parrington also describes the doctrines of the
Puritans, born of the philosophy of Calvin, as "rigidly aristocratic."
(*The Colonial Mind*: New York, 1927: p. 16.) In civil government, as
Preserved Smith has also pointed out, Calvin "preferred an aristocracy."
(*The Age of the Reformation*: New York, 1920: p. 597.)
[14]Ibid., p. 105.

a happy certainty, to roam after imaginary advantages in a new world."[15] Religious persecution, threat of confiscation of property, and other factors combined with a desire for freedom of worship (not freedom of worship for others but for themselves) undoubtedly did inspire the emigration of certain members of the upper bourgeoisie to America.[16] But these types constituted the exception instead of the rule. Thomas Shepard, for example, was the son of a grocer's apprentice; John Harvard was the son of a butcher; Henry Dunster was descended from yeoman stock; and even John Eliot, who became a Cambridge graduate, was born in a family of extremely humble circumstances. As a result, the mainstay of the Puritan leadership was more inclined to advocate the ascetic virtues of the petty bourgeois Dissenters[17] than the more cultivated virtues of the upper bourgeois Puritans of the Cromwellian and Hutchinson type in England. Certain of the leaders of the first generation, men like Bradford and Winthrop, it is true, were by training and temperament closer to the ideology of the upper middle class than that of the lower middle class, closer, indeed, to Hampden

[15] Robert Beverly: *The History and Present State of Virginia:* London, 1705: Part IV, p. 50.

[16] The religious force at that time, having acquired intensity and momentum from the economic conflict of which it was the cultural expression, was able in cases to work vertically as well as horizontally, although the exceptions were far less numerous than is usually supposed. To illustrate, certain wealthy merchants and owners of large landed estates who actually came over with the Bay Colony were men who, in the crisis of the conflict in England, had been driven to such a point of desperation that even the greater economic advantage which England may still have held out for them over that promised by New England was not sufficient to deter them.

[17] Puritanism in America, as Hall states, was "far more influenced by Dissent than Dissent was by Puritanism" (p. 107) from joining the colonists. The psychological process in such cases very often worked somewhat as follows: The economic conflict became so acute that its religious expression became more and more intense, so that in time the religious conviction with the individual became a far more determining factor than the economic. The same is true in other cases in which social or moral considerations instead of religious became a motivating factor. Of course, and it cannot be stressed too often, all these motivations were but ramified products of the economic order of the time. It is simply their personal, their individual expression which is not economic. In the case of early

and Hutchinson than to Praise-God Barebones. But those leaders were in the minority, and after the first generation they practically disappeared. But in the last analysis, it was the environment which made their type of leadership unable to continue. It was the nature of the native conditions of life which made it impossible for an upper bourgeois ideology to survive in America in the seventeenth century. The character of the frontier milieu favored instead the upward-struggling, self-denying, pleasure-hating ideology of the petty bourgeoisie.

This brings us to a new and revealing insight into the nature and place of art in American life. It makes it possible for us to understand better the basis of what may be called the American æsthetic attitude. Although the origins of this attitude are to be found in New England, its spirit, due to the spread of the same psychology, fostered by the evolution of similar economic circumstance, became dominant in the country as a whole. Subject as it was to all the carking handicaps of the colonial complex, it nevertheless absorbed only those parts of the mother culture which were conducive to its own avenues of thought. It is not to Puritanism, therefore, which we must turn in order to apprehend the character of New England life and literature. Puritanism in England, as we have noted, represented latitudes of variation which never found root on our soil. In America Puritanism proper, or at least its upper middle-class manifestations, exercised comparatively little influence upon our life. It was the lower middle-class philosophy of Dissent that established itself here, and that provided the background in which our con-

Christianity, for instance, the conversion of certain nobles to Christian doctrine, the sacrifices they underwent, the agonies they endured, cannot be said to have been motivated by economic logic; nevertheless, the struggle itself, which Christianity represented, was unquestionably a result of underlying economic conflict. Certain of the members of the upper bourgeoisie who came over with the Bay Colonists were instances to an extent of that reaction. Of course, in other cases, as in that of Winthrop, decline in economic possessions in the home country made them more inclined to venture the fresh possibilities of the New World rather than cling to the withering possibilities of the Old.

cepts were born. To understand the development and direction of our culture, therefore, we must first realize that it evolved almost wholly and completely out of a petty bourgeois concept of existence.

The importance of the petty bourgeois origins of American psychology, insofar as our art and literature are concerned, can hardly be overestimated. Even to-day, as we shall show in more detail in later chapters, the effects of that origin have not been destroyed. On the whole, we continue to be a nation of petty bourgeoisie in our attitudes and convictions. While the opposition to all art which did not serve a religious end has disappeared, and there has been created an artist group and following which scorn the petty bourgeois outlook upon things artistic, the American public as a whole, aside from that group and that following, has not yet escaped the æsthetic—or unæsthetic—philosophy of that class. The best proof of that fact is to be discovered in the unconcealed indifference to the finer aspects of art on the part of American leaders in almost every field of activity: political, economic, educational. An evidence of the extent of this influence upon American life to-day can be readily seen by contrasting the concern for art and literature on the part of the personalities which make up the Houses of Parliament and those that make up the Houses of Congress. No ruling class in the Western world to-day is so lacking in a cultural interest in the arts as our own. Encumbered by the sense of inferiority bred in him by the colonial complex, the American artist has been doubly handicapped by the addition of this petty bourgeois attitude toward his work which undoubtedly has retarded him as much by its later indifference as by its earlier hostility.

Furthermore, America is the only country of any importance in the modern civilized world where literature and art have grown up without the influence of an aristocratic tradition. There is scarcely any other cultural consideration which should give us greater pause. Whatever may be stated in attack upon the spirit and rule of modern aristocracies, their interest in the arts cannot be gainsaid. In keeping with the very nature of their life, aristocracies cultivated the arts as an exalted form of entertainment and amusement.[18] If they did not pamper the artist, they at least did not discourage him in the nature of his work. In general, the art which grew up under the protection of aristocracies, the art that flourished under Elizabeth, for example, or that which enriched the reign of Louis the XIV, was an art which was hedonistic rather than moral in motivation. Although it is "bourgeois art," as Howard Mumford Jones observes, that "runs to the didactic" (*America and French Culture*, op. cit., p. 294), it would be incorrect to say that it was "bourgeois art" which introduced the moral or didactic element into literature. After all, evidences of didacticism are to be discovered in the writings of such writers as Spencer, Sidney, Racine, and Fénelon, who were products of the aristocratic tradition. The important difference lies in the fact that didacticism is seldom more than incidental to aristocratic art, whereas it becomes fundamental to bourgeois art. It served to entertain, even to inspire, but rarely to instruct or reform. Its purpose was exquisitely useless. Like the fountains at Versailles which, as Walpole described, "to contradict utility, toss their waste of waters into the air in spouting columns," aristocratic art had little concern for the useful. The artist thus had but to impress and move. Within a tradition so elastic and cordial, his talents had ample opportunity to shape and mature.

In order to avoid misunderstanding in reference to the aristocratic factor, it is important to point out that it was not the aristocracy itself which created art, but merely the nature of its life which led it to encourage its creation on the part of others. Few important artists have been of aristocratic birth. Contradictiously enough, it was the nature of its life

---

[18]This was not as true of country aristocracies as of urban aristocracies. Country aristocracies on the whole were ignorant of art appreciation and showed little interest in culture. It was the urban aristocracies which patronized and cultivated the arts.

and its philosophy which discouraged its own talent from becoming creative in the arts that at the same time encouraged outside talents to become creative. In few instances, for that matter, was its encouragement very genuine. The artist, in its eyes, was a kind of exalted jester, to be patronized because he was an asset to a higher form of amusement. Few members of the Elizabethan or Augustan aristocracies, for example, were aware of the significance of the art to which they had indirectly given birth. Another point to be remembered is that when we speak of the aristocratic tradition, we do not mean a tradition which was created anew and originally by modern aristocracies. What was called the aristocratic tradition—an outgrowth of the mediæval cultural pattern, which in turn was derived from the Greek and Roman synthesis— was built upon the homogeneity of Western culture. The aristocracies did not create the tradition; they merely gave it a specific form, a form which in literature, for example, expressed itself as the aristocratic conception of tragedy. What the aristocracies did, in other words, was to provide the means, the wherewithal, which were necessary for the cultivation of a tradition. Uncreative themselves, they made it possible for the artists whom they patronized to be creative. They were not interested in the promotion of art as art, as an addition to culture, but as a form of pleasant and, perhaps, inspiring escape—escape not from reality but from boredom. Nevertheless it was the presence of that interest which made it possible for art to flourish under its influence.

It was within such a tradition that Shakespeare, Ben Jonson, Marlowe, Wycherly, Congreve, Racine, and Corneille developed. In every European country such a tradition played a most important part in giving character and cast to the art of the nation. It provided a background to which artists could cling and an inspiration which very often was able to survive antagonistic conditions and controls. Even when it was superseded by the bourgeois tradition, it never failed to function as a qualifying factor in literary evolution. The æsthetic attitudes of the upper middle class, as we have shown, were unquestionably affected by it in a very profound way. The poetry of Milton, to cite an example, springing as it did from the upper middle-class Puritan psychology, showed greater affinity for the aristocratic tradition than for that of the petty bourgeois. Even the literature, scant though it was, that emerged out of petty bourgeois origins in England, as evidenced in Bunyan's *Pilgrim's Progress* and *Grace Abounding*, was not entirely unaffected by the presence of the aristocratic tradition. No writer in fact that lived within the radius of an aristocratic tradition could completely escape its influence. Wherever social life became a conflict of tendencies and traditions—aristocratic, upper middle class, lower middle class—the subordinate ones were bound to be affected by the dominant one.[19] However hostile the petty bourgeois attitude was to the aristocratic, the very nature of the hostility, intensified by actual struggle with it, was certain to influence its spirit. Where the aristocratic tradition was absent, and there was no struggle to aggravate hostility, as was the condition in America, the petty bourgeois attitude toward art soon became more indifferent than antagonistic.

It was only in America that the petty bourgeois conception of life was able to gain complete and unchallenged control of a culture. The importance of that fact, I believe, is very great. Handicapped as our literati were by the centrifugal impact of the colonial complex, they were even more hampered by this lower middle-class[20] philosophy of life which looked upon art with an apathy allied to scorn. In England the petty bourgeoisie never rose to power and never acquired such control. It was the upper bourgeoisie, closer to the court than to the commoner, which was the victor there.

[19]The effect of the bourgeois tradition upon the aristocratic in nineteenth-century England is a splendid example of an amazing aspect of this process. When the upper bourgeoisie gained final control of English culture in the nineteenth century, during the Victorian era, we find the aristocracy itself becoming middle class in its faiths and ideals.

[20]To avoid confusion on the part of the reader, let me say that I have used the words "petty bourgeois" and "lower middle class" interchangeably throughout the volume. I have done this obviously in order to avoid the constant repetition of the same phrase.

Puritanism in England consequently was never what Puritanism, so-called, was in America. The petty bourgeois Dissenters, who established themselves in America, were able in a short time to dominate the psychology of the country. There was no aristocratic tradition to hold it in check, nor any upper-class influence to temper its asceticisms and asperities. Even those aristocrats such as Lord Baltimore who did come to American shores, and those who fled to Virginia in the 1650's came either as individuals and not as members of a class, or as exiles rather than emigrants.[21] They were in no more advantageous position to transplant their own tradition upon American soil than are the Russian emigrés to-day to extend their tradition into the various countries where they have fled. The very nature of the new environment would have thwarted any such attempts even if they had been made. Nor would the rich middle-class Puritans have been very much more successful had they endeavored to introduce their own practices and prejudices into a country at once so new and so alien. The hangings in Cromwell's bedrooms, depicting in colorful patterns the story of Vulcan, Mars and Venus, the garden decorations which he cherished, the statues of Cleopatra, Adonis, and Apollo which he loved to have about him,[22] expressed a taste for art and culture which was scarcely in keeping with the hard and unyielding demands of the New England frontier. It is doubtful whether the upper middle class could have survived had it striven to settle and rule here. Of course, having less to gain from such emigration, it naturally preferred England to America as its home. It was the lower middle class, which had more to gain in America, religiously as well as economically, that inevitably flocked over here in great numbers.[23] And it was that very same class which, by virtue of an amaz-

[21]Almost all the Cavaliers who came to Virginia after the defeat of Charles I returned to England as soon as Charles II was restored in 1660. Thomas Cuming Hall, op. cit., p. 113.

[22]Joseph Crouch: *Puritanism and Art*: London, 1910: p. 167.

[23]James Truslow Adams: *The Founding of New England*: Boston, 1921: p. 122.

ing and almost uncanny historical coincidence, succeeded so well here because its self-denying, hard-working, upward-struggling psychology fitted so exactly the needs of the pioneer environment.

This perfect harmony of psychology and setting gave the petty bourgeoisie an unprecedented advantage in establishing its foothold in America. It wrote its traditions into the environment and the environment into its traditions. From the very beginning its economic and psychological conquest was complete. It entrenched itself throughout the length and breadth of existence, in daily routine as well as in Sabbath ritual. Its outlook upon life dominated economics, politics, education, art, religion. No detail of behavior eluded its scrutiny. As a newly established ruling class, its power was supreme. It vied with no other class, had to wrest power from no other class. It was the source and centre of culture and control.

America, then, is the one country whose whole tradition grew out of an unadulterated petty bourgeois psychology. It is the one country which the petty bourgeois was able to control from the very beginning and shape in terms of its own destiny. In a very important sense, we can say that America is the great petty bourgeois experiment—just as Soviet Russia to-day is the great proletarian experiment. It was the psychology of the petty bourgeois, as we stated before, and not that of the upper bourgeois, which determined the course that our life was to follow. It formulated at once and almost ineradicably our attitudes toward religion, art, and the state. Forced to no compromise with other traditions, aristocratic and upper middle class, it gave no quarter to tendencies and aspirations which were in opposition to its own. It is not the psychology of Puritanism, therefore, which we must study, but the psychology of the petty bourgeois, if we are to understand the origin and development of American life and literature. Upper middle-class Puritanism which found its embodiment in the attitudes of such men as John Milton, Oliver Cromwell, John Glynn, and Sir Benjamin

Richard, never reached these shores; only the lower middle-class ideology of the Dissenters succeeded in spreading here. Even the Puritanism which did land here was the Puritanism of the lower and poorer elements in the movement, and was far more petty bourgeois than upper bourgeois in its perspective.

It is only to-day that we can appreciate how much of the inferiority of our literature, in both inspiration and achievement, is due to its having been dominated so completely by this petty bourgeois philosophy. The absence of an aristocratic tradition limited our literature from the start. It deprived us at once of an attitude toward art which was conducive to its creation. Without an American aristocracy to purchase his books or encourage his efforts in any of the arts, the existence of an English aristocratic tradition could have little meaning to the artist in America. "There was no Mermaid, no Will's in Boston," as Professor Murdock has stated, and, "such taverns as there were heard more of Indian raids, of crops, of fisheries, of trade, than of poetics or of wit. There was no royal court in Massachusetts. There were no idle or gay dilettantes to praise or condemn current poetry; no patrons to aid struggling authors; no book-buying public, except for such books that were tried and tested by time, or likely to be helpful in the day's work."[24] The American writer, therefore, had to write for the petty bourgeois audience which confronted him or not write at all. If there had been the neutralizing effect of an upper middle-class tradition, he would at least have had some choice. But with his entire culture monopolized by a class whose English heritage was hostile to art, and whose American attitude toward it was worse than apathetic, he was hemmed in on every side, in a spiritual prison which provided neither light nor food for his impulse.

[24] Introduction: *Handkerchiefs from Paul and, Being Pious and Consolatory Verses of Puritan Massachusetts including unpublished poems of Benjamin Tompson, John Wilson, Anna Hayden.* . . . Edited with an Introduction by Kenneth B. Murdock: Cambridge, 1927: p. xviii.

Now that we have cleared the way somewhat for a more careful consideration of the nature and evolution of American literature, we must look at the literature itself if we are to see the effects of this petty bourgeois psychology in action. It is to religion that we must turn first, for it is there that this psychology found its focal centre. In religion, the lower middle class had forged its most effective weapon. When we remember that the entire culture of the Middle Ages had revolved about a religious orbit; that even kings and princes had often been forced to accept its decision along with jester and serf; that all of life in those days was permeated with religious significances, from the infinitesimal to the infinite, we can easily understand why economic classes at the time of the Renaissance in France, Holland, Germany, as well as in England, expressed their revolt in religious instead of political or economic form. Religion was the great mask behind which everything was concealed. It was the only cultural form of expression to which men could resort. If change was in the air only religion could justify it. When feudalism broke down, and with the rise of commerce the town supplanted the manor, the individualistic spirit which emerged ineluctably assumed a religious guise.[25] Only later when the various Protestant religions, which vivified the individualistic revolt, emancipated themselves completely from Rome, did the religious insurgency begin to take on definite political form. The literature which expressed this revolt was almost as religious in its early developments as it was in its origins. For a long time, indeed, it was more of a religious literature than a literature with a religious motivation. Not until the revolt which it expressed advanced beyond the religious front into the political did it escape its theological background.

"A careful study of American church history is one of the prime requisites for the historian of American letters,"

[25]Oscar Marti: *Economic Causes of the Reformation in England:* New York, 1929: p. xxi; also Preserved Smith: *A History of Modern Culture:* New York, 1930: p. 9.

Howard Mumford Jones observed with philosophic shrewd-ness, "for the American Protestant churches have been the nurse and mother of our culture."[26] Professor Jones goes even further and speaks of the American church and American religion, but, penetrating as his comments are on this topic, he fails to distinguish between the religious psychology of the upper bourgeoisie and the lower, and though he realizes the difference between the American religious background and the European, he interprets the difference entirely in terms of the immediate environment without considering sufficiently the fundamental differences in class psychology and class dominancy which were involved. While Professor Jones understands better than perhaps any other American critic the influence of what he calls "the triumphant bourgeoisie" upon our religion and literature, he does not see that it was not the bourgeoisie as a whole but the petty bourgeoisie who, superimposing their psychology upon the environment, and in turn absorbing the environment into their psychology, gave American religion its Americanness. Nor does Professor Jones take notice of the fact that it was only the absence of another tradition to challenge or curtail its supremacy, that made it possible for the petty bourgeois philosophy of life to become so representatively and over-whelmingly American. The American church and the American religion to which he refers were the church and religion of the triumphant petty bourgeoisie. And it was this church and this religion, with all their ramifications, which gave form to the American mind and the American outlook upon æsthetics.

As we shall see in later pages in this chapter, practically all the religious leaders in the Puritan movement in America adopted the same attitude toward art as that entertained by the Dissenters. The American environment throughout the seventeenth century was a levelling force, emphasizing

[26]Cf. Howard Mumford Jones: *The European Background*, essay appearing in Norman Foerster's symposium: *Reinterpretation of American Literature*: New York, 1928: pp. 76, 79.

resemblances and obscuring differences. Calvinism broke down into Congregationalism; aristocratic attitudes tended to dissolve into democratic; and cultural conceptions acquired in the old country came to lose their meaning and distinction in the new. Nevertheless the fact that the Puritan clergy as a whole had descended from a more cultured tradition was sufficient in itself to endow it with intellectual advantages superior to those of the less-cultured traditions. In the application of that tradition, however, those differences became inconspicuous. Cotton Mather might have been more interested in science than any of the members of the Dissenting clergy, but with regard to the theatre, to dancing, to painting, his attitude was much closer to that of the Dissenters than to that of Cromwell. Without doubt the levelling force of the environment, favoring the lower middle-class attitude instead of the upper, was accountable for a considerable part of his reaction. Removed from a milieu in which such cultural values possessed meaning, and plunged into one in which they had none, there was no stimulus to make him other than he was. But more important than that was the fact, which we noted before, that the overwhelming majority of the colonists who surrounded him were members of the lower middle class and not of the upper.

In no other country did a tradition ever develop in which it was necessary to justify interest in art on the basis of circumstance or conscience. Yet that is just what the ascetic tradition of the lower middle class made necessary in America. When Joseph Tompson, one of America's earliest poets, allowed himself the privilege of versifying, he invariably defended his action as forgivable only because it did not interfere with more serious and sacred things. In one instance he even went so far in his Journal as to state that the only reason he permitted himself to write poetry on a certain day was "that day was the after part of the day taken from my business abroad by reason of the rain." The exigencies of economic life of the middle class in America favored no such idle, impractical pursuits as those falling under the head of

belles lettres. If a man would write poetry, he must not let
it become more than a moral pastime (pastime in the seventeenth-century sense of the word, and not the twentieth) and
it must always be with a pious ideal in mind. It was not until
the eighteenth century, when American middle-class psychology began to change as its supremacy evidenced itself
more in the political domain than in the religious, that a poet
could hazard verse that failed to edify. As in the case of Joseph Tompson's brother Benjamin, all poets in America
throughout the seventeenth and the first half of the eighteenth century bowed before the petty bourgeois philosophy
and "suppressed in themselves all art for conscience's sake."[27]

Even Michael Wigglesworth and Anne Bradstreet in this
respect advanced not a step beyond their lesser known contemporaries. Indeed, the very title of Wigglesworth's most
celebrated poem: *The Day of Doom or a Poetical Description of the Great and Last Judgement. With a short discourse about Eternity,* reveals the same tendency in one of
its most barren and bleak extremes. The very success of the
poem, which sold out its first edition of eighteen hundred
copies within a year, indicated how well its spirit fitted the
philosophy of the time. Although Wigglesworth was a Puritan, his attitude toward art was not of the upper middle-class
strain.[28] He embodied in his verse all the fanaticism of the
lower middle class dominant in the America of his day. One
can scarcely find in these lines, culled from his *Day of
Doom,* any traces of that Cromwellian psychology which
admired Titians and treasured busts of Apollo and Venus:

"They wring their hands, their caitiff-hands, and gnash their teeth
    for terror,
They cry, they roar for anguish sore, and gnaw their tongues for
    horror.
But get away without delay, Christ pities not your cry;

[27]*Benjamin Tompson: His Poems:* edited by Howard Hudson Hall:
Boston, 1924: with an introduction by H. H. Hall.
[28]Like most of the other Puritans in America, he was closer to the
ideology of the lower middle class than to that of the upper.

Depart to Hell, there you may yell, and roar eternally.
With Iron bands they bind their hands and cursed feet together,
And cast them all, both great and small, into that Lake forever,
Where day and night, without respite, they wail, and cry and howl,
For tort'ring pain which they sustain, in Body and in Soul.
For day and night, in their despite, their torment's smoke ascendeth,
Their pain and grief have no relief, their anguish never endeth.
There must they lie and never die, though dying every day;
There must they dying ever lie and not consume away."

Nor was there any deviation from this same tendency in his poem *Meat out of the Eater; or Meditations concerning the Necessity, End and Usefulness and Afflictions unto God's Children. All tending to Prepare them for and Comfort them under the Cross,* which was second only to *The Day of Doom* in popularity in America throughout the seventeenth and the early part of the eighteenth century. The one poem by his son, Samuel, *The Funeral Song,* followed in the same tradition.

Anne Bradstreet, who was scarcely more than a feminine counterpart of Michael Wigglesworth, typified the same artistic obeisance to conscience that afflicted the versifying proclivities of such theocratic poetasters as John Cotton and Urian Oakes. Imitative in every line, her stanzas show all the unfortunate effects of that synthesis of the colonial complex and the petty bourgeois philosophy of life. Although the enormously elongated title of her volume of collected poems—such elongations were characteristic of the titles of poems in England at that time—*The Tenth Muse, Lately sprung up in America, or Severall Poems, compiled with great variety of Wit and Learning, full of delight. Wherein especially is contained a complete discourse and description of The Four elements, Constitutions, Ages of Man, Seasons of the Year. Together with an Exact Epitome of the Four Monarchies, viz., The Assyrian, Persian, Grecian, Roman. Also a Dialogue between Old England and New, concerning the late troubles. With divers other pleasant and serious poems. By a Gentle woman in those parts*—suggested an interest in more material and mundane things, the verses themselves, with their stilted imitations and artificialities, clung very close to the New England ideology. She never forgot to reprimand and chide herself for sins of omission as well as commission. In such lines as the following one can appreciate this spirit in one of its most straightforward forms:

"Silent, alone, where none or saw, or heard,
In pathless paths I lead my wand'ring feet,
My humble eyes to lofty Skyes I reared
To sing some Song, my mazed Muse thought meet.
My great Creator I would magnifie,
That nature had, thus decked liberally:
But Ah, and Ah, again, my imbecility!"

Although she was one of the first poets to put nature into verse, it was a nature that was always bound up closely with her religious psychology, a nature infused with didactic allusion and import.

If Michael Wigglesworth, Anne Bradstreet, and Benjamin Tompson reflected the petty bourgeois attitude in their hopelessly mediocre verse, the early annalists afforded even better testimony of it in their simple but at times inspired prose. Bradford's *History of the Plymouth Plantation,* dealing as it did with the career of the Pilgrims in England as well as with their later experiences in Holland and America, was filled with the same scriptural severities which mark the rest of the literature of the period. Other annalists of the time such as John Winthrop, Edward Winslow, and Edward Johnson were scarcely less pious or dismal. This very piety became so imbued in our culture that in time it was identified with every detail of our life, however insignificant or infinitesimal. Not only did Cotton Mather devise a prayer for such simple things as brewing, baking, and washing, as we noted before, but as an illustration of the extremity of this attitude, he even insisted upon piety in connection with functions which later generations were to consider too vulgar to mention:

Accordingly, I resolved that it should be my ordinary practice, whenever I step to answer the one or other Necessity of nature, to make it an Opportunity of shaping in my Mind some holy, noble, divine Thought; usually by way of occasional Reflection on some sensible Object which I either then have before me, or have lately had so: a thought that may leave upon my Spirit some further Tincture of Piety!

To come face to face with this petty bourgeois psychology in its most obvious and outstanding literary form, one needs but to turn to the first book published in America: *The Bay Psalm Book*, printed in Cambridge in 1640. *The Bay Psalm Book* was written to replace the Geneva Bible of 1569.[29] This version deviated too sharply from the original Greek and Hebrew texts and was entirely too aristocratic in adjective and simile to suit the morbid scrupulosity of the New England theocrats.[30] The authors of *The Bay Psalm Book* were aware of exactly what they were doing. They wanted a Bible that would dovetail with their class psychology, departing not a whit from what they thought correct and sacred. As they stated in their preface—the book was written under the guidance of Richard Mather, Thomas Welde, and John Eliot—they were not apologetic for what might seem its literary imbecilities. Indeed, they defended its crudities in no uncertain words. "If therefore the verses are not always so smooth and elegant as some may desire or expect," they wrote, "let them consider that God's Altar needs not our polishing: Ex 20 for wee have respected rather a plaine translation, then so smooth our verses with the sweetness of any paraphrase, and soe have attended conscience rather than Elegance, fidelity

[29] Wilberforce Eames: *Bay Psalm Book:* New York, 1903: Introduction, p. v.
[30] The difference between this attitude and that which governed Milton's choice of words in *Paradise Lost* signified the difference between the upper middle-class attitude toward art and the lower. These theocrats were lower middle-class Puritans, and not upper middle-class ones. The American environment had cured any upper middle-class propensities they might ever have had. Typical of this attitude was the remark of the Reverend Charles Chauncy, who, a century later, was to express a wish that Milton's *Paradise Lost* be translated into prose so that he could understand it.

rather than poetry, in translating the Hebrew words into english language, and David's poetry into english metre." Nowhere else has the petty bourgeois attitude toward literature received so perfect an expression as in the words of that preface. Even when later on, as the cultural control of society receded from the religious front, and the petty bourgeoisie turned toward politics as their avenue of economic defense, they carried over this same attitude toward literature, and, in large part, have carried it over even until to-day.

The stress upon "plaine translation" and upon "fidelity rather than poetry" can be looked upon as expressive of the petty bourgeois psychology through every interstice of its life. It found as definite form in the *New England Primer* as in the *Bay Psalm Book*—or in John Cotton's *Spiritual Milk for Boston Babies*. It invaded newspapers and periodicals as well as books. *The Boston News-Letter*, and the *Gazette* disclosed its imprint on every page. In fact, when the first purely literary newspaper was published in New England, *The New England Courant*, a paper innocuous enough in its ethical tenor, it was attacked as an expression of the Hell-Fire Club because it dared put mundane matters before religious.[31]

Imprisoned by such a tradition, our early literature was inevitably religious. The poetry of Anne Bradstreet and Michael Wigglesworth meant far less to our cultural life than did the pious prose of such pre-Revolutionary hierophants as Cotton Mather and Jonathan Edwards.[32] From the beginning, American literature was exposed to the handicaps of a religious censorship—the religious censorship in Europe at the time was of a different character, controlled as it was by the religious representatives of the aristocracy instead of those of the petty bourgeoisie—and therein

[31]Thomas Goddard Wright: *Literary Culture in Early New England:* New Haven, 1920: p. 213.
[32]Only when, as we stated before, the petty bourgeois Weltanschauung managed to work out its defense upon a political instead of a religious front did our literature find opportunity to escape from this overmastering religiosity.

lay the significant difference—a censorship which has not ceased even to-day. When a press was set up in Cambridge in 1639, it was openly supervised by the University authorities. The Board of Licensers which later assumed control was not less religious in prejudice. As a result, individual authors turned to religious themes as much by force as by choice. There was so little room for publications of a non-religious variety, and so little inspiration for their composition, that between 1706 and 1718, for example, among 550 publications printed in this country "all but 84 were on religious topics, and of the 84, 49 were almanacs."[33] When the one outstanding male poet of the period wrote an apostrophe to heaven, and described the earth as a "prison," and the body as a "useless wight," and Cotton Mather devoted two hours to his church prayer and still more to his sermon, it is not surprising that literature that was not religious in motivation had no chance of success.

It is important to note that this lack of interest in the arts was as pronounced in the attitudes of such religious intransigeants as Roger Williams and Thomas Hooker as it was in those of such ruling theocrats as John Cotton and Richard Mather. Music and painting fared no better than literature. The opposition to dancing was unanimous. So rigid was this petty bourgeois opposition to art that it was quite possible, as N. H. Chamberlain has stated, "that there were not five copies, perhaps not one, of Shakespeare's plays in Massachusetts Bay for nigh the first hundred years."[34] While many differences arose among the New England religionists, resulting in both revolt and exile, they all revolved within the same radius. In short, they all expressed the same lower middle-class psychology,—even where certain class concepts came into conflict, as in the case of Roger Williams' fight for democracy against the prevailing theocracy, it was a re-

[33] Fred T. Pattee: *History of American Literature:* Silver, Burdett & Co., 1896.
[34] N. H. Chamberlain: *Samuel Sewall and the World He Lived In:* 1897: p. 236.

ligio-political conflict and not an underlying cultural one, as it would have been had it occurred in England where the cultural attitude of the Puritans was distinctly upper middle class. Neither Williams nor Hooker, for instance, nor any other leader in New England, ever made a defense of the upper middle-class outlook. The conditions of life alone, as we previously stressed, defeated such a possibility. The character of the American environment in the seventeenth century was still agrarian—agrarian in the petty bourgeois sense of the word. Large farms were uncommon. It was the small farmer who predominated. The Puritan theocrats, their Calvinism notwithstanding, had to deal with that small farmer psychology and not with the psychology of a successful upper bourgeoisie. While, therefore, the fight of Williams and Hooker took on political proportions that were important, it did not alter at all the attitude which prevailed toward *belles lettres*.

Only in Merry Mount did any deviation from that philosophy occur. There the presence of Thomas Morton, a Cavalier and a bona-fide member of the Church of England, gave life to a different tradition. Morton believed in all the vices of merriment which the poor farmers and merchants detested. An aristocrat in both psychology and origin, he continued to love the pagan outlook upon life which his class had long enjoyed. A haphazard personality, with the spirit of an adventurer compounded with the philosophy of a "heathen," he lent more color to the American scene than any other individual of his time. Fond of the Indians, he came to know them far more intimately than did any of the inhabitants of Salem or Plymouth. The most interesting part of his book, *New English Canaan*, or *New Canaan*, is the part dealing with Indian life and customs. His claim that "the Massachusetts Indian [was] more full of humanity than the Christians," which extended to the point where he even sold them firearms that later were used against the Puritans, was enough to stamp him immediately as a desperate enemy of the theocracy. His ridicule of the religionists of that day belonged to a tradition that did not survive his own disappearance from New England. It was snuffed out by its enemies before it had a chance to flame. The assault upon his Maypole festivities put a swift end to this one aspect of New England life which for a brief moment had escaped middle-class tyranny. Certainly, these verses of Morton, culled from the *New English Canaan*, and associated with the Maypole rites, echoed a tradition that was foreign to that of Michael Wigglesworth and Anne Bradstreet:

> "Drink and be merry, merry, merry, boys,
> Let all your delight be in Hymen's joys,
> Jo to Hymen now the day is come,
> About the merry May-pole take a Roome.
>
> Make green garlons, bring bottles out;
> And fill sweet Nectar freely about,
> Uncover thy head, and feare no harme,
> For hers good liquor to keep it warme.
> Then drinke and be merry, and
> Jo to Hymen, etc.
>
> Nectar is a thing assign'd,
> By the Deities owne minde,
> To cure the hart opprest with griefe,
> And of good liquors is the cheife."

It must not be thought, however, that Thomas Morton was the only one to criticize the philosophy of the ruling regime. The significant fact was that such attacks could not make great headway because of the ecclesiastical despotism which prevailed. Beginning with the notorious instance of the passenger who on his way to America "diverted himself with an hook and line on the Lord's Day" and who, when called to task for his sin, "protested that he did not know what the Lord's Day was; he thought every day was a sabbath day; for, he said, they did nothing but pray and preach all the week long,"[35] instances could be cited beyond number

[35]Lucy Hazard: *The Frontier in American Literature*: New York, 1927: p. 8.

which evidence the ill-will that existed in the minds of many toward the oppressing hand of the theocracy. Sewall noted in his Diary a satire, *The Gospel Order Revived,* which was perpetrated by Benjamin Colman and his friends in attack upon Increase Mather's *The Order of the Gospel.* Such verses as these indicate the sharpness of its sting.

> "Saints Cotton and Hooker, o look down, and look here
> Where's platform, Way and the Keys?
> O Torey what story of Brattle Church Twattle,
> To have things as they please.
>
> Our Merchants cum Mico do stand Sacro Vico;
> Our Churches turn genteel;
> Parsons grow trim and trigg with wealth wins and wigg
> And their crowns are covered with meal."

John Banister's satire on Cotton Mather's degree of Doctor of Divinity, which he received from Glasgow University, was not less scabrous:

> "The mad enthusiast, thirsting after fame,
> By endless volum'ns thought to raise a name.
> With undigested trash he throngs the Press;
> Thus striving to be greater, he's the less,
> But he, in spite of infamy, writes on,
> And draws new Cullies in to be undone.
> Warmed with paternal vanity, he trys
> For new Suscriptions, while the Embryo lyes
> Neglected—Parkhurst says, Satis fecisti,
> My belly's full of your Magnalia Christi,
> Your crude Divinity, and History
> While hot with a censorious age agree."

Less serious than these satires but more devastating in their effect, were the pranks and plots executed by the mischievous within as well as without the holy precincts of The Meeting House. As Sewall has again informed us, mischief-mongers one time placed "a sturgeon of about eight feet in length on the Pulpit floor . . . [which] caused such a Nauseous and Infectious stench that neither Minister nor People could by any means assemble in The Meeting House"; upon another occasion they scratched a "virulent Libel" upon the door of The Meeting House, disturbing thus the peace of mind of those who first attended the service. As early as the first quarter of the seventeenth century the young had already begun to grow beyond the control of their elders, and not even Cotton Mather was safe from their obstreperous irreverences. Mather's description of their antics shows that the theocracy, powerful though it still was at that time, was already beginning to weaken, and that refractory elements were willing to risk punishments which once would have intimidated and terrified them.

There are knotts of riotous Young Men in the Town. On purpose to insult Piety, they will come under my Window in the middle of the Night, and sing profane and filthy Songs. The last Night they did so, and fell upon People with Clubs, taken off my Wood-pile. Tis hightime to call in the Help of the Government of the punishing and suppressing of these Disorders.

Still others, rebellious against the theocratic suppression, made their retreat into the woods to live with the Indians. This *going native* at times became more than a sporadic practice. The case of Eunice Williams, who preferred the life of the Indians to that of the New England whites, and who refused to be inveigled back into Christian territory by moral appeal or admonition, is an excellent illustration of the sincerity of those who adopted that manner of escape.[36]

But these satires, strictures, pranks, and attacks were not perpetrated by the members of the ruling class. As in England the very lowest classes were much closer to the aristocracy in their ideology than to the petty bourgeoisie. They liked the amusements and sports and resented the tradesman's antipathy to them. It was they, therefore, who, like Thomas Morton, were glad to take advantage of any opportunity to ridicule, or escape the petty bourgeois domination

[36]Lawrence: *Not Quite Puritans:* Boston, 1928: p. 188.

of life and custom. The ruling theocracy, however, gave them little room for expansion. *It was only when the theocracy began to crumble, as the agrarian way of life was gradually superseded by the commercial, and the petty bourgeoisie shifted its economic emphasis into the political sphere, that such irreligiosities of conduct could manifest themselves with impunity.*

In the early days when the theocracy was unassailable, whatever controverted established custom was done in secret, for the powers of the theocratic state were omnipresent and omnipotent. The *tything-man,* who was the official detective of sin, was an important aid in perpetuating that power. The tything-man—a tything-man was appointed for every ten families in the community—was required, according to the law passed in 1679, to diligently "inspect all houses, licensed or unlicensed, where they shall have notice or have ground to suspect that any person or persons doe spend their time or estates, by night or by day, in typling or gaming, or otherwise unprofitably, or doe sell by retayle, within doores or without, strong drincke." The powers of this *tything-man,* it is clear, were almost unlimited. As Joshua Hampstead has recorded in his Diary, it was the task of this tything-man to apprehend "all stubborne and disorderly children and servants, night walkers, typlers, Sabaoth breakers, by night or by day, and such as absent themselves from the publicke worship of God on the Lord's Dayes." It is obvious from Hampstead's own words that the "stubborne and disorderly" were members of the lower strata of society. The *"children and servants, nightwalkers, typlers, Sabaoth breakers"* were not scions of the theocracy or members of the hard-working lower middle class, but underdogs in origin, indentured servants and hired laborers. The unmitigated ferocity of the New England Christians in their zeal for purity in religion and morals, then, was the expression of a state determined to suppress any sign of revolt against it, especially on the part of the lower orders. *The whipping post, the pillory, the branding iron, were more than devices for religious punish-*

ment; they were weapons of the state devised to fortify its power. All the advertising and publicity which were attached to punishment in those days, all the religious preliminaries, with open lecture and prayer, finding their morbid climax in public parade and execution, were encouraged by the state as much for political reasons as for religious. Motivated though it was by religious conviction, the petty bourgeoisie, having acquired power for the first time in its existence, utilized every despotic resort within the command of the political state to make its control indestructible.

This entire defense of religion in America during the seventeenth century, it is obvious, was at basis political. Its expression in literature was as patent as it was in every-day life. *The theocracy encouraged literature that was religious because it justified the established state.* It discouraged literature that was not religious because it had little value to the state and might sow within itself seeds of opposition to the state. Naturally, therefore, literature was watched over as carefully by the theocracy as was moral conduct. So complete was this dictatorship that almost all who dissented from it were immediately muffled. There was no place for their protests to be voiced in print. As a result, literature had but one path to pursue: the religious. To pursue another path was impossible.

It was only in the eighteenth century, with the weakening of the theocracy, that means were devised for the expression of the rising tide of revolt. *The New England Courant,* founded in 1721, was created to provide such protesting elements with a literary mouthpiece.[37] *The Boston News-Letter,* an organ of the older order, immediately assailed the *Courant* as "a Notorious Scandalous Paper" and described its contents as "full freighted with Nonsense, Unmannerliness, Railery, Prophaneness, Immorality, Arrogancy, Calumnies, Lyes, Contradictions, and what not, all tending to Quarrels and Divisions, and to Debauch and Corrupt the

[37]*Massachusetts Historical Society Writings:* paper by Ford: Boston, 1924.

Minds and Manners of New England." Oddly enough the
first clash which *The Courant*[38] occasioned circled about the
problem of inoculation against small-pox. While the theocracy favored inoculation, *The Courant* took a definite stand
against it.[39] Increase Mather's most bitter attacks were directed against *The Courant's* stand on this question. Both
the Mathers in fact joined in the attack with equal vehemence. But *The Courant* did not stop with such discussions.
Inoculation, a most controversial topic of the day, was only
a point of departure for *The Courant* in its general lines of
attack. It even went so far as to defend the early emergence
of the democratic idea. In its sixth issue (September 11,
1721) it had an article on *The Rights of People as Opposed
to Their Rulers*, maintaining that the people are nearly
always in the right, but do not revolt until their burdens
become intolerable. That the theocracy had not lost its power,
however, was revealed by the fact that, despite the mischievous innuendoes of James Franklin and other wits, the
clergy forced the paper to a point of apology on more than
one occasion.[40]

Contrary to the common notion, the colonists who settled
in America were not full-fledged capitalists in their philosophy. In the Massachusetts Bay Colony, for example,
they carried over a great number of feudal forms into their
economic life. While the capitalist philosophy of profit-
seeking had infected the minds of the petty bourgeoisie in
England and elsewhere long before they came upon the
American scene, it was a capitalist philosophy still in the
embryo, so to speak, which had yet to rid itself of many of
its feudal vestiges. It was the perpetuation of those feudal vestiges which prevented early capitalist society in the sixteenth

[38] The career of *The Courant* will be dealt with in more detail in the
fourth chapter.
[39] It is curious to note that the clergy should have been the progressive
side of the issue—George Bernard Shaw to the contrary notwithstanding.
[40] See especially issue No. 3 in which the publisher promised not to
print anything that "anyways reflects on the Clergy or Government, and
nothing but what is innocently Diverting."

and seventeenth centuries from becoming unqualifiedly individualistic in spirit. The Bay Colony, to illustrate, did not adopt a laissez-faire doctrine until the eighteenth century, when with the rise of commerce on large scale and the development of manufactures, it became necessary to shelve all traces of the feudal order with its various regulations and restrictions. The history of the Bay Colony reveals that change in striking detail. In the beginning the ruling group in the Bay Colony did not destroy feudal distinctions between the ranks and relations of men. It altered their emphasis but not their meaning. Instead of basing them upon inherited station it founded them upon economic assets. In the churches seats were assigned according to economic station. Even dress was regulated in keeping with class status. Connecticut, for example, regulated the apparel of all but "magistrates, their wives and children—military commission officers or such whose quality and estate have been above the ordinary degree though now decayed." Before 1649 about only one in fourteen people were allowed to use the title of Mister. Goodman and Goodwife were the forms of salutation permitted for the commoner. These class regulations, to be sure, were a direct hang-over of the feudal scheme.

As a result of this compromise economics, compounded of old feudal vestiges with new capitalistic concepts, finding a contradictory synthesis in the mercantile theory, social life revolved about a different pivot from that of a century later when that compromise and contradiction had disappeared. The Massachusetts colony, for example, advocated regulation throughout social life. It stood for legislative administration of all trade. In order to socialize production as well as distribution it tried to establish regulation prices as well as regulation wages. As early as 1641 in The Body of Liberties this attitude received explicit statement:

to appoint certain select man to set reasonable rates upon all commodities and proportionately to limit the wages of workmen and labourers. No increase to be taken of a pore brother or neighbor for anything lent unto him.

The wages of master carpenters, sawyers, masons, and wheel-wrights, were established by law, and stipulated to be not more than two shillings a day, and anybody who paid more or received more was fined ten shillings for the offence. Laissez-faire economics, thus, and the modern democratic conception of society, were not defended by the ruling class in the Bay Colony.

The New England theocracy could not have flourished except upon agrarian foundations. Its career was contingent upon the perpetuation of the agrarian way of life. It was inevitable, then, that the theocracy should begin to crumble as soon as commerce advanced and replaced agriculture as the dominant economic force in the community. With the growth of trade, which demanded the destruction of old economic regulations and restrictions that hampered individual enterprise, the social vestiges of feudalism broke down and disappeared, and with their passing the authority of the theocratic state was shorn of its power. This loss of power was anticipated by the theocrats long before it occurred. American literature at the time, chiefly in the form of diaries and sermons, voiced in no uncertain terms the change that had come to pass. As early as 1663 a well-known Salem clergyman, cognizant of the decline of theocratic power, warned his congregation that "worldly gain was not the end and design of the people of New England." If in 1673 Increase Mather in his two sermons against *The Sin of Drunkenness* admitted that "there [was] need of such houses and no sober Minister [would] speak against the Licensing of them," nine years later he was forced to confess that "sin and Prophaneness" had advanced so rapidly that religion was powerless to destroy them. "The time was," Mather said, "when in New England they durst not continue whole nights in Taverns, in drinking and gaming and misspending their Precious Time . . . Time was when in this Boston men durst not be seen in Taverns after the Sabbath had begun." Without understanding what had happened in economic life, Mather saw the change as due principally to the loss of respect for religion which had come over the people. Nothing was as ominous as his sermon: *The Signs of a Day of Trouble being Near.* "We can now see little difference between Church members and other men," Mather declared in one of his most spirited jeremiads, "whence is all that rising up and disobedience in inferiors toward superiors, in Families, in Churches and in the Commonwealth." In sermon after sermon Mather denounced the transformation of life which had occurred in New England. His words showed that all the social aspects of feudal practice which had been partially perpetuated by the early doctrines of mercantilism had been supplanted by the unmitigated individualism of the aggressive, commercial economy. While it was Cotton Mather who maintained that it was the kingdom of God which had perished, and the kingdom of Trade and Land, and Earthly accommodations which had superseded it, we know to-day that the succession of kingdoms had mainly to do with the conflict between an agrarian and a commercial economics, the former retaining a semi-social character and the latter expressing an anarchistically individualistic character.

Cotton Mather early foresaw the collapse of the semi-social spirit of the agrarian order. With an eye as keen for discrepancies in economic behavior as in religious doctrine, he struck more definitely at the root of the evil of his time than did most of his contemporaries. In 1715, in one of his most penetrating sermons, entitled *Fair Dealing Between Debtor and Creditor*, he delivered an unforgettable onslaught upon the growing individualistic economics of the day:

It has been complained, That tho' the Religion of God, be Professed with an uncommon Show among ourselves, yet among us, there are too often found such Iniquities in the Dealings of Men as are condemned even in the Judgment of the Nations.

In another sermon, "A Discourse Shewing what Cause there is to Fear that the Glory of the Lord is departing from New

England," he testified still further to the deterioration of the theocracy and the theocratic values and virtues. Even the ministers, Mather declared, were "not like their Predecessors, not Principled, nor Spirited as they were." After the earthquake of 1706, Mather made one of his most stirring appeals to the people of his day to preserve themselves against the evils that were springing up in their civilization. It is doubtful whether any of the American theological writers, with the exception of Jonathan Edwards, ever surpassed, in violent sincerity, this challenge of the American Isaiah:

Stage-playes and Mixed dancings, and those Diversions in which cruelty is Exercised on Dumb Creatures, which some Ungodly Youths in this Countrey have delighted themselves with; I mean that which they call Cock-Scaling and those infamous Games of *Cards* and *Dice*. Because of the Lottery which is in them . . . it is a matter of Lamentation that ever such things as these should be heard of in New England, and that with them. . . . And are there not some that Smoke away their time? An hours idleness is a sin as well as an Hours Drunkenness. . . . Moreover there are some who altho they are not altogether Idle, nevertheless, they spend their Time Unprofitably. *It may be in Reading unprofitable books. Some read Prophane Books. Such as come from the Stage, whose vile design is to corrupt good manners. Others spend their time in reading vain Romances.* It may be that if they had spent half that Time in Reading the Scriptures, and Books that shew unto them the way to Eternal Life, they might have been converted thereby. *But what are they the better for Reading Romantic stories?* It is mere loss of time. And do not some spend much Time in unprofitable Discourse? . . . What shall be said of the Tiplers? Prov. 23, 30. *They tarry long at the wine.* There are that spend much time in the Tavern, or in the Ale-House: They tarry long there. And what is their Discourse there? That which is very Unprofitable, and many times very Sinful. It may make a mans heart tremble to think what account some Church-members will give to Christ at the Day of Judgment, for the time they have spent at the Tavern and at the Coffee House.[41] (Italics mine.)

While Mather's fulminations stand well beside those of

[41] Mather's reference here to Prophane Stories and Tales and to the Stage is but another illustration of the petty bourgeois attitude toward art that was characteristic of the theocracy.

such English divines as Gosson, Stubbes, and Northbroke, they were unable to stem the tide of change that had already begun to overrun the country. All the diabolic persecutions of witches, the spying, and the harassing of the wicked and unclean, which reached an apex of intensity in the last decade of the seventeenth century, could not save the theocracy from destruction. The spread of commerce spelt the death of agrarianism and the inevitable disintegration of theocratic supremacy. Nevertheless the theocratic control of our culture did not disappear at once. Although, as a religious contemporary wrote, merchants and traders "would willingly have had the Commonwealth tolerate divers kinds of sinful opinions to entice men to come and sit down with us, that their purses might be filled with coyn, the civil Government with contention, and the Church of our Lord Christ with errors," the ecclesiastical leaders did not sacrifice their control without a struggle. Although the actual government by godly men came to an end in the 1660's their cultural rulership remained active until the last semblances of the old order were destroyed in the eighteenth century.

It was in the personality of Jonathan Edwards that the theocracy made its last stand. Jonathan Edwards recalled men to their divine mission, fired them with a holy dedication, and spurred them on to introspection as morbid as it was merciless. Caught in the wave of religious energy which had received a dynamic culmination in the preaching of the Englishman, George Whitefield, Jonathan Edwards made the Great Awakening in America into a vast revival, exploding every bridge behind him in his anxiety to race toward the millennium. Edwards' methods were desperately direct. He was no soft-gloved orator, tolerant of error and sin. His fortissimo outbursts derived their strength from the living wrath which burnt within him. Nothing so well represents his fear-inspiring eloquence as his famous Endfield sermon: "Sinners in the Hands of an Angry God." It was such sentences as these which made Edwards such a powerful spokesman for the theocracy of his day:

O sinner! consider the fearful danger you are in: it is a great furnace of wrath, a wide and bottomless pit, full of the fire of wrath, that you are held over in the hand of that God, whose wrath is provoked and incensed as much against you, as against many of the damned in hell: you hang by a slender thread, with the flames of divine wrath flashing about it, and ready every moment to singe it and burn it asunder; and you have no interest in any Mediator, and nothing to lay hold of to save yourself, nothing to keep off the flames of wrath, nothing of your own, nothing that you ever have done, nothing that you can do, to induce God to spare you one moment. . . .

While Edwards' defense of Idealism, which revealed almost a Berkeleyan climax in his essay on *God's Last End in Creation,* undoubtedly constituted his most important intellectual work, it was his more direct activity as a preacher that had most effect upon his generation. Already the spread of commerce, as we have indicated, had weakened the influence of theological thought upon the spirit of the time, and had forced the preacher to compete with other forces in society for cultural authority. The rebuff which Edwards himself met with at the hands of his own congregation showed not only how strong the forces of discontent had grown, but also how weak the clergy had become in the face of them.[42]

Edwards himself was keenly aware of the powerful forces that were arrayed against him and the whole theocratic outlook. He realized full well the part that wealth had come to play in vitiating religious morale, and the dangerous struggle which had already developed between the commercial interests and the ecclesiastical. In reply to many of the criticisms directed against religion by the representatives of the new commercial interests, criticisms that assailed the theocratic philosophy in its theory of trade restrictions and limitations, Edwards maintained that he could not see any virtue in the argument "that religion ought not to be attended lest it should injure our temporal affairs." Edwards' words indicate the nature of the arguments that were then being made

---

[42]The social significance of Edwards' dismissal by his congregation is dealt with in more detail in Chapter IV.

by the commercial powers in their fight against the old economics. In 1736, thus, Edwards found it necessary to defend
"eternal" things against temporal. A century earlier no such
defense had been necessary. Eternal and temporal things
then had been both united under the dominancy of the theocracy. Edwards, however, faced by an intractable situation,
attempted to reason with as well as denounce the forces
opposed to him. *Instead of defending religiosity for its own
sake he even went so far as to maintain that it served the
interests of commerce as well.* In fact, his contentions on this
score were not very different from those of many preachers
to-day who defend prohibition as an asset to industry and
business. His words, for example, in defense of the reaction
to the revival of religion are typical of his attitude:

> *Besides if the matter be justly examined, I believe it will be
> found, that the country has lost no time from their temporal affairs
> by the late revival of religion, but have rather gained:* and that more
> time has been saved from frolicking and tavern haunting, idleness
> and improfitable visits, vain talk, fruitless pastimes, and needless
> diversions, that has lately been spent in extraordinary religion; *and
> probably five times as much has been served in various ways, as
> has been spent by religious meetings.* (Italics mine.)

But Edwards fought a losing battle. The odds were too
heavy against him. The system of life which he advocated
belonged to an age that was already dying. His eloquence
had lost its force upon the people long before he died. The
victory went to his opponents who had learned to trim their
sails in keeping with the winds of change.

Once the grip of the theocracy was broken, new literary
forces could make headway and a literature which was not
overwhelmingly religious could arise. With the changes that
accompanied the expansion of commerce and the appearance
of wealth, the middle class steadily began to shift its emphasis from the religious into the moral plane. The growth
of trade made tolerance a necessity. The intolerant fanati-
cisms of the early theocrats had to give way before the more

easy-going and ever-yielding convictions of the rising com-mercial classes. *If these classes desired their literature to be moral, they did not demand that it be religious.* After all, morality was a more mundane matter and was necessary even in business. Religion which was more concerned with eternal values than with earthly ones was scarcely fitted to meet the needs of the new commercial era. Indeed, it soon became an obstacle to economic progress. Consequently, from that time forth the tendency to turn religion into a moral vehicle in-stead of a spiritual one gathered such momentum that a gen-eration or two later the one-time vigorous intolerances that had existed faded out into tepid tolerances which endured all differences without a murmur of protest. Thus the vigor of early American religion was undermined by the inevitable force of economic circumstances, and was converted into a sickly servant of the new order.

This new order, for a while, attempted to preserve the ethical aspects of the theocracy but not its spiritual. What it gained in latitude it lost in strength. In its own way, it pre-pared the ground for the advance of the fully-matured capi-talist ideology which was to overtake the nation early in the next century.

It was this decline in religious dominancy which marked the end of what has been commonly called the Puritanic philosophy of life in America. As we showed in the earlier part of this chapter, the so-called Puritanic philosophy of life here was not representative of Puritanism as a whole. The disintegration of what has been commonly called the Puritanic philosophy was concomitant with the decline of the theocracy. What is generally known as American Puritanism was an expression, as we have stressed, of the petty bourgeois ideology manifesting itself in theocratic form. This phase in American culture was concluded with the theocratic surren-der. What came after that was not Puritanism at all, but a dilution of it which was the expression of a different social order.

Notwithstanding the fact that it was this so-called Amer-

ican Puritan—in reality as we have shown he was more of
a Dissenter than a Puritan—who, with his petty bourgeois
instincts and antipathies, retarded the growth of the arts in
this country, it must be remembered that this same Puritan
embodied in his makeup virtues as well as vices which heretofore have been largely ignored. More than that, it should
be said at once that numerous as were the evils associated
with his outlook, there were—and still are—an even greater
number of evils ascribed to him than were his due. This
American Puritan has shouldered the blame for a score of
sins of which he was not the namesake.

Whatever else may be said in attack upon him, it can be
stated without hesitation that in many ways, as we shall have
occasion to show in subsequent chapters, his outlook upon
life was superior to that of the commercial and industrial
classes which followed him. As a merchant, for instance, he
was impeccably honest, for while he made a whole religion
conform to his economy he did not think of his economics as
something apart from his religion. The simple basis of his
life upon which his philosophy was founded prevented him
from being otherwise. As an individual he was close to his
goods, the goods he bought and sold; he stood up for them,
so to speak, was responsible for them, as he was for his own
character. Strict moral discipline governed every economic
transaction. As R. H. Tawney has shown, the Puritan lived
with the moral understanding that "they must not take advantage of the necessities of individual buyers, must not
overpraise their wares, must not sell them dearer merely
because they have cost them much to get." Sharp penalties
were meted out to the individual who failed to observe
moral discipline in his economic relations as well as in his
spiritual relations. As Bancroft has stated, the offenders were
first admonished, and, admonishment failing, excommuni-
cated. This philosophy was in keeping with the spirit of a
class struggling for supremacy; once its supremacy was established, however, its moral discipline weakened, and, with the
rise of commerce, the coming of machinery and the advance

of the manufacturing class, its spiritual meaning was destroyed in entirety. As soon as the early entrepreneur phase of industry was past, the manufacturer grew steadily farther and farther away from the goods he manufactured, and a new system of economic relationships was begun. Investment provided a common basis for economic organization and expansion, and very soon manufacturers were able to invest money in enterprise totally removed from their own interest or intimacy. Naturally, under such new conditions, moral discipline almost entirely disappeared as a binding factor in social life. Profits, in the unadulterated and extreme sense of the word, became the sole motivation of industry. The test of a man's worth then became a monetary matter in which morals played an increasingly small rôle beside reputation. Personal responsibility became a problem of economics instead of ethics. The double standard of morality, which every Puritan and Dissenter would have detested, thus became an accepted creed. Puritanic honesty was succeeded by capitalistic manipulation. Thus respectability, which was Puritan morality stripped of sincerity and a self-discipline, became the new ethic of the era.

The American Puritan, like the petty bourgeoisie in every country, represented in his whole ideology the unresting zeal of a merchant class which had to bend all its energy to fight the domination of the landed class. Its tradition derived its strength from that vast reorientation of culture which was first set in motion by the commercial revolution of the fourteenth and fifteenth centuries and which reached England in the sixteenth. Its philosophy, born out of strife, was a rigorous, rugged one, denying immediates for the sake of ultimates, and as tight in its discipline as the skin of a drum. The petty bourgeois had to arm himself against every weakness in the struggle that faced him. Living constantly in the camp of the enemy, he had to avail himself of every protection against defeat. Labor became a sacrament—and idleness a vice. Leisure was looked upon as an evil, inviting the mind to sin. Amusement was scorned because it weakened the will.

Books were despised unless they had a spiritual import. Life's vanities were abhorred because they divided man from God, encouraging indulgence instead of consecration. All the pent-up energy of the soul was concentrated toward one consuming end. The individual Dissenter and Puritan thus was a man of deep convictions, convictions that he never deserted through all that long deluge of attack that threatened to overwhelm him in the early decades of the sixteenth century. Above all, he was no hypocrite. He was stern, but as stern with himself as with others. He was willing to slave, to sacrifice, and even to die for his convictions. Caught in the swell of that vast flood of energy that broke across the world of his day, himself as much a part of it as the economic forces which had been set free by the collapse of the old order, he absorbed within himself the impact of that energy and transmuted it into intellectual form. His mind was charged with a new vision—a vision none the less exalted because of its economic origin. What he opposed, he sought to annihilate. There was nothing half-way, nothing luke-warm, or nothing squeamish about his attitudes. The expanding energies of his spirit demanded a new way of life for his people—nothing more and nothing less. There could be no compromise with the forces of evil, for, in the words of Bunyan: "There was a way of Hell even from the Gates of Heaven, as well as from the City of Destruction." It was his long and bitter fight with the aristocracy that drove the petty bourgeoisie to these extreme conclusions. It was the very nature of that fight, with its tragic consequences in religion as well as in economics, that early steeled him against adversity and taught him to risk comforts for the sake of convictions.

This petty bourgeois dedication to an ideal began to lose its force when the expansion of commerce broke down social controls. It was at that time that the individualistic philosophy rooted itself almost ineradicably into our soil. The coming of machinery, and the rise of the manufacturing classes sounded the death-knell of that ideal. If during a generation or two following the death of Jonathan Edwards something of that ideal lingered, its final vestiges vanished before the close of the century. The determining note of the theocracy was devotion to that ideal, a religious ideal that was hard, inelastic, and demanding, allowing for neither compromise nor deviation. The dominant note of the new ideology was *respectability*. Riding to power on the wheels of machinery, the manufacturing classes brought with them a new philosophy of life in keeping with the new organization of society which they led. Respectability was as necessary to establish credit in industry as to be approved in literature. It immediately became the test of the day, reflecting itself in every variety of endeavor. Even God was made respectable. The Jehovah-like deity of the Puritans, warlike in mien and merciless in judgment, was supplanted by a more gentlemanly and compromising Creator. Thus it was possible in the nineteenth century for capitalists who were exploiters of men six days of the week to be deacons in their churches on the seventh. In fact, by the end of the nineteenth century there were few churches, at least in the cities, that did not have the wealthy as their main deacons and trustees. The Puritanic fibre of Christianity in this way was robbed of its vigor. The test of character was no longer spiritual but material. The Christian who fasted and denied himself went out of fashion. The only virtue he had to respect in the nineteenth century was that of respectability. If he was respectable, no other virtues needed to be added unto him—for respectability was virtue *par excellence*. His moral code was simple. Reduced to a formula, it stressed two things, as Esme Wingfield-Stratford points out:

> "(1) It pays to be good.
> (2) If you must commit sins, at
>   least don't talk about them."

With the Puritan the stress had been upon character: with the wealthy bourgeoisie the emphasis was upon reputation. It was not what a man was that counted any longer, but what he was reputed to be. Reputation was indispensable for credit, and without credit industry could not be run. With the Puritan, failings in character were fundamental; with the wealthy bourgeoisie, on the contrary, failings in character were not of serious consequence if they were not known to the public, and, therefore, did not affect one's reputation.

This stress upon character instead of reputation saved the American Puritan from many of the hypocrisies with which he has been erroneously blamed. His literature is a direct testimony to this. The common notion of the American Puritan as evasive and prudish, for example, is based upon a totally false conception of his attitudes and ideals. Above all, he was not prudish. He was not afraid of sex. He condemned its laxer manifestations, but he did not deny or try to evade them. In fact, the Puritan was too simple and plain-spoken to be either evasive or prudish about important matters. It was the nineteenth-century bourgeoisie that was evasive and prudish. One needs only to turn to the writings of the Puritans, and then compare them with those of the nineteenth century, in order to realize that prudishness and evasion were the vices of the Victorian and not of the Puritan. Scarcely any better illustration of the influence of respectability upon nineteenth-century literature is to be found than in Harriet Martineau's remark that she was "unable to read *Vanity Fair* from the moral disgust it occasions." One can readily understand, then, the truth of Thackeray's comment that "no writer of fiction among us has been permitted to depict to his utmost power a Man. We must drape him and give him a certain conventional simper. Society will not tolerate the Natural in Art." Better still, as an illustration of the same influence, is Leslie Stephens' advice to Thomas Hardy that he should not portray a lady as "amorous" but as "sentimental." All such devices would have disgusted the Puritan.

In Cotton Mather's *Diary*, for example, one is met with a candor of speech unsurpassed by any Elizabethan. Mather never minced words in his comments or criticisms; he called a spade a spade at all times and made no ado about it. No bourgeois writer of the nineteenth century, for example, would have written about his son's moral indiscretion in the candid way that Cotton Mather did about that of his son Increase. Even better, note the words from a sermon of Thomas Sheperd:

Thy heart is foul sink of all atheism,—blasphemy, murder, whoredom, adultery, witchcraft,—so that, if thou hast any good thing in thee, it is but a drop of rose water in a bowl of poison, where fallen it is all corrupted.

And compare that with the review of *Oliver Twist* which appeared in *The Quarterly Review,* in which the critic claimed that "By such publications *the happy ignorance of innocence is degraded.* Our youth should not even suspect the possibility of such hidden depths of guilt." (Italics mine.) What we have here in this contrast needs little comment. The Puritan would never have stooped to such deceits as those recommended by *The Quarterly Review.* He would have scorned "the happy ignorance of innocence" even more than the contemporary critic. He reared his children in full awareness of evil, and rather than keep his youth from suspecting the existence of sin, he preferred to exaggerate its ubiquity. His children, who were taught to spell from the *New England Primer,* were regularly made to master such a word as "for-ni-ca-ti-on." It is curious to observe that there were only fourteen words of that length in the primer. Even such a book as *Onania* published in 1724 was allowed to circulate without threat of suppression. More than that, it went through ten editions and sold altogether over fifteen thousand copies. While the attitude defended in the book was most unhappy and unintelligent—the subtitle reveals that clearly: the heinous Sin of Self Pollution and all its frightful Consequences in both sexes considered—there was no hesitation in discussing it or employing language that came into explicit grips with it. It is no wonder, then, as Ralph and Louise Boas pointed out, that "when one realizes the complete lack of prudishness or even common reticence among Puritan men and women, the prevalent modern conception of the 'Puritanical' seems grotesque." It was the manufacturing class, with its creed of respectability, that encouraged "the happy ignorance of innocence," developed the science of deceit and the art of evasion, made children into the scions of storks, turned legs into limbs, and emasculated literature of all intimacy and intensity.

The pruderies and reticences in our literature developed after Puritanism as a living force was dead. They came with the rise of the new philosophy of the upper bourgeoisie, that of respectability, which candied over everything real with the surface of decency. The Puritanic philosophy of fortitude broke down, in the crucible of respectability, into the philosophy of sweetness and light. When the Puritans opposed the theatre they closed it. Only after the merchant class lost its warring aspect did it begin to moralize the stage.[43] It was the wealthy bourgeoisie which sentimentalized it. The Puritan would not have been guilty of the sick duplicity of Sumnerism, censoring serious plays and books for their moral deviations while allowing pornographic vaudeville and burlesque to run rampant. The Puritan would have been consistent. He would have censored both or none at all. Nor did the literature of the tired business man have its roots in Puritanism. The Puritan despised almost all literature that did not serve a sacred purpose. He would have sneered at the happy ending as a shallow, feminine device, demoralizing in effect. In fact, there is scarcely anything about nineteenth-century American literature which he would not have condemned. Bryant, Longfellow, Lowell, Howells, for example, would have met with his immediate and abiding contempt. He would have scorned the sentimentality of their poetry and prose as much as he would have loathed their *respectable* way of life.

The American Puritans with their petty bourgeois psy-

[43] In England the process of moralizing the stage began when the merchant class had already gained definite power after the Revolution of 1688.

chology did not encourage the arts, or cultivate literature in any other sense than the religious, because they were constantly concerned with an ideal which exalted values that were far removed from the æsthetic. Nevertheless, it was this petty bourgeois lack of esteem for art values, plus the influence of the colonial complex, which encouraged imitation instead of originality in whatever little art that was attempted, that kept American literature from coming of age before the twentieth century. American Puritanism died long before the Revolutionary War, but the petty bourgeois psychology which underlay it continued, in diluted form, to influence our culture, emphasizing moral values instead of religious, and making our literature into an adventure into ethics instead of æsthetics. The absence of any aristocratic tradition allowed this tendency to have full and unchallenged sway. If the presence of the colonial complex made it impossible for our literature to stand on its own legs, the influence of the petty bourgeois attitude toward art, in its moral as well as its religious form, prevented those borrowed legs from ever moving with freedom.

It is only to-day, with the developments which have taken place in the twentieth century, that American literature has escaped the more paralyzing effects of the petty bourgeois psychology as well as the more encumbering aspects of the colonial complex. It is only to-day, with the decay of the moral tradition of the upper bourgeoisie, and the growth of a definite revolt against its philosophy of life, that our literature, in the face of the prevailing chaos, has been able to express itself in new and more native patterns. Without those developments, our literature would have remained, as Gertrude Atherton described it at the beginning of this century, "as correct as Sunday clothes and as innocuous as sterilized milk."[44]

[44]This quotation is taken from a striking article which appeared as early as 1904 in *The North American Review* (*Why Is American Literature Bourgeois?*) in which Gertrude Atherton described American literature as "the expression of that bourgeoisie which is afraid of doing the wrong thing."

CHAPTER III

THE SOUTHERN PATTERN

ONLY when we begin to take inventory of this country as a whole do we come to realize its enormousness in size as well as spirit. There has really never been an America; there have been only Americas. Even after the Civil War, the phrase, the United States, continued to be, aside from its political import, a misnomer. To-day, for that matter, despite the spread of industry from coast to coast and the destruction of the Mason and Dixon line as a boundary between an industrial and an agrarian civilization, the country is still far from unified. In the past, at least previous to the Civil War, the only unifying bond between these Americas was that of language, and for a considerable period in sections of those Americas even language was not a connecting link. At the present time the unifying bond, which is rapidly making those Americas into an America, and which has endowed the country with a national consciousness, is industry.

When we learn to appreciate the fact that the history of a people is far more concerned with the nature of their culture than with the specific expression of their political life, we shall be in a better position to understand the operation of those social forces which determine the character of a civilization. A unified country depends not upon a political alliance but upon economic unity. No country can be spoken of as a unit, except in political terms, unless it has a unified economic life. Prior to the twentieth century, America was a divided entity. In fact, its only existence as an entity was political. The conflicts in its economic organization of life, conflicts that took on a tri-fold character, finding their varying expressions in the north, the south, and along the ever elusive frontier, created Americas instead of an America. The only force which influenced each of these Americas was the colonial complex. But even the effect of this complex upon these sundry Americas was tempered by each of their respective cultures. Their contradictions in economic life made cultural unity impossible.

We are confronted here again with another set of forces which have made our culture in general, and our literature in particular, follow a unique course. When modern European nations came of age, they had already begun to develop a relatively unified culture. Even in a country such as Germany where high German and low German existed in different regions, and political unity was not established until after the Franco-Prussian War, a unification of culture prevailed expressing itself in patent form in German literature. German literature thus, once manumitted of French influence, grew up as a single unit. French literature, likewise, pursued a comparatively parallel pattern. The development of English literature was also similar. This unification in each of these countries was primarily due to a similarity of economic life within each of their different territories. And it was this lack of unification of economic life which prevented such unification in American literature. The expanse of the country alone encouraged differences instead of resemblances and made the creation of varied and contradicting, and even hostile, economic systems almost inevitable. Thus again, in this way, American literature was in the very beginning shot off in conflicting directions, and divorced from the mainstream of energy which a unified culture would have provided.

The entire history of Southern culture, which its literature as well as its morals reflected, was an expression of a semi-feudalistic agrarian economy. The nature of Southern soil expedited the evolution of this semi-feudal order. Geographic factors thus, encouraging to agrarian economics, combined with a climate which has made slavery into a feasible surrogate for serfdom, rapidly established Plantation rule. It was this plantation ideology which made the political doctrine of State's Rights into the challenging philosophy of the South. It was the same ideology which gave Southern morality the leniency and latitude of a feudal society, institutionalizing by practice if not by precept its system of Negro concubinage as a substitute for the white concubinage which had prevailed in European feudal orders. And on the literary front it was this same ideology which manifested itself in contradiction to the ideology which dominated in the North.

This Southern ideology, however, expressing itself on every branch of the cultural front was a direct importation from England. Contrary to the old belief, which has been exploded by recent research, it was not the Cavaliers who superimposed a feudal philosophy upon the South. In the first place, it was not the Cavaliers who in the main settled the South. The Cavaliers came over in small companies from time to time, it is true, and during the period of the Commonwealth a number of them remained in America for more than a decade. But once the Restoration was accomplished, the vast majority of them returned to England. Only three families in Virginia, it has been established, were definitely a branch of Cavalier houses in England. As a whole the Cavaliers themselves even at the height of their emigration constituted an inconspicuously small percentage of the population. The South, in fact, was colonized by approximately the same people who settled in the North.[1] The same petty bourgeois and plebeian elements who inhabited New England populated also the shores of Virginia and Maryland.[2]

[1] Thos. Cuming Hall: *Religious Background of American Culture:* Boston, 1930: p. 113.

[2] (1) James Truslow Adams: *Provincial Society:* p. 10. (2) V. L. Parrington: *Main Currents in American Thought:* Vol. II, p. 7. (3) Thos. J. Wertenbaker: *Patrician and Plebeian in Virginia:* p. 7. (4) A. W. Calhoun: *Social History of the American Family:* p. 219. The only one whose opposition to this fact deserves any consideration at all is R. A. Bruce who in his *Institutional History of Virginia in the 17th Century* (New York, 1910) made a valiant attempt to defend the contention that the Southern colonies, particularly Virginia, were settled in considerable part by the genuine aristocracy. At the cost of indefatigable labor, he claimed that he copied himself eighteen thousand signatures of legal

They brought with them almost the same religious attitudes and the same moral shibboleths.

A survey of the laws and statutes of early Virginia reveal the same spirit as that which pervaded New England. Blue laws were enacted in Virginia which were just as severe as those that were passed in Massachusetts. The grand juries and vestries were as vigilant in reporting the offenses as the courts were in executing the punishments that were to be meted out to those guilty of profaning the Sabbath, inebriety, defamation, and sexual immorality. In 1649 a law was passed in Virginia forcing every person to attend church. Floggings, exposure in the stocks and heavy fines were very much in vogue. Laws concerned with limitations of dress were also common. Bishop Bayly's *Practice of Piety directing a Christian how to work that he may please God,* which was popular in Virginia as late as the eighteenth century, was scarcely less gravely admonitory in its tone than the sermons of the New England theocrats. Indeed, so saturated were the early Virginians with this ascetic religiosity that when the Indian Massacre of 1622 occurred the Virginia company attributed it to the "sins of drunkenness and excess of apparel"[3] which prevailed in the colonies. Virginians who went into battles with the Indians did so with prayers not less devout than those of the New Englanders, with strict prohibitions against profanity as part of their martial procedure.

Even in artistic matters their original attitude was not very different from that found in the colonies along the New England coast. While the coming of the Cavaliers during the first half of the seventeenth century had unquestionably tempered somewhat the petty bourgeois attitude toward art

documents in order to make a table proving that the aristocracy was literate. It is needless to add, however, that notwithstanding his research, recent investigations have shown the fallacy of his hypothesis. It should be added in fairness to Bruce, nevertheless, that he does point out in an earlier study—*The Social Life of Virginia in the 17th Century* (1907), p. 83—"that the most important section of the higher planting class during the seventeenth century were the families sprung directly from English merchants."

[3] Edward Eggleston: *The Beginners of a Nation:* p. 149.

and thus provided leeway for a degree of art appreciation if not art expression which did not exist in New England, the vast majority of the population was unaffected by this influence. Although Governor Berkeley may have approved of the theatre and even written plays himself, the populace with its petty bourgeois antipathy for art refused to be converted to his æsthetic philosophy. Long before Berkeley ever appeared on the American scene, actors were considered in Virginia as part of "the scum and dregs of the earth."[4] In fact as late as 1665 three men from Accomac county were arrested for staging a play known as *Ye Bare and Ye Cubb*.[5] Previous to 1665 it is doubtful if any Virginians would have hazarded such a violation of the petty bourgeois ethic. Even under the protection of Governor Berkeley play acting was only attempted as an amateur amusement in drawing-room and parlor. Literature itself was looked upon with affection only by the aristocratic exiles, or by those Englishmen, scions of the aristocratic tradition, who flocked about Berkeley. Even in the eighteenth century, when the structure of Southern society had already begun to alter, we frequently find references in *The Virginia Gazette* which testify to the persistence of the petty bourgeois contempt for *belles lettres*. Even after this petty bourgeois philosophy had been superseded by the semi-feudal plantation one, the attitude toward the artist as an individual did not become very exalted. It was easier to appreciate art than to appreciate the artist. Indeed, continuing even until to-day the individual artist in the South has scarcely come to be looked upon with much less contempt than had been his seventeenth and eighteenth-century predecessors. In general a man who turned to literature was viewed as one who could not succeed in more "honorable callings." Richard Henry Wilde, for instance, who wrote the *Captive's Lament*, a poem which Byron described

---

[4]P. A. Bruce: *Social Life of Virginia in the Seventeenth Century*: 1907: p. 102.

[5]Ibid., p. 102. At the same time that that arrest occurred in England Restoration drama was beginning to develop in real earnest, introducing a new era in the history of the comic tradition.

as "the finest poem of the century," refused for a time to admit his authorship of the poem, so unfavorably was versifying looked upon in the South.[6] The fate of William Gilmore Simms, whom Poe described as "immeasurably the best writer of fiction in America, leaving out of the question Brockden Brown and Hawthorne (who are each a genius)" was typical of the continuance of that attitude far down into the nineteenth century. The story told of Lord Morpeth and his attempt to discover the whereabouts of Simms in the latter's native city of Charleston is interesting in the light of this attitude. When Lord Morpeth discovered that the Charlestonians not only did not know where Simms could be found but that they did not even consider him an important man, he made a reply that was unforgettable:

"Simms not a great man," replied the astonished visitor, "then for God's sake who is your great man?"[7]

Paul Hayne described Simms' struggle as "a fight against the bitter prejudice, miserable provincialism of tone and sentiment . . . (which) awaits every true literary athlete whose intellectual battlefield happens to be in any part of this material, debased, provincial, narrow-minded South." The cold treatment which Poe received in the South was in consonance with the same tradition. The well-known Southern author, Hugh Swinton Legare, described this attitude in no uncertain words when he wrote to his friend T. C. Reynolds at Heidelberg and stated that:

There can be no doubt that throughout the Southern States at least, a taste for literary studies (much more than any serious or continued application to them) stands very much in the way of a young man in the pursuits of an active life. It raises a presumption among worldly people that he can never become practical, and such a notion whenever it has taken root in the public mind is beyond all comparison the most formidable obstacle a man of talents can encounter in such a state of society as ours.[8]

[6]C. Alphonso Smith: *Southern Literary Studies:* 1927: p. 47.
[7]William P. Trent: *William Gilmore Simms:* New York, 1892: p. 159.
[8]*Writings of Hugh Swinton Legare:* 2 vols.: Charleston, 1846: p. 206. Letter to T. C. Reynolds at Heidelberg, April 23, 1840.

Here is another episode which shows the presence of this attitude even at the close of the nineteenth century:

"Who is that man going along yonder?" an ex-Governor of Tennessee, now living, heard some one ask in the streets of Nashville.

"*Oh, he is nobody but the editor of a magazine*," was the almost contemptuous answer.[9] (Italics mine.)

Even to-day in the South this attitude has changed little. While contemporary writers such as Paul Green, James Branch Cabell, Du Bose Heyward, and Julia Peterkin, have emerged as expressions of the new South, it is doubtful whether they have derived very much inspiration from the communities in which they live. The truth of the matter is these writers have to work for the Northern market and not the Southern. Aside from *The Virginia Quarterly Review*, which is scarcely any more Southern in spirit than *The Nation*, there is no Southern magazine in the creative field to which they can contribute their work. It is for New York magazines that they must write their stories and articles, just as it is for the people of the North and West that they must write their books. They may use Southern materials but they must interpret them for non-Southern audiences. For the South to-day has continued to remain in its cultural attitude the same literary desert that it was in the seventeenth century.

The fact that Southern literature never came of age becomes all the more a problem when we realize that Southern culture managed to escape a considerable portion of the petty-bourgeois heritage which clung to New England culture until this century. But how did Southern culture, which in origin, as we have just shown, was just as petty bourgeois in its psychology as that of New England, succeed in partially emancipating itself from this heritage? This very

---

[9]*Southern Literature*, by William B. Baskervil, published in *Publication of the Modern Language Association of America*, Vol. VII, No. 2: Baltimore, 1892: p. 90.

emancipation was part of the process of making the South into a separate America.

The South continued in many ways to resemble the North as long as its economic organization developed in the same direction. As soon as this resemblance was destroyed, and the South began to carve out a new form of economic existence, dependent upon slave labor instead of free labor, with the plantation as its pivot, its cultural attitudes also took on a different character. From the very beginning, for instance, the religious elements in the South had much greater difficulty in enforcing their rules and regulations upon the people.[10] Of course, the fact that the ruling class religious elements subscribed to the Prayer Book and were not in revolt against the King and the Established Church[11] one might think would have made them more yielding and tolerant

[10]The expression of religiosity, however, during the early years of Southern colonization was not less devout than that found in the North. It is doubtful whether any New Englander would have written with greater fervor of his people than did John Hammond of Maryland and its inhabitants:

"The Country is very full of sober modest persons, with both men and women and many that truly fear God and follow that perfect rule of our blessed Saviour to do as they would be done by." (John Hammond: *Leah and Rachel, or the Two Fruitful Sisters Virginia and Maryland*: 1656.)

Better still are the words of Father Andrew White descriptive of the colony of Lord Baron of Baltimore:

"The first and most important design of the Most Illustrious Baron, which also ought to be the aim of the rest, who go in the same ship, is, not to think so much of planting fruits and trees in a land so fruitful, as of sowing the seeds of religion and piety. Surely a design worthy of Christians, worthy of angels, worthy of Englishmen. . . . The Indians themselves are everywhere sending messengers, to seek after fit men to instruct the inhabitants in saving doctrine, and to regenerate them with the sacred water. . . . Who then can doubt, that by one such glorious work as this, many thousands of souls will be brought to Christ?" (*Narratives of Early Maryland 1633–1684.*)

Of course there was the same attempt to shrewdly combine the material with the spiritual as is well attested by the following passage from the Annual Letter, 1681, of the members of the Society of Jesus to headquarters in Rome:

"Yet we trust in the goodness of God and the piety of the Catholics that, while we sow spiritual seed, we shall reap carnal things in abundance, and that to those who seek the kingdom of God the other things shall be added."

[11]E. L. Goodwin: *The Colonial Church in Virginia*: Milwaukee, 1927: p. 97.

than the New England theocrats. But they were not. Even
the witch-hunting craze found almost as secure a foothold
there as in the North.[12] Indeed a record of the trial of a
witch, a certain Grace Sherwood, in the County of Princess
Anne has been preserved. The inlet in which she was submerged—she was able to swim and unfortunately was trans-
ported to jail for more dire punishment—is still known as
Witch Duck.[13] In addition to persecuting witches we find
that the ecclesiastics forced through the Assembly laws that
were in every way as strict as those in New England.[14]
Certainly the following laws which were passed in Virginia
in 1662 were not more lenient than those enacted in Massachusetts:

"Every person who refuses to have his child Baptized by a lawful
Minister, shall be amerced 2000 pounds of Tobacco; half to the
Parish, half to the informer."

"The man and Woman committing fornication shall pay each
500 pounds of Tobacco and to be bound to their good behaviors."[15]

Why then did not religious rule become as tyrannous in
the South as it did in the North?

To answer that question we must turn to the field of economic and geographic calculus. Theocratic rule was no less
desirable by the ecclesiastics in the South than by those in
the North, but the conditions in the North which made such
rule possible were absent in the South. To begin with, it was
the presence of well-knit communities in the North out of
which cities soon grew that gave the theocrats the opportunity to enforce their power. The absence of cities in the
South rendered the clergy impotent. In the South, as the

[12]Carl Holliday: *Wit and Humor of Colonial Days:* Philadelphia, 1912.
[13]Campbell: *History of the Colony and Ancient Dominion of Virginia:*
p. 382.
[14]It is interesting to note that the hierophants in the South use the
same justificatory dialectic as did the Massachusetts theologians. In
truth the early Southern clergymen were just as convinced of their holy
mission as were the Puritans.
[15]Thos. Cuming Hall: *Religious Background in American Culture:*
p. 78.

community spread, life centred itself about plantations instead of cities, and hence neither the central authority of Church or State could exercise so powerful an influence over individuals as where the city was the unit and laws could be executed as easily as they were passed. The Virginia clergy might make the Assembly enact statutes, fining all who did not attend church, but topographical factors made it practically impossible to execute those statutes—especially after the population began to expand and string itself out along the shores of the river and the bay. Many parishioners could attend church only by sailing to it in their sloops, and if for reasons of their own they failed to attend it was very hard to get to them to mete out the punishment which was their due. With the church so far away—some parishes were as removed as thirty miles inshore—the churchmen found themselves helpless in their effort to impose their authority upon the people. Consequently, after the first few generations of expansion, Sunday in the South, at least among the growing plantation aristocracy, was seldom the solemn sanctimonious day which it was in the North. Virginians very often resorted to Indian villages for fun and sport, and Sundays in particular, associated thus with the paganism of the red man, became more heathen than Christian in spirit. It was not a far step from this habit to the more extreme ones which appeared later on in Southern life.

Two factors, then, prevented the South in pre-Civil War days from becoming as religious-ridden as the North; first, the presence of the Episcopal Church, the established church of the aristocracy and its followers in England as well as in America, which was the Church in power in many of the Southern colonies; and second, the topographical element, dividing instead of uniting the community as a whole, which made it impossibly difficult for the religionists to acquire control in the despotic manner of the theocrats in the North. Consequently we find that the cultural front in the South was soon dominated by the ideology of the plantation owner instead of the ecclesiastic, and the cultural energy of the

South was shunted off in the direction of political oratory instead of theological polemics. Politics there became the great art, with religion playing an ever-receding rôle in the administration of the social order. As a corollary of this condition, the high-spirited ecclesiastics who had come over in the early years of Southern colonization were followed a generation or so later by the easy-going, inferior-minded clergymen who made religion into an enterprise instead of an ideal. This new race of clergymen, who, as Eggleston said, "could babble in a Pulpit or in a tavern," soon bred the "horse-racing parson" who became popular in many places in the South. As in the instance of the famous old church on Miles River in Maryland, where the preacher and the congregation repaired to the horse races immediately after the service was over, sport and religion went hand in hand as part of the social process.[16] Naturally, the position of the clergyman deteriorated rapidly. The so-called "Maryland parson,"[17] known for the loose ways conspicuous among the Maryland ministry, became common throughout the South. *Pari passu* with this development, a considerable army of free thinkers arose in the South. *The Virginia Gazette* took note of the spread of these groups of so-called free thinkers, and even attempted to trace their origin:

> The religion of free thinkers, which makes so much noise in the world and is every day increasing, is a production of our age and

[16]As a matter of fact, it was this kind of a clergyman, or at least one who was not very dissimilar, that Virginians and Southerners in general desired. All one needs to do to realize the significance of this is to remember the kind of ecclesiastic that dominated in the North, the terror-inspiring Mathers and Edwardses, and then read this thoroughly honest and unexaggerated statement of the variety of clergymen that was preferred in the South: "Clergymen . . . should be persons that have read and seen something of the world . . . and have studied Man and business in some measure as well as books; they may eat like Gentlemen, and be facetious and good humored without too much freedom and licentiousness; they may be good scholars without becoming cynics, as they may be good Christians without appearing stoics." And one can understand then, without further ado, why religion played such a different rôle in the two cultures. (Hugh Jones: *The Present State of Virginia:* London, 1724: p. 97.)

[17]James Oneal: *Workers in American History:* p. 31.

seems to be composed of the four religions now reigning . . . of Paganism . . . of Judaism . . . of Mahometism . . . of Christianity.[18]

By the time of the Revolutionary War, as it became more common in the South to call the clergy "celestial asses" and other phrases even more opprobrious, these anti-religious groups had little difficulty in disseminating their ideas. No one was more outspokenly typical of the spirit of these groups at that time than the young Thomas Jefferson. It was a little later, when alarmed at the spread of this "free thinking movement," that George Washington, a conservative in such matters, made a direct attack upon the idea that morality could exist without religion.[19]

It was the combination of all these circumstances, then, which made the South so different from the North in religious tradition—and religion, it cannot be stressed too strongly, was more important than any other single psychological force in shaping the background of literary America. This difference, however, was not one which ran vertically throughout the length and breadth of Southern society. It was one which was confined mainly to the ruling class and its immediate dependents. The petty bourgeois elements, descendants of the Dissenting tradition, and many of whom eventually made up the vast yeoman class which developed with plantation economics, clung tenaciously to their creeds despite the lax attitude of the ruling class in religious matters. If these petty bourgeois elements at that time had been able to control society effectively in the South, they would have made it as God-fearing as New England. They were, and continued to be, as self-denying and pious as the ruling class was pleasure-loving and wanton. It was the women of this class who lived through what Corra Harris, the well-known Southern writer, so aptly described as "the candle-lit drama of salvation." To them religion was a con-

[18]*Virginia Gazette*, No. 579, February 12, 1762.
[19]George Washington: Advice to a nephew, from a letter to Bushrod W. Washington, Newburgh, January 15, 1783.

viction; to the ruling class it was only a form. In general the Established Church was anathema to them; it was to the evangelical faiths, the Baptists, the Presbyterians, and the Methodists, that they flocked.[20] While the petty bourgeois elements in general were unable to function with marked success in a cityless environment where emphasis on caste prevailed, they preserved their rigid ideology in towns and in those isolated communities which they dominated, and those of their group who merged into the yeomanry carried this ideology over, as has been observed, into the spirit of that class. After all, this yeomanry which made up the poor-white section of the community was more fitted by the economic nature of its life to preserve the petty bourgeois virtues than to verge over and adopt the aristocratic. But despite their great numerousness, it was not the yeomanry which constituted the ruling class in Southern society.[21] While many political leaders in the South derived from the yeoman group, they soon adopted the ideology of the ruling class once they became politically entrenched.

The South was not religious, then, in the sense that the North was, except in those places where the petty bourgeois psychology was able to resist the influence of the ruling class. Wherever that was the case religiosity in the South was not less excoriating in its extremes than in the North. Indeed, in specific communities in the South this religiosity, accentuated in places by climate and isolation, became more maniacal than anywhere else in America. The grandmother in Mary Johnston's novel *Hagar* evinces the appalling effect of this religiosity, when she avows with pride that she doesn't "pretend to be 'literary' or to understand literary talk. What Moses and St. Paul said and the way we've always done in Virginia is good enough for me."

[20] Francis P. Gaines: *The Southern Plantation*: New York, 1924: p. 144.
[21] It was this yeoman class, then still in the embryo, more than any other, which Nathaniel Bacon represented in his famous struggle against Governor Berkeley. Of course, at that time economic life in the South had not become definitely organized, and, classes still being in the process of formation, the ideology of the yeoman class itself had not yet crystallized into a programme.

Examples of the extent to which this religiosity ran in the South are numerous. One of them, which occurred recently, is an excellent illustration of the presence of the same religious temper on the part of petty bourgeois groups below the Mason and Dixon line as well as above it. This example which took place in Virginia on Tangier Island reveals an extremity of action which was never paralleled by the religionists in the North. A certain laxity was noted on the part of the younger generation growing up on Tangier Island in the second decade of this century, and the religious-minded poor whites of the community passed a law, stating that any one who did not attend church on Sunday unless confined to bed by illness would be subject to imprisonment and liable to be shot. On Sunday, the sheriff of the community discovered a young man sitting on his porch during church time; he ordered the youth to go to church, and when the youth refused, the sheriff shot him. (*Baltimore Sun*, June 19, 1920.)

But there was one colony in the South in which a different ruling class had established itself. While the plantation aristocracy dominated decisively in Virginia, Maryland, and South Carolina, it struck a snag in North Carolina. North Carolina was the one Southern state during colonial times which escaped the hegemony of a plantation aristocracy. The plantation aristocracy never established a final foothold there. North Carolina was the only Southern state which perpetuated its petty bourgeois ideology throughout the seventeenth, eighteenth, and nineteenth centuries. As Vance has pointed out the petty bourgeois of Scotch-Irish extraction who populated North Carolina constituted "the best *middle class* in the world."[22] (Italics mine.) While Vance's opinion of this middle class is entirely too exalted, the influence of the class itself cannot be denied. Due to topographical factors, the sweep of the Piedmont Plateau, the poverty of the sea coast, an insufficiency of great navigable rivers which ran exclusively within the state, commerce found little encouragement and vast accumulations of capital could not occur. In addition

[22] Ex-Governor Vance: *Sketches of North Carolina:* Norfolk, Va., 1875.

the absence of cities which would have provided active home markets, kept agriculture in a backward state. In fact the economic inferiority of the state drove away those who were ambitious of large land holdings, and attracted those who were content with small land possessions. Those interested in large plantation possibilities settled in Virginia or moved on to South Carolina, leaving the intermediate colony of North Carolina for the habitation of the small land owner. Consequently, as Professor J. S. Bassett has shown, "the genius of land owning in (North Carolina) remained to the Civil War on the basis of the small farm"[23]; while the western part of the state was settled independently of the eastern, the landholding situation was practically the same in both regions. The land west of Raleigh, for example, was deliberately sliced up into small holdings which seldom exceeded 500 acres. Indeed one of the earliest laws passed in North Carolina, enacted in 1670, stated that no surveyor should grant more than 660 acres to any one person unless the person had the particular permission of the Lord.[24] As a result the small upper class which eventually did evolve was never able to develop a plantation ideology such as characterized the ruling classes in Virginia and South Carolina. Class distinctions were never able to develop in North Carolina as they did in the two leading Southern colonies and, because North Carolina lacked the "intellectual tolerance, the pride of race, the assurance which mark an aristocracy," as Peter Mitchell Wilson expressed it.[25] The culture of North Carolina possessed little of the spirit of the culture of South Carolina and Virginia. The Established (Episcopal) Church which was foisted upon the colony by royal decree was swept away at the time of the Revolutionary War.[26] Because there was no plantation

[23]John S. Bassett: *Suffrage in the State of North Carolina:* Washington, 1895: p. 271.

[24]John S. Bassett: *Inholding in Colonial North Carolina,* from *Historical Papers* published by the Historical Society of Trinity College, Durham, N. C., 1898: p. 53.

[25]Peter Mitchell Wilson: *Southern Exposure:* Chapel Hill, N.C., 1927:p. 2.

[26]Steven B. Weeks: *Religious Development in the Province of North Carolina:* Baltimore, Md., 1892: p. 11.

aristocracy to lend it stable support, the Established Church in North Carolina was never able to effect the persecutions that it did in other Southern colonies, although it was viewed as an oppressor by the petty bourgeois population of the state. Naturally, therefore, the Established Church had very little influence over the life of the people. It cultivated none of the amenities of existence which were associated with its form of life elsewhere. The "strict attendance on the worship of Almighty God" demanded of every North Carolinian was not an outgrowth of its presence.[27] It was the petty bourgeois who enforced such a regulation in the state. As a corollary of these conditions, what little education was undertaken in North Carolina was conspicuously religious. The arts were given no encouragement there, for "a love of polite literature was considered a little less than a sin and was fatal to a legal reputation. To accuse a man of writing poetry was little less than an accusation of crime."[28] The theatre fared ill also. Indeed, it can be said without exaggeration that, as a result of this petty bourgeois domination, culture advanced so little in North Carolina that when one speaks of Southern culture one never thinks of North Carolina as being a part of it at all.

It is obvious thus that religion has played a unique and contradictory rôle in Southern life. While communities that were dominated by the petty bourgeois were overwhelmingly religious in character, the rest of Southern society, in particular the ruling class and the Fourth Estate, in every colony but North Carolina, were even less ardent and ascetic in their religious outlook than the English aristocracy. One thing is certain, that with the exception of North Carolina the plantation aristocracy never allowed the petty bourgeois ministry to command public opinion.

It was the control of public opinion by the theocracy in the

[27] Wm. Henry Foote: *Sketches of North Carolina*: New York, 1846: p. 13.
[28] Steven B. Weeks: *Libraries and Literature in North Carolina*, from the *Annual Report of the American Historical Society for the Year 1895*: Washington, 1895: p. 352.

North which, as Thomas Jefferson said, created a condition, as it also did in North Carolina, in which "no mind beyond mediocrity dared there to develop itself."[29] This conviction of Jefferson was shared by Southern intellectuals in general and the ruling class as a whole.

Such was the condition then which prevailed in the South until the Civil War.

The Civil War ended plantation rule. The passing of plantation economics in the South, and the rise of commerce and industry, marked the beginning of a new South, with a new economics, and a new ruling class. The new ruling class was the petty bourgeoisie which supplanted the plantation aristocracy. For a number of years after the Civil War, to be sure, no one class was dominant in the South. The plantation owners did not surrender without a struggle, and it was only after several decades when the smoke of that struggle had vanished that the power of the petty bourgeoisie was finally established. Southern life then began to centre itself about cities instead of plantations, until to-day the plantation has practically disappeared as a force in Southern affairs. The city has superseded it. While plantations still remain, their owners have receded steadily in influence and power. In many instances these plantations are not even self-supporting units, but are clung to by the old generation as relics of an age of gold which has now given way to an age of steel. The petty bourgeoisie, adapting itself readily to the new way of life which commerce and industry have created in the South, soon seized control of the reins of government, and, aided by the new economic forces at its command, superimposed its ideology upon the changing environment. In every field this petty bourgeoisie, comprising the urban shopkeepers, traders, merchants, and poor whites who aspired to be traders, and the small farmers who dominated in the towns, extended its tentacles of control. Abetted by the alli-

---

[29] *Jeffersonian Principles:* Extracts from the writings of Thomas Jefferson selected and edited by James Truslow Adams: New York, 1928— letter to Horatio Gates Spofford, January 10, 1816: p. 139.

ance with Northern capitalism, it lent its new-found energies to the scrapping of everything old, the worn-out agricultural régime, the hopeless, broken-backed agrarian tradition, and bent the rest of its energies to the construction of a
South that was to be entirely new. Before the end of the
nineteenth century the outline of this new South already
had become clear and the effects of its new tradition had revealed themselves in Southern culture. In politics the change
was catastrophically precipitate. The Calhouns and Ran-
dolphs, political representatives of the old order, the plantation aristocracy, were supplanted by the Heflins and Hoke
Smiths, the political spokesmen of the new order, the petty
bourgeoisie. With this change in economic life, which chalked
off the passing of political power on the part of the plantation aristocracy, the whole plantation ideology collapsed like
a mountain of sand before the advance of a typhoon. Ellen
Glasgow in her novel, *The Battle Ground,* traced something
of the conditions of decay which led to this melodramatic
collapse.

In a little while, journalism, religion, and education underwent sharp changes in consonance with the ideology of
the new ruling class. D. A. Tompkins, one of the first successful Southern engineers, and the owner of *The Charlotte
Observer,* described very precisely the nature of this change
in journalism when he wrote:

> The ante-bellum newspaper of the South was essentially a po-
> litical institution. Its patrons were chiefly planters and slave-owners.
> . . . But politics is no longer the one subject of public interest to
> Southern people. . . . *Southern people are becoming more and
> more interested in manufactures*—in diversified manufactures, and
> in education.[30] (Italics mine.)

The status of religion changed even more rapidly than that
of journalism. While in colonies such as North Carolina, the
petty bourgeois of Scotch-Irish extraction had managed to
monopolize mental instruction by controlling practically all

[30]Edwin Mims: *The Advancing South:* 1926: p. 85.

the private schools in the State,[31] they had not succeeded in other states in throttling every progressive sign of intellectual impulse. It was only after the Civil War, when this petty bourgeoisie became the ruling class throughout the South, that it was able to institute its reign of intellectual terror. Since that time, in particular in the last few generations, as a result of this petty bourgeois hegemony, the South has been as religious ridden as was the North in the seventeenth century. In other words the South to-day is intellectually 200 years behind the North, afflicted as it is with the onus of a petty bourgeois ideology which has not yet been tempered by the rise of an upper industrial bourgeoisie for whom religion means less than politics and economics. Consequently freedom of thought in the South to-day, like an echo from the catacombs of a buried past, revolves about an issue which was fought out and downed in industrialized communities many generations ago. Not that religion, in a meeker, milder way, and with elasticities which have made it respectable instead of respected, has not been preserved by the industrial bourgeoisie! It certainly has. But the industrial bourgeoisie has no longer made it the inexorable test of human values. Politics and economics, as we have shown, have taken its place as more important shibboleths. In educational institutions controlled by the industrial bourgeoisie, such as the leading colleges and universities in the North to-day, religion is no longer a vital test. Politics and economics, however, are. A professor at Harvard or Columbia, say, can be an avowed free thinker on religious matters, but he dare not be an avowed free thinker on political and economic matters if his free thinking leads him in the direction of communism. The truth of this statement is to be seen in the fact that there are scarcely more than four or five professors in American universities to-day who are known as avowed communists. Wherever such individual professors have been discovered, and there have been several who have been thus detected,

[31] Ex-Governor Vance: *Sketches of North Carolina:* Norfolk, Va., 1875: p. 52.

they have been immediately eliminated from the institution. Politics and economics, then, constitute the battleground for the industrial bourgeoisie to-day—and not religion. With the petty bourgeoisie on the other hand, it is religion which still remains the challenging test, for the nature of its economic life has not yet effected that tolerance in religious matters which is inevitably created by an industrial order. Revealingly enough, many individual professors in the South have found economic radicalism in much less disrepute than religious heterodoxy. This is true, of course, in those places where the labor movement has caused little friction and the evidences of class struggle are obscured.

Undoubtedly the present advance of industry in the South, which has already resulted in vicious economic clashes in Gastonia, Elizabethton, Marion, and Danville, will shift the social emphasis from religion to economics. But that shift will not occur until an industrial bourgeoisie has established itself throughout the Southern states, instituting its own ideology in the place of that of the petty bourgeoisie, and thus accomplishing the transformation of the South from an agrarian into an industrial community. At the present time, however, that transformation is only in a state of transition. So long as the industrial bourgeoisie must function in isolated centres and is unable to extend its way of life over the South as a whole, it will be impossible for it to supplant the ideology of the petty bourgeoisie with its own. The petty bourgeoisie to-day is still in control, and the emerging industrial bourgeoisie has not yet begun to shed very much of its petty bourgeois psychology. This petty bourgeois control, focussing itself on the religious front, is effective in education as well as in politics. The recent race of anti-evolution bills which have been forced through various Southern legislatures and barely defeated in others has been one of the most exciting illustrations of this bourgeois activity in the educational field.[32] The influence of Bishop Candler whom Corra Harris

[32]Of course, one of the important factors which has rendered Southern culture so backward and the Southern masses so illiterate is to be found

described in *My Book and Heart* as "the greatest church-man of his times" is typical of this ideology in its most menacing form. Bishop Candler's opposition to such "free thinking" institutions as Harvard and Yale, and his hostility to independent educational institutions and state universities is characteristic of this philosophy as it expresses itself in educational thought. Without question there are bishops and parsons in the North who share the views of Bishop Candler, but the difference is that these Northern bishops and parsons have little influence and less power, while Bishop Candler has great influence and enormous power. And it was such influence and power shaping the cast of Southern culture, which provoked the Dayton fiasco, and made the South into a spectacle of stupidity in the eyes of the modern world. This same spirit was manifest in the Southern condemnation of Paul Green's now defunct magazine *The Reviewer* as "The Devil's Instrument."[33]

---

in the very nature of agrarian economy. In agrarian communities education is a luxury instead of a necessity. An illiterate working class is preferable to a literate one. There is no spur to education even on the part of the petty bourgeois except in so far as the practical necessities of its life demand. Moreover the lack of surplus fluid capital militates against extensive social expenditures such as would be involved in a well-organized and entirely adequate state-protected instead of church-controlled educational system. It is only in industrial communities where educated workers are a necessity in order successfully to carry on the business of commerce and industry that illiteracy is eradicated. In addition, it is only in industrial communities that sufficient fluid capital accumulates to make it possible to make those social expenditures for education which are necessary to combat ignorance and illiteracy. Again here we can observe at once the difference between the public-school education which exists in communities dominated by the industrial bourgeoisie and those dominated by the petty bourgeoisie. Northern schools, for example, which fall under the former category, stress comparatively little the religious element; in Southern schools on the contrary which fall under the latter category religion still continues to be an important factor. This educational tie-up with religion which is the product of an agrarian petty bourgeois philosophy, is what has given fundamentalism its foothold in the South.

[33] *The Reviewer*, it is interesting to observe, has less than fifty subscribers in the whole state of North Carolina, the state in which it was published under Paul Green's editorship. It is doubtful whether it had any larger subscription list proportionately in the South as a whole when it was published in Virginia, with Emily Clark as its editor.

Even among the more liberal educators this same religious-tinged attitude persists in slightly adulterated form. Although the influence of the industrial bourgeoisie is beginning to percolate here and there in independent colleges and universities in the South, it has not yet escaped the impact of religious rule. After the Dayton episode, for instance, Chancellor Kirkland of Vanderbilt University stated, in what was considered in the South a very liberal address, that "a remedy for a narrow sectarianism and a belligerent Fundamentalism is the establishment on this campus of a school of religion, illustrating in its methods and its organization the strength of a common faith and the glory of a universal worship." Harry W. Chase, president of the University of North Carolina, who fought the anti-evolution bill in the legislature, has not advanced much further in his religious stand than Chancellor Kirkland. Victimized still by the petty bourgeois religious outlook, he is willing to fight against its Fundamentalist pretensions—but that is all. "North Carolina," he maintained, "is a deeply and genuinely religious state. It is in no denial, rather in a positive affirmation of its faith, that it has taken the stand that faith in God and the free pursuit of knowledge are handmaidens each to each, that the priesthood of science can be at the same time the priesthood of the living God."

It is to such a pass, then, that petty bourgeois domination has brought culture in the South to-day. Without libraries that are genuinely interested in the promotion of literature,[34] without bookstores to cultivate the sale of books, without publishing houses and magazines to stir a consciousness of

[34] In North Carolina, for example, as Doctor L. R. Wilson has shown, only thirty-five out of sixty-two towns have public libraries; these libraries are inferior in every way to libraries in the North, both in quantity and quality of books. More than fifty per cent of the common schools in the state do not even have libraries. Even the largest libraries in the South are pathetically small and inadequate when compared with those in the North. The condition of periodical literature is no improvement over that of book literature. (For further details concerning this aspect of Southern culture to-day, or lack of it, one can turn with profit to Edwin Mims' study, *The Advancing South*, chapter entitled "Scholar and Critics.")

literature in the environment,[35] the condition of literature in the South to-day is no better than when Sidney Lanier (one of the few worthwhile American authors to come out of the South) wrote to his brother that, in his soberest moments, he could "perceive no outlook for that land." "Our people," asserted Lanier, "have failed to perceive the deeper movements, under-running the times: they lie wholly off, out of the stream of thought, and whirl their poor dead leaves of recollection, round and round, in a piteous eddy that has all the wear and tear of motion without any of the rewards of progress." Those authors who have emerged out of the South in the last decade have done so by virtue of Northern environment rather than Southern. The few individuals who have striven to oppose these conditions in a

[35]A recent sign of change was to be seen in the week-end party of Southern writers which was held at the University of Virginia last October (1931). Instigated originally by Ellen Glasgow, and presided over by Doctor James Southall Wilson, the affair, which definitely tried to avoid the aspect of a conference, turned out to be an interesting success from the point of view of its aim. Over thirty writers, including such diverse types as James Branch Cabell, Julia Peterkin, Isa Glenn, Emily Clark, Caroline Gordon, John Peale Bishop, Du Bose Heyward, Paul Green, and William Faulkner, appeared in response to the invitation to attend the literary house party. In terms of cultural significance, however, the affair signified nothing of importance. The writers themselves, with the exception of Paul Green, made no particular contribution which indicated that they really understood what is happening in the South to-day. While Stringfellow Barr stressed the unwillingness of Southerners to purchase books, no one seemed to appreciate the cultural factors at work in the South to-day which make that the case—or to understand what factors are needed in order not to make that the case. Ellen Glasgow, Mary Johnston, and James Branch Cabell adopted a stand as reactionary in spirit as that of any Civil-War Confederate. "Charity towards the well-bred" constituted the essence of their stand, according to Emily Clark. (*Herald Tribune Books*, November 8, 1931, p. 2.) "I find my sympathy shifting to that outcast from the machine civilization, the well-bred person," Miss Glasgow stated, justifying her belief that compassion is "the most essential element of a great literature." Is it not revealing that Miss Glasgow and her literary regionalists expressed no compassion for the workers and poor farmers who are ground down to agony and starvation in an attempt to survive in the South to-day?

And, in the last analysis, every one of the Southern writers in attendance at the party knew full well that his success depended upon the North far more than upon the South, and that however Southern many of them might be they realized it was the North rather than the South toward which they all commonly gravitated with their work.

more realistic way have been lost in the shuffle, as it were, and forced to operate in isolation. Individual writers, such as L. P. Wilson, who has carefully studied and criticized the library situation in the South, Edwin Mims, who has challenged Southern educators to free themselves from the religious yoke, and Julian Harris, who has made the bravest fight of all in his struggle against the Ku Klux Klan, religious intolerance, and lynching—these men and a few others have carried on a vigorous struggle against the cultural backwardness of the South of to-day. That their struggle has not been a more successful one is not due to lack of courage on their part, but to the forces in the environment which have thwarted their efforts and resisted their influence. Even such magazines as *The Virginia Quarterly Review*, *The Sewanee Review*, and *The Southwest Review*, which all represent a spirit of advance which is far superior to the environment in which they exist, rally perhaps as much of their support from the North—if not more—than from the South. Nevertheless, these individuals and these magazines do indicate signs of advance—signs which will become more conspicuous as industry spreads in the South and breaks down the provincialism which now prevails.

To-day a group of Southern writers are in active revolt against the Southern environment, and in a recent symposium, *I'll Take My Stand*, they declaimed against the petty bourgeois South which has grown up since the Civil War, and in verbiage charged with indignation announced their stand in favor of a pre-Civil War Dixie. Donald Davidson, who edited the symposium, challenged his fellow Southerners to act before action is too late. This whole group is anxious to restore the old South with its plantation ideology and its agrarian economics. Only such a restoration, these writers are convinced, can release the South of to-morrow from the death hand of the petty bourgeoisie. Hopeless as is their hostility to what is already an ineradicable tendency, they have not allowed themselves to be discouraged as yet by the vast army of opposition which surrounds them. In fact, the very intensity of their challenge has a kind of corner-driven desperation about it. Full of intellectual TNT as their words are, they voice nothing more than the expiring spirit of a dead cause. At best, the plantation ideology having lost its economic *raison-d'être*, this group can do nothing more than stand apart, without the support of its environment, fighting a futile battle, modern Don Quixotes stabbing at steel windmills, hoping to destroy them by the gesture.

II

Without understanding the religious character of American culture, in the North, in he South, and along the shifting frontiers, it would be impossible to appreciate the development of American literature. It was in terms of religion that American culture with its petty bourgeois emphasis first expressed itself, and it was out of that religious background that our literature grew. The vicissitudes of religious ascent and descent, and the various mutations in the religious temper, revealing as they did the religious ideology of the respective ruling class, have had more to do with the shaping of the American literary tradition than has been realized by our critics. As we have seen in the evolution of New England literature, it was the religious attitude of the regnant theocrats that determined its spirit and direction. In the case of Southern literature, it was the absence of such theocrats that saved it, prior to the Civil War, from that type of devitalization. In the early beginnings of Southern culture, as we have noted, the same religious domination occurred, for essentially the same petty bourgeois elements who colonized the North settled also in the South. Only differences in topographical and telluric environment, resulting in differences in economic life, prevented those same petty-bourgeois groups from acquiring control of the Southern society in the same despotic way that they secured control of Northern. It was the growth of a plantation aristocracy which thwarted the petty bourgeois control of Southern morals and manners antecedent to the Civil War.

In the seventeenth century, before the plantation aristocracy established itself as the ruling class, the attitude toward religion and art in Virginia was not very different from that in Massachusetts. Although the petty bourgeois in Virginia did not stem from the same Puritan stock as did the New England theocrats they were descendants of the same Dissenting tradition which rooted itself much deeper than Puritanism proper into the matrix of our culture.[36] It was this Dissenting tradition which endeavored to make the South as sacrosanct as the North.

Now let us turn to the theatre. In the early part of the seventeenth century play-writing and play-acting were prohibited in Virginia. If that Dissenting tradition of the petty bourgeoisie had not been driven to retreat by the semi-aristocratic tradition of the plantation owners, the stage would have fared as ill in the South in the seventeenth and eighteenth centuries as it did in the North.

The plantation aristocracy finding its religious expression in the Episcopal Church, the Established Church of England, did not develop a hostility to art such as was common to the Puritanic and Dissenting traditions of the petty bourgeoisie in both the North and the South. The Episcopal Church, indeed, was a perfectly shaped upper-class instrument. It provided for all the latitudinarian privileges which an upper class desired, cultivated virtue without too strongly denouncing vice, exalted form more than faith, and was more willing to condone than to condemn. It was not an accident of choice or fate therefore that made the Episcopal Church the church of the wealthy planters, but a distinct ideological affinity which made them inevitable kin.[37]

[36] Thomas Cuming Hall: *The Religious Background of American Culture:* Boston, 1930: p. 108.

[37] In fact the Episcopalian clergymen were so loose in habit and behavior that instead of discouraging immorality they encouraged it. Commissaries Blair of Virginia and Bray of Maryland repeatedly reported to the Bishop of London that the meagre support of the clergy and the slight honor in which they were held prevented them from making honorable

The Episcopal Church, because it represented the aristocracy instead of the petty bourgeoisie, was friendly to art. While the religious leaders of the petty bourgeoisie, in both the North and the South, were opposed to music and dancing, and even forbade the introduction of organs into their churches, the Episcopalian clergymen were no more averse to musical entertainment than they were to horse racing or theatre going. Music, therefore, was able to advance in the South with much greater ease than in the North. In New England Cotton Mather described ministers who permitted the psalms to be sung in their churches as "Cathedral Priests of an Anti-Christian spirit," and so successful was the theocracy in the North in its battle against music

marriages and led them into disgraceful connections. A love-letter still survives written by a Maryland clergyman to a planter's daughter, in which he argues at length that inasmuch as his suit was allowable on other grounds, the fact of his being in Orders ought not to be an insuperable barrier. The clergymen provoked contempt and allowed themselves to be treated like lackeys. Governor Nicholson led out one who was drunk in the church, and caned him soundly with his own hand; clapped the hat over the eyes of another; and sent billets-doux to his mistress by a third. He hectored and browbeat a whole Convocation and drove them to sign an adulatory testimonial to his own religious devoutness. Commissary Blair writes: "The governor rules us as if we were a company of galley slaves, by continual reviling and thundering, cursing and sneering, base, abusive, Billingsgate language, to that degree that it is utterly incredible." One commissary was given the lie in his own house by the governor; and the wife of another was pulled out of Lady Berkeley's pew by the wrist because her husband had offended its owner by "preaching a little too near home against adultery." There were always present in these colonies some clergy of exemplary life and high character, but neither their example nor their reproof was able to redeem their brethren. Most of them were planters, and did priestly duty now and then to eke out their income. They hunted, played cards, drank punch and canary, turned marriages, christenings, and funerals alike into revels. One bawled out to his church warden at the Holy Communion, "Here, George, this bread is not fit for a dog." One fought a duel in his graveyard. Another, a powerful fellow, thrashed his vestrymen one by one, and the following Sunday preached before them from the text, "And I contended with them, and cursed them, and smote certain of them, and plucked off their head." Another dined every Sunday with his chief parishioner, and was sent home in the evening drunk, tied in his chaise.

Now that plantation life had grown easy, and a ready fortune was to be gathered, and the people themselves had declined in manners, so many of Coode's sort came that we shall find ministerial unworthiness to be a painful feature of the Church for more than a generation—indeed, in the Southern colonies, quite up to the Revolution. (McConnell: *History of the American Episcopal Church:* London, 1916: p. 57.)

that, as George Hood informs us in his *History of Music in New England,* "the knowledge and use of notes had so long been neglected, that the few melodies sung became corrupted, until no two individuals sang them alike." At the same time, then, that the North was weighed down with an ideology that associated music with sorcery, the South came to look upon music as an elevating diversion. The first musical society in America, the St. Cecilia Society, for instance, was founded in Charleston, South Carolina, in 1762.[88] Twenty-seven years before that same city had welcomed the first opera staged in America. The first orchestra used in America was in Upper Marlborough, Maryland, in connection with the Kean and Murray production of the *Beggar's Opera*[39]—a production, we can rest assured, which was not witnessed by those with a petty bourgeois psychology.

The same conditions which encouraged the development of music in the South favored the growth of the theatre there. In every Southern colony with the exception of North Carolina, where the petty bourgeois dominated, these conditions prevailed. The pastoral soliloquy recited by the students of William and Mary College in 1702 was perhaps the first instance of public drama staged in America.[40] We have no record of the plays that were possibly produced in drawing-rooms during the years when the Cavaliers were exiled in America but we can be reasonably certain that they were private and not public performances. The first professional production in America appeared in 1703.[41] This performance was put on by Anthony Aston, an English actor. It was in Williamsburg, Virginia, in 1722, that the first play house was opened. The first travelling companies of actors therefore found their happy haven in the Southern states and not in the Mid-Atlantic and Northern. Lewis Hallam's Company which arrived in Yorktown in 1752 and

[88]John Tasker Howard: *Our American Music:* p. 26.
[39]Ibid., p. 27.
[40]Arthur Hobson Quinn: *A History of the American Drama:* New York, 1923.
[41]Ibid., p. 5.

staged its first play in that same year in Williamsburg, gave the American theatre its first definite start. The moment he took his company to New York and Philadelphia, however, where the petty bourgeois instead of the plantation ideology predominated, he was faced with extremely troublesome difficulties, and it was only after altercations with the authorities and the strategy of a petition which he issued to the people of New York combined with the promise that he would produce "nothing indecent or immoral" that he was able to stage any of his plays at all.[42] The experience of David Douglass who followed Hallam six years later was similar. A ban was placed on his theatre at once in New York, and even the subterfuge of calling his playhouse "A Histrionic Academy" was not sufficient to lift the ban until he was able to placate the authorities with the promise not to produce dramas that condoned immorality. When he arrived in Philadelphia a bill was passed forbidding the production of all drama because it was considered subversive to the order of all morals preserved in this government. Although later on Douglass managed to produce a number of plays in that city, it was only in the face of great difficulty and discouragement. In Newport, Rhode Island, in order to escape persecution he was driven to change the title of *Othello* to *Moral Dialogues, in Five Parts*. In Providence, Rhode Island, he was forced to call his theatre "a school house" in order to conciliate the authorities. Only the South was cordial to his coming. Throughout Maryland, Virginia, and South Carolina his American company was most appreciatively received.[43] In Annapolis and Charleston, so enthusiastic was his reception, theatres were built for him by popular subscription.[44] This contrast in response to the thea-

[42]Walter Long: *The Sociological Criticism of the American Drama: The Modern Quarterly*, Vol. II, No. 3, p. 183.
[43]Walter Long: *The Sociological Criticism of the American Drama: The Modern Quarterly*, Vol. II, No. 3, p. 186.
[44]It should be observed here that among four plays written by Americans, which Douglass staged between 1760 and 1766, two of them appeared anonymously, the authors wishing to save their reputations from so unhappy an association with as low an enterprise as the theatre.

tre, negative in the North and positive in the South, was a direct reflection of the antithetic ideologies of their respective ruling classes.

It was only as the industrial bourgeoisie brought into being a new social order in the North, based upon laissez-faire economics, that the theatre there had any chance to grow. The decline and disappearance of the theocracy, shifting the cultural front from the religious field to the political, was an aspect of the same change. This loss of power on the part of the theocracy, a loss caused by this change in the nature and ideology of the ruling class, resulting from the replacement of agriculture by commerce as the new way of life, was what directly made possible the development of a theatre in the North, emancipated from religious circumscriptions. Just as in England, in keeping with the change which came over the petty bourgeoisie as it became more commercial than agrarian, the religious emphasis was superseded by the moral. Dramas became possible when they were entitled "Spectaculum Vitæ"; *Hamlet* could be staged when it was called "A Moral and Instructive Tale as Exemplified in the History of the Prince of Denmark," or as in another instance when it was entitled "Filial Piety"; the *School for Scandal* became fit to witness when it was captioned a "Comic Lecture in Five Parts on the Pernicious Vice of Scandal." Royall Tyler was able to meet with approval with his non-religious play *The Contrast,* for instance, simply because it scrupulously observed and sanctified the petty bourgeois ethic. Although after 1814 there were scarcely any states of the Atlantic seaboard which still forbade stage performances, as late as 1845 Phineas T. Barnum found it necessary to call his theatre in New York a "Moral Lecture Room" as a subterfuge to ward off attack. After the Civil War, however, as great cities sprang into life, and the relationships of men became at once more intricate and remote, even the moral ideals of the industrial bourgeoisie lost their compelling and conforming vigor, and as reputation became more important than character social life began to revolve more about secular virtues than religious. It was more important that a man's credit be good than that his church attendance be perfect; a free thinker who paid his bills was preferable to a devout believer who did not—and since it was possible, in the new economic world that was emerging, to pay bills and to accumulate wealth without being religious, it was not long before virtues became tested by secular instead of sacred standards. As this new test of worth evolved, new attitudes toward mundane matters were precipitated. The theatre was immediately affected by these new attitudes. A considerable section of the industrial bourgeoisie which was not motivated by the old petty bourgeois religiosity began to take a more tolerant attitude toward life as a whole. This section, part of the *nouveau riche* of the time, influenced by the inevitable laxities and leniencies which come with wealth, began the building up of a background out of which an audience for the theatre in the North was to arise. By the end of the nineteenth century the influence of this group, aided by the multiplication and magnification of cities, had become sufficiently widespread definitely to affect the development of the theatre and of every other art. While the petty bourgeois and those sections of the industrial bourgeois who still clung with vestigial conviction to the petty bourgeois ideology, continued to oppose the theatre, this new group, whose influence also won the allegiance of those members of the intelligentsia who escaped their religious background, afforded a new source of strength for the theatre in the New England and Mid-Atlantic cities. With the appearance of New York as the great metropolis, where, due to the enormous complexity of the city itself, it was impossible for the religious and moral forces of the petty bourgeois to exercise marked control over the way of life of the population, the theatre found an ideal haven. For decades now the theatre in the North has revolved about New York as its inevitable radius. The economic superiority of the city gave the theatre unsurpassed advantages there from a commercial point of view, but even those advantages would not have been sufficient if they had not been accompanied by freedom from the dictatorship of petty bourgeois morals and ideals. It was the combination of those advantages which has made New York the theatre centre of the entire country.

At the same time that the theatre made headway in the North it lost ground in the South. Before the Civil War as we have seen the home of the theatre in America was the South. After the Civil War the home shifted to the North. The plantation aristocracy in the South before the Civil War had welcomed the theatre; the petty bourgeois who became dominant in the South after the Civil War discouraged the theatre. As a result of this change the South has lost its standing as a theatre community and New York companies even to-day are loath to make a Southern tour. The fate of the theatre in the South thus has been similar to that of religion. When the plantation aristocracy predominated, the theatre succeeded in escaping the religious tyranny of the petty bourgeois; when the petty bourgeois became dominant the theatre withered. In North Carolina where the petty bourgeoisie was dominant before the Civil War as well as after, the theatre was never welcomed. Curiously enough, it has only been since the World War, with the advance of industry in that state, that a more tolerant attitude toward the theatre has managed to spring up in sections of the community, finding its most promising voice in the work of the North Carolina Players. It is logical to presume that this type of little theatre is likely to spread in the South as the influence of the secular-minded industrial bourgeoisie becomes more penetrating and far reaching, supplanting that of the religious-minded petty bourgeoisie. For the time being, however, the signs of such changes are unexcitingly and uninspiringly few.

III

In view of the fact that the South was the only part of America in which an aristocracy, albeit a plantation aristocracy, existed as the ruling class, it should be a matter of considerable concern to know why that aristocracy was so sterile in the creation of art. We have abundant evidence to show that art was appreciated earlier in the South than in any other part of America; we know that not only were the first music halls and the first theatres opened in the South, but that many private homes there contained virginals, hand lyres, violins and flutes, and that the walls of those homes were often adorned with the canvases of Reynolds, Gainsborough, and Stewart.[45] Even the study of music was encouraged in Virginia and talented performances were not uncommon in many parts of the state.[46] Not only did the theatre meet with a happy response in the South, but in Charleston theatre-going among the plantation aristocracy became the vogue. Women as well as men attended the performances, and it was the women, no doubt, even more than the men who made theatre attendance into so fashionable a habit. Indeed, as many as two hundred and fifty ladies often appeared in a single audience.[47] Painting, too, notwithstanding the fact that Thomas Jefferson asserted that painting and sculpture were "too expensive for the state of wealth among us,"[48] received better support from the Southern planters than from the New England theocrats. Literature, also, although cultivated with less enthusiasm than the other arts, was certainly provided with a more fertile environment in which to grow than that afforded in the North. Nevertheless, no great artist arose in the South, in music, in painting, in the theatre, or in literature. Indeed, it can be said at once that, despite the superficial advantages of milieu, the artists produced in the South, on the whole, were inferior to those developed in the North.

An examination of the nature of the Southern plantation

[45]M. J. Moses: *Literature of the South:* New York, 1910: p. 105.
[46]T. S. Wertenbaker: *Patrician and Plebeian in Virginia:* Charlottesville, 1910: p. 126.
[47]Arthur Hobson Quinn: *History of the American Drama:* New York, 1923: p. 31.
[48]Suzanne La Follette: *Art in America:* New York, 1929: p. 8.

aristocracy will reveal immediately why it was not artistically productive. In the first place it plainly was not a genuine aristocracy in terms of the European tradition. In a word, it was a fake aristocracy. Its entire pretence at an aristocratic way of life was of the sickliest order. Derivative from the English petty bourgeoisie instead of from the English aristocracy, its attempts to pose as an aristocracy were often little more successful than the efforts of various members of women's clubs to appear cultured. Even where the Southern aristocracy was friendly to art, in consonance with the attitude of the English aristocracy, it affected to be so more to keep up appearances, as it were, than because of a genuine appreciation of the æsthetic. Its reactions were those of a social climber instead of those of a social superior. The merchant's strain ran too strongly through it to be disguised. The business spirit, accompanied by all of its shrewdness, hardnesses and chicaneries, stultified its ideals. It thought like a merchant but tried to act like an aristocrat. In other words, it tried to imitate the aristocracy in the external details of its life, but endeavored to preserve the petty bourgeois virtues of its ancestors in its inner convictions.

It was not until after the Revolutionary War, with the swift advance of slavery in the South, that the plantation aristocracy actually began to disencumber itself of its more obvious middle-class characteristics and substitute in their stead the so-called chivalric virtues which have become so commonly associated with the Southern tradition. It was only then that the Southern lady became exalted, for before her position in society had been scarcely superior to that of the middle classes in England at the time.[49] Undoubtedly the exaggerated exaltation of the white woman in the South was part of the defense mechanism set up by the Southern white man to mitigate the importance of the system of Negro concubinage which he had created.[50]

But not only was the plantation aristocracy in the South a

[49] Wertenbaker: *Patrician and Plebeian.*
[50] Walter White: *Rope and Faggott:* New York, 1929: p. 62.

parvenu aristocracy, saddled with that contradiction between aristocratic aspirations and middle-class motivations,—more than that it was a false aristocracy, imitative instead of creative in character. Emulative of everything English, it grew up like an artificial plant which derived its strength from the heat of a hothouse instead of from the natural heat of the sun. England was that cultural hothouse in which its artificial tradition was nurtured. Without question European aristocracies had often been influenced by the cultures of other aristocracies, and at times had even copied them, but no European aristocracy ever developed a creative tradition of its own except when it distilled such influences into a new compound, or forsook copying for the sake of a new conception. The Southern aristocracy displayed neither the energy nor the initiative to form a new compound or to create a new conception. Another important point to be noted is the fact that country aristocracies even in Europe had revealed little interest in art. It was the urban aristocracies that had encouraged art—and artists. The Southern aristocracy, being almost exclusively a country aristocracy, tended, like most country aristocracies, to shower more of its interests upon horseracing and gambling than upon the production of painting and literature. It simply imitated and continued to imitate English tradition, without adding to it or transmuting it. So slavish was its imitation that it copied with exasperating fidelity to detail almost every aspect of English life. Creating little if anything of its own out of the environment of which it was a part, it was impossible for it to provide a creative cultural tradition for its artists. Instead of building up an aristocratic tradition in terms of the American environment it lent its aid to the construction of an aristocratic tradition which had less to do with the American environment than with the English. Every effort was made to make that tradition follow the English pattern, while no effort was made to allow for the infiltration of American elements into that pattern which in the osmotic process might have provided materials for the making of a new pattern. What was worse, actual barriers were set up to prevent such infiltration of American elements lest they mar the pattern. It was almost as if American elements were foreign and English elements were native, so scorned were American tendencies and so extolled were English.

The *colonial complex*, thus, had an even more overwhelming and disastrous effect upon the ruling class in the South than upon the ruling class in the North. While Northern culture emulated English culture in every respect, Southern culture simply copied it. Moreover the fact that Southern culture endeavored to copy aristocratic models, although at best it was only a hybrid aristocracy with middle-class limitations, while the New England middle class strove to emulate nothing more than middle-class models which had been as genuinely theirs in England as in America, afforded the latter a distinct advantage over the former in the cultural process. At least New England culture had the virtue of that consistency which was lacking in Southern.

It was just because of these differences that the revolt against the colonial complex never took on as sharp a character in the South as in the North. While Poe and Simms, as we noted in the first chapter, openly fought its presence we must not forget that both of them fought it mainly when they were not on Southern soil. Just as the name of Warm Springs was changed to Bath in deference to the English resort, a change which Captain Bayard in 1791 attacked as part of that "imitative mania (which) is a bad symptom and augurs ill for the nation,"[51] so Southern writers deferred in theme and technique to English models without ever daring to deviate from them in an attempt to create new ones of their own.[52] It is perfectly proper and expedient, argued W. J. Grayson, "to imitate the poetry of Queen Anne's time as well as the tables and chairs."[53] George Tucker saw no ob-

[51]Captain Bayard: *A Journey into the Interior of the United States to Bath, Winchester, the Shenandoah, etc., during the summer of 1791.*

[52]*The South Carolina Gazette*, for example, did little more in its editorials than copy verbatim editorials from London magazines.

[53]W. J. Grayson: *The Hireling and the Slave*: Charleston, 1856: Preface, p. xv.

jections to the fact that the South adopted English fashions
with uninspired fidelity "in dress, customs and manners, and
followed them throughout all their capricious changes."
"Public taste in that country (England)," he went on to add
in an appreciative vein, "cannot fail to influence our opinions
on the more important subjects of religion, morals and literature."[54] Although in several editorials in the *Southern Literary Messenger,* the leading magazine of the South, regret
was expressed that Southern authors "slight the familiar
materials which everywhere surround us, and resort to those
hacknied and frequently distorted pictures of trans-Atlantic
manners," it counter-balanced such regrets with literary ad-
monitions to the effect:

> That the preservation of a pure English diction is not sufficiently
> aimed at in America. It is an *English* not an American language
> which we are called upon to nurture and perfect. . . . If we de-
> part from this we not only fall to pieces at home, but eventually sever
> our literature from that of the mother country: a mishap to be
> deprecated by every man who wishes his posterity to drink at the
> "well spring of English pure and undefiled," *or who desires our
> authors to be honored in Great Britain.*[55] (Italics mine.)

In another issue of the same magazine a year later—already
this was sixty-one years after we had signed the Declaration
of Independence—in an article entitled *The Rights of
Authors* we find this attitude confirmed in a not less emphatic manner:

> To emulate the literary zeal and character of our mother coun-
> try is certainly creditable to our national mind: to do them honor
> and render them justice is unequivocally our duty; and when this
> is done we secure our own advantage and place our own character
> on a secure foundation.[56]

When we bear in mind that these attitudes were being
expressed about the same time that Emerson and Willis

[54]George Tucker: *Essays on Various Subjects of Tastes and Morals:*
Georgetown, 1822: p. 45.
[55]*Southern Literary Messenger*, Vol. II, No. 2, January, 1836.
[56]Ibid., Vol. III, No. 1, January, 1837.

were becoming most vociferous in their struggle for our literary Declaration of Independence, we can see the difference in spirit which existed in the two regions. The South, plainly, was less resistant to the colonial complex than the North, and while both regions were blighted by its influence, the North as the nineteenth century moved on was given to protest much more vigorously against its presence than the South.

Such servility of spirit, unhappily cultivated by the plantation aristocracy, prevented Southern culture from acquiring strength or initiative. Furthermore, the petty bourgeois background out of which the Southern aristocracy emerged, combined with the telluric factors which gave form to its features, tempered its outlook in such a way that while it did not discourage art, so anxious was it to simulate the English aristocracy, it did discourage the artist, so obviously were its cultural attitudes infected by the petty bourgeois motivations. Thus it was that the very region which welcomed English actors and playwrights was so little interested in creating American—or Southern—actors and playwrights of its own. All this was an undoubted reflection of the false relationships set up by the Southern environment, reaching a climax in the creation of this artificial aristocracy which was willing to accept a culture that was provided for it[57] but which had no desire or will to create a culture of its own

---

[57] While this Southern aristocracy was ever so anxious to keep up with literary tradition in England, it was very disrespectful of literary manners in New England. This little conversation, reported by John Davis at the beginning of the nineteenth century, is typical of this latter attitude:

"What spelling book do you use? What spelling book, sir? Indeed—really upon my word, sir,—any—oh! Noah Webster's, sir."

"Ah, I perceive you are a New England man, by giving preference to Noah Webster."

"Sir, I beg your pardon, I am from Old England."

"Well, no matter for that, but . . .

"*Mrs. H.*—*who is an excellent speller never makes use of any other but Mather Carey's spelling book.* It is a valuable work, the copyright is secured."

(John Davis: *Early Travels in America, 1798–1802:* Boston, 1910: p. 68.)

construction.[58] It is no wonder, then, that "cotton in Carolina and horse-racing in Virginia were the prevailing topics of conversation,"[59] and that Southern planters, however charmed they might be by the romance of Scott and the poetry of Moore, were more interested in productive pursuits and the patronage of sport than they were in the less material substance of art. Unlike the English aristocracy, they were forced to pay much closer attention to the productive pursuits and, therefore, were less concerned with the unproductive, and it was into this latter category that art fell in the eyes of the Southern gentleman. For the Southern aristocrat art was a luxury: for the European aristocrat it had long before become a necessity. At best, then, art was an addition to Southern life but not an intrinsic part of it. It was a superfœtation, an excrescence, which lived on but not within the matrix of Southern culture.

As a result of this condition the creative life was thwarted in every direction. The best illustrations of the extent of this frustration are to be found among those artists and intellectuals who, in the face of these handicaps, attempted to pursue the path of creative work. Hugh Swinton Legare described his own struggle in no uncertain words:

*I have found my studies in Europe impede me at every step of my progress. They have hung around my neck like a dead weight—*and so to this very day. Our people have a fixed aversion to everything that looks like foreign education. They never give credit to any one for being one of them who does not take his part in life early, and do and live as they do. Nothing is more perilous in America than to be too long learning, and to get the name of bookish.[60]

[58]Thomas Jefferson very early realized the faults and shallow character of this patrician order, this Southern aristocracy, and stated that Southerners should "annul this privilege, and instead of an aristocracy of wealth, of more harm and danger than benefit to society, (they should) make an opening for the aristocracy of virtue and talent which nature has wisely provided for the direction and interests of society." (*Jeffersonian Principles. Extracts from the Writings of Thomas Jefferson:* Selected and edited by James Truslow Adams: New York, 1928: From *Extracts on Natural and Artificial Aristocracies:* p. 15.)
[59]Ibid., p. 118.
[60]*Writings of Hugh Swinton Legare:* Charleston, 1846: p. 206.

Even John Randolph confessed to his son that he would "find nothing in our solitary and deserted habitation to raise (his) spirits."[61] Lanier claimed that aside from his father he "had not been able to find a single individual who sympathized in such (literary) pursuits enough to warrant showing him our little production—so scarce is 'general cultivation' here."[62] The declaration of John R. Thompson in 1852, namely that the "passion for literary distinction (is) detrimental to the letters and arts,"[63] is typical of the attitude which prevailed toward literary aspirations and literary aspirants. It is no surprise therefore that many individuals who ventured into literature in the South concealed their identity beneath a pseudonym, or even went further and adopted anonymity as a safer protection.[64]

The Southern aristocracy then was willing enough to adopt a ready-made culture which could be had at a low price; it was not willing, however, to try to nurture a culture of its own. It was content that culture remain as a form of ornamentation, an attractive veneer. In such an environment, it is clear, authors could not grow. By a curious irony thus, the part of America which first welcomed art was the last to encourage its creation. Although it was active enough to purchase books, it was not intense enough to want to create them. While the claim of the publishing house in Columbia, South Carolina, for instance, that it had printed "an amount of literature which even in the palmiest days of peace would swamp any but the largest establishment in the country"[65] was guilty of egregious hyperbole, it indicated something of the interest in books that existed in the

[61]*Letters of John Randolph to a Young Relative:* Philadelphia, 1834: p. 123, Letter written May 11, 1812.

[62]*Cambridge History of American Literature:* New York, 1910: From the section, *The New South*, by Dudley Miles—letter from Lanier in Georgia to a Northern friend: p. 334.

[63]Quoted from Grace Warren Landrum: *Notes on the Reading of the Old South: American Literature* (magazine), Vol. III, No. 1, p. 61.

[64]The case of Richard Henry Wilde, which we cited earlier in this chapter, is an excellent illustration of this gesture.

[65]Grace Warren Landrum: *Notes on the Reading of the Old South: American Literature*, Vol. III, No. 1, March, 1931, p. 63.

South in Confederate days. Even in Macon, as early as 1831, there was a reading room "open to subscribers (containing) a considerable number of papers together with several foreign magazines . . . and most of the valuable reviews and magazines of the United States."[66] There was even a circulating library in that city in 1832. Moreover, it is well known, for instance, that Scott, Byron, Bulwer, Campbell, and Mrs. Hemans were popular in many parts of the South. In Williamsburg, even Wycherly and Congreve were read with enthusiasm and Addison, Pope, and Dryden were revered as well as read.[67] At the same time, however, that the South showed widespread appreciation of these English authors, it failed to appreciate or to encourage its own writers.

Undoubtedly, a considerable part of the lethargy of spirit which characterized the ruling class in the South and which made it more interested in indolent leisure than in creative leisure and more given to an appreciation of a ready-made culture instead of an individually-made one of its own was to be traced to the institution of slavery. Nevertheless the importance of this factor must not be exaggerated. There was very little difference between the status of slavery in the South and the condition of serfdom which existed as part of the aristocratic culture in Europe. Almost all the critics[68] who have accounted for the uncreativeness of the South on the basis of the maleficent influence of slavery have neglected entirely to observe the failure of such a condition in nineteenth-century Russia to effect a similar condition of stagnation. The status of the serf in czaristic Russia was not superior to that of the slave in the South; Russian nobles treated their serfs with even less kindliness than was bestowed upon Negro slaves by many Southern planters, and

---

[66]Ibid., p. 66, taken from the *Macon Telegraph*, April 4, 1831.
[67]Montrose J. Moses: *The Literature of the South:* New York, 1910.
[68]Brander Matthews was one of the most guilty critics here. In his book, *Aspects of Fiction and Other Ventures in Criticism* (New York, 1896: p. 31), he contended that the real cause for the cultural sterility of the South was the evil effects of slavery upon the spirit of the people.

there was little difference between the way serfs and slaves were bartered off or made the pawns at card game or auction block. Nevertheless, Russian literature surrounded by such conditions of feudalistic slavery was enormously creative, with its Pushkin, Lermontov, Goncharov, Dostoyevsky, Chekov, and Tolstoy, while Southern literature, faced by a not dissimilar condition of feudalistic slavery, was unutterably sterile. Serfdom even in France under Louis XIV represented an equally degraded status, and yet the magnificent Augustan literature flourished as an expression of its life, or rather of the life of the aristocracy whose dominancy was dependent upon the existence of this serfdom. Greek society, which in various periods was weighed down also with the incubus of slavery, produced a literature whose greatness in no way seemed tempered by the existence of that institution. The presence of slavery therefore cannot be used as the sole or the main cause of explanation for the literary backwardness of the South, for even if the conditions of slavery in that region were somewhat different from those in European countries and ancient Greece, the psychological effects of the institution, contingent upon its degree of extensity as well as intensity, were approximately the same wherever it prevailed. The relation of slave to slave master was essentially the same in the pre-Christian city of Athens as in the Christian city of Charleston; the dependence of the slave owner on his slaves for labor, with its consequent effect upon his psychology, inducing him to indolence, driving him to ungovernable passions in his attempts to fortify his authority, brutalizing his feelings toward all forms of life that were not part of his own class, petrifying his sensibilities to pain on the part of others and paralyzing his perceptions of human values which were contrary to the life he knew—all these were as characteristic of slave owners in Greece, or in France, as in America.

If we cannot then account for the stagnation of Southern culture as a result of the presence of slavery, since other ruling classes equally dependent upon slavery have produced advanced cultures, we should not deny for that reason the influence that this feudal institution did exercise over the South. The first thing that we should note is that while slavery has been characteristic of feudal cultures wherever they have occurred, there is a marked difference between an aristocracy which is bred to the tradition of having slaves and a petty bourgeoisie which acquires slaves by virtue of a new economic situation and thereupon affects to emulate aristocratic attitudes and ideals. It was this contradiction, which we dealt with before, and which resulted in the creation of a slave-owning aristocracy shot through with middle-class motivations, that made slavery more baneful in its effect upon Southern culture than upon European cultures. It was this contradiction which made it necessary for the Southern ruling class, faced as it was by the purely middle-class civilization that had come to dominate most of Europe, to rationalize the slave basis of its society. Aristocratic societies in the past as well as the czaristic aristocracy of the nineteenth century had never resorted to such rationalization. In their eyes slavery was an established and eternal reality sanctioned by the natural order of things, the necessary creation of a divine plan. They expended no energies in defense of what needed no justification. Their order of society was for them a living faith. And it was the very absence of this living faith, this confidence within itself, this imperturbable assurance, which helped to make the plantation aristocracy of the South into so impotent a ruling class. Immediately after the invention of the cotton gin toward the close of the eighteenth century until the Civil War, the South spent more than half its intellectual energy, trying to justify the existence of slavery in its midst. Every cultural means was employed to strengthen this defense. Theologians went back to the Bible for evidence, and politicians turned to past history for support. The Negroes were suddenly discovered to be descendants of Ham whom God had punished, and their slavery was thus stressed as part of a God-ordained plan. All these rationalizations, all the energy consumed as a result of them,

were an undoubted testimony of the intellectual uncertainty
and inferiority of the Southern ruling class. They were not
due to slavery *per se,* but to the character of the ruling class,
which, caught between an aristocratic-bourgeois contradiction, and driven to the corner by a middle-class civilization
in the North—which had discovered long before with the
coming of industry that wage-slaves were more profitable
than bond slaves—was mastered by the institution of slavery
instead of becoming its master.

IV

All these changes and crises in Southern culture have
found their immediate and revealing reflection in Southern
literature. Beginning with the early Southern diaries and
running up to the literature which has sprung up in the South
since the Civil War we can trace as on a chart the evolution
of Southern culture. The three stages which we have hitherto noted: first the stage in which the petty bourgeois dominated; secondly, the stage in which the plantation aristocracy
supplanted it; and thirdly the stage in which the petty bourgeoisie returned to power, all stand out in bold relief in the
history of Southern letters.

The first two of the above stages find a most interesting
and illuminating reflection in the characters and careers of
the Byrd family. As Wertenbaker has shown in considerable
detail, the three men who all bore the name of William
Byrd, father, son, and grandson, typified to perfection the
spirit of the times in which each of them lived. The father,
who embodied the psychology of the last part of the seventeenth century, when the petty bourgeois ideology still prevailed, "possessed to an extraordinary degree," as Wertenbaker shows, "the instinct of the merchant taking quick advantage of any opportunity for trade that the colony afforded; . . . even to stinginess . . . he was predominated
by the spirit of gain." This elder Byrd was interested in
every form of bargaining; in his stores he sold cotton goods,

window glass, lead, solder, and pills; he made profit off the sale of white servants, importing them from England and then merchandising them in the colony; he even traded with the Indians, procuring from them at the cost of a bauble furs and hides which he was able to sell at profiteer rates to English merchants. His son, William Byrd, the second, betrayed at once the effects of the change that was coming over the ruling spirit of the colony. What happened to the Byrd family was very similar to what happened to many of the other petty bourgeois families in the South. It was as these families acquired wealth and began to constitute an upper class capable of having the land which they had purchased cultivated by others instead of themselves that the background of the plantation aristocracy was formed. William Byrd, the second, symbolized the transition between the dissolution of the petty bourgeois ideology and the rise of a pseudo-aristocratic one. Although still a business man he lacked the shrewdness of his father and was far less successful with his mercantile ventures. If his iron mines did not afford him great profit and his Indian trade met with frequent disasters, it was partly because his mind was already interested in other matters—less productive matters, his petty bourgeois father would have exclaimed—than those entirely concerned with business. Although he was not "an aristocrat with wide sympathies," as Mark Van Doren described him,[69] he was unquestionably, as Wertenbaker observed, "more the Cavalier than his father (and), less the merchant." The grandson, William Byrd, the third, living in a time when the plantation aristocracy had already begun to take on clear-cut form, marked the definite departure from the petty bourgeois ideology in favor of a feudal aristocratic one. Uninterested in business, and lacking all the cunning which goes with mercantile enterprise, he succeeded at the cost of economic ruin in making himself into the only really cultivated gentleman of the Byrd family. Constantly in financial distress, owing

[69] William Byrd: *A Journey to the Land of Eden*: edited by Mark Van Doren: New York, 1928: p. 6.

large sums to English merchants, forced to mortgage his slaves at times, he nevertheless continued to be contemptuous of economic gain and to focus his main interests in gambling and horse racing. It was this William Byrd, the third, then, who must be looked upon as exemplifying the beginning of the aristocratic ideology in the South. If his individual life was somewhat different from that of the individual lives of members of other families in this rising aristocratic set, the Bowlings, the Lees, the Carters, the ideology which he represented was not different, but of the same strain.

In the writings of William Byrd, the second, one is immediately struck by their fidelity to the character of the time. In his *History of the Dividing Line*, we already note the early signs of the hostility which existed between the North and the South and which eventually, as the economic order of the two regions more decisively diverged, was to emerge in the final conflict of the Civil War. Byrd's words in this connection are as interesting as they are betraying:

> We also saw a small New England sloop riding in the sound, a little to the south of our course. She had come in at the new inlet, as all other vessels have done since the opening of it. This navigation is a little difficult, and fit only for vessels that draw no more than ten feet of water. The trade hither is engrossed by the saints of New England, who carry off a great deal of tobacco, without troubling themselves with paying that impertinent duty of a penny a pound.

But more striking than his comments upon New England are his reactions to North Carolina. The conflicts between the ideologies of the two states, Virginia and North Carolina, had begun to take shape by this time and the contempt which the pseudo-aristocratic Virginian gentlemen had for the petty bourgeois civilization of North Carolina found definite voice in Byrd's narrative:

> The truth of it is, the inhabitants of North Carolina devour so much swine's flesh that it fills them full of gross humors. For want too of a constant supply of salt, they are commonly obliged to eat it

fresh, and that begets the highest taint of scurvy. Thus, whenever a severe cold happens to constitutions thus vitiated, it is apt to improve into the yaws, called there very justly the country distemper. This has all the symptoms of *syphilis*, with this aggravation, that no preparation of mercury will touch it. First it seizes the throat, next the palate, and lastly shows its spite to the poore nose, of which it is apt in a small time treacherously to undermine the foundation. This calamity is so common and familiar here, that it ceases to be a scandal, and in the disputes that happen about beauty, the noses have in some companies much ado to carry it. Nay it is said that once, after three good pork years, a motion had like to have been made in the house of burgesses, that a man with a nose should be incapable of holding any place of profit in the province; which extraordinary motion could never have been intended without some hopes of a majority.

Some borderers, too, had a great mind to know where the line would come out, being for the most part apprehensive lest their lands should be taken into Virginia. In that case they must have submitted to some sort of order and government; whereas in North Carolina, every one does what seems best in his own eyes.

Surely there is no place in the world where the inhabitants live with less labor than in North Carolina. It approaches nearer to the description of Lubberland than any other, by the great felicity of the climate, the easiness of raising provisions, and the slothfulness of the people. Indian corn is of so great increase, that a little pain will subsist a very large family with bread, and they may have meat without any pains at all, by the help of the low grounds, and the great variety of grass that grows on high land. The men, for their parts, just like the Indians impose all the work upon the poor women . . . It is a thorough aversion to labor that makes people file off to North Carolina.

Or consider the sharp irony of this:

And considering how fortune delights in bringing great things out of small, who knows but Carolina may, one time or other come to be the seat of some other great empire?

A later observation of Byrd in the same account "That the clergy is rarely guilty of bestriding such as have the misfortune to be poor" reflected the growth of an aristocratic attitude toward religion which was rapidly replacing that of the petty bourgeoisie. Similar observations and animadversions are to be found in other papers of this same William Byrd, especially in his *A Journey to the Land of Eden,* but few of them are as remarkably illuminating as those which we have just quoted from his narrative which dealt with the argument over a border line between Virginia and North Carolina. No doubt the fact that Byrd's writings were not penned for publication had much to do with their untrammelled frankness of utterance. Unquestionably a good deal of their simplicity of style is to be accounted for on that basis. Certainly such simplicity was an unfortunately rare virtue in early Southern writing, for beginning with George Sandys and continuing down the generations, Southern writers seemed to eschew simplicity as if it were a sin.

While it is true that many of the early Southern annalists, Captain John Smith, Edward Maria Wingfield, William Strachey, and John Hammond,[70] wrote with comparatively little affectation and assumed elegance, those writers that followed them swiftly deserted their excellent example. Influenced more by the petty bourgeois attitude toward literature than by the aristocratic these annalists naturally turned their pens in the direction of candid, unadorned speech rather than toward the purple-patched euphuism of the aristocratic tradition. This petty bourgeois spirit is so unmistakably apparent in John Hammond's comment in *Leah and Rachel: or the Two Fruitful Sisters Virginia and Maryland:*

> I can conveniently affirm, that since my being in England which is not yet four months I have been an eye and ear witness of more deceits and villainies (and such as modesty forbids me to utter) than I either ever saw or heard mention made of in Virginia, in my one and twenty years abroad in those parts.

It is just as conspicuous in *Babylon's Fall in Maryland* which was published by Leonard Strong in that colony in 1655. Although many of these annalists were far from being as religious minded as the petty bourgeois annalists in the

---

[70]George Alsop, whom we referred to before, proved an exception. In his account of the *Character of Province of Maryland, 1666,* he employed a style that was reprehensively artificial and grandiloquent.

North, their attitudes toward the sacred and the profane in life and literature were part of the same substance.

It was after these petty bourgeois groups lost influence that their style of writing disappeared. Although it is true that most of their annals were written in defense of their colonies Virginia and Maryland, in order to counteract the false pictures of them that prevailed in England, their value as representative of the dominant spirit in their part of America at the time is not therefore to be questioned. With all their exaggerations, they were as faithful to their petty bourgeois tradition as George Sandys was to the aristocratic one. Side by side with them, in the same external environment, George Sandys, while sojourning in Virginia, translated Ovid's *Metamorphoses*. In a more exact sense, to be sure, George Sandys preceded certain of them since his translation was practically completed in the early sixteenth century when he made his stay in America. Both Eggleston and Angoff contend that Sandys should not be considered an American author since he lived in America for so brief a time and wrote nothing about America itself. Although there is a certain soundness to this point of view, it must be noted that there is a difference between an Englishman living in a newly founded English colony, and holding an important office there, and an Englishman living in France, say, or in Germany. In the former case, which was that of Sandys, he could not but participate in an active sense with the life about him, while in the latter case he would be forced to look upon himself as an alien, an outsider. Sandys, then, cannot be so easily dismissed from the history of American letters. The very fact that he could translate Ovid's *Metamorphoses* when faced by an environment which was well-nigh a wilderness is of no little significance. The petty bourgeois annalists were not interested in Ovid and had they been concerned at all with Sandys' translation, they would have condemned it as a waste of time. Ovid belonged to that profane category of writers who had meaning to the aristocratic lovers of profane literature. Sandys' translation, then, marked the first presence of the aristocratic tradition on Virginia soil, just as the writings of the early annalists signified the beginnings of petty bourgeois literary expression in that part of the continent. With the exception of the well-known poem: *Bacon's Epitaph, Made by his Man,* which expressed the petty bourgeois ideology of the yeomanry who supported Bacon in the rebellion, Robert Beverly's *History of the Present State of Virginia* and Byrd's narratives which we previously discussed, Lawson's *History of North Carolina,* Garden's volume on South Carolina, Hugh Jones' *The Present State of Virginia* and Tailfor's *A True and Historical Narrative of the Colony of Georgia,* there was practically no other literature worth noting that was published in the South in almost a century.

It is only in the nineteenth century that a few Southern writers begin to take an active interest in belles lettres. None of them, however, with the exception of Poe and Lanier managed to lift his work beyond the horizon of mediocrity. Undoubtedly the conditions which we have described that made Richard Henry Wilde, one of the most interesting of Southern poets, conceal the fact that he wrote verse, discouraged the appearance of literary talent throughout the South and prevented that which did appear from being anything more than tenth rate. Certainly one cannot describe the work of Paul Hamilton Hayne, James Mathew Legare, James Barron Hope, Thaddeus Oliver, John R. Thompson, Francis Orray Ticknor, Margaret Junkin Preston, Albert Pike, Theodore O'Hara as falling into a more exalted category. Even the poetry of Henry Timrod, who was commonly known as the poet-laureate of the Confederacy, attained a no more elevated distinction. In all this poetry there was a singular devotion to place, a regional loyalty, which in the case of the older poets rose to a point of chauvinistic climax in the Civil War.

The literary output of the South in prose was scarcely superior to its outpourings in verse. Excluding political writings which had literary pretensions and oratorical outbursts

and made claim to literary power, William Gilmore Simms
and Edgar Allan Poe were the only prose writers of any
importance in pre-Civil War Dixie. Even Simms, when all
is said, is important only in recollection. All his novels were
of inferior quality. Even his well-known frontier novel, *The
Yemassee*, which once inspired the critics of his time, reads
like a stilted melodrama to-day. It was in the North that his
work received a hearing; in the South it was either ignored
or scorned. A member of the petty bourgeoisie, Simms felt
like an alien in aristocratic Charleston. Simms' own words
reveal this reaction in no uncertain manner:

> Charleston, which has never smiled on any of my labors, which
> has steadily ignored my claims, which has disparaged me to the last,
> has been the last place to give me its adhesion, to which I owe no
> favor, having never received an office, or a compliment, or a dollar
> at her hands; and with the exception of some dozen of her citizens,
> who have been kind to me, and some scores of her young men, who
> have honored me with a loving sympathy and something like rever-
> ence, which has always treated me rather as a public enemy to be
> sneered at, than as a dutiful son doing her honor.

There was no Bryant in that city to befriend him and no
Harper's Magazine to open its pages for his prose. The
plantation aristocracy, as we previously pointed out, was
more interested in English authors than in American, and
while they might buy many volumes of Pope they would
never be inclined to patronize a native talent in their midst.
Even his novel *Guy Rivers*, centring about a plantation aristocrat and a frontiersman, evoked a much warmer response
in the North, and even in London where it was reprinted in
1835, than it did in the South.[71]

Although Simms' work was not of a high grade or lasting
quality, the prose and poetry of both Edgar Allan Poe and
Sidney Lanier were unquestionably of excellent calibre. Poe
reflected less of his native culture in his writing than he did

---

[71] *The Southern Literary Messenger*, of course, provided some opportunities for the Southern writer, but, it must be admitted, it illustrated in
its attitude an exception rather than the rule.

of European. In fact, along with Simms he fell in with the Northern writers of his day, and deviated little from them in outlook and spirit. In that sense, Poe can scarcely be looked upon as a product of Southern culture at all. Eccentric genius that he was, and possessed of a style that surpassed in magnificence the styles of all his American contemporaries, he belonged less to the American scene than any other American writer of his period. A Castle of Otranto artist, caught in the bystream of European romanticism, Poe's imagination succumbed to the weird adumbrations of the European horror-mongers of post-Waterloo days.[72] If we explain Poe's affection for the story of horror, his deep concern with the morbid, as purely a result of an individual neurosis, or rather psychosis, we should be guilty of that same inadequacy of analysis which has characterized most of the work of the biographers of Poe. The fact is the story of horror was not Poe's particular cultivation. It did not express Poe's peculiar psychosis. The story of terror grew out of post-war romanticism in Germany, a romanticism that became almost a religion in its intensity and fervor, and which in the art of Hoffman reached a point of perfection rarely equalled. This reaction of the romanticists had a direct social causation in the changing European conditions of the day. In brief, nevertheless, we can say that this movement afforded the idea, supplied the substance, for the story of terror; Poe afforded the personality, supplied the mechanism, to develop and intensify it. The influence of Hoffman on Poe is not hard to detect. But not Hoffman alone influenced Poe. Tieck and Richter and other members of the German ro-

---

[72] We are speaking here entirely of Poe as a creative artist. In the critical field, where he also did significant work, he kept his eye fastened more closely upon the American scene, and if many of his judgments to-day have been reversed it was not because Poe was weak in critical theory but because he was bad in putting his theory into practice. It is interesting to observe that Constance Rourke and even Lewis Mumford have suggested the presence of the frontier force in Poe's fiction. The likeness which Miss Rourke stressed between the frontier tradition of *Tall Tales* and Poe's stories of terror does not strike me as very convincing, although without doubt Poe's work, like that of so many Americans of his day, was not unaffected by the frontier force.

manticist school also indirectly affected his work. Thus Poe, who in his critical work declaimed with ardor upon the necessity of American literature becoming American, surrendered just as easily to the influence of the colonial complex as did his other contemporaries, except that he turned to Germany instead of to England for his inspiration.

Unlike Poe, Lanier is really part of the Southern tradition. However backward he thought the South was, and however often he emphasized its deficiencies and cultural desolation, his work was definitely a part of the Southern pattern. A product of the post-Civil War epoch, for it was in the seventies and eighties that his literary talents attained fruition, Lanier nevertheless was close enough to the prewar South, having fought in the Civil War as a youth, to understand its spirit sufficiently to realize the wisdom of living in Baltimore instead of in Macon. Although before the Civil War the South had provided an unhappy enough environment for the artist, Lanier realized that after the war that environment had become impossible. In Baltimore, where he settled after exploring New York, and where he stayed almost until his death except for his occasional hegiras South in search of health, he dedicated himself to the pursuit of poetry and music. In his letters to Bayard Taylor, who was so impressed by Lanier's poem *Corn* that he succeeded in having him chosen to write the cantata for the opening of the Centennial Exposition at Philadelphia, Lanier described the terrible odds which weighed against the Southern writers of his day. A descendant of the petty bourgeois tradition—his earliest ancestor was Jerome Lanier, a Huguenot refugee—he carried over this tradition into his verse. From his earliest days he was concerned with "ascertaining God's will with reference to (him)" and to the very day of his death he was convinced that it was through "a knowledge of Him . . . which cometh . . . daily in fresh revelations" that he was able to communicate beauty in his art. In *Marshes of Glynn, Ballad of the Trees and the Master* and *The Crystal* this religiosity manifested itself in intimate form.

Strengthened by the growing religious fever, which had taken hold of the South with the accession to power of the petty bourgeoisie after the Civil War, his infectious faith in the infinite had more meaning to the Southern populace than it would have had in the first half of the nineteenth century. Indeed his poem *The Crystal* can be looked upon as a harbinger of that religious spirit which was to overwhelm the South shortly after his death. It is doubtful whether the religious attitude of the post-bellum South attained finer expression than in the memorable closing line of *The Crystal*:[73]

"Jesus, good Paragon, thou Crystal Christ."

Nowhere is the difference between the backward Southern tradition and the progressive frontier tradition better revealed than in Lanier's reaction to Whitman:

Whitman is poetry's butcher. Huge raw collops slashed from the rump of poetry, and never mind gristle—is what Whitman feeds our souls with.

As near as I can make it out, Whitman's argument seems to be, that, because a prairie is wide, therefore debauchery is admirable, and because the Mississippi is long, therefore every American is God.

Lanier's personal reply to Whitman's conception of democracy discloses even more subtly the contrast between the spirit of the two regions:

My democrat, the democrat whom I contemplate with pleasure, the democrat who is to write or to read the poetry of the future, may have a mere thread for his biceps, yet he shall be strong enough to handle hell; he shall play ball with the earthy; and albeit his stature may be no more than a boy's, he shall still be taller than the great redwoods of California; his height shall be the height of great

[73]Lanier's criticism has found its best embodiment in his *The Science of English Verse*, and *The English Novel* was fortunately free from most of the religiosity which penetrated into almost all his poetry. Oddly enough it was Lanier who, in criticism, defended the scientific approach, contending that "the best conceptions cannot be save where science and genius are," and in a letter to E. C. Stedman maintained that poetry is suffering from the shameful circumstances that criticism "was without a scientific basis for even the most elementary of its judgments."

resolution, and love, and faith, and beauty, and knowledge and subtle meditation; his head shall be forever among the stars.

Lanier's democrat smells of the lamp: Whitman's springs from the soil itself.

Since Lanier poetry in the South has practically died. The religious dominancy of the new ruling class was too great a handicap for the artist to overcome. It hung like a pall over the land, stifling every sign of growth. The only poet to emerge during those fallow years was the Negro poet Paul Laurence Dunbar. In a geographic sense Dunbar, having been born in Ohio, belongs more to the West than the South. By tradition, however, he falls within the Southern school. Dunbar's importance must be confined to dialect verse. Like Robert Burns, Dunbar was at his best when he wrote in the language of his people and not in the language of the poets. Although Dunbar was far from a first-rate poet or even a significant one in terms of the poetic tradition, he was more important than Adah Isaacs Menken or any other of his Southern contemporaries, with the exception of Lanier. In truth it can be said that limited as was his dialect verse it achieved in its own genre an excellence that surpassed the verse of Timrod, Hayne and the other members of the earlier Southern school. It was Dunbar too who began the development of that Negro school of poetry which in the twentieth century achieved such distinction in the verse of Langston Hughes and Countee Cullen. Unfortunately Dunbar was so handicapped by the nature of the prevailing culture that in spirit he became nothing more than a Negro prototype of Longfellow. The crispness of vision and fervor of challenge which were to dominate Negro poetry in the twentieth century did not pervade his verse. He belonged all too obviously to the Booker T. Washington school of yes-men.

Since the World War, which marked the beginning of another change in Southern culture, poetry has made a slight advance in the South. The founding of *The Fugitive* in the twenties still stands as the first symbol of that advance.

Although *The Fugitive* is now dead, many of its contributors, in particular Allen Tate and Donald Davidson, have matured into able writers. Inevitably, however, the success of these writers has been more decisive in the North than in the South. And their recent stress upon the necessity of restoring the pre-industrial South has been an open confession of their inability to work in their present environment. The very fact that Donald Davidson has been forced to give up the literary page that he was editing for several Southern newspapers is further evidence of the extent of indifference to culture which still exists in the South.[74]

If we turn now to the prose which has been written in the South since the Civil War we shall be confronted with a no less uninspiring picture. The novelists who succeeded Kennedy and Paulding displayed neither greater talent nor superior vision. Thomas Nelson Page's *Red Rock*, to cite an example, showed no definite or significant advance over John Pendleton Kennedy's *Swallow Barn*. The main difference between Kennedy's novels and Page's, aside from the fact that Kennedy's were more sketchy and less symmetrically organized than Page's, was in their spirit. This difference in spirit, to be certain, was entirely environmental; Kennedy's spirit discovered its origin in a living glamour, Page's in a dead glamour. Kennedy wrote of the plantation when it was a vital reality; Page wrote of it when it was scarcely more than a lifeless recollection. Both were sentimentalists however, the one about that which he saw or imagined he saw, the other about that which he never saw and regretted that he could never see. The exuberant optimism of Kennedy and the reminiscent melancholy of Page reflected the change in status of the plantation aristocracy; in the days of Kennedy, the plantation was "as rich as a castle," while in the days of Page it had become a bankrupt vestige.

The plantation motif, then, did not die after the Civil War. Indeed, as the years passed, it began to gather strength

[74]The only other literary page in the South to-day that deserves praise is the one which is edited by Mrs. Green, Paul Green's wife.

in retrospect, and to surround itself with the halo of a romantic tradition. Inaugurated by John Pendleton Kennedy, W. A. Carruthers, John Eston Cooke, and James W. Hungerford, this tradition after the Civil War continued to find an expression in the fiction of Opie Read, Mary Johnston, Thomas Dixon, Walter H. Page,[75] and to-day, in the revolt of the Donald Davidson group, it has received striking intellectual defense.

Ellen Glasgow was one of the few Southern writers who resisted the sentimental appeal of the past and who has actually dealt with the materials of life which have surrounded her. Nevertheless, even she did not turn to the new South for the substance of her narratives. Her first work was concerned with Virginia in Confederate days and it was only later that she came closer to the contemporary scene. Even her later novels have dealt with the influence of the new South upon the remnants of the old South, revolving about the ghost-like figures of the fast withering plantation aristocracy and the semi-aristocrats who will cling to as much of the old as they can preserve amidst the new.

Now that the plantation aristocracy is dead and plantation life has been invested with the romance of the remote it is not surprising that many Southern writers, depressed at the dominancy of the religious-minded petty bourgeoisie who have reduced the South to a state of cultural anemia, have turned to the plantation past for renewed inspiration. Seeking the cultural life which once prevailed in Charleston, "the gayest in America" as Crevecœur at one time described it, preferring the plantation owner who could gamble away his plantations without losing his poise to the petty bourgeois who counts his every cent, these writers have had to turn to that dead plantation world for escape. The choice that confronted them was crucial. Either they had to turn back to that romantic feudal world, rose-rimmed in recol-

[75]Of course, in this same tradition fall many of the works of A. W. Tourgee, Frances C. Tiernan, and many others whose novels belonged distinctly to abolition literature.

lection, with its "rose order of Southern women," as James Lane Allen phrased it, its gay gentlemen brave to the point of duel, and "its singing niggers"; the world which stirred Stephen C. Foster, even though not a part of it, to immortalize it in his popular melodies, *My Old Kentucky Home, Old Folks at Home* and *Old Black Joe;* or like James Branch Cabell to invent a new world of their own, a Poictesme of intellectual refuge. Even George W. Cable, who tried to keep his eye closer to the earth, found the Creole background of New Orleans far more interesting than the background of his own people. To face the real world in which these Southern writers lived was but to recoil from it in despair.

No greater proof of this latter fact is to be found than in the nature of the work of those contemporary Southern writers who have neither succumbed to the plantation dream nor invented a new world of their own. Desiring to write about the world in which they live rather than escape to mythical worlds of the past or future, and yet realizing the barrenness of the civilization which surrounds them, they have turned to the Negro with an almost inevitable unanimity for their materials.[76] In a word, it is only the Negro in the South to-day who can provide them with artistic inspiration. Like Joel Chandler Harris in the previous century they have turned to the Negro for those rich human possibilities which are latent in his forthright, dynamic reaction to life. Harris in his *Uncle Remus* sketches returned to the old days for his facts and fables. Harris, however, belonged to the romantic

[76] It is interesting to observe that one of the few exceptions here, Mary Noailes Murfree, who wrote under the pseudonym of Charles Egbert Craddock, turned to the retarded mountaineers for her subject in her most successful work, *In the Tennessee Mountains* (1884). The Tennessee mountaineers attracted Mary Murfree because their lives were removed from the petty bourgeois world in which she lived, and gave promise of a form of life which could be more easily translated into art than the form of life which surrounded her. Other Southern writers have adopted a similar form of escape from their immediate environment. Fiswoods Tarlton in *Bloody Ground* and *Some Trust in Chariots* has followed in Mary Murfree's path, centring his attention, however, in the Carolina hills. Even Kroll, one of the newest writers of the Southern group, has pursued the same route. In *The Cabin in the Cotton* he has focussed his attention upon the poor whites in the Mississippi Delta country.

plantation tradition and to the lineage of Thomas Nelson
Page rather than to that of the moderns. These new Southern writers want to deal with the facts and fables of the
Negro which have been carried down into the present. Paul
Green's plays, in particular *In Abraham's Bosom* which won
the Pulitzer prize several years ago, Julia Peterkin's novels,
Black April and *Scarlet Sister Mary*, which also won the
Pulitzer prize not long ago, DuBose Heyward's *Porgy* which
was one of the great theatric successes in the late twenties
and his novel *Mamba's Daughters* which was very popular
shortly thereafter—all these products of this new group of
Southern writers have revolved about Negro life and character. The Negro alone, living in a different world of motivation, has retained enough of his simplicity and charm
and irresponsible gaiety to attract writers for the next generation. While the white man's world, spiked in on every
side by religious ramparts, has become desolate of cultural
stimulus, the black man's world has taken on fresh meaning.
Yet it is not the new black man's world where the new Negro
is the protagonist which appeals to them, but the old black
man's world in which the new Negro has little part. The
new Negro is part of the new South, the South which has
grown up since the Civil War and which in this century has
opened wide its doors to the coming of industry. This new
Negro, represented at one extreme by the Negro bourgeoisie,[77] and at the other by the Negro intellectual who is
largely a product of that bourgeoisie, does not interest the
Greens, the Peterkins, and the Heywards. This new Negro
has already become too much like the rest of the South in his
desires and ambitions. It is only the old Negro whose life is
still uncorrupted by the influence of the petty bourgeoisie, or
the struggling but defeated Negro, who as in *Abraham's
Bosom*, meets frustration at every turn, that arouses the interest and sympathy of this new school of authors. In this
sense, however successfully they have managed to avoid the

[77] Franklin Frazer: *Le Bourgeoisie Noir: The Modern Quarterly*, Vol. 5,
No. 1, p. 78.

sentimentalities of the old plantation school, these writers
are much closer to the plantation tradition than they suspect.[78]

Nowhere, then, is there a forward-looking tendency in
Southern literature. Everywhere the logic of escape prevails,—escape to a plantation recollection, an imaginary
Poictesme, or to a backward Negro living out of tune with
his time.

[78] In this connection it is important to remark that, despite this interest in the Negro by many Southern writers and despite the rise of many
Negro writers, the hostility felt for the Negro is just as active to-day in
the South as it was twenty years ago. This hostility is just as pronounced
in many ways in literature as in life. *In the sixteen-volume library of Southern Literature, for example, not a single Negro writer's work is included.*
While the biographical section gives mention to Frederick Douglass,
Booker T. Washington, and W. E. B. Du Bois, it does not quote a single
selection from their works. Paul Laurence Dunbar is not even mentioned
in the entire sixteen volumes. Needless to add, dozens of Southern writers
whose works are greatly inferior to those of Douglass, Washington, and
Du Bois are included, with ample space provided for their ofttimes inferior selections. Equally revealing is the fact that Professor Fred L. Pattee in his recent volume, *American Literature Since 1870*, does not even
mention a single Negro writer, although he discusses hundreds of white
writers, many of whose works are of no more than microscopical importance. Such promising Negro poets as Langston Hughes and Countee
Cullen are not even mentioned in the index; Eddie Guest, on the other
hand, is given two pages of discussion—and partial praise.

CHAPTER IV

FROM REVOLUTION TO REACTION

WITH the rise of commerce as the new way of life, and the creation of a mercantile aristocracy with economic power at its command, the back of the theocracy was broken and its authority destroyed. The acquisition of wealth created new attitudes, new outlooks, and new aspirations. The attitudes and aspirations of the theocrats were not those of the mercantile aristocrats, and since the increasing wealth of the community had come to inhere in the hands of the latter instead of the former, the clergy soon found that it had far less influence upon matters of state than the merchants. The old order which had found its embodiment in the religious idealism of Cotton Mather was replaced by a new order which discovered its embodiment in the moral precepts of Benjamin Franklin.

The rulership of the theocracy had been dependent upon the dominancy of the petty bourgeois groups that had settled in New England. In fact, the theocracy was a direct reflection of this petty bourgeois ideology, embodying as it did the petty bourgeois vision of Utopia. What the theocrats accomplished in Massachusetts approximated what the petty bourgeois groups in England as well as elsewhere would have liked to put into effect had they been able to acquire power. Religion and politics were identical for them. Political power was merely the means of putting their religious ideology into effect. Even their economic philosophy was expressed in religious nomenclature. It was religion which tied together all the various threads of their life.

This religious ideology, born of the adverse environment against which the petty bourgeoisie in Europe had had to struggle for survival, was a product of war rather than of peace. It was better fitted for struggle than for success. As long as the environment in America remained adverse enough to foster struggle, the petty bourgeois ideology with its theocratic manifestations was bound to survive. In fact the early American environment, as we showed in an earlier chapter, provided an ideal setting for the implantation of the petty bourgeois philosophy of life. The struggle which the petty bourgeoisie had been driven to in its fight against the upper classes in Europe fitted it admirably for the struggle which it had to wage against the physical environment of America. Once the acuteness of that struggle was over, however, or was shifted to the Western frontier, the petty bourgeois philosophy with its rigorous asceticisms and homely aspirations lost more and more of its direct application to the New England scene. As the environment became subdued and wealth began to accumulate, and the Atlantic seaboard became transformed from an agrarian into a commercial community, an upper bourgeoisie arose to replace the petty bourgeoisie which had preceded it. This upper bourgeoisie, which soon constituted a mercantile aristocracy, developed interests and attitudes that its petty bourgeois ancestors would have scorned—and which those who continued to perpetuate the petty bourgeois ideology at that time did scorn. It was the coming of wealth, then, and the rise of the wealthy upper class, which caused the deterioration of that petty bourgeois idealism which is commonly described as Puritanism, and at the same time undermined the power of the clergy.

If the seaboard had continued to be agricultural, the power of the theocracy might have persisted, for part of the success of the theocracy had been directly dependent upon the agrarian fact, and the course of eighteenth-century life in New England and the Mid-Atlantic states would have followed a different pattern. The triumph of commerce over agriculture, however, spelt success, and, as we stated before, it was success which the petty bourgeois ideology could not withstand. When success favored it, it could no longer remain petty bourgeois, but changed into upper bourgeois—at least, the ruling class did. In an agrarian community such as New England had represented in the seventeenth century, even the life of the ruling class had been fraught with enough hardship to prevent it from developing that softness of temper which results from the artificial advantages of life that wealth brings in its wake. The theocracy, therefore, which had been able to thrive in an agrarian environment with which its petty bourgeois ideology was in harmony, was unable to maintain its position of authority in a commercial community in which the accumulation of wealth had created an upper bourgeoisie to supersede the petty bourgeoisie in power.

By 1730 this change in culture tendency had already acquired swift momentum. The "codfish aristocracy," which replaced the petty bourgeois theocracy as the dominant class in eighteenth-century American society, was a direct descendant of the petty bourgeois merchantry of the seventeenth century. The members of this "codfish aristocracy" were not English merchants who had come over from England to increase their wealth, but were American merchants born of American soil, who had risen to success on the basis of American conditions. The change in outlook which they brought into American life was a direct outcome of their elevation in economic status. In this elevation we discover the small shopkeeper and simple agriculturist transformed into the large merchant with maritime aspirations. This new merchantry owned and chartered vessels and dispatched them into the remote parts of the world in search of profits. Possessed also of whalers and coasters and all manner of fishing craft, it lacked little which was necessary for commercial success in those days. It participated in private banking enterprise and even became involved in insurance ventures. "Commerce occupies all their thought," wrote Brissot de Warville,[1] commenting upon the rise of this new ruling class which had transformed America from an agricultural

[1] Quoted from Samuel Eliot Morison: *The Maritime History of Massachusetts, 1783–1860:* New York, 1921: p. 42.

into a commercial community. Although this new class clung to the old religion of their fathers, they learned at this time to embrace it more as a form than as a fact.

The theocracy crumbled as this merchantry multiplied. Every idea for which it stood was driven to defeat by an economic force that was too strong to resist. While the theocrats continued to wage a brave battle in defense of their stand, and their sermons testify to the courage of their convictions, year by year their influence decreased. Their vigorous intolerances gave way to the weak tolerances of this new era—and it is at this time, and not before, that tolerance, a progeny of trade, is born on the Atlantic seaboard. The importance of individual character which the theocracy had exalted was supplanted at this time by the greater significance of individual reputation. The asceticism which the theocracy had urged was replaced by the leniences of luxury. In a word, an upper bourgeoisie endowed with almost unlimited wealth had succeeded in undermining the ideology of a petty bourgeoisie which by its very nature was limited in wealth.

One of the most striking evidences in the decline of the power of the theocracy was to be found in the loss of prestige of the ministry among eighteenth-century youth. In the seventeenth century, the ministry was the most exalted vocation. It held out the greatest promise of position and power in the community. In the eighteenth century, on the other hand, especially after the turn of the first quarter of the century, American youth, or at least the parents of that youth, came to realize that that position and power had waned. Samuel Johnson's son deliberately avoided the ministry as his profession. Such men as Stephen Sewall and Jonathan Trumbull definitely forsook their original intention of becoming ministers for the greater appeal of civil life.[2] In the colleges, this declining attraction of the ministry was conspicuous. During the administration of President Witherspoon only twenty-three per cent of the grad-

[2] James Truslow Adams: *Provincial Society, 1690–1763:* New York. 1927: p. 235.

uates of Princeton entered the ministry.[3] In Yale, Harvard, and Dartmouth a similar decline occurred. In Brown, the decrease was even more marked. The ministers themselves supplied even better testimony to the decline in their power. The Reverend Jonathan Mayhew, for example, made open apology upon one occasion for venturing without his province in discussing political issues.[4] Better still as an illustration of this change of attitude toward the clergy are two master's theses which were submitted at Harvard in 1763 on the theme *Ought Ministers of the Christian Religion to Preach Politics?*[5] That the authors of both these theses vetoed the intervention of ministers in politics is an even more significant revelation of the success with which the civil state was subordinating the theocratic.

The improvement in the status of the law developed in direct ratio with the decline in the position of the ministry. As commerce spread, and the upper bourgeoisie expanded in numbers and magnified in enterprise, lawyers became important social servants in the administrative process. In the seventeenth century, when the theocracy was powerful and the ministry symbolized the highest profession, lawyers occupied an unimportant position in the community. Preachers as well as merchants in those days qualified as lawyers, and members of the judiciary achieved their appointments regardless of their lack of legal experience.[6] By the middle of the eighteenth century this condition had almost completely changed and by the time of the Revolutionary War lawyers along the Atlantic seaboard had already become far more important than ministers in the social life of the day.

The rise of the legal group was a direct testimony to the breakdown of the old regulations of the agrarian order. As commerce advanced the social regulations which the theoc-

---

[3]George P. Schmidt: *The Old Time College President:* New York, 1930: p. 20.
[4]James Truslow Adams: op. cit., p. 315.
[5]Ibid., p. 315.
[6]Michael Kraus: *Inter-Colonial Aspects of American Culture on the Eve of the Revolution:* New York, 1928: p. 205.

racy had tried to enforce lost their efficacy. There came into being a more individualistic type of individual who paid less and less attention to the social regulations which his ancestors had stressed. Cunning replaced caution and promises became meaningless unless certified by contract. Business rapidly developed into the enterprise of getting the better of the other man, repudiating thus the virtue of social relations for the sake of individual gain. Contrary to the teachings of the seventeenth-century Puritans and Dissenters, a man's standing became determined not by his uprightness of attitude in his dealings but by his success in outwitting other men. In this way, this new condition of life prepared the way for the disappearance of the social emphases of the earlier way of life, and for the rise of the purely—or impurely—individualistic emphases of the capitalistic, laissez-faire one.

The mercantile system, which was capitalism in embryo, preserved enough of the social vestiges of feudalism to appease the religious spirit of the petty bourgeoisie, and at the same time provided enough leeway for economic enterprise to permit sufficient opportunity for individual advance. In the seventeenth century, for example, the mercantile logic attempted to regulate wages and prices, and in this way keep alive certain of the social aspects of economic life. In the eighteenth century, on the contrary, with the accumulation of wealth which resulted from the broadening of commercial enterprise, and with the rise of an upper bourgeoisie which by the very virtue of its life became more individualistic as its power increased, these social vestiges faded into vapid fictions. Individual profit, with money as its sanctified symbol, became the dominant incentive. Everything that tended to thwart the acquisition of profit was swept aside by this new force. In this manner the way was paved in advance for the coming of laissez-faire economics which, with its competitive individualism divorced of social restrictions, was to form the basis of the industrial order that was to make its appearance in America in the nineteenth century.

As the wealth of this upper bourgeoisie multiplied its

morale gradually altered. Victorious as it was in its fight against the economic restrictions which the theocracy attempted to impose upon it, it soon began to adopt those amenities of existence which its petty bourgeois forefathers had denounced as aristocratic. Indeed, like the upper bourgeois Puritans in England, it cultivated a fondness for feasts and pageants, and even became enamored of the dance. It built palatial mansions, ostentatiously contrived in imitation of English styles, and attired itself in fancy raiment which at once evoked the vexation of the clergy. In short, it inaugurated a new way of life in the North, cultivating new attitudes and tastes as it grew.

The new attitudes and tastes which this upper bourgeoisie brought into being in the North should not be misconstrued, however, as the products of a new social class. They were the products of the ideology of the same social class to which their forefathers belonged, except that their expression was modified by the advantages which wealth contributed to their life. In other words, this upper bourgeoisie did not become aristocratic in its outlook, but remained consistently bourgeois throughout its career extending down until to-day. What it did do, was to temper its former tension, soften its earlier severities of outlook, and develop an elastic instead of a rigid code of values. Very soon it made God over in its own image and acquired the gift of being able to hide its vices and extol its virtues. It transformed the harsh relentless Jehovah of the seventeenth century into the more merciful and humane God, the Father, of the eighteenth century. In religion it began to exalt good works over faith, and before the century was over morality rather than piety became its touchstone of virtue.

The literature of the time reflected in minute detail all the changes which we have recounted. In *The American Magazine and Historical Chronicle,* for instance, the change in religious attitude which we have described, made itself unmistakably manifest. By the 1740's criticisms of religion had begun to appear with frequency. In an article entitled *A*

Parallel between Superstition and Enthusiasm, Commonly Mistaken for Religion this criticism had mounted into a challenge:

> As to the just notion we ought to entertain of the Supreme Being, Superstition and enthusiasm equally corrupt them; they both represent Him a cruel, fanatical, arbitrary Master. . . . Thus religion is overthrown where either of these evils prevail. . . .
> Upon the whole it cannot be well determined which of these two vices (grown to their height) is most flagitious and destructive in Society; but when they both happen to unite their forces they accomplish every evil that can be practiced to all the absurdities that can be imagined.[7]

Such a declaration, it is obvious, was a far cry from the spirit of the theocracy.

But not only were the superstitions and enthusiasms of religion exposed to criticism; the whole self-denying rationale of petty bourgeois religiosity was summoned forth for attack. The right to enjoyment was openly defended, and the right of religionists to prevent the enjoyment of others was vigorously denied. In an essay on *Pleasure,* in *The American Magazine,* the author levelled his attacks against the pleasure-haters who had dominated in the century previous:

> There are some who are so rigid and timorous that they avoid all diversion and dare not but abandon lawful delights for fear of offending. These are hard tutors, if not tyrants to themselves and whilst they pretend a mortified strictness, are injurious to their own liberty, and to the liberality of their maker.[8]

These words are an index to what was happening to the morale of the mercantile aristocracy. They show the decided change that had already come over the old Puritanic-Dissenter temper. But more important than the defense of

[7] *American Magazine and Historical Chronicle:* issue of December, 1743, p. 157.
[8] *The American Magazine:* issue of April, 1744, p. 334.

pleasure which was being undertaken by many of the leading spirits of the day was the different conception of religion which was evolving out of the new conditions of American life of that period. Not only were superstition and enthusiasm censured, but the entire religious outlook was transformed. Everywhere writers began to conceive of religion as performing a very different function from that which it had served in earlier generations. While the old religion had bred vigorous, self-abnegating men and women, dour in aspect and cheerless in disposition, the new religion encouraged a sweeter, softer type of votary who looked upon this world as well as the next in a more kindly and benignant way. "The spirit of true religion," wrote an author in *The American Apollo*, evincing this change which we have noted, "breathes gentleness and affability. . . . It is social, kind, and cheerful; far removed from that gloomy, illiterate superstition which clouds the brow, sharpens the temper, and dejects the spirits."[9] A little later on in *The Columbian Phenix and Boston Review* similar animadversions upon the old type of religion appeared with frequency. In an article on *Reflections on Devotion*, the editor maintained that "the character of devotion has frequently suffered from the forbidding air, which has been thrown over it by the moroseness of bigotry, on one hand, or the gloom of superstition on the other. When freer and more cheerful minds have not had occasion to see it accompanied with the feelings of delight and benevolence which naturally attend it, they are apt to be prejudiced against piety at large, by mistaking this ungracious appearance for its genuine form."[10] Even the interior of the churches was condemned. In another article in *The American Apollo* on *Hints for the Improvement of Public Worship*, the writer urges that every one should "reprobate those gloomy, solitary cells (the churches) which deform the building no less to the eye of taste than to the eye of benevo-

---

[9] *American Apollo*, August 4, 1792.
[10] *The Columbian Phenix and Boston Review*, Vol. I, No. 1, January, 1800.

lence."[11] Little of the old order, then, with its dim religious gloom, was left unassailed.

This new attitude toward religion soon had its effect upon mundane literature. Literature in the seventeenth century had been entirely religious. In the eighteenth century, in response to the changes in the environment indicated, it gradually began to shed its religiosity and venture forth into the more promising field of *belles-lettres*. As the upper bourgeoisie became more devoted to things civil than to things religious, its cultural interests naturally shifted in directions that would have been anathema to the seventeenth-century clergy. While it never learned to appreciate or cultivate art in the manner of an aristocracy, it slowly began to discard something of the hostility for art which its petty bourgeois progenitors had bred. The reaction of John Adams to painting illustrates something of the change in the attitude which had already developed in the later part of the eighteenth century. When he visited the studio of Charles Wilson Peale, a portrait painter, he found himself face to face with a new world, a world, incredible as it may seem, of which he knew nothing. In that studio he met persons and things that challenged him by their very newness. Writing to his wife at the time he described with a betraying naïveté the artist, Francis Hopkinson, whom he met there. "Mr. Hopkinson," he observed, "is liberally educated, and is a painter and a poet. I have not met with anything in natural history more amusing and entertaining than his personal appearance—yet he is genteel and well bred and is very social." Nothing could be more characteristic of the reaction of the bourgeois to the artist type than Adams' comment on Hopkinson's personal appearance, and his following concession that, however eccentric, the artist was genteel and well bred. Later in the same letter he added that he wished he "had the leisure and tranquillity of mind to amuse myself with those elegant and ingenious arts of painting, sculpture, statuary, architecture

[11] *The American Apollo*, October 5, 1792.

and music. But I have not."[12] As his words reveal, his attitude toward art was no more than a condescending one at best—but what is important is that it was not a hostile one. It even had a touch of the curious about it, an element of the tolerant, which augured better for the future than had the attitude of the preceding generation.

But Adams was not alone in reflecting the growth of this more latitudinarian attitude. In the Foreword to the first issue of *The New England Magazine*, published in August 1758, the editor asserted that there were many men "placed in such an exalted rank in the world as allows them much leisure and large opportunity to cultivate their reason, and to beautify and enrich their own and the minds of others, with various knowledge." Trumbull in *An Essay on the Use and Advantages of the Fine Arts*, delivered at the commencement in New Haven on September 12, 1770, assigned literature the most exalted place among the arts, and derogated the petty bourgeois indifference to art which had crushed all æsthetic incentive. "They (the arts) are considered as matters of trifling amusement," he stated, "and despised in comparison with the more solid branches of learning."[13] It was the same John Trumbull who along with Timothy Dwight and Joel Barlow was to constitute one of the first members of the school of American letters.

Before this period it had been practically impossible for a profession of letters to arise. The lack of wealth in the community, and the absence of a ruling class which would have been able to afford to cultivate art if it had desired it, made it impossible for an artist to survive if he pursued his art as a vocation.[14] Before this time, therefore, literary men had to win their livelihood in other fields than literature. Literature consequently could only be practiced as an avocation. At this time, however, as art came to hold forth something of the

[12]Moses Coit Tyler: *Literary History of the American Revolution:* New York, 1897: p. 162.

[13]Ibid., p. 208.

[14]Frederick C. Prescott and John S. Nelson, editors: *Prose and Poetry of the Revolution:* New York, 1925: Introduction, p. v

promise of a livelihood, even the petty bourgeoisie lost a considerable part of its scorn for the artist. These observations of an obscure New England writer in the eighteenth century epitomized that change in a perfect manner:

> The Plowman who raiseth grain is more serviceable to Mankind than the Painter who draws only to please the eye. . . . When a people grow more numerous and part are sufficient to raise necessaries for the whole then tis allowable and laudable that some should be employed in innocent arts more for ornaments than necessity. *Any innocent business that gets an honest penny is better than idleness.*[15] (Italics mine.)

Since art was beginning to pay for itself, as it were, or was able to win pay from those who could afford to purchase its creations, it could no longer be categorized as an unproductive pursuit. At least, as the foregoing writer confessed, it was superior to idleness. In earlier generations it had been all too frequently associated with idleness—a product of aristocratic vice. Even worse, it had been thought of as iniquitous, an evidence of sin. Now it had become innocent instead of iniquitous, worthy of toleration if not of encouragement.

It was at this time that the "tired business man's" attitude toward art began to formulate itself into an æsthetic, or rather unæsthetic, philosophy. Repelled by the gloom-ridden world of the theocracy, and seeking a world of balmier aspect, this upper bourgeoisie cultivated pleasure as a means of escape. Escape from what? From the world in which their traditions had been born, the theocratic world of their forefathers. They did not seek pleasure as an end in itself which would have led them to the appreciation of art as æsthetic reality, but pleasure as a relief from fatigue. Nowhere in eighteenth-century literature was this attitude expressed with better candor and precision than in these words which appeared in *The American Magazine:*

> The end therefore of pleasure is to support the offices of life and

[15]James Truslow Adams: *Revolution in New England:* Boston, 1923: p. 31.

to relieve fatigue of business and to reward a regular action. Pleasure and recreation of one kind or another are absolutely necessary to relieve our minds and bodies from too constant attention and labor.[16] (Italics mine.)

The aristocratic attitude toward art had never been handicapped by such an incubus. A class which did not have to work, since it lived on the work of other classes, the aristocracy never had to escape from fatigue. The tired business man's attitude toward art, therefore, found no shelter in its philosophy.

The entire literature of the period reflected in abundant detail the growth of this "fatigue" theory of art. The periodicals were replete with reference to its wisdom, and as the century advanced one had but to turn to the pages of almost any of them in order to have its argument thrust before him in editorial, article, and essay. Even gayety as an escape was recommended. In a striking article, *In Praise of Gayety*, which appeared in *The American Magazine*, the author asserted that "gayety, so-called, is the *sine qua non* of a fine gentleman, and indeed comprehends in itself . . . *a knowledge of most polite authors*, a good-natured, generous, courageous mind." (Italics mine.) The allusion to polite authors was an important indication of the spread of interest in a secular literature. Farther on in the same article, the author justified gayety in defense of the "fatigue" theory. "What odds is there between the man of business," the author continued, "and his shop, his warehouse, or his papers? His body is only the shop to his soul; there it lies a dull, heavy, inactive load. They therefore who would taste the sweets of life must have recourse to sprightliness and gayety."

The fatigue theory marked a second state in the cultural development of American literature. It signified the transition from a religious to a moral emphasis. In the seventeenth century our literature had been preponderantly re-

[16] *The American Magazine*, April, 1744, p. 334.

ligious. In the eighteenth century it became predominantly moral. The upper bourgeoisie might become enamored of a pleasure instead of a pain theory of behavior, but it would not allow its pleasures to become immoral. It might oppose the religious conception of life but not the moral one. In fact what it did was to supplant the religious conception by the moral conception.

This new change was borne out in the entire evolution of American literature in the eighteenth and nineteenth centuries. When Durget of Yale, for example, maintained that novel reading need not be classed as a sin if the novels were of a moral character he voiced this change in definite form. Nevertheless, he did not extend his defense of the novel to the stage. He warned his students against the theatre as a den of vice and classified actors as "the very offal of society."[17] At Harvard Kirkland also recommended secular literature to his students, and even endorsed works of a light and amusing character.[18] But neither did Kirkland extend favor to the theatre. The theatre remained for some time to come an unacceptable institution to the upper bourgeoisie.

Of course, there were certain individuals in the new social line-up, who, in the vanguard of the time, as they were, and learning to be more imitative of the aristocracy and at the same time more contemptuous of the pleasure-hating ideas of their forefathers, developed a less scornful attitude toward the theatre. This change in attitude toward the theatre was reflected in the magazines of the day. In *The New England Magazine*, for example, this new attitude achieved revealing embodiment in the following passage:

That there should be some gloomy spirits in all sects averse to theatrical representation in general is not to be wondered at. But if these have inveighed against plays, they have likewise bitterly inveighed against each other's religious principles and practices and if they have agreed in condemning the theatre they have likewise

[17]George P. Schmidt: *The Old Time College President:* New York, 1930: p. 194.
[18]Ibid.

agreed in condemning very innocent things, as the wearing of periwigs, the taking of snuff and the smoking of tobacco. Where superstition mixes with religion she frequently points the Deity as a
morose sour Being, disgusted with cheerfulness and gaiety in his
children.

But the bountiful creator has given man an eye to be delighted
with beautiful appearances, an ear to enjoy hearing and a taste to
relish not only the variety of food intended him, but every convenience and even elegance of life.[19]

But that was as far as the upper bourgeoisie would go at the
time in countenancing the theatre. In other words, it was
willing to be captious of the "theatre burners" but it was not
willing to put its stamp of approval upon the theatre as an
institution. As late as 1804, for example, we discover *The
Boston Weekly Magazine* still active in condemning the
stage:

With the beauties of poetry, the surprise of incident and force of
action are united to favor the vices of human nature, to make the licentious gaiety of the fashionable world appear agreeable and inviting, and the sober modest regular conduct of the virtuous and religious world formal, sour and disgusting. If this be the general
object of that species of dramatic representation called Comedy, we
shall easily see how disadvantageous (it is) to the morals of society.[20]

The sentiment expressed in *The Boston Weekly Magazine*
was little different from that which governed the decision of
the Massachusetts General Court in 1850 when it definitely
forbade the production of plays. Nor was it much of an improvement over the article on the stage which appeared in
1768 in *The Essex Gazette,* a Salem publication—the article
was entitled: *Another High Road to Hell. An essay on the
pernicious nature and destructive effects of Modern entertainments.* Nevertheless, the attitude toward the stage was
no longer a united one. The petty bourgeois opposition to it
had already undergone attack. As a matter of fact in the same

[19]*New England Magazine*, No. 2, November, 1758, p. 14.
[20]*Boston Weekly Magazine*, Saturday, November 17, 1804: article on
Dramatic Entertainments: p. 14.

year that *The Essex Gazette* article was published, Richard Cumberland's *The Fashionable Lover* appeared in New York.

Naturally, also, as the upper bourgeoisie became more contemptuous of its petty bourgeois background, the opportunity for theatricals was improved. Beginning with the furious controversy which raged in Boston in 1770 when the clergy attacked the stage as "the high road to hell," after which even more stringent laws were passed against play acting, this petty bourgeois psychology became more and more stupid as the opposing forces grew. Lingering on, however, despite its decline in power, we still have its manifestations present with us to-day in the personages of John S. Sumner and Will Hays. The whole moral censorship idea is derived from this petty bourgeois background, and there is no better testimony to its continued influence than the American cinema of to-day. The whole moving-picture industry in this country has been constructed to appeal to the petty bourgeois populace. Indeed, a good part of the failure of the American film is due to the fact that the cinema censors in almost every city are so severe in their condemnation of anything that suggests a violation of petty bourgeois morality that film producers are prevented from becoming either adventurous or advanced. As a result the American cinema is an infantile product, uninspiring from beginning to end— the dime novel projected on the screen.

II

The eighteenth century in America, then, supplied the battle ground for the conflict between the ideology of the petty bourgeoisie and the upper bourgeoisie.

This conflict, as we shall see, has continued ever since or at least until the end of the last war, to provide the dominant dividing line of attitudes and issues which have colored our history. The real struggle, of course, has been between the proletariat and the bourgeoisie, but the petty bourgeois-mindedness of the proletariat has obscured the true character of the struggle. In truth, we can venture to say at this point that practically every rallying cry which has been raised in this country has sprung out of this conflict. More than that, the ideas and ideals which have determined the character of the American mind have grown directly out of the same root. This is apparent in our educational and philosophic ideas as well as in our economic and political ones. As we pointed out in the second chapter, America has never had an aristocratic ideology to influence its spirit, and, consequently, the underlying conflict of aristocratic and bourgeois culture has never exercised any influence over our manner of living or habit of thought. Of almost equal significance is the fact that America has never had a genuinely proletarian ideology take root upon its soil. Our so-called proletarian movements prior to the World War were essentially petty bourgeois in psychology and programme. Aside from certain class-conscious phrases which have been strewn about by radical groups in various periods in the past, and possibly with the exception of the direct appeal to class which was made at the beginning of the seventies by the Knights of Labor, there has been no proletarian ideology developed here. The proletariat has been appealed to almost invariably in terms of the catchphrases of the petty bourgeois. This tendency, as we shall see in the next chapter, has been an inevitable product of those conditions created by the frontier which gave the American proletariat a petty bourgeois outlook. With a proletariat which was petty-bourgeois-minded, there was no chance for a proletarian ideology to develop and influence the course of American life and thought. Naturally, therefore, proletarian organizations succeeded to the extent that they could harmonize the immediate interests of the workers under the banner of petty bourgeois ideals. The American Federation of Labor typifies this contradiction in its most active and vicious form. Beneath the guise of petty bourgeois ideology, the real interests of the workers are weakened instead of strengthened, and the spirit of social solidarity which characterizes proletarian movements in every country in Europe is undermined and corrupted here. But even radical groups did not escape that contradiction. No party represented it more clearly than the pre-War Socialist party which, despite its admission of the class struggle, won a considerable part of its support on the basis of such a petty bourgeois slogan as "down with the trusts," and which made a more ardent fight in defense of bourgeois civil liberties than in behalf of a proletarian state.

In succeeding chapters we shall trace the development of this conflict in the nineteenth century and then down through the changes which have occurred to-day, showing in just what ways it has affected and shaped the nature of our literature in particular and our culture as a whole. Already in this chapter we have considered certain of the differences of outlook which resulted from the beginnings of this conflict, that is, as the upper bourgeoisie diverged definitely from the petty bourgeoisie in the nature of its economic life and cultural interests. As differences in wealth increased between the two groups their economic attitudes came into more decisive clash. The petty bourgeoisie was anxious to hold on to the social environment of the past with its economic restrictions and religious regulations. The upper bourgeoisie, on the contrary, was eager to escape those economic restrictions and religious regulations of the past and carve out a new individualistic world which would be in better harmony with its rising desires. This upper bourgeoisie, therefore, swept aside every trace of feudal economics which the petty bourgeoisie had perpetuated, and converting the seas into its legal tender it plunged into that exploitation of foreign markets which, with the advent of industry, was to form the foundation of capitalistic imperialism. In this manner, the upper bourgeoisie prepared the way for the realization of *laissez-faire* economics. At the same time that its struggle for unrestricted commercial rights reached its political peak in the Revolutionary War, Adam Smith formulated its economic theory in his study, *The Wealth of Na-*

tions. The fact that the Declaration of Independence and *The Wealth of Nations* appeared in the same year was not the result of chance or coincidence. On the contrary, both were tied up with the same economic force and were intrinsic parts of it. Both served as an intellectual defense, one in the political field and the other in the economic, of the new bourgeois world which was coming into being, and which with the coming of industry was to be known as capitalism.

This upper bourgeoisie in America soon became much more interested in opposing English legislation which hampered its economic rights in this world than in defending its heavenly rights in the other world. Moreover, it was determined not to let anything stand in the way of its progress. Whatever opposed it had to be annihilated, sacrificed in defense of its economic destiny. It was this class, which made money its sole incentive, that laid the foundation for that materialistic philosophy of life which Europeans inevitably interpret as American. The truth of the matter is this materialistic philosophy has very little to do with national characteristics but very much to do with class characteristics. The English upper bourgeoisie, or the French upper bourgeoisie, were—and still are—no less monetary-minded than the American upper bourgeoisie. The reason why the American nation has come to be looked upon as exclusively materialistic, and devoid of the cultural interests and spiritual values which characterize European nations, is the fact that in America this upper bourgeoisie acquired complete control of the national culture, while in Europe the upper bourgeoisie was never able to establish such undisputed dominance. In Europe, as we pointed out in the second chapter, the differential fact was the presence of an aristocratic tradition which informed the prevailing culture with a philosophy of life that was the very antithesis of the bourgeois. That aristocratic culture, to be sure, was not the product of the aristocracy. It was the outgrowth of that homogeneity of culture which had been transmitted to the modern world by mediæval civilization, which in turn had been built upon the

basis of the Roman and Greek tradition. What the aristocracy did was to give a special tone to that culture, a special
emphasis, cultivating it as an aristocratic ideal. It must also
be noted that in European countries the proximity of aristocratic culture tempered the character of bourgeois culture,
that is the culture of the upper bourgeoisie. The lower bourgeoisie, alone, as we observed, resisted that influence. In
America it was the absence of an aristocratic tradition to
leaven the influence of the bourgeois which proved historically speaking so disastrous to our cultural experience. It
was that condition which made it possible for America to
exalt monetary values above cultural ones as soon as the
more social-minded, religious idealism of the petty bourgeoisie was vitiated by the individualistic-minded, pragmatic
materialism of the upper bourgeoisie. While the psychology
of the petty bourgeoisie in the eighteenth century was an
upward struggling one, with the economic fact intruding as
an impelling force, its religious resolution preserved its sense
of social continuity. It was idealistic to the extent to which it
made its individual members subordinate their lives to its
religious ends.[21] They did not make money into their consuming motivation; indeed, they even waged war against
"profiteers" in the community and ostracised them from po-
sitions of influence. Interested though they were in the material substance of money, and it would be absurd to deny that
the petty bourgeoisie in America at that time did not have
such an interest, they were also moved by the immaterial
aspect and other-worldly promise of religion. Religion with
them was a social force, constraining their individualistic im-

[21] This does not mean that its religious attitudes were not directly connected with the shift in economic life of the day. They most certainly
were. As we emphasized in the second chapter the very asceticism which
dominated its religious logic was a distinct product of its economic way
of life. Even the nature of its religion, exemplifying the advancing individualistic spirit which was the outgrowth of the Reformation prepared
the way for the coming of the unrestricted individualistic temper of capitalism. A link between the social spirit of feudalism and the ultra-in-
dividualistic spirit of capitalism, the petty bourgeoisie clung to enough
of the former in the sixteenth and seventeenth centuries not to succumb
completely to the latter.

pulse. With the upper bourgeoisie, on the other hand, religion was a convenience which they bent this way and that in order to affirm instead of deny their individualistic impulse. It was easy, then, for money to become their supreme objective.

The reason why America is looked upon as more money-minded than Europe is the fact that when one thinks of the American nation one thinks of it, because there is no other way to think of it, exclusively in terms of its bourgeois aspects; but when one thinks of European nations one thinks of them in terms of their total culture, their aristocratic background as well as their bourgeois foreground, and even of the mediæval culture, and the vestiges of Greek and Roman culture, upon which the culture of modern aristocracies was built. If one thought of European nations in terms of their bourgeoisie alone one's reaction to them, or opinion of them, would not be vastly different from the European reaction to America. The English bourgeoisie, the French bourgeoisie, the German bourgeoisie, were not, and still are not, widely different from the American bourgeoisie in their attitudes and reactions. The middle-class Englishman, Frenchman, or German, is as interested in money-making as the middle-class American. Furthermore, the European bourgeois is just as concerned about the preservation of middle-class economics, politics, education, and morality as the American bourgeois. The European bourgeoisie, however, because it was constantly challenged by the aristocracy, and because it had an aristocratic tradition which it could utilize by converting it to its own ends, was able to develop a culture superior to that created by the American bourgeoisie. Had the European bourgeoisie had as untrammelled a career as the American bourgeoisie, acquiring complete control of culture without conflict with aristocratic forces, the ineluctable propensities of its economic life would have driven it in the same direction as the American bourgeoisie. It was the conflict with the aristocracy, therefore, and the presence of a total culture from which it could borrow sustenance, which saved the European bourgeoisie in part from becoming as definitely anti-cultural and anti-artistic as the American bourgeoisie.

But even more important than those differences was the fact that in Europe it was the upper bourgeoisie which gave cast and character to the bourgeois culture which sprang up, while in America it was the petty bourgeoisie which shaped our cultural attitudes from the very beginning of our civilization. America was the only country, as we have shown, in which this was the case. Nowhere else was the petty bourgeoisie able to secure or assume so important a rôle in the cultural process. Naturally, therefore, our culture was not only handicapped by the absence of an aristocratic tradition —and the totality of culture out of which aristocratic culture emerged—but it was further handicapped by a petty bourgeois attitude of mind which viewed this aristocratic tradition as the product of weakness and vice. The upper bourgeoisie, in England and on the Continent, as we have illustrated, was never so desperately antagonistic to aristocratic culture as to disabuse itself entirely of its service and significance as a cultural stepping-stone to a higher culture of its own construction. It wished to purify aristocratic culture of its sexual abandon and excess, but it did not insist upon destroying its very shadow. It wished, in the words of Steele, to "please by wit that scorns the aid of vice," and hoped:

> ". . . with breeding to refine the age,
> To chasten wit, and moralise the stage."

The petty bourgeoisie, on the contrary, would have nothing to do with such a midway course. It not only would not compromise with aristocratic culture, but what was more extreme, it demanded its destruction. Its attitude was just as extreme in England and France as it was in America. If the petty bourgeois Huguenots had secured control of American life and culture instead of the petty bourgeois Puritans and Dissenters, there is little likelihood that the destiny of seventeenth-century America would have been very different from what it was. In practically every European country at that time the petty bourgeois ideology was relatively similar.

It believed in revolution and not evolution, and religion was its revolutionary watchword. Its opposition to art was based upon the fact that art was without religious meaning, that it contributed to the irreligious instincts of the aristocracy, and was a servant not of God but of Mammon. When it opposed the theatre of the aristocracy, it did not attempt to "moralize" it; it closed its doors, or burned it if necessary, imprisoned its actors, and punished its spectators. When it opposed secular literature, it did not debate about it in the manner of the eighteenth and nineteenth century liberal, but it set up, as in New England in the seventeenth century, a dictatorship of the press which made it impossible for secular literature to be printed.

Now it was just that class, the Puritanic-Dissenter petty bourgeoisie, with the type of ideology which we have described, that laid the cornerstone of American culture. American culture did not start at scratch, as many have contended, but with this distinct petty bourgeois heritage which has influenced the course of American life and thought ever since. In fact, as we shall see in later chapters, this influence is not dead to-day. It has advanced and receded as the vicissitudes of American life have dictated. More significant than that, it has been able to establish itself as a standard, the original American standard. Even when the upper bourgeoisie emerged and came into definite conflict with the petty bourgeoisie, it did not break completely with that standard. It set up a different standard of its own, it is true, but it was different in degree and not in kind. Even where it deviated most widely from the original standard, it obscured rather than stressed its deviations. In short, it never got to the point, not even to-day, where it boldly denounced its earlier attitudes, and disembarrassed itself entirely of all trace of its petty bourgeois heritage. To this very time it continues to use petty bourgeois phrases to cover up its upper bourgeois ambitions. It employs them in education, religion, politics, and economics. In other words, in order to placate instead of alienate its petty bourgeois adversaries, it has never completely deserted its petty bourgeois ideology, never completely forsaken the traditions of its fathers. To have done so, to be sure, would have been suicidal in a political scheme which bases control upon ballots, for despite the rise of the upper bourgeoisie to supremacy the petty bourgeoisie inevitably remained the more numerous. After the Constitutional Convention, of course, this danger had been averted by limiting the vote to a small percentage of the population. In the nineteenth century, however, as industrialism set in and the petty-bourgeois-minded frontier became too vigorous to resist, the fight between the upper and lower bourgeoisie became more acute, and the upper bourgeoisie from that time forth has had to use petty bourgeois political slogans in order to win the majority of the populace to its side. The fact of the matter is both sides used petty bourgeois slogans, and still continue to do so, with the result that to-day the majority of the American people vote the Republican or Democratic ticket for reasons which have nothing at all to do with the realities in the case.

III

During the period which we are concerned with in this chapter, the conflict between the upper and lower bourgeoisie had become aggravated to a point where bitterness of opposition could no longer be concealed. The clergy in the main continued to fight for the position of vantage which it had occupied in the seventeenth century. Cotton Mather spent his last years denouncing the loose type of life which commerce had created in New England. As wealth increased, and the rich bourgeoisie began its importation of luxuries from the old country, luxuries of apparel, of decoration, and amusement, the hell-threatening condemnations of the clergy became more thunderous. But the upper bourgeoisie was not to be terrified. The petty bourgeoisie however, which lacked the opportunities and advantages of life that wealth affords, and, therefore, had as much if not more to gain from the other-world than this, could still be intimidated by such hell-lashing threats and maledictions—as it still is to an extent to-day by such religious mountebanks as Billy Sunday and Aimee McPherson. The rich bourgeoisie merely went its way, disregarding hell and heaven in its attempt to exploit the world in which it lived. The conflict between the clergy and the wealthy bourgeoisie could not continue in this fashion, however, without a show of power by one side or the other in the controversy. The crisis came toward the middle of the eighteenth century when Jonathan Edwards was discharged from his church by his parishioners.

Indeed we can look upon the discharge of Jonathan Edwards as an important turning point in American history. In the first place it symbolized the end of the theocracy; and in the second place, it definitely marked the accession to power of the upper bourgeoisie. The theocratic state was now supplanted by the civil state. The clergy, henceforth, would play an ever more and more inconspicuous rôle in secular life.[22] Jonathan Edwards made the last stand in defense of the religious idealism of the petty bourgeoisie. With his defeat, every trace of that idealism disappeared, and religion became nothing more than an unprotesting agent of the status quo. The edge taken off its fighting spirit, its vigor gone, religion speedily became—what it is to-day—the personification of a yes-man in social and economic life.

There were several other elements of social significance which were involved in Jonathan Edwards' dismissal. Edwards' dismissal did not result from his attacks upon wickedness and vice as a whole, or even from his attacks upon the richer classes in general, but from his deliberate attempt to examine the wickedness and vice of individual members of his parish, exposing their sins in open display before his

[22]This will be just as true in the South to-morrow as it came to be true in New England and the Mid-Atlantic states in the late eighteenth and nineteenth centuries. When wealth accumulates in the South and an industrial bourgeoisie wrests power from the present petty bourgeoisie, the religious elements will recede in power, and be succeeded by the secular.

congregation. The petty bourgeoisie had believed in the debt of the individual to the community and had allowed little leeway for the individual to permit his right hand to do what his left hand could not see. It had insisted upon virtue as a daily necessity and not as a Sabbath convenience.[23] It had assailed the wickedness of individuals as well as wickedness in general, and had minced no words in its condemnation. But such methods could not be perpetuated in a community in which wealth had arrived, and where a rich middle class was able to succeed only by denying on weekdays the virtues which it extolled on Sundays. Naturally, therefore, when Edwards threatened to disclose the truth about the individual lives of the members of his congregation there was but one recourse, namely, to dismiss him. And such has been the treatment which has been accorded every ecclesiastic in America who has attempted to pursue Edwards' method of attack, or who, like Bouck White or Bishop Brown, has dared to defend the social ethics of primitive Christianity against the individualistic ethics of capitalism.

In literature *The New England Courant* represented one of the first definite reactions against the theocracy. Insolent, coarse, and violently bitter in its manner of attack, it whipped the clergy into a tantrum of fury with each successive issue. It insulted Cotton Mather and reviled the clergy at every opportunity it could find or invent. No longer could the clergy remain in the background, and confine its replies to the pulpit. In a short time *The New England Weekly Journal* was founded by Samuel Kneeland in order to provide a voice for "a Select number of Gentlemen who have had the happiness of a liberal Education."[24] The select number of gentlemen, it need scarcely be added, were gentlemen who would give no offense to religion. In fact, two of its three editors and correctors of the Press were ministers: the

---

[23]As we showed in the second chapter, this attitude of mind was consistent with its entire social philosophy at that time.

[24]Elizabeth Christine Cook: *Literary Influences in Colonial Newspapers:* New York, 1912: p. 36.

Reverend Thomas Prince, and the Reverend Mather Byles, the nephew of Cotton Mather. One of the earliest expressions of retaliation on the part of *The New England Weekly Journal* was the appearance of a poem celebrating the death of *The New England Courant* which went out of existence in 1727. *The Elegy on Old Janus* was the reply of the ecclesiastics to the insults which had been fired at them by *The Courant* when it was alive.

> "Mourn, all ye scribblers who attempted fame,
>   Screened by the umbrage of his pow'rful name."

Weak as was this Dunciad of the young ecclesiastics, it undoubtedly filled them with a sense of great achievement, burying, as they thought they were, one of the last of the anti-religious papers.

But just as no change is ever so sharp as it seems, since it is always preceded by a series of microscopical permutations of which it is but the culmination, so no ideology can be said to have begun here or ended there, nor any way of life be defined in terms of a fixed origin or finale. Fluidity rather than fixity should be stressed in all interpretations of cultural processes. Culture is constantly in a state of imbalance, shifting this way and that in response to changes in the environment which affect the attitudes of classes and the minds of individuals. It is only at periods of revolutionary crisis that attitudes suddenly snap and break down into their opposites; it is only at such a time that individual minds make sudden revaluations and accept with equal suddenness a new set of conceptions. When such a crisis is absent, attitudes tend to change in a more gradual and inconspicuous manner, and it is only after a considerable period that the nature and extent of the change are fully realized. This is true especially where the change occurs within the same class and does not result from a revolution between two classes.

But revolutions, so-called, are very often not revolutions between classes at all. In that sense, to be precise, they are not really revolutions. A score of South American revolutions, for instance, have signified little more than the usurpation of control by various cliques, one supplanting the other as the vicissitudes of state permitted. And the American Revolution to extend this logic further, while a more significant revolution than any that have occurred in South America, was not fundamental in character. The Revolutionary War accomplished no change in ideological emphasis. It freed America from the economic bondage of England but, as we have already noted, it did not destroy her cultural bondage. The upper bourgeoisie and the plantation aristocracy which were in power before the Revolutionary War remained in power after it. If anything it is very possible that our Revolutionary War had almost as much influence upon English ideology as upon American. In England, the victory of the Colonies unquestionably weakened the influence of the aristocracy and lent strength to the forces of the bourgeoisie. In America it merely strengthened the power of the upper bourgeoisie and the plantation aristocracy without changing the dominant ideology in any significant way. The only effect which it did have was in creating a national consciousness which evaporated shortly after the war and which did not acquire cultural expression until more than a century later.

One of the most important effects of the war, nevertheless, was in destroying the last remnants of feudalism in the New England and Mid-Atlantic colonies. It had been largely through the English crown that feudal land-grants had been introduced in America, and with the disappearance of English sovereignty those grants ceased. More important than that, most of the living recipients of those grants, once the war was begun in earnest, fled from America, sacrificing thus their estates and power. In religion, too, the war was not without effect. The strong ties which had bound together the Episcopal and Methodist churches in both countries, for instance, were severed as the result of the war. For a time, it is true, it looked as if both of those churches, having taken the Tory side in the conflict, could have no future in America. When they did revive, however, a few years later, it was as American churches, disassociated entirely from their English brethren. In the case of the Scotch Presbyterians who were largely patriotic during the war, such severance of connections had been practically established before the war had begun.

It was the feudal aspect of the American ruling class, then, which was removed by the American Revolution. In that sense the defeat of Jonathan Edwards and the rise of the ideology of the upper bourgeoisie to power was, culturally speaking, almost as revolutionary an event as the Revolutionary War. It marked the retreat of an old ideology and the rise of a new. What the Revolutionary War did was to strengthen the reversal of power which had taken place at the beginning of the century, and which had reached a decisive turning point in the Edwards episode.

Even before Edwards' downfall, however, in response to the same forces which had brought about his dismissal, a new type of clergyman was beginning to arise. Just as we saw before that fewer youths were entering the clergy at this time than in previous generations, so we are now able to note that those youths who emerged as young clergymen were of a different character from their forefathers. They were without the old ferocity of the seventeenth-century theocrats, without their vigor and overmastering certainty of conviction. Already they had become a milder, meeker type, sweeter in disposition and gentler in approach. It was this type of clergyman who fitted in so much more satisfactorily with the changing scheme of things. He attacked less and forgave more. Indeed, it was this new type of ecclesiastic who made forgiveness into a salient virtue. The old type had forgiven little and demanded much; the new type forgave much and demanded little. Without this change in ecclesiastical type, religion would have had no future among the successful, the well-to-do. The old type of clergyman, following Edwards' tact, would have found himself so busy condemning his congregation that in time he would have had no congregation left to condemn. The new type, by subduing the thunder of the older, and by closing his eyes to that which it was better for him not to see, became more like a shepherd who learned that it was wise to sleep while his sheep grazed than like a faithful watch-dog who found no time for idleness from dawn to dusk.

One of the first signs of this change in type appeared in the person of the Reverend Mather Byles. While Mather Byles was very far removed from the later type of clergyman who emerged from this change, he was also considerably different from the theocrats who preceded him. Cotton Mather, for example, had scorned all pleasure which did not contribute to the religious emotion and had even refused to allow his mind to turn to poetry except in a religious sense. Mather Byles, on the other hand, broke the bonds of that religious straitjacket, and became openly interested in pleasures that had nothing at all to do with what his uncle had described as the religious instinct. The cleverest punster of his day, who punned at the very time when he was put on trial for aiding the British in Boston in 1777,[25] he combined in his personality those elements which stamped him as a type of clergyman who had not been seen before in New England. While he was able to deliver a vigorous sermon on *The Vileness of the Body*, at the same time he was able to make puns on the future of the soul. Moreover, he became an avowed advocate of poetry, and recommended it as an inspiring *pleasure-giving* art. Further than that, as a poet himself he became concerned with the technique of verse as well as its conception. Poetry became of more interest to him than religion, so instead of thinking of poetry in terms of religion, as Cotton Mather had, he tended rather to think of religion in terms of poetry. A wide

[25]When brought before his judges at the time of his trial they requested him to sit down and warm himself. "Gentlemen," was the reply, "when I came among you, I expected persecution; but I could not think you would have offered me the fire so suddenly." (E. A. and G. L. Duyckinck: *Cyclopædia of American Literature*: New York, 1856: p. 119.)

change this! An admirer of Pope, he corresponded with the latter, and became his literary disciple. Evincing his sycophantic admiration, he addressed Pope in the following fashion:

"O, Pope! thy fame is spread around the sky
Far as the waves can flow, far as the winds can fly!"

The heroic couplet became Byles' poetic model, and little that Pope attempted did the latter fail to imitate. When Byles turned to prose it was Addison who became his idol. Shaping his style on the Addisonian pattern, he even copied at times Addison's similes and metaphors and employed Addison's analogies and allusions. By way of illustration, Byles—who was in all likelihood the author of the essay in *The New England Weekly Journal*—described the unfortunate lady, who had been bled to death by the prick of a needle, as a "Martyr to Good Housewifery." Addison in *The Spectator* had originally described the same woman as a "Martyr to Diligence and good Housewifery."[26] Other examples of imitation were equally servile. In short, Byles became the American Pope in verse and the American Addison in prose.

Although the whole Hell-Fire Club had striven to write like *The Spectator,* and had adopted the very phrases of that English journal, even to the point of modelling its first page on that of *The Spectator's* first page, nothing illustrated so well the devastating influence of the colonial complex as the intellectual servitude which *The New England Weekly Journal* revealed in its introductory note. In order to point out the extent of this servitude, one needs but to compare the first sentence of the inaugural issue of *The Spectator* with the first sentence in the initial literary article in *The New England Journal*. In *The Spectator* the first sentence was printed as follows:

I have observed that a reader seldom peruses a book with pleasure until he knows whether the writer of it be a black or a fair man,

[26] Elizabeth Christine Cook, op. cit., p. 51.

of a mild or choleric disposition, married or a bachelor, with other particulars of the like nature, that conduce very much to the right understanding of an author.

In *The New England Weekly Journal* the beginning sentence appeared in this form:

> An ingenious Author has observed that a Reader seldom peruses a book with pleasure, till he has tolerable Notion of the Physiognomy of the Author, the year of his Birth and his Manner of living, with several other Particulars of the like nature, very necessary to the right Understanding of his works.

Even the names of fictitious characters in American papers were modelled upon names which appeared in English periodicals. Nathaniel Henroost, for example, in *The Spectator* became Ichabod Henroost in *The New England Courant*, and Mr. Honeycomb became Mr. Honeysuckle in *The New England Weekly Journal*. From format, then, to contents these papers copied English matters and models.

It was in these early papers however, which sprang up in response to the new environment, that the beginning of a new emphasis in American literature could be noted. This new emphasis was moral instead of religious in character. In the seventeenth century the entire stress of our culture had been religious. The Wigglesworths and Bradstreets constantly sought religious meanings in the universe. Little else concerned the writers of that period. In the eighteenth century, however, especially after the fourth decade, as the hierophantic dictatorship disappeared and the wealthy bourgeoisie rose into power, this religious concern faded into moral didacticism. Mather Byles represented this new tendency in literature as well as in life. Practically all of Byles' work in *The New England Weekly Journal*, as well as most of the other material which appeared in that journal, was moral instead of theological in spirit. Byles was more interested in making moral men than religious men. Morality became the new watchword of the time. Even belles lettres, as we have seen, could be encouraged if it was moral, and

Byles' ventures into belles lettres, in imitation of Pope, were pre-eminently moral in tone. The very fact that Byles adopted Pope as his master was indicative of this change from the religious to the moral emphasis. The change which had taken place in American life in the eighteenth century was already making it possible for America to appreciate an aspect of English culture which it had hitherto disregarded and disesteemed.

In England, as we have indicated, the petty bourgeoisie had never gained control of culture; it was the upper bourgeoisie, from the very beginning, which gave English culture its middle-class direction. Before the end of the seventeenth century, for instance, the moral motif had imprinted itself indelibly upon English literature. The petty bourgeoisie, however, would have nothing to do with this milky mid-way course, and in America the "moralized" stage of Steele and Cibber received no encouragement at all. It was only as the upper bourgeoisie arose in America and asserted its power that this moral motif received recognition. Byles represented one of the earliest signs of this change in reaction. Under his editorship, Lillo's *The London Merchant* was published in *The New England Weekly Journal,* and Addison's moral essays were slavishly imitated in style as well as in sentiment. In Mr. Timothy Blunt, who was the American edition of the English Sir Roger de Coverley, this moral spirit found its literary personification. Blunt was different from de Coverley only in that he retained certain of those New England petty bourgeois characteristics which de Coverley would have scorned. Blunt, to illustrate, with Yankee parsimony would carry two bottles of milk to town with him in order to minimize his expenses en route.[27] Other personages in sundry American papers of the period revealed in various ways the same petty bourgeois characteristics—characteristics which have come to be known familiarly as Yankee, but which in reality were class characteristics and not regional— which the characters in *The Spectator* would have contemned

[27] Ibid., p. 43.

and ridiculed. Translated in simple words, it merely meant that the upper bourgeoisie in America had not succeeded as yet in shedding its petty bourgeois heritage. Nevertheless, this upper bourgeoisie no longer demanded religious consecration as the test of character. It was content with morality as a criterion. And it was in reply to that new test that the moral motif was able to make headway in American literature, beginning at this time to formulate itself into a tendency which continued to dominate American literature until close on to the end of the nineteenth century.

But why should the upper bourgeoisie have turned from the religious motif to the moral motif in its scale of values? The reason is not difficult to discern. In the first place the wealthy bourgeoisie depended almost in entirety upon trade for its livelihood and trade in itself created necessities which were very different from those which grew out of agriculture. The religious intolerances of the petty bourgeois theocrats could succeed in an environment in which agriculture and not commerce was the mainstay of economic life. The theocracy itself for that matter was able to survive as long as it did only because the agrarian environment supported its premises. Agriculture encouraged a domestic economy in which the restrictions and regulations of the theocracy could actually be put into execution. It was the rise of commerce which made that execution impossible. Trade transformed that domestic economy into a maritime one, and broke down the provincial barriers which the earlier economy had erected. The intolerances which had been supportable in the agrarian environment of the seventeenth century became impossible in the commercial environment of the eighteenth. The inexorable exigencies of a commercial economy destroyed the narrow intolerances of an agrarian economy, for trade must be undertaken with every one who can be traded with, regardless of whether he is Jew or Gentile, Protestant or Catholic, Christian or heathen. Above all, religion could not be allowed to interfere with the advance of trade. A merchant might believe what he wished in private, scorn

Catholics, despise Episcopalians, loathe Jews, and consider the heathen as eternally damned but in public he had to conceal his personal predilections when he traded with these people in the open market. Difference of religion became inconsequential where the objective was exclusively monetary. It was inevitable, therefore, that tolerance should replace intolerance in this new economic world which the wealthy bourgeoisie was building upon the dead world of its fathers. Not only did tolerance become established among the Christian sects, but tolerance for the heathen also became part of the new credo. In our treaty with Tripoli in 1796, for example, this attitude had advanced so far that the American government openly stated that:

(Art. XI.) *"As the Government of the United States of America is not in any sense founded on the Christian religion;* as it has in itself no character of enmity against the laws, religion, or tranquillity of Mussulmen; and as the States never have entered into any war or act of hostility against any Mehomitan nation, it is declared by the parties, that no pretext arising from religious opinions shall ever produce an interruption of the harmony existing between the two countries." (Italics mine.)

A far remove, this, from the intolerant attitude which prevailed in the seventeenth century. Once the religious differentiation disappeared as a barrier between peoples only the moral remained. While the upper bourgeoisie became apathetic as to the form of religion practiced by the people with whom they carried on their transactions, they became most concerned with the moral element involved in the matter of whether those peoples paid their debts and fulfilled their promises. Morality in this sense, then, became extolled because it was so important in the new economic life.

This moral motif, however, was not concerned with morality as the Greeks and Romans viewed it. It was morality conceived of entirely in terms of the bourgeois way of life. While it condoned completely the essential immorality embodied in the nature of its economic enterprise, justifying the buying cheap and selling dear theory of conduct, it was most astringent, by way of compensation no doubt, in its insistence upon the recognition of moral obligations in every other descending relationship in the economic scale. In other words, granted the underlying immorality in its profiteer economy it was the most moral class, or at least prided itself upon being such, in every other detail of life. Without question the exaggerated stress upon morality which the middle class was guilty of was in part an unconscious attempt to cover up the fundamental immorality of its existence. In a more practical sense, however, this stress developed as a direct protection of its interests. As in George Lillo's *The London Merchant* it emphasized the duties of employees to their employers and not the obligations of the employer to his employees. It demanded honesty of its inferiors but rewarded the dishonesty of its superiors. It condemned sex outside the domestic circle because it tended to disrupt the continuity of the family-unit in which its economic inheritance was preserved. It exalted thrift, frugality, sexual fidelity and family devotion and made them into the cornerstone of its morality.

When the moral motifs of the middle class first began to take precedence in literature, it denounced all the vices which the bourgeoisie was opposed to in life. In *The New England Weekly Journal* as well as in *The Spectator* those vices were summoned forth for ridicule and attack. In the former journal there were numerous essays on the evils of idleness, covetousness, and loose living, and also equally revealing ones recommending work as the best cure for unsavory moods. Later on, however, when the conflict between sexual impulse and social ethic became more acute, the moral emphasis in middle-class literature began to revolve about the element of love. Morality became a matter of exalting love and denying sex—a tendency which in the nineteenth century produced a literature as viceless as it was artificial. The great problem which was created by the suppressive morality of the middle class was that of keeping individuals from violating its ethical code. As a consequence the bulk of middle-class literature in the nineteenth century, for example, was concerned with the struggles of individuals who succeeded in observing that code or who failed to observe it. In considerable part, literature became a triangular affair in which the tug of sexual impulse and the pull of moral duty provided the main source of conflict. The attitude of mind thus, which made the Greek critics upbraid Euripides for picturing the maudlin spectacle of a woman in love, was completely reversed, and in point of fact, it was the woman in love who became the cynosure of middle-class literature. Beginning in England with *Pamela* in the eighteenth century, this love motif did not strike root in American literature until the nineteenth century, when it gathered force and became a pervading influence.

Before the Revolutionary War, however, the moral motif in American literature was unembarrassed by the love factor. It was only when the novel developed toward the end of the eighteenth century that the love element appeared, and morality and love became almost synonymous entities. In the seventeenth century the Puritans and Dissenters had exalted religion and not love and while marital devotion had been extolled by them, it had not been associated with anything romantic. It was not until the end of the eighteenth and the beginning of the nineteenth century that love took on a romantic turn in American literature.

IV

It was Benjamin Franklin who in pre-Revolutionary days extended Byles' moral motif into mundane life. Franklin, indeed, was the perfect representative of the moral motif in literature. An opponent of the seventeenth-century theocracy and of religious rule in every respect, Franklin took up the cudgels in defense of a morality based upon a shopkeeper's economics. A social hybrid, as it were, Franklin opposed the religiosity of the petty bourgeoisie but defended their economic position. Caught in the chaos of a rapidly changing world, Franklin represented all the contradictions of a man who managed to succeed in that world by keeping afloat on all its various seas of change. Assertive in his ideas, he always observed a most politic caution in his actions. While an avowed deist in religious outlook and, therefore, a convinced opponent of the churches of his day, he donated money to almost every church in his adopted city, Philadelphia. More than that, as Bernard Faÿ, one of his most recent biographers, has pointed out, he saw "A certain advantage in the multiplicity of churches in the world, as that made for competition and competition made for trade." And therein lies the clue to Franklin's character. He was above all a shopkeeper in his logic—and it was out of that shopkeeper's logic that his morality sprang. Curiously enough, despite that rise of the upper bourgeoisie in his time Franklin managed to succeed without allying himself with its cause. Beginning his political career as a member of the lower orders in a fight against taxation imposed by the upper, Franklin continued throughout his career to champion the cause of the oppressed instead of the oppressors. Whatever else may be said in attack upon Franklin's inconsistency, this aspect of his career, attaining a stirring climax in his solitary defense of democracy in the Constitutional Convention,[28] cannot be assailed. He believed in a shopkeeper's world, but it was a world of many small shopkeepers and not one of a few large shopkeepers. His entire defense of the backland yeomanry, his whole dedication to the concept of democracy can be traced to that source.

Already the struggle between the lower and the upper bourgeoisie which marked that period in American history had begun to sharpen, and Franklin, forced to take sides in it, joined the army of the petty bourgeois in opposition to that of the plutocrat. In point of fact, he believed more firmly in the virtue of agriculture than in that of commerce, and it was the ideology of the small farmer even more than that of the small merchant that he defended. His faith was

[28]James Oneal: *Workers in American History:* New York, 1921: p. 50.

in the capacity of individual man to achieve happiness out of the land if allowed to possess and till it. "There seem to be but three ways for a nation to acquire wealth," he wrote in 1769, "the first is by war, as the Romans did, in plundering their conquered neighbors. This is robbery. The second by commerce, which is generally cheating. The third by agriculture, the only honest way, wherein man receives a real increase of the seed thrown into the ground, in a kind of continual miracle, wrought by the hand of God in his favor." This intellectual defense of agriculture, which was an American expression of the physiocratic doctrine of the day, made Franklin distrustful of manufactures as well as merchantry. "No man," Franklin contended, "who can have a piece of land of his own, sufficient by his labor to subsist his family in plenty, is poor enough to be a manufacturer, and work for a master." In those words, anachronistic as they seem, was embodied the quintessence of what is familiarly known as the American ideal. The ideal of American individualism interpreted in terms of the soil! It was this possibility of possessing the land, the gratification of individual ambition translated into land hunger, which, as we shall see in the next chapter, constituted the great petty bourgeois ideal. It was this possibility which made our proletariat bourgeois-minded, and which created an alliance between the small merchantry of the towns and cities with the yeomanry of the South and the West. Herein also resided that concept of agrarian democracy and equality of which Jefferson as well as Franklin became an exponent.

It was in Franklin's literary work that this petty bourgeois materialism, common then to the petty bourgeois shopkeepers in the cities as well as to the petty bourgeois farmers in the backlands, achieved its representative utterance. Much ink has been wasted in castigating Franklin for the cheap and uninspired nature of his doctrines,[29] but when we realize that Franklin did nothing more than crystallize the spirit

[29]Charles Angoff: *A Literary History of the American People:* New York, 1931: pp. 295–310.

and sentiment which characterized the changing petty bourgeoisie of his time, we can see that it is not Franklin who
should be attacked but the class and the country that produced him. Without doubt, Franklin represented that class
and that country better than any other individual who might
be singled out from that period, for in his life and in his
works he embodied both the virtues and the vices which
were—and to an extent still are—the inevitable concomitants
of that way of life in America, and for that matter, with
but few qualifications, in most countries. In the seventeenth
century, as we have noted, the petty bourgeois who had
settled and dominated the Atlantic seaboard had been religious-minded, and had striven to harmonize their economic life with their religious ideals. In the eighteenth century, however, with the theocracy in ruins, and a wealthy
bourgeoisie harassing it on every side, the petty bourgeoisie
was forced to adapt itself in a score of ways to the new commercial world into which it had been so mercilessly plunged.
While it did not desert its religiosity, and has not until this
day, it soon found it necessary to spend more time on material considerations than on spiritual. The theocracy, a
product of its own ideology, had worked in harmony with
its needs; the wealthy bourgeoisie, on the other hand, which
had become the new ruling class, contradicted its needs at
every point. It was this latter fact which drove the petty
bourgeoisie in the East to ally itself with the laborers and
artisans[30] in its midst and with the farmers in the backlands
in a common struggle against the tyranny of the rich. This
alliance alone, breaking down still further the intolerances
of the previous century, diverted a considerable part of the
religious energy of the petty bourgeoisie in the direction of
politics and converted their religion from a spiritual into a
moral issue.

   If Franklin's literary work contributed nothing else to
American culture, it certainly provided the petty bourgeoisie
with a convenient handbook of vices and virtues, a simple

[30]Van Tyne: *Causes of the War of Independence:* Boston, 1922: p. 424.

gospel of economic wisdom. The wealthy bourgeoisie, modelling itself upon the English upper classes, disdained such vulgar appeals to popular taste. But Franklin did not essay to be elegant, nor to appeal to those who preferred elegance to simplicity. In the case of *Poor Richard's Almanac*, for example, he knew his market and he wrote in a language which would attract it. His explanation of the aim of the *Almanac*, that it "inculcate industry and frugality, as the means of procuring wealth, and thereby securing virtue," expressed his philosophy in snapshot style. It was in terms of such virtues that Franklin—and the petty bourgeoisie—had come to envision life. The incandescent fervor of seventeenth-century religiosity had already begun to burn out and lose its glow. Frugality not as a religious virtue but as a source of economic saving had begun to acquire appeal. Wealth had become a means of "securing" virtue and not virtue of securing wealth.

It was as the open spokesman for the entrepreneur psychology and as its moral defender, that Franklin won his popularity with the American masses. In such proverbs as these Franklin pinned down the petty bourgeois philosophy of life to such a point of precision that even to-day they have not lost their quotability with the millions:

"Early to bed and early to rise, makes a man healthy, wealthy, and wise."
"One to-day is worth two to-morrows."
"If you would know the value of money, go and borrow some; for he that goes a borrowing goes a sorrowing."
"What maintains one vice would bring up two children."
"Industry pays debts, while despair increaseth them."
"Laziness travels so slowly that Poverty soon overtakes him."
"He that riseth late must trot all day, and shall scarce overtake his business at night."
"Drive thy business or thy business will drive thee."
"The sleeping fox catches no poultry."

If one turns from the epigrams which made *Poor Richard's Almanac* into a best-seller in its time to Franklin's *Autobi-*

ography, one finds it scarcely more than an intimate edition
of the *Almanac,* in which Franklin changes places with Poor
Richard and proves the truth of the latter's proverbs by
applying them to his own life. In Franklin's enumeration of
his thirteen virtues one merely discovers Poor Richard venturing to present himself in a more serious and less epigram-
matic mood. One needs but to compare a few of the virtues
to realize the resemblance:

INDUSTRY

Lose no time; be always employed in something useful; cut off
all unnecessary actions.

ORDER

Let all your things have their places; let each part of your business have its time.

TEMPERANCE

Eat not to dullness; drink not to elevation.

FRUGALITY

Make no expense but to do good to others or yourself; i.e., waste
nothing.

CHASTITY

Rarely use venery but for health or offspring, never to dullness,
weakness, or the injury of your own or another's peace or reputation.

Every activity in life, thus, was chiselled down to its material end. Nothing must be undertaken but with an eye for
practical advantage or gain. Even sex was to be resorted to
only for health or offspring—and not for the enjoyment of
it, for such enjoyment might interfere with the more serious,
economic virtues which were the sine qua non of bourgeois
existence.

While Franklin was not opposed to art in the manner of
the seventeenth-century theocrats, he did little more to encourage it than his predecessors. As a matter of fact, his interest in utility made him indifferent to pursuits which
seemed to serve no useful end. Like the New England
writer whom we quoted before, Franklin would have had

no objection to arts that were able to eke out "an honest penny," but he certainly was not inspired to aid art sheerly because it aimed to beautify. The merchant princes of the time, emulative of the English aristocracy, might encourage a portrait painter upon occasion or even support a musical society such as William Selby sponsored, and listen with patience if not enthusiasm to renditions of Handel and Bach, but not so the petty bourgeoisie, not so Franklin. There was no reference to art in Franklin's ritual of virtues, nor any sign of interest in it in his other observations upon life's significances. There is no better proof of the influence of the petty bourgeois ideology upon art-attitudes than is to be discovered in the case of Benjamin Franklin. Franklin was an uncommonly learned man for his day. He read extensively, was a shrewd student of political thought, and was widely travelled. In addition to that he had risen from being the Lorimer of his time into becoming the super-Colonel House of his generation. Nevertheless, he remained pre-eminently practical throughout his life, concerned himself only with material values, and allowed the entire world of art to move outside of him, unwitnessed and unfelt, as if it belonged in another hemisphere of existence.

While Jefferson would not have attempted, as Franklin did, to replace the poetry of the King James version of the Bible by the prose of eighteenth-century speech, it should not be thought that Jefferson's attitude toward art was very different from that of his Philadelphia contemporary. To be precise, the attitudes of the two men resembled each other more than they differed. Although Jefferson was a member of the plantation aristocracy which had risen to power in the South, the conditions of life there had not yet rubbed the edge off the petty bourgeois background out of which that plantation aristocracy had emerged, and Jefferson himself had not advanced very far beyond the cultural attitude which preceded. His interest in the arts was purely practical—just as practical as Franklin's interest in virtue. As a consequence, architecture, the most practical of the arts, was the only art which really absorbed him. "It is desirable," he wrote, "to introduce taste into an art which shows so much." Sculpture and painting interested him but little, for "being too expensive for the state of wealth among us, they are worth seeing but not studying." Indeed, he even tried to defend what little interest in the arts he showed by explaining to his friend Madison that he was not ashamed of it since "its object is to improve the taste of my countrymen, to increase their reputation, to reconcile to them the respect of the world and procure them its praise." At best Jefferson's concern for art, despite his argument that for the sake of literature he would be in favor of the expulsion of the Turks from Greece, was scarcely more than epidermal. If he actually took more interest in galleries than Franklin, if he really gazed at the Maison Quarree "like a lover at his mistress," if he did declare that "music is the favorite passion of my soul," it cannot be said that in actual life he took art very much more seriously than Madison, who advised his friend Bradford to give up poetry for law, because, when all is said, Madison declared, he had discovered that the arts "deserve but a moderate portion of a mortal's Time and that something more substantial, more durable, more profitable befits our riper age."

The political direction which Jefferson took confirmed rather than contradicted his attitude toward the arts. By a curious coincidence of interests, his logic led him in the same path as Franklin. The conflict which arose after the Revolutionary War between the agrarian interests in the South and the commercial interests in the North drove Jefferson, in search of political strength, into an alignment with the petty bourgeoisie. His vision of utopia, derived from impact with the same French and English ideas which influenced Franklin, plus the impinging force of the American environment, was aggressively agrarian. He believed in an America of small farms, where each and every individual would have full freedom of possession, retaining all the individual rights and liberties which are inherent in such a condition of life.

Convinced by his own limited experience in that respect that men should live in an agrarian instead of an urban environment, and dedicated, therefore, to a decentralized theory of state power, Jefferson rapidly won the allegiance of all those petty bourgeois groups in the agricultural regions in the South and West, and later on the petty bourgeois elements in the North also, which united in their opposition to the centralized control of the rich bourgeoisie in the cities. In consonance with this conviction, Jefferson fought the growth of manufactures even more vigorously than Franklin, claiming that they would only produce a surplus, turn us into an exporting nation, and thus involve us in international competitions and wars.[31] Besides that, he argued, they would lead us to adopt a policy of protection, necessitate a strong armed force on both land and sea to maintain their defense, and result in the oppression of the farmers and the destruction of individual liberty.

The truth of Jefferson's prediction has been corroborated by the developments which have occurred in American history in the twentieth century. Nevertheless, Jefferson's stand was reactionary in terms of his time, reactionary in the sense that his agrarian utopia was a composite of fancy rather than of fact. He understood well enough what he wanted, but he did not understand well enough the forces in American life which made what he wanted unattainable. In fact we can even say that in terms of America as a whole his position was just as reactionary then as is the stand of those Southerners to-day who hope to oppose the advance of industry in the Southern states, and restore the plantation-ruled South of pre-Civil War days. Indeed, we can go even further, and state that his stand was as futile as has been the entire position of the petty bourgeoisie in its struggle against the wealthy bourgeoisie in the last two centuries. There was no more chance of Jefferson stemming the advance of manufactures and insuring the success of agrarian democracy than there was of anti-trust laws preventing the centralization of in-

[31]Gilbert Chinard: *Thomas Jefferson:* Boston, 1929: p. 328.

dustry. Franklin was shrewd enough to relinquish his fight against manufactures later on in life, but Jefferson, despite the concessions to state power which he made while president, remained adamant to the end. Inspiring as was his fight, it was unfortunately in defense of a losing cause. The whole nature of our economic world, then but in the embryo, ordained it to defeat.

It was Alexander Hamilton, the intellectual representative of the rich bourgeoisie, who was victorious because he had history on his side. Hamilton believed in everything that Jefferson opposed. Jefferson believed in agrarianism, democracy, individual rights and liberties, states' rights, decentralization, because these were the means of protecting the needs of the petty bourgeois farmers, petty bourgeois merchants, and petty bourgeois frontiersmen of the time. They were the sesame to the petty bourgeois dream of Utopia in the eighteenth century. Hamilton believed in commercialism, plutocracy, centralization, and in the subordination of the rights of individuals to the economic needs of the state. He was convinced that America must be "rescued from democracy," and in one speech even went so far as to advocate the creation of a "monarch (who) ought to be hereditary and to have so much power that it would not be to his interest to risk much to acquire more." More than any other individual of his time, he prepared the way for the rise of industrial capitalism by encouraging manufactures, establishing a National Bank, and concentrating the financial resources of the country in the North where they could be used to dominate economic enterprise. By thrusting the burden of taxation upon the farmers instead of upon the manufacturers, by granting subsidies to the latter from time to time, and by protecting them by means of high tariffs, Hamilton laid the foundation for the success of the upper bourgeoisie in the nineteenth century.

If Jefferson and not Hamilton has won the sympathy of the American public, it is not because that public if faced with the realities in the case would claim that Jefferson's agrarian vision was the right one, but because Jefferson symbolized in his fight against the commercial interests of his day the underlying spirit of the whole struggle which the petty bourgeoisie has waged for two centuries now against the tyranny of the upper bourgeoisie. The struggle, to be sure, is not over to-day, although the strength of the petty bourgeoisie has been practically wiped out by the crushing advance of the upper bourgeoisie, which has driven the farmer to the wall, bankrupting its better possibilities and shunting over a large section of it into the proletariat. Notwithstanding that fact, the rallying cries of the petty bourgeoisie still linger, and Jefferson has been made a hero, thus, by the petty bourgeois elements in our population, who have come to identify their own fight against the upper bourgeoisie with the fight against it which Jefferson undertook in his own day. While Jefferson was in the wrong, then, insofar as economic destiny was concerned, he was in the right insofar as his defense of the oppressed against the oppressors was concerned—in the right in the sense that all leaders who fight for the weak against the strong, the poorer against the richer, are viewed as nobler than those who stand with the group in power. To-day, of course, it is the struggle of the proletariat which is important and not the struggle of the petty bourgeoisie; the Jeffersonian challenge as a result has become anachronistic, except with those who continue to believe in an anachronistic ethics and an anachronistic economics.

Before the Revolutionary War this conflict of classes was a regional and not a national one. After the war was over the issues more or less resumed their regional character until the time of the Constitutional Convention, when again they became national in scope. Before the war the conflict in the South was between the small farmers and the growing plantation aristocracy: in the North it was between the petty bourgeois agrarians and the small merchants on one side and the mercantile aristocrats and rising manufacturers on the other. Once the Constitutional Convention attempted to weld the country into a national unit, the struggle resolved itself into the new pattern which emerged in the conflict between the Hamiltonians and Jeffersonians, and which received a new impact and direction with the drafting of the backland regions into the union.

I have taken so much space to discuss this struggle because it marked the early beginnings of the conflict which has charted out the course and current of American history ever since. Nothing of literary permanence arose directly out of it, unless we single out certain of Jefferson's writings and appraise them for their literary as well as political merit. Indirectly, however, one literary figure did emerge—Philip Freneau. Freneau, who was regarded in New England as "that rascal Freneau," and who was despised by Washington as a sneak and a snake, was the first American poet to break away completely from the religious tradition of the Wigglesworths and Bradstreets and turn his verse in the direction of political satire. Mather Byles and his immediate contemporaries had levelled their weak Dunciad at the Anti-Christs of *The Courant,* but there they stopped, hesitant to venture further in their attack. And such Dunciads as they wrote were of that Sunday-school variety which amuses more than it stirs. Their poem: *On the Death of Old Janus* (*The Courant*) revealed that weakness in every line. But the iconoclastic spirits in *The Courant* itself had not displayed superior poetic calibre in their attacks upon the theocracy. In fact it was not until Freneau appeared that satire in America acquired literary distinction.

Philip Freneau was more than the product of the Revolutionary War. He was the product of the petty bourgeois forces which were let loose in the Revolutionary War, and which dynamited against the citadel of wealth that was erected by the upper bourgeoisie after the Constitutional Convention and the election of Washington. His early revolutionary poetry was impregnated with the incendiary zeal of a genuine sansculotte. In 1775 he delivered, in the form of eight poems, each published individually, his first series of attacks against British rule. Freneau was no half-way enthusiast, no Franklin hesitating to admit the necessity of independence until the very last, no literary debater weighing pros and cons in the manner of a senile pundit; he was a forthright revolutionary, who was unalterably convinced of the righteousness of his cause and who hit hard whatever or wherever he struck. His satires were not gentle; they were bitter and merciless. Their popularity no doubt sprang up in response to the righteous fury embodied in their challenge. In a word, Philip Freneau was the Thomas Paine in poetry of the Revolution.

While during the Revolution Freneau had contributed some of his most interesting poems to *The United States Magazine,* a patriotic magazine edited by Brackenridge in Philadelphia, it was in *The Freeman's Journal or North American Intelligencer,* organized near the end of the war and of which he was the silent editor, that Freneau's more mature work was published. Little that the British undertook in the Revolution escaped his satiric thrust. In addition to that he wrote patriotic poems in praise of American triumphs. But more important than his satires and apostrophes at this period was the initial editorial which he wrote at the time of the appearance of this magazine:

> At no period of time, in no era of important events from the first established social government, have the liberties of man, have the rights even of human nature, been more deeply interested than at the time in which we presume to address you. While Liberty, the noblest ornament of society, and without which no community can be well organized, seemed to pine and sicken under the trammels of despotic restraint in every land of the earth, it fairly promises to resume its pristine majesty here, and the new world begins to emerge from the fangs and tyranny of the old.[32]

It was the intensity of the revolutionary crisis which lent strength to such words. They embodied the battle-cry of the era. They provided the rallying centre of patriotic appeal.

[32] Frederick Lewis Pattee: *Philip Freneau:* Princeton, 1902. This is an excellent study of Freneau as a man of affairs as well as poet.

All classes, in the fury of the fight, subscribed to them, swore eternal allegiance to them. They became the fighting faith of the whole revolutionary movement.

When the war was over, however, and "the insolent foe," as Freneau described the British, had been vanquished, those words were robbed of much of their meaning and promise. As the country resumed a more peaceful character, and the problems of reorganization arose and demanded solution, the challenge of liberty was lost in the confusion. The mercantile aristocracy had been willing enough to employ such words in an attempt to rally the masses in defense of its cause, but it was far from willing to put the meaning of those words into effect once its cause won. Just as in the last war Western nations appealed to their masses to fight "to end war" and "to make the world safe for democracy," but once the war was over, set about making a more warlike world than before, with democracy reduced to an empty fiction, so the mercantile aristocrats after the Revolutionary War proceeded to establish a nation based upon a complete betrayal of what it had ostensibly defended.[33] But the petty bourgeois masses who had fought that war believed in those words, believed in the virtue of their application and the fruits of their promise. Moreover, the advance of their interests was contingent upon their fulfillment. But the advance of the interests of the wealthy bourgeoisie was dependent upon their not being fulfilled—and therein lay the cause of the struggle which ensued.

Freneau's part in that struggle was in defense of that petty bourgeois faith, in defense of Jefferson, who, as we have noted, became the Moses of the hour, promising a new Canaan—an American edition of Rousseau's perfect conception of a petty bourgeois utopia—to the petty bourgeois farmers and tradesmen who would follow him out of the

[33]Of course, the Revolutionary War was a progressive war in that it eventually benefited the country as a whole as well as the wealthy classes —and thus has its social value. The World War, on the contrary, was a reactionary war, a source of unmitigated social evil from start to finish.

wilderness of commerce and finance. As editor of *The National Gazette*, Freneau became a thorn in the side of the Federalist administration, assailing upon every possible occasion those violations of democratic faith which were perpetrated by the Hamiltonian party in power. Not even Washington escaped his scathing attacks. Hamilton's attempt to prove that he was working in a conspiracy with Jefferson, Freneau's affidavit to the contrary, the suspicion cast upon his oath by Hamilton in counter-reply, Jefferson's vigorous denial of any connection in the matter—all these developments were but the superficial manifestations of the underlying struggle which was being waged between the liberty-loving petty bourgeoisie of the time and the wealth-loving upper bourgeoisie.

Egged on by the intensity of the fight, the vanguard of the petty bourgeois forces even went so far as to challenge the place of religion in the new world of things. Freneau, for example, did not hesitate to write a stanza as devastating as this:

> "Virtue, Order, and Religion,
>   Haste, and seek some other region;
>   Your plan is fixed to hunt them down,
>   Destroy the mitre, rend the gown,
>   And that vile b-tch—Philosophy—restore,
>   Did ever paper plan so much before?"

But that mood did not continue. In the excitement of the Revolution, when everything was in a state of tempestuous flux, and every form of demagogery that inspired the masses to further revolt was encouraged, even religion could be attacked with impunity. Within a few decades, however, when law and order had been restored, attacks upon religion went out of vogue. Religion by that time had already become a docile servant of the *status quo*, meriting support, therefore, rather than censure. When Thomas Paine's *Age of Reason* appeared, then, it met with a storm of denunciation which increased instead of decreased with the years.

In this sense religion was the one social bond between the two classes, which could still be exploited by the upper in order to win the support of the lower. Even to-day, for that matter, religion continues to be the one instrument which the upper bourgeoisie can still exploit to good effect in an effort to win the support of the petty bourgeoisie in political elections. The defeat of Al Smith in the 1928 election was an outstanding illustration of the persistence of the religious factor in American politics.

Philip Freneau can be described as the first man of letters to appear on the American continent. All the writers who preceded him were individuals occupied with other interests or professions who made of literature an avocation instead of a vocation. Freneau made literature his profession. Fortunately, the rise of journalism in his day made it possible for a writer to earn his livelihood in an editorial capacity. As contributor to *The United States Magazine* and editor of *The Freeman's Journal* and later on of *The National Gazette*, he was able to support himself financially and at the same time find time to write his poetic satires and nature lyrics. It is true that even if he had wished it he would not have found it possible to devote his talents exclusively to belles lettres, but when all is said very few American writers even in the century that followed were able to make belles lettres their exclusive concern. Hawthorne discovered it necessary to accept a position as a customs-office clerk; Longfellow remained a college professor most of his life; Holmes continued to be a doctor as well as a poet; Bryant and Lowell both turned to public life as well as to literature for their interests. In Freneau's time, it is hardly necessary to observe, the situation was much more difficult for the author than in Longfellow's. Indeed, it was only a happy coincidence of events that made it possible for Freneau to survive as a writer in his day. The environment at the time was still apathetic if not hostile in its regard for literature. Mather Byles's interest in Pope and concern for poetry in general had not been enough in themselves to break down the barriers of indifference and opposition to art which the petty bourgeois ideology of the seventeenth century had erected. The upper bourgeoisie, as we have seen, was just beginning to desert the religious and adopt the moral motif, and it was chiefly in response to the tirades of satire, intense with moral indignation, which Freneau charged at the British that the latter earned his early reputation. His nature poetry and even his Indian verse were unappreciated save by a microscopical few. Freneau felt this limitation of the environment and attacked it with vigor. "Barbers cannot possibly exist as such among a people who have neither hair nor beards," he observed, and then satirically added, "how, then, can a poet hope for success in a city where there are not three persons possessed of elegant ideas?"[34] He was forced, he said, to write alone, "assisted by no poets of the plain." Assailing the cultural desolation of the American scene, he penned this revealing stanza:

> "Long have I sat on this disastrous shore,
> And sighing sought to gain a passage o'er
> To Europe's towns, where as our travellers say
> Poets may flourish, or perhaps they may."[35]

The editor of *The United States Magazine,* who had printed one of Freneau's better poems, *The House of Night,* in his periodical, confirmed Freneau's judgment when he declared that the bulk of the American people "inhabit the region of stupidity, and cannot bear to have the tranquillity of their repose disturbed by the villainous shock of a book. Reading is to them the worst of all torments."[36]

It should not be a matter of surprise, then, that we find American artists driven to almost every form of economic escape in order to survive in the environmental struggle. Not only was Freneau discouraged thus by his surroundings, and made by them into a better editor than poet, but practically every aspiring artist of that day as well as for many days to come was forced to equip himself in a diversity of ways to

[34]Ibid., p. xxxvi.   [35]Ibid., p. xxv.   [36]Ibid., p. xxix.

meet the exigencies of the environment. This condition continued far down into the nineteenth century. Robert Fulton and S. F. B. Morse, who attained international fame in the technical fields of transportation and telegraphy, were both painters who abandoned their art by compulsion and not by choice. Henry Sargent, John Trumbull, and Rembrandt Peale, painters whose work is still valued to-day, resorted to the military field, business and state offices for sustenance.[37] In music the situation was similar. William Billings, who was the first American composer, and the leading American musician throughout the latter part of the eighteenth century, found the economic struggle so difficult that after he forsook tanning for music he constantly lived on the verge of starvation, and died without leaving enough money to provide for a tombstone.[38] In the middle of the next century, another American composer, William Henry Fry, contended that the situation had grown worse instead of better. In Paris the director of the opera had told him that "In Europe we look upon America as an industrial country—excellent for electric telegraphs, but not for art . . . they would think me crazy to produce an opera by an American"—and when Fry returned to America he discovered that the Parisian director was correct. Indeed, with the influence of the whole colonial complex to overcome on the part of conductors and managers as well as the public, and with the composer helpless before them, the plight of the musician was even worse than that of the writer and painter—and has continued so even until to-day.

Influenced by the aggressive frenzy of the Revolution, in which everything British became hated with a vigor that defied reason, in which Samuel Adams led the parties in Boston that tarred and feathered the Tories, and in which almost every other form of violence was perpetrated in defense of the native cause, it was inevitable that a widespread revolt against the colonial complex should set in. At once every-

[37]Suzanne La Follette: *Art in America:* New York, 1929: p. 73.
[38]John Tasker Howard: *Our American Music:* New York, 1930: p. 53.

thing English was condemned, English songs, English science, English speech. The patriots of that day were determined to let nothing that was English remain; everything suddenly had to be made into American, made native. Very little, even to the most trifling things, was unaffected by this transforming process. The song "Four and twenty blackbirds" was rewritten by Samuel L. Mitchell, a well-known medical scientist of the day, in order to purge it of its royal reference. The stanza in which the pie is set before the King was changed to read this way:

> "When the pie was opened
> The birds they were songless,
> Was not that a pretty dish
> To set before Congress?"

Dr. Benjamin Rush was more interested in writing than in songs, and in 1781 in *The American Museum* delivered himself of the following observation upon the future of style in America:

Even modern English books should cease to be the models of style in the United States. The present is the age of simplicity of writing in America. The turgid style of Johnson, the purple glare of Gibbon, and even the studied and thick-set metaphors of Junius are all equally unnatural and should not be admitted into our country.[39]

But Benjamin Rush did not stop there. The Americanization of language was only one of his interests. Science was of even greater concern, particularly medicine. A physician himself, he was especially interested in the development of an American system of medicine. It was Noah Webster, of course, who succeeded in first giving this revolt systematized direction in his treatise on grammar, and more than a quarter of a century afterwards crystallizing its challenge in his famous Dictionary. The memorable words which he addressed to the American people, in 1783, urging them to reject the old and

[39]Henry L. Mencken: *American Language:* New York, 1919: p. 2.

create a new, he attempted to fulfill in his *American Diction-ary of the English Language:*

> For America in her infancy to adopt the present maxims of the Old World would be to stamp the wrinkle of decrepit old age upon the bloom of youth, and to plant the seed of decay in a vigorous constitution.

The Dictionary was dedicated to the simplification and standardization of English spelling in hopes of bringing it into better harmony with American usage. The prediction which Webster made in the introduction to his Dictionary, namely, that "in fifty years from this time (1828) the American English will be spoken by more people than in all the dialects of the language; and in 130 years by more people than any other language on the globe," was typical of the spirit of the era. Even Jefferson maintained that an American dialect would be an inevitable product of the new nationalistic environment. Few American writers of the period failed to assert themselves in favor of things American as opposed to things English. Freneau, as the following stanza testified, was unequivocal in his denunciation of British influence:

> "Can we never be thought
> To have learning or grace
> Unless it be brought
> From that damnable place?"

It was as an outgrowth of this revolt that American writers began to turn their attention to the American scene. Freneau became interested in the Indian and the natural environment of America as a whole and began that struggle with American materials which, as we saw in the first chapter, the American writer had to carry on for more than a century afterwards before he could come to grips with them. In New York not many years later, Drake engaged in the same fight, contending that America represented all the background necessary for poetic transcription. Robert C. Sands, another Knickerbocker poet of the period, joined vigorously in the same defense. Even Washington Irving, who for a long time was more attracted by Europe than America, stated that "never need an American look beyond his own country for the sublime and beautiful of natural scenery."[40]

But all this struggle for cultural independence, as we showed in an earlier chapter, resulted in nothing more than an ineffective sacrifice of energy, which found no creative resolution until a century later. Freneau's nature poetry and Indian verse could just as easily have been written in England as in America. Drake's poetic cry:

> "Shame! that while every mountain, stream, and plain
> Hath theme for truth's proud voice or fancy's wand,
> No native bard the patriot harp hath ta'en,
> But left to minstrel of a foreign strand
> To sing the beauteous scenes of nature's loveliest land"——

remained unanswered for a long time to come. Native bards sang of American things but in a foreign way. Even Fitz-Greene Halleck, to whom Drake had especially addressed his verses, could not respond to the "wild Niagara roar," not even when he described his caricature of an Indian in *Red Jacket*. In fact once the two wars with England were over and belonged definitely to the past, the hatred for things English lost much of its previous sting. While the majority of the nineteenth-century literati were anxious to escape British influence, the growing dominance of the upper bourgeoisie, whose attitude towards things English became more kindly once England could no longer hamper its advance, helped create a pro-English movement to counteract the American. This pro-English movement, combined with other factors with which we have previously dealt, unquestionably tended to make our colonial complex into an almost indestructibly enduring phenomenon.

So definite had this movement become in the nineteenth

[40]Nelson Frederick Adkins: *Fitz-Greene Halleck:* New Haven, 1930: p. 44.

century that when James Fenimore Cooper published his first novel he refused to sign his name to it, and had it appear as *Precaution, by an Englishman.*[41] *Port Folio,* to which we referred before, under the editorship of Dennie, deliberately endeavored to exterminate every trace of Americanism in literature in order "to win the coveted stamp of English approbation."[42] As a result American literature was soon sneered at as much by Americans as by Englishmen.[43] Indeed Dennie, himself, was forced to admit later on that, in consequence of this condition, "American critics seem in almost all cases to have entered into a confederacy to exterminate American poetry. If an individual has the temerity to jingle a couplet," Dennie continued, "and to avow himself descended from Americans the offense is absolutely unpardonable." This whole tendency reached a high point in Irving's crude mutilation of Bryant's poetry in order to placate the English public. In response to Bryant's eager desire to be published in England—a response, product of the colonial complex as we showed in the first chapter, which dominated in an overwhelming sense the mind of almost all the nineteenth-century American literati—Irving, acting upon the suggestion of Verplanck, who functioned as an intermediary between the two writers, set forth upon the task of finding an English publisher for the American poet. A publisher found, Irving

[41]Albert H. Smith: *Philadelphia Magazines and Their Contributors, 1741–1850:* Philadelphia, 1892: p. 9.
[42]Ibid., p. 9.
[43]Even an American enthusiast of the type of Joel Barlow did not escape the influence of this change. While he did not sneer at America, but rather defended it, he freely and soundly averred that though our government was American, our "manners are European. The people of that country (America) have always been accustomed to borrow their maxims as well as their manners, from the various nations of Europe from which they emigrated . . . fashions, and a taste for expensive modes of living are imported with other merchandise.

"The Americans cannot be said to have formed a national character. The political side of their revolution, aside from the military, was not of that violent and convulsive nature that shakes the whole fabric of human opinions, and enables men to decide what are to be retained as congenial to their situation, and which should be rejected as the offspring of unnatural connections." (Joel Barlow: *Advice to the Privileged Orders:* Paris, 1793.)

proceeded to edit the book and dedicate it to Samuel Rogers, who stood for all that was anti-American in London at that time. Worse than that, he wrote an apologetic letter to Rogers in which the following sycophantic sentence, which infuriated Bryant, appeared in the concluding paragraph: "Neither I am convinced will it be the least of his (Bryant's) merits in your eyes that his writings are imbued with the independent spirit and buoyant aspirations incident to a youthful, a free, and a rising country."[44] What was even more outrageous, however, was that in Bryant's poem, *The Song of Marion's Men,* Irving changed the line:

"The British foeman trembles"

to

"The foeman trembles in his camp."[45]

Irving stated that he made this change lest the volume might "startle the pride of John Bull on your first introduction to him."[46] Irving, himself, was not less shrewd in connection with his own work in England. In the American edition of his *Tour on the Prairies* he wrote a preface, fulsomely extolling his native country; in the English edition of the same book he eliminated the preface.[47] But this kow-towing to English influence, as we have seen, did not stop with Irving and Bryant. Close on to the twentieth century, Joel Chandler Harris, cognizant of the persistence of the colonial

[44]William Aspenwall Bradley: *William Cullen Bryant:* New York, 1905.
[45]Ibid.
[46]It is interesting to note the way in which Bryant's poems were received in England. The reviewer in Blackwood's, for example, stated: "All their (American) writers are but feeble dilutions of English originals. Some of the pieces of Bryant *having found their way by piecemeal into England, and having met with a little newspaper praise which was repeated with great emphasis in America,* he is set up by his associates as a poet of extraordinary promise; but Mr. Bryant is not more than a sensible young man of a thrifty disposition, who knows how to manage a few plain ideas in a handsome way. 'To a Waterfowl,' though beautiful, has no more poetry in it than 'The Sermon on the Mount.'" (Parke Godwin: *Biography of W. C. Bryant:* New York, 1884.)
[47]William Cullen Bryant: *Essay on Washington Irving,* in *Prose Writings:* New York, 1884: p. 357.

complex, still argued: "Why should there not be an American culture as distinctive in its way as the culture that is English? Why should Americans strive to be anything else than American?"[48]

In the way of language alone, this pro-English movement, as Mr. Mencken has excellently illustrated, prevented American writing from developing a spontaneity and spirit of its own and helped make it still further into a carbon copy of English models. Not only did such philologists as Witherspoon, Worcester, Fowler, and Cobb oppose as Mr. Mencken stated "every indication of a national independence in (American) speech," but as late as the twentieth century, in fact as late as 1920, Rupert Hughes asserted:

> But let us sign a Declaration of Literary Independence and formally begin to write, not English, but United Statish. For there is such a language, a brilliant, growing, glowing, vivacious, elastic language for which we have no specific name. We might call it Statesish, or for euphony condense it to Statish. But whatever we call it, let us cease to consider it a vulgar dialect of English, to be used only with deprecation. Let us study it in its splendid efflorescence, to be proud of it and true to it. Let us put off livery, cease to be the butlers of another people's language, and try to be the masters and the creators of our own.[49]

In other words, in linguistic-servility the colonial complex is with us yet. While I should disagree here with Mr. Hughes in that I believe there are abundant signs to indicate that in language as well as in literature American writers to-day have succeeded in escaping the major aspects of the colonial complex, it would be absurd to maintain that his argument is pointless. Although most American writers to-day are using American speech as their model, few of them realize how very new and how very important is the change which they represent. Without that change the elasticities of style which characterize the work of John Dos Passos, Sinclair Lewis,

---

[48]Joel Chandler Harris: *Miscellaneous Political and Social Writings.* Edited by Julia Collier Harris: Chapel Hill, N. C., 1931: p. 189.
[49]H. L. Mencken: *The American Language:* p. 24.

Michael Gold, and Ernest Hemingway could not have been realized. In another part of his article, Mr. Hughes pictured the condition of the American author in a way that admirably illustrated the handicaps which he experienced in his attempt to express himself in his own language:

Could any one imagine an English author hesitating to use a word because of his concern as to the ability of the American readers to understand it and approve it? The mere suggestion is fantastic. Yet it is the commonest thing imaginable for an English author to wonder if the word that interests him is good "English," or, as the dictionaries say, "Colloquial U. S." The critics, like awe-inspiring and awe-inspired governesses, take pains to remind their pupils that Americanisms are not nice, and are not written by well-bred little writers. When you stop to think of it, isn't this monstrosity absurd, contemptible, and servilely colonial? . . . Why should we fail to realize that all our arts must be American to be great? Why should we permit the survival of the curious notion that our language is a mere loan from England, like a copper kettle that we must keep scoured and return without a dent? Have we any less right to develop the language we brought away with us than they have who stayed behind?[50]

The effects of this condition linger in an active form still in our university life, where, as Professor Foerster has pointed out, American literature has never been made into a branch in itself but remains as part of the department of English literature "annexed either as another large field to be conquered or, more often, as a hobby that may be tolerated."[51]

As wealth increased in the colonies and the upper bourgeoisie spread in influence, the economic and cultural centre of America shifted from the New England states to the Mid-Atlantic. Philadelphia and New York became the main cities in which the new cultural life penetrated. When Philadelphia was made the capital, of course, it made cultural strides

[50]Ibid., p. 23. Both of these references to Hughes, and also the quotation in connection with Witherspoon, Forster, Fowler, and Cobb, are taken from Mr. Mencken's study which covers this field in a way that is as brilliant as it is exhaustive.

[51]Norman Foerster: *Re-Interpretation of American Literature* (A Symposium): New York, 1928: pp. x, xi.

which later on slowed up and slackened. Freneau, to be sure, had been active in Philadelphia for a time, but he was only one of a galaxy of writers who came to figure in the cultural life of that city.

By the turn of the nineteenth century the mercantile aristocracy had reached a point of security which made it possible for it to become interested in art. Its new economic status no longer made it necessary for it to share the petty bourgeois hostility for art, and before long it not only tolerated but even encouraged and began to patronize art. As early as 1805 Charles Brockden Brown's *Literary Magazine* recorded the opening of the "Academy," the Academy of Fine Arts, which was devoted to the cultivation of architecture, painting, and sculpture:

A number of gentlemen in Philadelphia (the article reads), have united in a plan, for promoting the charming studies of sculpture, painting, and architecture. A liberal subscription has been raised for purchasing ground and building a house, suitable for the reception and display of the finest monuments and models, which can be procured from abroad or supplied at home. Sufficient funds have already been formed for these purposes. A plan for a building has been furnished by an amateur of great taste, and it is expected that a temple will speedily rise, in the most airy and desirable situation in the city.

This design is highly honourable to the spirit of those who have adopted it. Our country is generally considered as youthful, or rather, in some respects, an infantile country, whose imbecile and growing state requires corporeal nutriment and exercise, rather than intellectual; but the success of this project is a proof that we are not altogether occupied in those coarser cravings.

A large supply of the best models has already been engaged from France and Italy, and the zeal and liberality of those engaged in the undertaking will, no doubt, procure new and constant accessions to the collection, after it is begun.

Whatever justice there may be in the contempt with which the literary and scientific spirit of America is regarded by Europeans, we are surely remarkably distinguished for our genius for the arts.[52]

The Port Folio noted the appearance of the "Academy" also. In literature the same interest was manifest. In Philadelphia

[52]Burton Alva Konkle: *Joseph Hopkinson:* Philadelphia, 1931: p. 150.

in 1786 the total book printing undertaken had been less than 500 octavo volumes; by 1813, as Joseph Hopkinson showed in his presidential address before the Academy of Fine Arts, the total exceeded 1,000,000. In that same address, Joseph Hopkinson made another observation of significance when he stated that the task which faced his contemporaries was to encourage "the arts in our country at this time, and to remove the objections and prejudices which may impede their progress."[53] Hopkinson even went further and maintained that our merchants should patronize art as well as pursue commerce.[54] As a matter of fact, Hopkinson himself in later life became a patron of artists. A number of obscure artists, Charles W. Leslie, Charles B. Lawrence, S. V. Clevenger, benefited directly by his patronage. Two of Stuart's best portraits were those he painted of Hopkinson and his wife. Besides being the author of *Hail Columbia* and many other poems, Hopkinson was, it is clear, just as close a friend of painting and sculpture. In addition to that he revealed an interest in Shakespeare, conspicuous in his essay on *Timon of Athens,* which would have ill-fitted a seventeenth-century mind—or even an eighteenth-century mind of the type of Charles Chauncy, quoted elsewhere, as wish-

[53]Ibid., p. 162.
[54]A generation or two before such an attitude would have been taboo. At that time the arts were still being inveighed against by men and women in the high places of mercantile society. In *The American Magazine,* for instance, as late as February, 1788, an article appeared condemning a university education lest it interfere with the forming of good business habits ("what is now called a liberal education disqualifies a man for business") and induce the mind to "contract a fondness for ease, for pleasure, or for books which no efforts can overcome." (*American Magazine,* February, 1788, p. 160.) In fact, as late as 1821, to show that the old attitude had not disappeared but had only been challenged by the appearance of a new, Timothy Dwight observed that in Boston "a man who is not believed to follow some useful business can scarcely acquire or retain even a decent reputation." (Timothy Dwight: *Boston at the Beginning of the 19th Century:* Boston, 1821: p. 15.) In other words, an artist in Boston had more than a little difficulty in commanding "a decent reputation." It was natural enough, therefore, as we shall see in the next chapter, that Emerson, Thoreau, and Whitman should turn their eyes more toward the West than upon their home environment.

ing "that some one would translate *Paradise Lost* into prose, that he might understand it."[55]

Important as Hopkinson was as a writer—and as a judge also—and worthwhile as his influence was as a patron of arts in the city in which he lived, it is as a symbol more than as an individual that we are interested in him here. Hopkinson was a lawyer and a judge—not a merchant. In that difference resides a significant clue as to what was happening in American life at that time and its transforming effect upon our culture. In the seventeenth century, as we have noted, the position of lawyer was inferior in both rank and income. By the time of the Revolutionary War and the end of the eighteenth century the position of the lawyer was elevated to one of great distinction and power. As the upper bourgeoisie progressed, the complications of its commercial life necessitated increasing resort to litigation of one kind or another, and the lawyers necessary to carry out this litigation were placed in a position where they could take advantage of the multiplying wealth which directly or indirectly passed through their hands. Being close to the owners of wealth the lawyers could profit by that wealth without having to become merchants to make it. Consequently, as the legal group grew and waxed wealthy in turn, it very soon cultivated a liking—or at least a number of its members did—for certain aspects of life which the merchants had had but little time to cultivate even when they had begun to evince an interest in them. It should be a matter of no surprise that the class for which Joseph Hopkinson stood as a symbol should often bend to turn up its nose at the crass form of life which the logic of the merchantry had encouraged. Shutting its eyes to the fact that its own growth had been dependent entirely upon this rise in merchantry, this group very often did not hesitate to exhort the merchants to pay less attention to foreign imports than to native culture.

This reaction, it should be stressed, only marked the be-

[55] Duyckinck: *Cyclopedia of American Literature*: New York, 1856: Vol. I, p. 95.

ginning of that confusion in values which has resulted from our losing sight of their source. Once civilization became complicated by the ramifications of commerce, and the origins of wealth became obscured by the machinery of finance, the problem of values became lost in a misty labyrinth of abstractions. The agrarian, whether feudal land-owner or small farmer, knew whence his wealth came, knew what his interests were, knew what he wanted and valued. But this was not so with the types of individuals produced by the complexities of mercantile and manufacturing life. Those who actually undertook the mercantile and manufacturing endeavors knew well enough what they were about, but those who profited by the civilization which was built upon those endeavors came to know less and less what it was about. To-day, to take a single example, that vast class of experts, managers, industrial engineers, laboratory and research men, in other words all those types which constitute the technical superstructure of our civilization, represent an element of great significance in our society, and yet an element which has different interests and objectives from the industrialist and financier, however dependent they are in the last analysis upon the industrialist and financier for their existence. What this element does not see, and what most of the intersecting and criss-crossing groups in society to-day fail to realize, is the nature of the economic base upon which our type of civilization is built, and their ultimate dependence upon that base for survival in their present form. In a society built about another economic base, a use instead of a profit base, that element would become part of a new alignment of forces, its objectives would be harmonized with social needs instead of constantly being forced into conflict with the hampering demands of individual and class profits, and its relationship to society as a whole would become as clear as the relationship of the peasant to the soil. It is that clarity which has been lost by the anarchical character of capitalistic economy—a loss which has made it possible for selfish objectives to be concealed behind altruistic slogans, has made ruling classes able to exploit the democratic formula and force the masses to believe that the interests of the rich and the poor are identical, and has made nations, dominated by the interests of industrialists and financiers, able to sacrifice the lives of the masses in wars waged in defense of those interests.

As a result of this confusion of sources, this obscuring of cause and effect, this contradictory creation of seemingly rootless values, or at least of values which make claim to be rooted in nothing deeper than individual logic, and to have little if anything to do with socio-logic, many groups in our society have been able to build up interests and affections which, in their eyes at least, seem to have nothing to do with the fundamental nature of their cultural economy. These groups in turn often tend to scorn the consuming economic concern which dominates the minds of the rest of the populace, never appreciating the fact that their own interests and affections are, in an indirect way, the product of the same forces, and are, as in the case of the æsthete, distorted in their emphasis by their very attempt to escape the impact of the prevailing attitudes which those forces have created. It was out of this conflict that the escape motivation developed into an important element in modern literature, achieving its most exaggerated expression in the form of the æsthete at the end of the nineteenth century.

V

The interest in art which began to manifest itself in America at the beginning of the nineteenth century, then, was a result of the impact of a multitude of forces, all revolving about the rise of the wealthy bourgeoisie and the new form of life which that rise precipitated. While for a span Philadelphia played a dominant rôle in American cultural life, the creation of Washington as the national capital robbed the former city of many of its official advantages, and before long it was forced to surrender its leadership as the cultural centre of the nation. During Philadelphia's cultural hegemony, when "Philadelphia led all the cities of the country in culture, in commerce, in statecraft, and in authorship,"[56] when a Philadelphia writer did not hesitate to predict that "*The Columbian Phenix* which was to be published in Boston was bound to be short-lived," for, as he said, "literary projects almost always prove abortive in Boston,"[57] practically every new venture in literature was first attempted in its midst. Later on literary ventures became less concentrated, although it was not long before Boston again became their centre of inspiration.

Altogether it was a period when America was beginning to become art-conscious. In 1826 John Trumbull addressed a letter to the President of the country in which he outlined a plan for developing the fine arts in America. The letter is a memorable document in our cultural history:

Sir—I beg permission to submit to your consideration the following plan for the permanent encouragement of the fine arts in the United States; a public protection has already been extended, in a very effectual manner, to various branches of the public industry employed in manufactures of different kinds; and I wish to call the attention of the government to the arts, which, although hitherto overlooked, may, I trust, be rendered a valuable, as well as an honorable branch of the national prosperity, by very simple and inexpensive means. . . .

By giving, in such a way as I have here taken the liberty to suggest, a right direction and suitable encouragement to the fine arts, they may be rendered essentially subservient to the highest moral purposes of human society, and be redeemed from the disgraceful and false imputation under which they have long been oppressed, of being only the base and flattering instruments of royal and aristocratic luxury and vice.[58]

[56]Albert H. Smith: *The Philadelphia Magazines and Their Contributors:* Philadelphia, 1892.

[57]The entire quotation is most revealing of the spirit of the time, and I, therefore, am giving the rest of it here. "Many attempts have been made to establish periodicals in that small town; but miscellaneous readers ask in vain for a magazine, or a review, or a literary journal in the capital of New England."

[58]Wm. Dunlap: *History of the Arts of Design in America:* edited by Bayley and Goodspeed: Boston, 1918, C. E. Goodspeed & Co.

A little later in another letter apropos of the same project Trumbull, in an overaboundingly optimistic mood, wrote:

Talent for all the elegant arts abounds in this country, and nothing is wanted to carry other votaries to the highest rank, of modern or even ancient attainments, but encouragement and cultivation, and altho all cannot hope to rise or be sustained in the most elevated rank still the less successful competitors would become eminently useful by turning their abilities to the aid of manufacture.[59]

Trumbull's letters revealed in explicit form the distinct advance of the moral motif in the arts of the nineteenth-century bourgeoisie. The arts, he observed, were to be "rendered essentially subservient to the highest moral purposes of society"—but, more revealing still, they were to be rescued from "royal and aristocratic luxury and vice," which, in other words, was but to say that they were to be the products of a bourgeois and not an aristocratic tradition. Now the moral motif which he stressed was but another way of stating that the arts would serve an economically useful instead of an exquisitely useless function in society. The arts would be more interested in being instructive than in being decorative. By virtue of their moral design they would even add to the "national prosperity by very simple and inexpensive means." In fact, as his letter shows, he even harbingered the coming of commercial art when he declared that "the less successful competitors would become eminently useful by turning their abilities to the aid of manufactures." Nor did Trumbull stand alone in his position. Indeed, he did nothing more than voice what had become the prevailing spirit of his time.

The upper bourgeoisie and its offshoots might become interested in art, but it was not an art born of an aristocratic background and tradition. It had to be a bourgeois art if it was to be encouraged and patronized. Above all, it had to justify itself as being *useful*—and the most obvious way in which art could justify itself as being useful in bourgeois so-

[59] Letters Proposing a Plan for the Permanent Encouragement of the Fine Arts by the National Government, by John Trumbull: New York, 1827.

ciety was in defending bourgeois morality. Where religion, as we stated before, was the shibboleth of petty bourgeois society, morality became the shibboleth of upper bourgeois society. Only when art aspired thus to be moral, and hence useful, could it grow in the middle-class environment of the period.

If we turn to the newspapers and magazines as well as to the writers of the time we shall see how clearly this attitude was expressed. In the Foreword to *The Columbian Phenix* the editor commented on "that indifference or rather apathy to genius and genuine literature which has been so often, and he would believe falsely, represented as an inherent quality of Americans."[60] In a later issue in the same publication, however, an article appeared which was more important in disclosing that aspect of the petty bourgeois state of mind which carried over into the nineteenth-century environment:

America personified, is a vigorous young man, cast upon the world, without the guidance of a parent, or the aid of a friend whom necessity has compelled to choose the forest, as the scene of his present enterprise, and future grandeur—whose persevering industry has been uncommonly successful in subduing the wilderness and reaping from the bountiful soil an ample reward in the necessaries of life, and who has been equally intent in furnishing his mind with every kind of knowledge which his circumstances would admit, or his situation required.

America in this situation seems to address our writers in becoming language. At all events my stories must be replenished; as soon as I am able my library shall be enlarged. The laborious ploughman and the hardy sailor must be honorably paid in preference to those who voluntarily wield the pen for my amusement.

When in more advanced age, the produce of my assiduous labor has put me in position of affluence and ease I will then confer an ample reward, not only on the laborious and useful, but the amusing writer. *But remember, at present, I pledge myself only for the useful. If I occasionally purchase the works of fancy and the flowers of taste it is from the impulse, perhaps the whim of the occasion. It is out of my usual line and ought to be considered as a gratuity.* I

[60] *The Columbian Phenix or Boston Review*, January, 1800, Vol. I, from Foreword.

must therefore be candid and tell you plainly that in my present situation, if you continue to draw your extravagant bills upon me, for your mere fancy ware, I shall in no case bind myself to answer them.

Who would not choose to see the daughters of Columbia employed with the needle and distaff rather than to see them "from morn to eve, from even to morn" led thru fairy fields, to the bedlam of the novelist. Who would not rather see our own sex intent on the farm, or in the counting-room, adding strength, riches to the nation than to view from day to day, like the literary epicure, rummaging a library, gormandizing without digesting and more absurd than the miser, hoarding up treasures of ideas, which are not communicated to others, and cannot unless he becomes author, descend to posterity.

The pandora box of venal literature has never been opened to curse our country. *Too much learning has not yet made us mad.* We leave as much as we could acquire on our infant state. Less would have done us honor. More may be added. Knowledge is fought by most. The useful preferred by all. The useful writer alone is patronized; and his patronage is equal to his *reasonable* expectation.[61]

Eleven years before *The Massachusetts Magazine or Monthly Museum* had anticipated the same sentiment in an article on *The Progress of the Arts:*

The mind set free from the importunities of natural want, gains leisure to go in search of superfluous gratifications and adds to the uses of habitation the delights of prospect. Then began the reign of symmetry; orders of architecture are invented and one part of the edifice is conformed to another, without any reason than that the eye may not be offended.

The passage is very short from elegance to luxury. Ionic and Corinthian columns are soon succeeded by gilt cornices, inlaid floors and petty ornaments which shew rather the wealth than the taste of the possessor.[62]

The same use-motif with its moral implications obtruded everywhere, in newspapers, magazines, and books. In *The*

[61]*The Columbian Phenix or Boston Review,* Vol. I, No. V, May, 1800, p. 300. *The Eagle:* No. VII: *Patronage of American Literature.*
[62]*The Massachusetts Magazine or Monthly Museum,* April, 1789: *On the Progress of the Arts.*

Weekly Magazine, in an article on *Hints to Authors,* this revealing passage appeared:

There are three motives for writing: the best and noblest is to convey useful information; the next is to gain a livelihood, and I have heard an instance of a third—of a man whose thoughts were so troublesome that he was in the daily practice of committing them to paper and as regularly committing the paper to the flames. This last method I would most sincerely recommend indiscriminately to all the writers of plays, novels and those essays which require a translation into intelligent language and have no useful end in view, but are written merely to show the authors' ingenuity in saying a great deal about nothing.[63]

Even the novel was still looked upon askance. In another article of *The Weekly Magazine,* on the *Character and Effect of Modern Novels,* readers were warned against the seductions of fiction:

I have heard it said in favor of novels that there are many good sentiments dispersed in them. I maintain that good sentiments being found scattered in loose novels render them the most dangerous, since when they are mixed with seducing arguments it requires more discernment than is to be found in youth to separate the evil from the good; they are so nicely blended; and when a young lady finds principles of religion and virtue inculcated in a book, she is naturally thrown off her guard by taking it for granted that such a work cannot contain any harm; and of course the evil steals imperceptibly into her heart, while she thinks she is reading sterling morality.[64]

In still another article, this one on the *Importance of Female Education* which was published in *The American Magazine* a decade earlier, we are confronted with the same attitude:

With respect to novels so much admired by the young and so generally condemned by the old, what shall I say? Perhaps it may be said with truth that some are useful, many of them pernicious— and most of them trifling. A hundred volumes of modern novels

[63]*The Weekly Magazine,* Vol. II, No. 16, Saturday, May 19, 1798: Philadelphia: *Hints to Authors.*
[64]Ibid., Vol I, No. 6, March 19, 1798: Philadelphia.

may be read without acquiring a new idea. Some of them contain entertaining stories and where the descriptions are drawn from nature and from character, and events in themselves innocent, the perusal of them may be harmless.

Young people, especially females, should not see the vicious part of mankind. At any rate, novels may be considered as the toys of youth. They are the rattle-boxes of sixteen. The mechanic gets his pence for his toys, and the novel writer for his books, and it would be happy for society, if the latter were in all cases as innocent playthings as the former.[65]

Whatever else was uncertain, religion, ideas, convictions, moral virtue at least was the one eternal certainty. "But we all know the unquestionable path of virtue," wrote Francis Hopkinson. "Let us pursue that path with unremitting diligence."[66] "A virtuous people," stated *The Massachusetts Magazine*, "makes a virtuous administration of government."[67] "All truth is immutable and eternal as God himself," declared Timothy Dwight, "the morality therefore which is one thing at one time, and another at another cannot be true morality at both periods. If it be proved to be true at one period it must be false at another; for it is impossible that what is immutable and eternal in its nature can change, but must remain forever the same."[68] Bourgeois morality then was not just another morality, but was *the* morality— the unchanging, everlasting, ideal morality. While religions might veer and vary, morality remained an eternal constant.

If Joseph Hopkinson wished to defend the cultivation of the arts, he did it from a moral standpoint;[69] if John Trumbull wished to persuade the president to encourage the arts he stressed their moral significance; if an individual poet

[65]*The American Magazine*, May 1, 1788: *Importance of Female Education*: p. 369.

[66]Francis Hopkinson: *Essays and Occasional Writings*: Philadelphia, 1792.

[67]*The Massachusetts Magazine or Monthly Museum*, July, 1789: *The Politician*: No. 1, p. 431.

[68]Timothy Dwight: *An Essay on the State*: London, 1824. From Preface, p. 56.

[69]*The American Magazine*, May 1, 1788: *Importance of Female Education*: p. 369.

sought to win a public for his verses he emphasized their moral vision; if a novelist hoped to overcome the prejudice against his art he became an apostle of moral virtue. Charles Brockden Brown, in the capacity of editor of *The Literary Magazine and American Register*, avowed that he was "the ardent friend and the willing champion of the Christian religion," and promised to dedicate his magazine to the inculcation of the highest virtues. Poetry was still unacceptable at that time without moral justification. Longfellow defended poetry against its enemies, who still considered it a form of dissipation, declaring that "the legitimate tendency of poetry is to exalt, rather than to debase—to purify, rather than to corrupt." Lowell, in furtherance of the same defense, maintained that "poets are the forerunners and prophets of changes in the moral world." Bryant rising to battle in the same cause, expatiated upon the "virtues" of poetry at great length:

Everything that affects our sensibilities is a part of our moral education, and the habit of being rightly affected by all the circumstances by which we are surrounded is the perfection of the moral character. . . . Every good action has its correspondent emotion of the heart given to impel us to our duty, and to reward us for doing it. Now, it is admitted that poetry moves these springs of moral conduct powerfully; but it has sometimes been disputed whether it moves them in a salutary way, or whether it perverts them to evil. This question may be settled by inquiring what kind of sentiments it ordinarily tends to encourage. Has it any direct connection with vice? for, if it has not, the emotions it inspires must be innocent, and innocent emotions are emphatically healthful. . . . Do we not know that poetry delights in inspiring compassion, the parent of all kind offices? . . . It luxuriates among the natural affections, the springs of all the gentle charities of domestic life. It has so refined and transformed and hallowed the love of the sexes that piety itself has sometimes taken the language of that passion to clothe its most fervent aspirations. . . . All moral lessons which are uninteresting and unimpressive, and, therefore, worthless, it leaves to prose; but all those which touch the heart, and are, therefore, important and effectual, are its own.[70]

[70] Wm. Cullen Bryant: *Literary Essays: The Value and Uses of Poetry.* Edited by Parke Godwin: Appleton & Co., 1884: p. 16.

Even Emerson was convinced that "the high poetry of the world from the beginning has been ethical."

The popular literature of the period was pervaded with the same spirit. Turning back for a moment to the latter part of the eighteenth century, we discover the moral motif manifest in the dedication of Sarah Wentworth Morton's novel: *The Power of Sympathy, or the Triumph of Nature founded in Truth.* The dedication was worded thus:

> To the Young Ladies, of United Columbia. These Volumes, Intended to represent the specious Causes and to expose the fatal Consequences of Seduction; To inspire the Female Mind with a Principle of Self Complacency, and to promote the Economy of Human Life, are Inscribed, with Esteem and Sincerity, By their Friend and Humble Servant."   The Author, Boston, Jan. 1789.[71]

All the many journals which sprang up in Boston, New York, Philadelphia, and Charleston during the early part of the nineteenth century were manifestly moral in character. Their aim was everlastingly to improve and purify the mind. The editors invariably promised never to admit material which could "call a blush to the cheek of innocence," but always to present articles and fictions "to please the learned and enlighten the ignorant, to allure the idle from folly and confirm the timid in virtue."[72] A host of magazines appeared, followed by an even greater host of books, which were devoted to the moral education of young girls. These publications, one more sentimental than another, in time became almost countless. There was scarcely a city of any size that could not boast of a *Misses Magazine,* a *Young Ladies Mentor,* or a *Ladies Literary Companion* to protect its womanhood from vice.

The art in literature which developed, therefore, was the

---

[71]Anne Russell Marble, M.A.: *Heralds of American Literature; A Group of Patriotic Writers of the Revolutionary and National Periods:* The University of Chicago Press, 1907: p. 280.
[72]McMaster: *History of the People of the United States:* Vol. V: New York, 1921: p. 270.

moral art of the bourgeoisie. In being moral it was able to serve a useful end. Forsaking the hostility for art which had been entertained by the religious-minded petty bourgeoisie of the seventeenth century, the upper bourgeoisie, nevertheless, accepted art only when it was expurgated of its aristocratic aspects and moralized to suit its own taste. When the American painter, John Vanderlyn, was commissioned to copy a European painting for a member of the American upper bourgeoisie, John R. Murray, he found himself in a most embarrassing situation, when, without considering the moral attitude of his fellow citizens, he copied Correggio's *Antiope*. Murray's remark upon it was characteristic of the moral attitude of the time: "What can I do with it? It is altogether indecent, I cannot hang it up in my house, and my family reprobate it."[73] But even Emerson's attitude toward literary masterpieces of an *immoral* order was scarcely superior. His words describing Boccaccio's *Decameron* are in the same spirit as those of Murray:

> There is no greater lie than a voluptuous book like *Boccaccio!* For it represents the pleasures of appetite, which only at rare intervals, a few times in a life time, are intense, and to whose acme continence is essential.

Thoreau was even more decisive in his insistence upon the moral motif in literature. Sex, in his opinion, ought never to be alluded to or discussed except in a manner "as reverent and chaste and simple as if it were to be heard by the ears of maidens."

It was this moral attitude which dominated nineteenth-century art and literature in America. In time, it became, in a less conscious way perhaps, as suppressive a force as religion had been in the centuries previous. All those vast energies of impulse which revolve about the sexual instinct were dammed up by this suppressive force, and sublimated in that romanticized and sentimentalized form which prevented literature

---

[73]Wm. Dunlap: *History of the Arts of Design in America*: edited by Bayley and Goodspeed: Boston, 1918: C. E. Goodspeed Co.

from pursuing the path of reality and truth. In short, for the sake of virtue, an artificialized and deceptive virtue which concealed the basic economic lie upon which its moral life was built, our literature for several generations to come was emasculated of all claim to vigor and veracity.

CHAPTER V

THE FRONTIER FORCE

I T was the frontier force which created a new America. It was the frontier which freed America from the cultural bondage of Europe, destroyed the dependence of the American mind upon the European mind, and released those energies of impulse and aspiration which the individual petty bourgeois had been forced to repress in varying degrees in almost every other environment in which he had lived.

The petty bourgeois is essentially an individualist who aims to create an environment in which his right to individual possession and his ambition to promote it, be it farm or shop, is unmolested by the restrictions of church or state. His religious revolution in Europe had grown out of the struggle for that privilege. His economic individualism, tempered at first by the constrictions of the environment, craved always a freedom from those constrictions, and as soon as commerce advanced and the more successful of his group acquired wealth and came to constitute an upper bourgeoisie, church and state were both forced to fiddle for him. But this very condition of change worked havoc for those members of this group who were not so successful, and who instead of becoming members of the wealthy bourgeoisie remained members of the poor bourgeoisie. As this upper bourgeoisie grew stronger, it inevitably began to concentrate wealth into its hands, working greater and greater hardship on the petty bourgeoisie who in turn had to draw in its reins instead of releasing them. It was in the eighteenth century that this struggle began in America, and by the end of the century, as we have perceived, in the conflict between Hamilton and Jefferson, it had already reached an early fever point. As the conflict of the two bourgeoisies continued, the difference between their interests became more and more clear-cut and challenging. The upper bourgeoisie sought a strong centralized state, with power in the hands of the few, and with the functions of the individual limited by the necessities of commercial enterprise and industrial advance. Its theory of laissez-faire demanded that it be "let alone" to exploit the resources of the earth; "let alone" to exploit the workers it needed to accomplish its aims; "let alone" to rule the country as befit its purpose. It had no interest in the plight of the small farmer or merchant whose individual rights it trampled upon with ever stronger tread. The theory of laissez-faire which the small farmer and the petty merchant came to defend was to be found in their plea that they be "let alone" by the state which taxed them and by big business which undersold and cheated them; that their rights as individual owners be protected against the predatory power of industry and finance. It was the small farmer and the poor merchant, therefore, who raised the cry of liberty and democracy—not the upper bourgeoisie. The upper bourgeoisie, as the Constitutional Convention revealed and as its entire history has confirmed, was interested in power for the few and not liberty for the many. In government it was and still is interested in plutocracy and not democracy.

As the struggle between those conflicting forces grew more acute, the conditions of life of the poorer elements of the population became more distressing, and out of deprivation and despair the movement westward changed from isolated and scattered expeditions into a literal migration. The trail-breakers, the trapper, the hunter, the trader, were followed by the poorer elements from the cities, the towns, and the villages; these elements with their petty bourgeois psychology came to settle and build and not merely to trade and plunder. Advancing from diverse sections of the East, this vast army of occupation spread its tentacles of control now this way, now that, driving the wilderness before it at the progressive rate of seventeen miles a year. Past the Alleghanies, past the Mississippi, it moved, skirting the gulf on one side and the Great Lakes on the other, and finally past the Rockies and on to the coast it went, thus completing by the end of the nineteenth century the greatest migration of peoples in the modern world.

Just as the Atlantic coast had been originally settled by the religious-minded petty bourgeois elements from England and other parts of Europe, and not by the wealthy bourgeoisie, so the West was settled by men and women who were either descended from approximately the same strata of society, or who at least, due to the conditions of the environment, were dominated by the same psychology. Many of the pioneers, of course, who plunged into the West, were not small farmers or poor merchants; many of the pioneers, indeed, as time went on, were laborers and artisans, mill workers and factory slaves. When they went westward, however, it was not as proletarians, imbued with a proletarian psychology, but as land-hungry individualists governed by a petty bourgeois psychology. The frontier environment, to be sure, gave that petty bourgeois psychology a different cast, endowed it with renewed vigor in terms of the times, and infused it with a democratic vision which had more practical meaning in the uncongested areas of the West than in the wealth-shackled cities of the East.

It is important to keep in mind the petty bourgeois ideology of the frontiersman, for if we do not we shall be bound to confuse the rôle which he played in the American scheme of things. The frontier background, because of rather than despite its hardships, provided an ideal environment for the realization of petty bourgeois ideals. The individual freedom from molestation on the top by the big bourgeoisie, gave the frontiersman that sense of personal security and self-reliance which endowed individualism with a meaning in America that it never acquired in any other country. Frontiers are never places which are pioneered by the rich; the very possession of riches militates against pioneering which by its very nature is too precarious a risk for those who have much of consequence to hazard. Just as in the founding of America it was the petty bourgeoisie who actually did most of the settling and not the wealthy bourgeoisie—in total percentage, as we showed earlier, the number of wealthy bourgeoisie who came to America was almost microscopical as compared to the petty bourgeoisie—so likewise on the frontier it was the petty bourgeois elements, particularly as time went on the petty-bourgeois-minded workers, who, following the trail-blazers and Indian fighters, mowed down the forests, forded the rivers, constructed the cabins, and laid out the farms—and not the rich bourgeois.

The rich bourgeoisie, as in the settling of America, might organize the companies, finance the stocks, and even procure the vessels, but it was the petty bourgeois elements who did most of the emigrating, embarked on the vessels, and established the colonies. As we showed in the second chapter, only extenuating circumstances could move the upper bourgeoisie —or the aristocracy for that matter—to emigrate. (The Cavaliers came over to Virginia in numbers as we have noted, only when, during the Cromwellian era, England became unendurable for them, and then went back, as soon as Charles II was restored.) The very fact that they had riches tended to make them, despite opposition and oppression, cling to the country in which they lived rather than desert that country at the risk of losing those riches in a new country which had nothing but insecurity to offer them in exchange. While religious attitudes, as we have seen, played a determining part in the matter, the religio-cultural attitudes of the upper bourgeoisie in England were of a different type from those of the petty bourgeoisie, and it was that difference, reflecting their disparity in economic status, which also helped to disincline the upper bourgeoisie as a whole from venturing upon an emigration which the petty bourgeoisie, having less to lose culturally as well as economically, was eager to undertake.

Now the New England emigration was different from the Western emigration, however, in one signal particular. In the founding of New England, as Morison convincingly showed, the religious motivation was often uppermost; in the founding of the West on the other hand, religion played an inconspicuous and infinitesimal part—it was the economic motivation there which was paramount. While in a fundamental sense, as we have endeavored to emphasize throughout this book, the religious motivation itself—the nature, intensity, and depth of it—is rooted in the economic basis of the culture, as historical materialism has constantly contended, the actual expression of it in personal motivation, for instance, may at times contradict the logic of economic advantage. The individual, in other words, is moved often by reasons which arise from other sources than the economic, although the economic basis of his culture creates the reasons, be they religious, moral, or political, which governs his possibilities of choice. Thus in the case of the founding of New England, there were some members of the upper bourgeoisie who did come over, especially in the instance of the Bay Colony, for reasons that were religious instead of economic, although the overwhelming majority who came from other countries as well as England were of petty bourgeois extraction, men of the lower middle class who had little to lose in their fatherlands and were possibly to gain much in the new country.

The upper bourgeoisie, then, in the eighteenth century, did not venture into the wilderness, or undertake to found the farms, although as conditions changed, and the West assumed a more promising prospect, it was not loath to take economic advantage of the new environment created by the petty bourgeoisie, finance groups to go West, and exploit the land values which had been developed by those who had already gone. The petty bourgeois belligerency which the West soon came to represent, however, plus the unstabilizing effect which Western migrations exercised upon the economic life of the East, swiftly aroused the antagonism of the ruling class along the Atlantic seaboard. In fact, once the West became a force that antagonism developed into one of the most virulent factors in American politics—a factor which is still operative to-day.

The history of the United States, it should be obvious at this point, has been the product of three cultural patterns. In the seventeenth century it was the petty bourgeoisie in both the North and the South which determined the nature of the prevailing cultural institutions. By the end of the seventeenth century or a little before the end of it, to be more precise, the plantation aristocrats had wrested power from the petty bourgeoisie in the South, except in North Carolina, and had laid the foundations for what has been familiarly known as pre-Civil War Southern culture. Since the Civil War the South has had a return to petty bourgeois dominance. In the North, the wealthy bourgeoisie superseded the petty bourgeoisie before the middle of the eighteenth century. On the frontier, on the other hand, the petty bourgeoisie retained its dominancy until after the Civil War, when the inroads of industry and finance crippled its vigor and influence. While differences in environment have made these petty bourgeoisie different in many superficial respects, they have not made them different in fundamental character. When they are in power, as in New England in the seventeenth century, or as in the South to-day, they are suppressive; when they are out of power, and have their individual rights trampled upon by the rich bourgeoisie, or, as in the South before the Civil War, by the plantation aristocracy, they are liberty-loving and ardently democratic. If the petty bourgeoisie of the frontier, and of the West, which emerged as the frontier moved farther and farther toward the Pacific coast, did not develop the same tendencies, it was due to two factors, namely, the territorial immensity of the country which prevented the concentration of control and power, and the fact that the petty bourgeois elements in the West, the small farmers as well as the lower middle-class merchants, were constantly forced to carry on a defensive war against the economic encroachments of the East. Now it was the first of those factors, the territorial factor, which created a different cultural pattern in the West, and which, aided by the second factor, converted the West into a force that made American ideas and ideals take on a form indigenous to this country and to no other.

The cultural pattern of the North, once the theocracy was overthrown and the civil state based upon the commercial interests of the time acquired control, was dominantly upper bourgeois; the cultural pattern of the South, once the plantation system had taken form, and continuing down until the Civil War, was pseudo-aristocratic. Both these patterns, as we have noted, were imitative instead of creative in character. The cultural pattern of the frontier was petty bourgeois until near the end of the nineteenth century—in fact even to-day the West has not lost most of its petty bourgeois characteristics—but petty bourgeois as we pointed out in the foregoing paragraph, with a difference. And it was that difference which made the realized individualism of the West into such a dynamic, driving element, and which made its cultural pattern more creative than imitative in type.

But let us examine a little more closely the conditions which made frontier life into such a unique and creative force in American culture. In the first place, its geographic remoteness from the Eastern coastline and European influence made it depend less upon England and Europe for commercial sustenance and cultural inspiration. As a whole, until it reached a surplus stage at least, it was practically a self-supporting unit whose conflicts were more with the East than with England. In the second place, the majority of the inhabitants of the frontier regions were discontents from the East, men who were in revolt against the East because it had not provided them with the opportunity for advance which they had sought. They had gone West to find conditions which would be more favorable to their rise. In the third place, in going West they were plunged into a stage of existence which they had never known before—and which will never be known again—and which brought them face to face with realities and possibilities that infused their individualistic psychology with a new vision. But the frontier originally began in New England; then how can one say these eighteenth and nineteenth century frontiersmen ventured upon a new stage of existence? Was it not similar after all to the stage of existence entered upon by the New England and Virginia frontiersmen? The answer is a significant negative. The coastal frontier was settled in the main by Englishmen who knew what they were about, and who brought with them a cultural form which had already begun to crystallize in their minds in England and which they tried to put into execution in the new country. Most important of all in this connection is the fact that these groups came over with special-class concepts in mind, and that they put those concepts into practice shortly after they had arrived. The New England and the Southern colonies established class distinctions from the very beginning, and as wealth grew those distinctions were accentuated instead of obscured. On the Western frontier, on the other hand, all such distinctions were absent. The Western frontiersmen advanced into the wilderness as equals, fought as equals, and established their communities upon an equalitarian basis. Class distinctions could have little meaning in an environment that demanded individual initiative, energy, strength, courage, and a willingness to work rather than willingness to live on the work of others. Society took on a fluidity which it had never experienced before and will never experience again. Individuals found themselves for the first time in their lives unfettered by class or rank, unencumbered by the cultural and economic vestiges of the past. The air tingled with new possibilities, the promise of a petty bourgeois millennium.

Out of that new condition, out of the challenge of those new possibilities, out of the illusory promise of that Utopia, sprang forth, in full-bodied, vigorous form, that spirit of individualism which determined the direction of so much of American thought, and which gave it a distinctly different twist from European. Individualism in the frontier environment became a reality, with an impact and an intensity, that shook the minds of men. The economic millennium at last unfolded opportunities for the individual that were unconfined by social status—opportunities which were limited only by the environment. But the environment was seemingly illimitable! The geographic enormity of the country alone promised to prevent exhaustion. The sources of power in the country covered what then appeared to be an unconsumable area. The individual felt that he could go on and on, fulfilling his petty bourgeois aspirations without end. Even with the coming of modern means of transportation and the invention of machinery, industry could spread in the frontier regions without undue concentration. It was only in such a state of economic flux, where the social structure was so fluid that individual advance was comparatively unimpeded, that such a philosophy of petty bourgeois individualism could drill itself so deeply into the lives of a people.

But this frontier force did not stop with the frontier. In a very significant way, it affected all of America. Moving ever farther and farther West, opening up new possibilities as it spread, the frontier provided a psychological as well as an economic outlet for the pent-up populations of the cities. It not only supplied a means of escape for the oppressed petty bourgeoisie in the East, but it also held forth an ever-promising escape for the worker, who, by virtue of its promise, adopted a petty bourgeois psychology instead of developing a proletarian one. Although the workers in the East felt the pressure of class subordination, the ever-stirring prospect of the West prevented their minds from becoming proletarianized in any lasting way. Even when they organized themselves into unions in the nineteenth century, it was under the banner of petty bourgeois demands and not proletarian ones that they fought. To this very day, as a matter of fact, the official labor movement in America is nothing more than a tail kite of the petty bourgeois movement.

It was the frontier, then, which produced not only an individualistic type of mind in its own domain, but which in turn affected the mind of America in every other domain, charging it with something of the same spirit. It is impossible to understand the American mind, the mind of the American masses, unless we can appreciate the verticalizing influence which the frontier factor exercised upon the general character of our life. Horace Greeley's admonition—"Go West, young man" had become part of the American creed long before it was uttered, and was believed in by workers as devoutly as by the petty bourgeoisie. Now the mistake which is often made is that of looking upon this belief as a myth or fiction. What we must realize is that that belief was based upon a reality as firm as the foundation of a skyscraper. It was not the mere existence of the frontier that perpetuated the faith in individualism, retarded the social organization of the workers, and prevented the sharp rigification of classes in America. It was only because the frontier actually *did provide those conditions necessary for the growth and continuation of individualism that individualism was changed from a philosophy into a religion.* If its promise had been merely an illusory one its influence would have been ephemeral. The frontier, with the wide areas of territory which it constantly opened up for new settlements, new towns, and new cities, afforded a spur to individualistic enterprise which spread from coast to coast. When we remember that in 1840, primarily as a result of the frontier, almost one-quarter of the total population of the United States was classified as land-owning, we can easily enough realize why the petty bourgeois ideology rooted itself so deeply into the mind of the nation. Moreover, because of the tremendous sweep of territory on the frontier, congestion could not swiftly occur, nor the individual be mowed down as readily by the machine. As a result of those factors, *individualism secured in America a foothold that it never acquired in any other country*—a foothold in the mind of the nation, as it were, rooting itself like a religion into the very essence of our culture.

In England, save for a brief period, individualism was primarily the property of the middle classes. It did not mean enough to the workers for them to adopt it as part of their philosophy. While before 1870 the English workers dallied with middle-class ideas, after 1870 that dalliance ceased. Before 1870, the frontier force had even played a part in English life. The frontier prospects of South Africa, and even of Australia and Canada, did not lose their appeal until the seventies. But even at their height of appeal they never exercised the influence over the English masses which the frontier force in America did over the American masses. The geographic disparities alone prevented that possibility. Only in America, as we have seen, and for the reasons which we have recounted, did individualism become a propelling motivation with the working class as well as with the bourgeoisie. It was that fact which made the American working class adopt a petty bourgeois philosophy of individualism instead of developing a proletarian philosophy of collectivism. It was that fact which made the workers think of themselves as potential bourgeoisie rather than as inevitable proletarians. It was that fact which made it possible for them to become wage-conscious without becoming class-conscious. It was that fact which made it possible for petty bourgeois ideals to become the embodiment of what is commonly described as American idealism.

II

It was this petty bourgeois idealism of the frontier, then, which provided the basic psychological determinant in our national ideology. It was the influence of that individualism which accomplished our release from European culture, undermined the force of the colonial complex, and laid the foundations for the development of an indigenous American culture.

But before we turn to the literary aspects of that culture, let us consider its religious background, for, as we have frequently stated in preceding chapters, it is in the form of religion that our culture reached its first focal point. The religious sects who populated the frontier regions were almost exclusively members of the various Dissenting denominations, particularly Baptists and Methodists. They were evangelical in type, and democratic in ecclesiastical conviction. Hating the theocratic dictatorship of the Massachusetts colony, the Baptists had made Rhode Island, which Roger Williams had founded in the name of religious liberty, their first centre of occupation. But the Baptists had made only limited gains in America prior to the middle of the eighteenth century. Although it was the coming of the Great Revival, gathered at first around the figure of Jonathan Edwards who later was to repudiate many of its more extravagant manifestations, which afforded the Baptist movement its first driving impetus, it was the frontier which gave it its great momentum.[1] The Methodists, who, like the Episcopalians, were almost wiped out in the East in consequence of their reactionary support of England during the Revolutionary War, also found the frontier the most fertile territory in which to spread their doctrines. In fact, it was only such doctrines as the Evangelical religions espoused that could have any appeal on the frontier.

What was there about the doctrines that these religions espoused which made them win such sweeping support in the West? In the first place, they were doctrines that in the East had represented the extremity of petty bourgeois independency of outlook, doctrines which appealed to the poorer elements in the population far more than to the wealthier.[2] The theocracy had stressed class divisions in church as well as in society; places in church had been determined by economic station; and authority had rested in the hands of the ecclesiastics and not in the hands of the individual members of the congregation. In other words, it was dictatorship and not democracy which prevailed. With the Baptists and Methodists, the situation was reversed. Appealing to the poorer

[1] William Warren Sweet: *Religion on the American Frontier* (The Baptists): New York, 1931: p. 18.
[2] Ibid., p. 17.

classes, these evangelical religions were overwhelmingly democratic in their emphasis. They threw their entire stress upon the individual and the right of the individual to salvation. They were not interested in theological differentiations and declarations. It was the inner reaction of the individual that counted, the inner vision of the soul which could perceive God and be saved. Redemption and salvation with these evangelical groups was far more of an emotional than an intellectual experience. There was nothing predestinate about their creeds, nothing Calvinistic; salvation was a matter of individual volition, attainable by all. The only test was individual faith, a faith which the individual could establish with his Maker without the intercession of an established clergy. It was emotional conviction and not theological purity in which they were interested. In their churches, therefore, the division between preacher and laymen was practically destroyed.[3] The qualities necessary to make a preacher revolved less about theological training than about religious emotions and insight. Men could become great preachers without theological study if they were religiously inspired. It was this belief that made it possible for lay preachers to become so instrumental in the spread of these doctrines—and for laymen to feel an intimacy, an intense, emotional intimacy, with their religions which had been impossible in the more theological creeds.

Now, it was just these individualistic, democratic, emotional aspects of the Baptists' and Methodists' creeds which made them capture the imagination of the frontiersmen.[4] To be sure, a considerable part of the frontier was settled by men and women who before they deserted the East were members of one or the other of those congregations, but the

[3]"Although I universally heard religion spoken of with 'respect' . . . yet they think much less of the necessity of a minister than the people of the North." (Timothy Flint: *Recollections of the Last Ten Years in the Valley of the Mississippi:* Boston, 1826: p. 76.)
[4]Even the Presbyterians, whose creedal origins were very different from those of the Baptists and Methodists, were forced to adopt the same attitudes and practices in the Western regions.

vast majority who joined them were converts made in the new territories. Those religions fulfilled a definite need in the virgin environment. They defended the cause of the frontiersman in politics,[5] lent validity to his economic form of existence and provided an outlet for his emotional life which otherwise, in surroundings as barren as those on the frontier, would have been pent-up and suppressed.

Indeed, the revivalistic type of Christianity created by the frontier,[6] running riot in every form of emotional extreme, and finding its anachronistic repercussions even to-day in the antics of the Holy Rollers, and the obscene theatrics of Billy Sunday, was a phenomenon which perhaps has never been seen elsewhere in the modern world.[7] It represented a form of religiosity in which the individual became a vital participant, in which he projected himself, plunged himself with primitive abandon. It provided him with a sesame to truth. It made him the divine possessor of a wisdom that no one else could rob him of, that no one else could surpass, for it was the wisdom of origins and ends, the wisdom that was greater than worldly wisdom, the wisdom that mundane minds, critics, scholars, professors, might attack but could never weaken or destroy. It was the possession of this wisdom, this inner light, which helped give the frontiersman his impregnable confidence, fortified his faith in himself as an individual, made him unashamed of his ignorance and illiteracy, and strengthened his scorn for the culture and punditry of the East. With this individual inner light to guide him, he could defy the rest of the world, defy reason, learning, science.

[5] William Warren Sweet: *Religion and the American Frontier:* New York, 1931: pp. 15, 16.

[6] "Protestant sects," stated Rusk, summarizing the whole tendency, "succeeded in the pioneer West in inverse ratio to their intellectual attainments and in direct ratio to their emotional appeal. R. L. Rusk: *The Literature of the Middle-Western Frontier:* New York, 1925: p. 18.

[7] The only other country in the modern world which provided any parallel was czaristic Russia. Along many stretches of the Russian frontier, the peasants were given to spasms of religiosity not unakin to those on our frontier. But the element of individualism which saturated frontier religion in America was undeveloped there.

This development of religiosity, of course, did not intensify in the West until the nineteenth century. In the eighteenth century, the frontier territory was still too sparsely settled to encourage the growth of sufficient communities in which the church could implant itself as an institution. In fact, as R. S. Cotterill has observed, in Kentucky in the eighteenth century there was a notable "absence of piety in the land." Less than one-tenth of the population in 1792 were church members.[8] Crevecœur related in his *Letters from an American Farmer* how, in the absence of a church and pastor, he had gathered the people in his vicinity into an improvised meeting-place, and preached to them himself in his own simple, humble way. On the extreme boundaries of the frontier, boundaries which were being steadily swallowed up into the interior as the population moved onward, religion did not penetrate at all, save as an individual frontiersman observed it in his hut or in the familial homestead.

After the Revolutionary War, however, when conditions on the coast became economically unstable, due in part to the closing of the ports of the British West Indies, and to the difficulties in trade which grew up between the new government and France and Spain, the prospect of the West became a compelling allurement. From that time on, the Westward migration became a force in the affairs of the nation, attracting hordes of pioneers who were determined to found new communities wherever they ventured. It was those communities, increasing in size as the migration continued, which made it possible for religion to grow and disseminate in the West, and finally to extend itself, through the agency of lay preacher as well as established cleric, into the remote places of the frontier.

While many of the pioneers set out to create a "new England of the West," as the Ohio Valley was described,[9] it was

---

[8] R. S. Cotterill: *History of Pioneer Kentucky:* Cincinnati, 1917: pp. 241–243.

[9] W. H. Venable: *Beginnings of Literary Culture in the Ohio Valley:* Cincinnati, 1891: p. 225.

really a new America which they founded. The intolerances of the East lost their meaning in the environment in which the possibility of control concentrating itself in the hands of a few was removed. Moreover, the individualistic, democratic tendencies of mind which the new conditions of life inevitably bred inspired divergence instead of unity of outlook. Where each individual was prone to think himself an authority, where it was the individual inner light which glowed within him and not the outer guiding light of church or state that determined his convictions, dissent was certain to prevail.[10] As a result, the religious history of the West soon became marked by the rise and fall of various sects, one more fantastic and hysterical than the other, and with the splits and divisions of those sects which survived in the struggle.[11] Within all sects, ranging from the Baptists, Methodists, Presbyterians, Campbellites, and Disciples of Jesus, to the Shakers, Groaners, Muggletonians, Come Outers, New Lights, and Mormons, this spirit of independence flared.[12] In no other country has religious liberty ever raced

[10] Indeed, it was in such a soil that the religious traditions of the Dissenters could root themselves with best success. (Thomas Cuming Hall: *The Religious Background of American Culture:* Boston, 1930: p. 170.)

[11] Terrified at the individualistic nature of frontier religions, many New England preachers advocated that missionaries be sent into the West in order to introduce "the social and religious principles of New England among them." Already, as a result of such superciliousness, the antagonism of the West to the East developed into an issue. In reply to the words of the New England clergymen the frontier periodical, *The Western Monthly Magazine,* discharged a sharp rejoinder:
"New England's desolate sons are called upon to go among the desolate population of the West for the purpose of sowing virtue in the minds of an ignorant generation. But they are to come not in a mass to excite an envious feeling—how kind! how philanthropic! to spare us the mortification of witnessing the concentrated brilliancy of a mass of cultivated intellects from the glowing East!" (*Western Monthly Magazine:* December, 1834, p. 655.)

[12] The Mormons constituted a conspicuous exception to that rule. Instead of organizing their communities in the haphazard devil-may-care manner which characterized most of the other Western communities, they pursued a plan of state socialism, and organized their life about a social instead of an individualistic pivot. Centralized control prevailed from the very beginning. Indeed, part of the opposition to the Mormon settlements grew out of this contradiction between their economic way of life and that of the rest of the frontier. To be certain, the differences re-

—or been able to race—to such wild and riotous extremes. The stamping and screaming preachers who populated the frontier, and who were noted for stripping off their upper garments, leaping out of their pulpits at times and clapping their hands in frenzy between sentences in their sermons,[13] constituted even less of a spectacle than their congregations which often exceeded them in their orgies of enthusiasm. Crooning congregations, moaning congregations, shaking congregations, jumping and howling congregations, rolling and wrestling congregations, were popular throughout the West. Camp meetings tumultuous with men and women swaying to strange macabre rhythms, stripped naked often as they were in the excitement of their ecstasy,[14] spread far west of the Mississippi. In a camp meeting of Presbyterians and Methodists held at Cain Ridge in August, 1801, thousands of people gathered for an extended service, lasting uninterruptedly for nearly a week. Over one thousand people fell as a result of the excitement and frenzy of preaching and singing.[15] No excess was too great to prevent these hysterically minded masses from exploiting it in pursuit of the religious experience. Religion consequently took on a militancy among these people which shattered almost every evidence of restraint. When emotion moved them, no matter how trivial the cause, sects and even new congregations split themselves

flected in religion, and even in moral concepts, were active elements also in the conflicts which arose between the Mormons and their neighbors. In the far West Brigham Young determined to irrigate the desert land, "believing that the close organization of the Mormon church (the central authority) could carry it through, whereas the individualistic and poor, typical farmers of the frontier, could not imitate it. As the colony grew through the arrival of converts, new sub-colonies were marked out, but they were not planted in the go-as-you-please manner of most frontier developments. Instead of this, the officers of the church made the reconnaissance, selected the state, and then told off enough of the members of each craft or line of business to make the venture a success." (Frederic L. Paxson: *History of the American Frontier:* Cambridge, Mass., 1924: p. 346.)

[13]Ibid., p. 180.

[14]Dorothy Anne Dondore: *The Prairie—and the Making of Middle America:* Cedar Rapids, Iowa, 1926: p. 176.

[15]R. L. Rusk: *Literature of the Middle-Western Frontier:* New York, 1925: p. 46.

asunder and set up new sects and new congregations.[16] The Presbyterians in Lexington, Kentucky, fought each other over a disagreement on psalmody[17] and split themselves in two as the result of the clash. The Society of Friends divided themselves into the orthodox and the Hicksians—the latter following the leadership of Elias Hicks.[18] The Baptists split themselves up into the Regular Baptists, the United Baptists, the Hard Shell Baptists, the Particular Baptists, the General Baptists, and the Primitive and Free Will Baptists. Feuds sprang up everywhere without the slightest provocation. Religious debates became a common occurrence. Various sects organized their own papers and periodicals which devoted most of their space to spreading their own propaganda and exposing that of their adversaries. In short, every means of defense and attack was exploited by these religionists in an attempt to establish their varied and conflicting creeds.

Without question it was the territorial factor which not only made these splits possible, but which also, paradoxically enough, established tolerance among them as a necessary principle. A majority movement could never force a minority to do its will in an environment where all the minority had to do was "to pick up stakes," as the American phrase of the time expressed it, and implant itself in another region where it could become the majority. Even on the New England frontier, it was the presence of that possibility which made the Puritans unable to establish their intolerance with unmitigated sway. When Roger Williams objected to the rule of the theocrats, he was not forced to endure it in silence, or to protest futilely against it as the Dissenters had done against their religious oppressors in the mother country. All

[16]"The worshippers split on trifling differences. The more trifling the more pertinaciously they cling to them, and where but a few Sabbaths before all seemed union, you soon find that all is discord." (Timothy Flint: *Recollections of the Last Ten Years in the Valley of the Mississippi*: Boston, 1826: p. 113.)

[17]W. H. Venable: *Beginnings of Literary Culture in the Ohio Valley*: Cincinnati, 1891: p. 225.

[18]Frederic L. Paxson: *History of American Frontier (1763–1893)*: Cambridge, Mass.: p. 342.

he had to do was to forsake the Massachusetts environment and move on to Rhode Island where he established his own colony, dedicated to that toleration which the Bay Colony had denied him. It was this possibility of the American environment that early created tendencies here which gave to the nation as a whole a cast that no other country possessed. But the possibilities on the New England frontier were small when compared with those on the ever-receding frontiers of the West. After all there were not scores of Rhode Islands or Connecticuts to occupy, for the cultivable territory in the East was severely limited. In the West, on the other hand, once the migration was in swing, the territorial possibilities which faced the pioneer were seemingly illimitable. Moreover, with such vast areas of fertile land staring them in the face, individual groups, armed against the Indians who very often could be placated instead of fought, had little fear in venturing forward into new regions, spurred on, as they were, more by economic hope than by religious conviction.

It was this lack of congestion, this lack of centralization, therefore, which saved the West from the early intolerances of the East. The individual groups that set up their own interpretation of divine truth in terms of their special religions would have been just as intolerant as the Puritans if they had had the chance! It was the environment alone which prevented their exercising such tyranny. And then, too, in addition to the physical environment, there was the fact that while the inhabitants of the West were "emigrants from all quarters of the Union, and from different parts of Europe," as B. Drake and E. D. Mansfield observed, "yet there (was) no portion of them from any particular district so numerous as to cause a general adherence to the peculiar prejudices and manners in which they have been educated."[19]

It was this individualism, then, this petty bourgeois individualism of the small farmer, which came to stand as

[19] B. Drake and E. D. Mansfield: *Cincinnati in 1826*: Cincinnati, 1827: p. 88.

the symbol for the West. It was this individualism which gave character to western economics, to western politics, to western religion—and, as we shall see, to western literature. It was this untrammelled petty bourgeois individualism, and not the upper bourgeois individualism which prevailed in the East and was dominant in Europe, that made Emerson declare that "in all my lectures, I have taught one doctrine, namely, the infinitude of the private man." It was this unalloyed petty bourgeois individualism, which was able to flourish in a land "where men of leisure and fortune are few or none"; where there were "neither St. Georges, St. Andrews, St. Patricks, nor New England societies to foster those prejudices in favor of distant lands"; where "an entire freedom from political restraint favors the assimilation of all classes to each other";[20] and where "wealth is moreover pretty equally distributed . . . and industry, temperance, morality, and love of gain"[21] are the governing virtues—it was that petty bourgeois individualism of the West, built upon a structure of agrarian economy, which stamped itself into the American mind and created the first signs of an American pattern.

III

By way of recapitulation, then, it was this petty bourgeois individualism of the frontier which provided the basic psychological determinant in our national ideology. It was the influence of that individualism which accomplished our release from European culture, undermined the force of the colonial complex, and laid the foundation for an indigenous American culture.

Fortunately, there is abundant evidence to-day to show that many American writers in the East in the nineteenth century were not unaware of the importance of the frontier as an emancipating influence. Emerson early showed that he

[20]Ibid., p. 88.
[21]George W. Ogden: *Letters from the West:* New Bedford, 1823: p. 92.

understood what was going on when he declared that "America begins with the Alleghanies." New England was not America; the South was not America—they were but slices of Europe transplanted in a new country. The West was America, the real genuine America which was unique, fresh, spontaneous. Such was the meaning of Emerson's words. N. P. Willis saw in the frontier the great hope of the American literature of the future. "Give us five years of the home tide of sympathy that is now setting westward," he wrote, "and we will have an American literature that will forever prevent the public taste and patronage from ebbing back to England."[22] Envisioning in the West that Divine Democracy which he unrestingly extolled throughout his life, Walt Whitman was moved to write, "Solitary, singing in the West, I strike up a new world." All these men and many other of their contemporaries sensed in the West, then, the development of a great force; a force which would revolutionize the foundations of our culture, and create a new America—more, a new world.

This was indeed a Golden Day of aspiration for the intellectual enthusiasts of the time. Hope pulsed through their prophecies; optimism became their accepted creed. The belief in the common man, which had been disavowed by the upper bourgeoisie, became a revived faith. They created, as Lewis Mumford described it, these Emersons, Whitmans, and Thoreaus, "an heroic conception of life."[23] Overwhelmed by the spectacle of a West which was created by men and women of common stock, of obscure heritage, men and women who made the soil their own, ploughed it, fertilized it, populated it in the beginning with huts, cabins, and crude homesteads and then with villages, towns, and cities, these literary men of the East saw in this spectacle, this intrepid undertaking of the average man, the promise of a great future for the human race. It filled them with renewed hope, charged them with fresh vision. It provided them with a

[22]*The Prose Works of Nathaniel P. Willis*: Philadelphia, 1852: p. 701.
[23]Lewis Mumford: *The Golden Day*: New York, 1926: p. 90.

living faith in the potentialities of man as an individual. Individual man in their eyes became a creative force. His place was in the centre and not on the periphery of things. He was a cause and not an effect—a cause which could create whatever effects it desired. He was free to make his own future, free to serve his own destiny.

It was this anarcho-individualism, born of the frontier, which constituted the essence of what Mr. Mumford has called "an heroic conception of life." In fact, as we shall see later on, it was this anarcho-individualism, in recent days more familiarly known as rugged individualism, which came to characterize the spirit of the American creed. With the exception of Whitman no one in the East responded to this force so consciously and so completely as Emerson. Indeed, we can say that the centrehood of Emerson's philosophy was a direct outgrowth of the frontier force. The so-called "heroic conception of life," ascribed to Emerson, was a "pure product of the frontier."[24] In truth, it was those elements in his philosophy which were not derived from the influence of the frontier, those springing that is from European and Oriental origins, which muddled his mind and confused his logic. Furthermore, we can be definitely certain to-day that those ideas of Emerson which influenced American thought and which continue to attract American intellectuals to-day, are those which were inspired by the frontier and not by foreign sources. His optimism, his eloquent defense of democracy, his belief in the individual, his stress upon personal independence and self-reliance, were all generated in his mind by the impact of the frontier.

[24]In the case of Emerson we are faced with another of those interesting contradictions among American literati in the nineteenth century. One of the most ardent nativists, emphasizing constantly the importance of America's signing its Declaration of Literary Independence, and responding as enthusiastically as he did to the American elements in the frontier, Emerson was as much influenced by the colonial complex the moment he turned to the field of creative literature, an influence conspicuous in almost every line of his verse, as he was not influenced by it in his critical conceptions. Whitman alone at that time, as we noted in the first chapter, was able to effect a revolt in the creative field as well as in the critical.

While in his earlier years Emerson had expressed a preference for aristocracy,[25] and later on had become even dubious of his democratic convictions, as when he saw the frontier in action during the Jackson administrations, in the main he stuck by his faith in man as an individual. It was this faith and this belief, rooted in the moving spirit of the frontier, which endowed Emerson's philosophy with those heroic proportions that have engaged the admiration of so many critics in the last few generations. But let us see out of just what materials the heroic elements in Emerson's philosophy sprang. In the first place, they sprang out of his belief in the individual's power to achieve, to work out his own destiny, notwithstanding the nature of society or environment. His faith in "the infinitude of the private man," translating itself upon other occasions into the statement that "man is stronger than a city," and again in his open declaration that "it is only as a man puts off all foreign support and stands alone that I see him to be strong and to prevail. He is weaker by every recruit to his banner. Is not a man better than a town? Ask nothing of man, and, in the endless mutation, thou only firm column must presently appear the upholder of all that surrounds thee"—it was this faith in man the individual, this faith in the individual isolated from society, the individual independent of society, a concentrated personal integer, as it were, that endowed his doctrine with the

[25] "Aristocracy is a good sign. It must be everywhere. 'Twere the greatest calamity to have it abolished." (*Works*, I, p. 311.) While Emerson wrote this in his early twenties, at other times he recurred to the same idea, as when he described "majorities (as) the argument of fools, the strength of the weak." (*Journals*, Vol. VII, p. 148.) These expressions of aristocratic temper, however, were not common in Emerson. They represented the influence of the East upon him—and also the effects of his ideas when he actually saw them in practice, as during the administrations of Jackson and Van Buren. In that sense he reminds one very much of many of the revolutionaries in czarist Russia, who, when they saw a revolution in reality, became horrified, and who, because they were not prepared for the ruthless tasks of carrying a revolution to its inevitable conclusion, became the most bitter opponents of the Bolsheviki who put the revolution into actual practice and made it work. It was much easier for Emerson, or let us say, for the Mensheviki, to defend democracy or revolution while they remained concepts, than it was to accept them when they saw them in operation, in the flesh, as it were.

spirit of challenge. If Carlyle spoke through Emerson's *great man* theory, it was the frontier, with its trumpetings of petty bourgeois individualism and independence, which voiced itself in Emerson's panegyrics on self-reliance. But Emerson's beliefs in this connection were based upon forces which were far more material than spiritual. Emerson understood the practical philosophy of the petty bourgeoisie much better than most of his critics have realized; and he above all others of his time, understood the meaning and basis of this philosophy in terms of the frontier. "Prudent men have begun to see that every American should be educated with a view to the value of land," he avowed, and later on added that "I think we must regard the land as a commanding and increasing power on the citizen, the sanative and Americanizing influence, which promises to disclose new virtues for ages to come." The frontier had opened up possibilities for the individual which European life had never disclosed; the frontier had given the individual a chance to possess land, to possess power as an individual owner, and to turn that possession and power to his own individual advantage. It was those possibilities which Emerson saw realized, and came into intimate, lifelike contact with on his lecture tours in the western regions; it was those possibilities which infused his belief in the individual with dynamic conviction, and convinced him that the road to security and happiness lay in the possession of the land by private individuals who could exploit it for their personal gain. It was this petty bourgeois philosophy of individual possession which he believed in and encouraged; it was this petty bourgeois conception of life which made him suspicious of social movements, distrustful of all forms of social organization, and an open scoffer at the social philosophy of the Utopian Owenists and Fourierists as well as an implicit enemy of the scientific socialism of Marx.[26] "I am afraid that in the formal arrange-

[26]While it is doubtful whether Emerson knew anything of the works of Marx or the Marxian socialists, there can be no question that if he had, the whole direction of his philosophy would have made him their instant opponent.

ments of the socialists," he wrote in reference to the application of the doctrines of Owen and Fourier, "the spontaneous
sentiment of any thoughtful man will find that poetry and
sublimity still cleave to the solitary house." Emerson did not
want the land socialized—neither in the sense that the members of the New Harmony colony at that time desired nor
in the sense that the Soviet Union is carrying into effect to-
day. "Concert," Emerson was irrevocably convinced, "is
neither better nor worse, neither more nor less potent than
individual force. All the men in the world cannot make a
statue walk and speak, cannot make a drop of blood, or a
blade of grass, any more than one man can." Indeed, Emerson extended the petty bourgeois philosophy of the frontier
to its farthest anarchical extreme, extolling at times attitudes
that were as definitely antisocial in their implications as the
activities of the frontiersmen who early defied every semblance of state, authority, and tradition. "Hence, the less
government we have, the better," Emerson wrote, defending
the laissez-faire principle of the bourgeoisie, "the fewer laws,
and the less confided power. The antidote to this abuse of
formal government is, the influence of private character, the
growth of the Individual." In fact, without wishing it, Emerson gave sanction by virtue of his doctrines to every type of
exploitation which the frontier encouraged. "A man," he
contended, "contains all that is needful to his government
within himself. He is made a law unto himself. All real good
or evil that can befall him must be from himself." Eternally
then, Emerson's stress is upon self, the individual self, the
personal ego. Society can take care of itself, or go hang, as
the frontiersman would have put it. It is the individual who
must be stressed, the individual who must learn to stand
alone, and become sufficient within himself. But, as we said
before, Emerson kept his eye upon the earth far more than
he has been given credit for doing, especially by those critics
who have erroneously traced the underlying substance of his
doctrines to European instead of to American sources,[27] and

[27]One of the best correctives of that interpretation of Emerson's phi-

he knew that without the land-promise of the frontier all talk of self-reliance and self-sufficiency would be without meaning. Seldom did Emerson's eye lose sight of the land and its promise of a petty bourgeois Utopia. "Though the wide universe is full of good, no kernel of nourishing corn can come to him," Emerson asserted, *"but through his toil bestowed on that plot of ground which is given him to till."* Every man, in other words, must have his own ground to cultivate, every man must be responsible to himself for the cultivation of that ground—and for the cultivation of himself.

Even Emerson's religious ideas were permeated by the influence of the frontier. The same petty bourgeois individualism which attained such flagrant expression in frontier religions, where Dissent was carried to its farthermost pole of revolt, received its philosophic justification in Emerson's exaltation of individual insight and truth. While the defense of individual faith as superior to ecclesiastical wisdom had originally grown out of the Reformation, and had become a cardinal doctrine of Dissent, it had seldom if ever advanced to the point of individualistic exaggeration which it achieved in the religious philosophy of Emerson and in the religious practice of the frontiersman. Emerson justified entirely the frontiersman's stress upon the superiority of the religious intuition of the individual to the wisdom congealed in the theological dogmas or ecclesiastical organizations. "God builds his temple," he averred, "in the heart of the ruins of churches and religions." It was the sacredness of the individual and not the so-called holy authority of the church which interested and moved him. "The faith that stands on authority is not faith," he maintained, for "nothing is at last sacred but the integrity of your own mind. Absolve you to yourself, and you shall have the suffrage of the world. No law can be sacred to me but that of my own nature." In these

losophy is to be found in Professor Ernest Marchand's superlatively fine study of *Emerson and the Frontier* which was published in *American Literature*, Vol. III, No. 2, May, 1931, pp. 149–174.

words Emerson voiced the religious spirit of the petty bourgeois frontiersman. In agreement with the frontier religionists he was firmly convinced that "the reliance on authority
measures the decline of religion, the withdrawal of the soul."

But Emerson's response to the frontier force was not the
reaction of an individual who knew by intuition what was
going on in the remote territories to the west of him, and
then tried to re-embody that intuitive knowledge in philosophic form. On the contrary, Emerson's response was that
of a man who witnessed what he interpreted, who saw and
felt the changes in life which occurred at the time, and who,
out of personal experience as well as philosophic contemplation, transmuted what he saw and felt into genuine literature.[28] From 1850 to 1870 he went into the West in person,
as a lyceum-lecturer, and came into intimate contact with life
in those regions, experienced its hardships, and met and con-
versed with its people. His Journals are replete with references to his reactions to the West, and the experiences he
underwent there. In the impending mud of the prairies,
where, as he wrote, "it rains and thaws incessantly," and
where his "chamber was a cabin," he nevertheless anticipated the birth of something new, a new race of men, with
new concepts and new principles. "In the prairie," he maintained, with an enthusiasm that characterized the spirit of
his time, "we are new men just come and must not stand for
trifles."[29] In time he came to know most of the country east
of the Rockies, slept in homely hotels and taverns in the
Ohio regions, travelled upon the crudely constructed railroads of the day, the first to line the West, resorted to wag-
ons and sleighs when those railroads broke down, watched
towns spring into cities, witnessed booms in the process of
becoming, investigated newly sunk mines, mingled with

[28]Of course, many of Emerson's essays revealing frontier influence were
written before he ever went West, and were indirect rather than direct
products of western influence.
[29]For many quotations in this immediate connection, I am directly indebted to Professor Marchand's study of *Emerson and the Frontier*—the
articles to which I referred before in an earlier footnote.

farmers and business men, and all in all came closer to understanding the life of the West than any other Easterner of his period. His comments on towns which expanded into cities with breath-taking swiftness, on the sudden growth of population over the country as a whole, on the ease with which the individual could acquire wealth in those vast, uncongested domains, and the security with which men and women could look to the soil for their sustenance, reflected his appreciation and understanding of the economic and psychological meaning of the frontier process. While Carlyle in a letter to Emerson in 1835 had shrewdly observed that "blessed are you where what jargoning soever there be at Washington, the poor man shoulders his axe, and walks into the Western Woods, sure of a nourishing Earth and an overarching Sky! It is verily the Door of Hope to distracted Europe; which otherwise I should see crumbling down into blackness of darkness," Emerson realized what Carlyle could not foresee, namely, that the West was not only an escape for the downtrodden and oppressed, but, more than that, it was the source of a new America, in culture as well as in economics. Hostile as he was at times to the Jacksonians, not hesitating to describe them often in the most denigratory fashion, he did not close his vision to the fact that these frontiersmen "heedless of English and all literature—a stone cut out of the ground without hands—may root out the hollow dilettantism of our cultivation in the coarsest way, and the newborn may begin again to frame their own world with great advantage." That in an economic sense the West had also created the possibility of the making of a new American Emerson asserted upon many occasions. He saw full well that the frontier had communicated to America the "general conviction . . . that every young man of good faculty and good habits can by perseverance attain to an adequate estate; if he have a turn for business, and a quick eye for the opportunities which are always offering for investment, he can come to wealth, and in such good season as to enjoy as well as transmit it." It was out of the consciousness of that conviction, out of the petty bourgeois promise which it conveyed, that his doctrines of self-sufficiency, self-reliance and self-dependence were engendered. In fact, he was not unconscious of the connection himself. His own words are sufficient proof of that fact. While the whole country had tended to breed the "wonderful personal independence" of individualism, it was particularly the West, Emerson was convinced, "where a man is made a hero by the varied emergencies of his lonely farm" that brought into relief the "presence of mind, self-reliance, and hundred-handed activity" which had come to be known as singularly American. Moreover, Emerson understood that American individualism, the extreme type of which he philosophically extolled, was born out of the "paucity of the population, the vast extent of the territory, and the solitude of each family and each man" . . . and recognized the fact that so long as the individual could declare that "here in the clam-banks and the beech and chestnut forests, I shall take leave to breathe and think freely. If you do not like it, if you molest me, I can cross the brook and plant a new state out of reach of anything but squirrels and wild pigeons," he could never be subordinated by state or society. Only in such an environment could his petty bourgeois propensities be allowed full freedom. Taking the stand Emerson did, it was inevitable that he should recommend the individual to "do what he can" for "every one must seek to secure his independence," thus leaving out of consideration the matter of social consequences—the disastrous effects of which we are only beginning to realize to-day—and to declare that each individual man "was created to augment some real value, and (for himself) not for a speculator." It was out of this America, then, out of the teeming plenty of the country and the vast promise of its resources, that Emerson derived his conception of self-reliance. Although he gave to the concept the spiritual character of a philosophic principle, his own words, as we showed before, revealed its concrete origin in materials overwhelmingly earthy and economic. In his essay on *The Fortune of the Republic*, he made especial note of the fact that "in proportion to the personal ability of each man he feels the invitation and career which the country opens to him. He is easily fed with wheat and game, with Ohio wine, but his brain is also pampered with finer draughts, by political power and by the power in the railroad board, in the mills, or the banks. *This elevates his spirits and gives, of course, an easy self-reliance.*" (Italics mine.) In a word, the philosophic idealism embodied in the doctrine of self-reliance was but a subtle camouflage, however unconscious, for the petty bourgeois materialism which was concealed beneath its inspiration.

Influenced as Emerson's doctrines were, then, by the spirit of the frontier, and sympathetic as he was toward the possibilities of individual man, even the common man, his attitudes toward the frontier in action, as we indicated in an earlier paragraph, and toward the power and purpose of wealth, were subject to those contradictions which were not unnatural in a man, who could never entirely escape the Brahmin traditions of New England in which he had been bred, and who was unalterably convinced, as Philips Russell well expressed it, that "he was only an inspirer and distributor of ideas . . . incapable of putting them into practice."[30] It can be said without exaggeration, I believe, that Emerson's belief in the common man as an abstraction was thoroughly sincere; it was when that common man arose in his might, and, in the election of a frontier president, emerged from an ideal abstraction into a crude reality, that Emerson became alarmed, and was moved to defend caste against mass, and side with the upper bourgeoisie against the petty bourgeoisie. At one time he asserted, in his lecture, *Man the Reformer,* that "the whole interest of history lies in the fortunes of the poor," that "the state must consider the poor man, and all voices must speak for him," and at another that he was happy to affirm that "ours is the country of poor men. Here is practical democracy; here is the human race poured out over the continent to do itself justice; all mankind in its

[30]Philips Russell: *Emerson:* New York, 1929: p. 196.

shirt-sleeves; not grimacing like poor men in cities, pretending to be rich, but unmistakably taking off its coat to hard work, when labor is sure to pay." At still other times he voiced his open admiration for the lowly farmer; "men of endurance—deep-chested, long-winded, tough, slow and sure, and timely." When these frontier democrats threatened to carry out the very virtues of self-reliance and self-independence which he had advocated, however, he denounced them as "rank rabble," and berated their political activities as cheap, tawdry, and vulgar. It was at such moments, and those closely akin, that he made his manifest defense of the wealthy classes. "The mass are animal," he decided, "in a state of pupilage, and nearer the chimpanzee." It is the upper class which "should possess and dispense the goods of the world," for, he added, in words suggestive of the apologists for the wealthy classes to-day, "the consideration the rich possess in all societies is not without meaning or right. *It is the approval given by the human understanding to the act of creating value by knowledge and labor.*" (Italics mine.) It is obvious, then, that Emerson's social outlook was not an unmixed one. Possessed at one time of a fortune of over $22,000, and caught by contradictions within his own nature which rendered him unable to carry out the doctrines which he preached, it is not surprising that he should have become agitated at the prospect of having his own security destroyed by masses which he might have extolled in theory but which he could not abide in practice. In theory, Emerson was an undoubted ally of the petty bourgeois elements on the frontier; in practice, however, at least in times of seeming seriousness, he took his stand on the side of the upper bourgeoisie.

It was as prophet of the petty bourgeoisie, however, that Emerson served his great function. He gave its material objectives philosophic formulation and justification. But further than that, he saw in its struggle in the West the coming of something new, the forging of a new America. He perceived more clearly than most of his contemporaries the meaning of the West, and the emancipating effect it would have upon our national culture. He hailed the influence which he was certain the West would have upon our literary outlook, and realized that it would be through its agency that we would be able to escape from the bondage of the colonial complex.

In description of the East, Emerson stated: "We all lean on England, scarce a verse, a page, a newspaper, but is writ in imitation of English forms; our very manners and conversation are traditional, sometimes the life seems dying out of literature, and this enormous paper currency of Words is accepted instead." Only the West, he believed, could provide us with something new, something our own, something original. In *The American Scholar*, he directed the attention of his contemporaries to the new movement which he prophesied would endow America with cultural orginality:

. . . the same movement which effected the elevation of what was called the lowest class in the state, assumed in literature a very marked and as benign an aspect. Instead of the sublime and the beautiful, the near, the low, the common was explored and poetized. That which had been negligently trodden under foot by those who were harnessing and provisioning themselves for long journeys into far countries, is suddenly found to be richer than all foreign parts. The literature of the poor, the feelings of the child, the philosophy of the street, the meaning of household life, are the topics of the time. It is a great stride. It is a sign—is it not? of new vigour, when the extremities are made active, when the currents of warm life run into the hands and feet. I ask not for the great, the remote, the romantic; what is doing in Italy, or Arabia; what is Greek art, or Provençal minstrelsy; I embrace the common, I explore and sit at the feet of the familiar, the low. Give me insight into to-day, and you may have the antique and future worlds.

It was only the West, therefore, Emerson recognized, with its emphasis upon American things instead of European things, which would make it possible for us to sever our slavish allegiance from Europe. "We have listened too long to the courtly muses of Europe," Emerson asseverated, and upon another occasion added: "our Religion, our Education, our Art look abroad, (as) does our spirit of society"—but such could not continue, he maintained, if we were ever to become a people in our own right. "The millions that around us are rushing into life," he pointed out, with his finger stretched toward the West, "cannot always be fed on the sore remains of foreign harvests." In the introduction to *Nature*, he reiterated the same challenge:

> The foregoing generations behold God and Nature face to face; we through their eyes. Why should not we also enjoy an original relation to the universe? Why should not we have a poetry and philosophy of insight and not of tradition, and religion by revelation to us, and not the history of theirs. . . . Why should we grope among the dry bones of the past? . . . There are new lands, new men, new thoughts. Let us demand our own work and laws and worship.

It was the West, then, with its illimitable possibilities for the individual, its predication of a new America, that fortified Emerson's belief in the future of the country and its people. It should be so easy for America, he observed, in his essay on *The Young American*, "to inspire and express the most expensive and humane spirit; new born, free, healthful, strong, the land of the laborer, of the democrat, of the philanthropist, of the believer, of the saint."

But Emerson did not stand alone in his convictions. He was not a solitary giant living out of tune with his time. "Greek head on right Yankee shoulders," as Lowell had characterized him in his *Fable for Critics*, he transmuted so successfully his Platonic idealism into realistic American form, spiritualizing thus what was so crudely material, that it was not long before he became the dominant philosopher of the epoch. Indeed, contrary to the common belief, the whole Transcendentalist movement, of which Emerson was the most striking incarnation, was based upon this same subtle combination of idealistic background with materialistic motivation.[31] Emerson's conception of Transcendentalism, there-

---

[31] Lucy Lockwood Hazard in her book, *The Frontier in American Literature* (New York, 1927), has an excellent chapter dealing with the materialistic logic which underlay the Transcendentalist philosophy.

fore, as well as that of the other Transcendentalists, was not, as many critics have contended,[32] purely imitative in character. In truth, it was more native than foreign in the source of its impulse. The Platonic world, which Emerson said he "might have learned to treat as a cloudland" had he not met Alcott who made it "as solid as Massachusetts to (him)," was nothing more than a poetic smoke-screen behind which he was able to conceal the practical character of his philosophic principles. Not that Emerson was aware of that fact. Obviously, he was not, or he could not have gone on with his work. Emerson, to be sure, was not the only philosopher who employed that device. As a matter of fact, it was just that device which has vitiated so much of social philosophy. By retreating to a world of abstractions, by basing one's principles upon *absolute* realities, one is more easily able to escape the practical implications of one's logic. The Transcendentalist movement in America profited by just that device.[33] Arising out of the changing environment of the time, responding as it did to the individualistic impulse which, accelerated by the spirit of the frontier, swept over America like a predatory invader, it obscured its immediate identity by ascribing its origins to the ancient past. Plato, Plotinus, Proclus, Kant, all played their part in giving metaphysical and mystical form to its credo. With Alcott, it was the mystical element provided by Plotinus and Proclus which afforded him the chief inspiration of his ethics.[34] With Emerson, it was Cudworth, Berkeley, and Kant as well as Plato who supplied in the main his transcendentalist ammunition. Regardless of what their specific philosophic sources were, and regardless of how remote their concepts may have seemed from the life of that day, they absorbed, these Tran-

[32] Woodbridge Riley: *American Philosophy*: New York, 1907: p. 12.

[33] For contrasting opinions, see Frothingham's *Transcendentalism in New England* (1876) and George W. Cooke's *Poets of Transcendentalism: An Anthology with an Introductory Essay* (1903)—and also his *An Historical and Biographical Introduction to Accompany The Dial* (1902).

[34] *American Literature*, Vol. III, No. 1, March, 1931. Austin Warren, article entitled: *The Orphic Sage: Bronson Alcott*: pp. 1–13.

scendentalists, by a kind of intellectual osmosis, that very life which they affected to transcend, and reflected in their conclusions the practical consequences of that life rather than the immaterial and spiritual consequences of their dialectic. While the "Transcendental Club" was organized, as Bronson Alcott declared, "because its members imagined the senses did not contain the mind,"[35] in refutation of the Lockian conception of the sensory origin of knowledge, the ideas which grew out of its discussions, and out of *The Dial* which it inspired, had less to do with absolute principles than with concrete and mutable realities. Emerson's unforgettable aphorism: "hitch your wagon to a star," came far closer to the kernel of his philosophy—and that of most of the transcendentalists—than any of his muddled observations on "the over soul." Even Alcott, who was an emanationist, of Plotinian extraction, and a far less practical man than Thoreau, Ripley, Parker, or Emerson, was swayed by the chaotic clash of events which bestirred America at that time. The influence of frontier individualism penetrated into the most exalted heaven of his Plotinian fastness, and filled it with the smell and impact of earth. His words: "Where is the individual who boldly dares assert opinions differing with pre-established notions—dares to think for himself? . . . Dare to be singular; let others deride," could have been written by Emerson as easily as by himself. His defense of self-reliance, his contempt for institutions, his belief in progress, his optimism, manifested in his reaction to the America of his day: "Yes, even here, we find progress. . . . 'Tis no time to doubt. Indeed, is it not time for the liveliest hope?"—all these reflected the earthy reality of his doctrines once they were translated into action. In one way, however, Alcott did differ from Emerson and most of the Transcendentalists; that was in his advocacy of the socialization instead of the individualization of personality. In his Fruitlands experiment, he endeavored to put into effect his social ideas, fan-

[35] A. Bronson Alcott: "Conversation" on the Transcendental Club and *The Dial*. (Reprinted in *American Literature*, Vol. III, No. 1, March, 1931, p. 14.)

tastic and futile though they were. Influenced by the Utopian socialist ideas of the period, which Emerson, we should not forget, had repudiated, Alcott managed to escape enough of the seductions of the individualistic philosophy, at least in its wilder extremes, to see through its shams and to be cognizant of its consequences. In one of his "conversations" before the Transcendental Club, he delivered himself of several observations on this score which show how well he understood certain of the dangers which inhered in the individualist philosophy:

That tendency of our teaching, a good deal has been rather to favor individualism—to confirm the student or inquirer in what was peculiar to himself, more than to lead himself forth into what belongs to all mankind. . . . We are so very individual that we meet with difficulty. . . . Well, very good, if we can at last get free of our individuality, and become persons indeed—partake that which unites and relates us to one another. I suppose that all doctrines, heretofore, have been aiming at that; but, unfortunately, they dropped out the mother word. Socialism was an attempt to bring men together into institutions, but it was found, by those who undertook it, that men were too individual, and the success has not warranted the outlay. Each person has taken away in his own culture the fruit of his own experiment, but is left alone, where he was before he entered, in a great measure.

In other places, to be certain, he revealed the same individualistic tendency which he deplored in the foregoing "conversation." Like most of the transcendentalists Alcott's philosophy was caught up in a mesh of confusion and contradictions. He was overwhelmed by the world which confronted him, a world in which everything was in a sea of flux, in which tiny wires suddenly were made into the conductors of great energy, in which inert metals were made into moving machines, and in which all values were juggled about in a state of chaos, the new becoming old before it had a chance to crystallize and mellow. Trying to find oneself in that world, as the transcendentalists primarily tried to do, was like trying to poise a stone in midair. It is no wonder, then, that Alcott and his transcendentalist friends turned to the past for anchor; it is no wonder that they seized upon Plato, Plotinus, and Kant for intellectual stability, for it was only by such a retreat that they could establish the illusion of permanence. The confusion in their logic arose out of their unhappy attempt to reconcile their philosophy with the world in which they lived. Had they remained in their neo-Platonic towers of contemplation, they might have escaped that confusion and retained a form of consistency in their argument. Descending to the earth as they did, however, was too much for them, and, as a result, their logic lost all trace of consistency and betrayed them into contradictions upon every occasion. Faced by this fact, they had no other recourse but to justify their contradictions on the basis of individualistic principle. While Alcott erected no such defense, Emerson and Whitman supplied it for him. "Why drag about this corpse of your memory," Emerson wrote, "lest you contradict somewhat you have stated in this or that public place? Suppose you should contradict yourself; what then?" Whitman, of course, as is well known, surpassed Emerson in that respect, and gave the whole attitude a poetic and almost Olympian turn in his lines:

> "Do I contradict myself?
> Very well, then, I contradict myself."

Thoreau at least, despite his belief that we changed from day to day, was consistent in that he practised what he preached. Of all his contemporaries, he was the only one to extend to its ultimate extreme the revolt of the "transcendentalist individual." In truth, it can be said that Thoreau represented the zenith of the individualistic revolt of his day. He did not extol the sufficiency of the individual, stress the significance of self-reliance, and rhapsodize about the inspiration of the lonely solitudes where man could become intimate with himself, and then, as did Emerson, live in an urban environment where he could seldom be alone and where he was dependent upon society for the fulfillment of his needs, and relied upon other individuals, servants of the house as well as of the state, instead of upon himself for sustenance and sufficiency. No; Thoreau, whatever else may be said against him, was a greater idealist than that. He carried his beliefs into action. In a sense, he was the best individual product of that petty bourgeois ideology of the frontier which captured the minds of so many of the literati of his day; for while he never became social-minded, he never became interested, on the other hand, in the acquisition of property, never built up a small fortune and never speculated in stocks as Emerson did,[36] or built and sold houses as did Whitman in his early thirties.[37] To the very end, he remained faithful to his convictions. Confirmed in his belief that he had "found nothing so truly impoverishing as what is called wealth," and convinced that to "inherit property is not to be born—to be still-born rather," he organized his life in such a humble way that it was impossible for wealth to come his way and vitiate his impulse. When he declared that he "must not lose any of (his) freedom by being a farmer and landholder" and advised men to "cultivate poverty like sage, like a garden herb," he did it as one who lived as he wrote and urged.

In his retreat in Walden, Thoreau came closer than any one in his age to putting into effect the doctrine of self-reliance which his friend Emerson preached and which most of his transcendentalist contemporaries advocated. There he achieved the comparatively untrammelled individual freedom which others talked about but never attained. Absurd as Thoreau's retreat may strike many to-day, it must be admitted that it was but a rational outcome of the individualistic philosophy which the frontier had inspired. If Emerson and others had literally believed in practising what they preached they would have followed Thoreau to the woods—and to jail. Emerson, however, preferred to remain the "seeing

---

[36] Philips Russell, op. cit., pp. 192–6; and *Journals:* Vol. IV, p. 122.
[37] John Addington Symonds: *Life of Walt Whitman:* London, 1893: p. 23.

eye" but not "the working hand." Emerson loathed the crushing weight of institutions and the interfering power of the state; he maintained that "no law (could) be sacred to (him) but that of (his) nature"; but in the last analysis he preferred compromising with the state to fighting it. Thoreau's remarkable reply to Emerson, when the latter visited him in jail, where he had been confined for carrying out his doctrines to their ultimate conclusion by refusing to pay the poll-tax which the state had imposed upon him, reflected the difference between the two men at once:

> *Emerson:* Henry, what are you doing in there?
> *Thoreau:* Waldo, what are you doing out there?

It was the same clear-cut logic, the same direct application of doctrine to life, which made Thoreau go to Walden in an attempt to fence himself off from society and live as an *individual*—a self-reliant, self-sufficient, self-perfected individual. If later events have tended to make Thoreau appear a little ludicrous, behaving and living as he did, we should remember that it is really not Thoreau but his doctrine that has come to look ludicrous. Emerson was saved from that ludicrousness because he never tried out what he advised, because he never tested what he taught. If there was a Quixotic element about Thoreau, it was the Quixoticism of the extremist—the man who, refusing to compromise, dauntlessly follows his logic where it leads.

If Emerson transmuted the petty bourgeois individualism of the frontiersman into philosophic doctrine, Thoreau tested that doctrine in practice. He opposed the state, despised the law, and scorned tradition—in action as well as in speech. "The man for whom law exists—the man of forms, the conservative," Thoreau wrote, "is a tame man." "A free-spoken man of sound lungs," he declared upon another occasion, "cannot draw a long breath without causing your rotten institutions to come toppling down by the vacuum he makes. Your church is a baby-house made of blocks and so of the state. . . . I will not consent to walk with my mouth muzzled, not till I am rabid, until there is danger that I shall bite the unoffending and that my bite will produce hydrophobia." But Thoreau did not confine the venom of his attacks to the church and the state. "The school, the magazine, think they are liberal, free! It is the freedom of the prison-yard. I ask only that one fourth part of my honest thoughts be spoken aloud. . . . Look at your editors of popular magazines. I have dealt with two or three of the most liberal of them. They are afraid to print a whole sentence, a round sentence, a free-spoken sentence. They want to get thirty thousand subscribers, and they will do anything to get them. They consult the D.D.'s and all the letters of the alphabet before printing a sentence."

Stinging words, those, quick with the dynamite of revolt —the revolt of an individual against the oppression of the society in which he lived. But they are more than that; they are also the words of an individual who believes in himself, in the possibilities which live in him, and also in the possibilities of individual man once he is freed from the fetters of society and the state. In an exalted way they expressed the spirit of the petty bourgeois frontiersman who hated the state because it taxed him, and who hated society because, dominated as it then was on the coast by the upper bourgeoisie and the plantation aristocracy, it thwarted his freedom of enterprise and advance. The West provided an opportunity for freedom from that oppression, an opportunity which the East denied. In the expansive areas that spread out beyond the Alleghenies, along the Ohio and far into the prairies, men were able to feel the unconfining and uncarking sense of freedom which no other country had ever proffered. The lack of a wealthy class, the lack of congested communities, made that freedom into a living thing. Not cultured enough in early years to articulate his freedom into a philosophy, it was in the works of such men as Emerson, Thoreau, and Whitman that the philosophy of the frontiersman found its first voice. It was the impact of the frontier force which spurred the minds of those men with new vision. "I am freer than any planet," Thoreau wrote, expressing the independent spirit of the frontiersman as well as his own, "I can move away from public opinion, from government, from religion, from education, from society."

The individualist philosophy which swept over a large part of Europe toward the end of the eighteenth and the first half of the nineteenth century, and which in the form of romanticism attained its most dynamic literary expression, never exercised the profound influence upon the masses —and upon culture as a whole that it did in America. American individualism was different from European individualism. In England, for example, or even in Germany after the Franco-Prussian War, individualism made its main appeal to the middle classes. The proletariat in those countries organized themselves about a social instead of an individualistic base, and developed a collective instead of a petty bourgeois outlook. The conditions of life in European countries hemmed in the workers as soon as industry was able to get a foothold and concentrate; limitations of territory made the process of concentration short and swift. There was no Door of Hope, as Carlyle described the American frontier, open for the workers and farmers in Europe (the only door of hope they had was America), for not only did the swift concentration of industry in European countries rapidly reduce the workers into robots, *but the feudal ownership of the land held the farmers just as fast to their lowly lot*. Individualism in America was different because of the absence of those conditions. In the first place, there were no vestiges of feudal land tenure to overcome in the West; and since land was there to be possessed by all who were willing to go after it and exploit it, the opportunity of the individual was greater than in any other country in the world. In the second place, the enormity of habitable and fertile territory, surpassing by far that provided, for instance, by Australia or Canada, not only increased the possibilities of land-possession but also made it feasible for industry to spread instead of to concentrate, thereby opening up greater opportunities for the individual in the industrial field as well as in the agricultural. Thus it was that, as we pointed out in an earlier section of this chapter, individualism in America became a mass phenomenon instead of a class one. It was not confined to one class in this country but extended through and included all classes. Or, to be more precise, it made all of America into one class in its ideology—middle class. The only class divisions that arose were within that middle class, divisions between the rich bourgeoisie and the poor bourgeoisie. The workers as well as the farmers developed an individualistic outlook, and adopted an unconcealed, petty bourgeois psychology. The whole country became afflicted with the psychology of the entrepreneur. The where and how of individual advance absorbed the interest of the poor as well as the rich. Men and women of all classes became more interested in the improvement of their individual lot than in the amelioration of their social lot. The individual and not society became the centre of their concern, and individualism became their sesame to utopia.

It was this type of individualism, this American individualism, which Emerson and Thoreau extolled, the one in words and the other in action. Individualism with them, as with the American people, was more than an economic doctrine, significant to the middle class as the *sine qua non* of political philosophy—it was in fact a religious belief, a spiritual principle. However economic its origin, it was transformed in their minds into a flaming faith. Their belief in the individual, their worship of the great man, their exaltation of the hero, were born on the wings of that impulse. Their overwhelming confidence in themselves, their intellectual audacity, their conviction that they had found the truth, were products of the same force. Little mattered save what went on in their individual minds. "If I were confined to a corner in a garret all my days, like a spider," Thoreau asserted with his accustomed vigor, "the world would be just as large to me while I had my thoughts." It was not by facing the world but by facing himself that man could find the truth. The dependence of oneself, of what oneself is, upon the world, never dawned upon their minds. To have realized that dependence would have been to undermine their whole philosophy, for their philosophy was a voluntaristic and not a deterministic one. In an environment in which man seemed free to make of himself what he would, free-will doctrine was bound to prevail. Indeed, it was out of that environment of the western frontier that the free-will philosophy which has dominated American thought acquired its meaning and momentum. Asking nothing of men, carving his life as he chose, Thoreau could not have been persuaded to believe that anything in the environment helped to determine his destiny or that of man as a whole. Man, in his eyes, was a free-agent, capable of choosing good from evil, capable of being what he pleased. If he failed it was not because the environment was too much for him, but because his inner self, his individual self, was not great enough to succeed. "The highest law gives a thing," he maintained, "to him who can use it." To find truth, then, did not necessitate an understanding of society but an understanding of oneself. "How shall I help myself?" he asked. "By withdrawing into the garret and associating with spiders and mice, determining to meet myself face to face sooner or later. . . . The most positive life that history notices has been a constant retiring out of life, a wiping one's hands of it, seeing how mean it is, and having nothing to do with it."

This anarcho-individualism of Thoreau inevitably led him to oppose movements or tendencies which demanded group action or emphasized social impulse. He believed in the individual as an individual, and insisted upon the fact that he could remain an individual only so long as he stood alone. The moment he became a member of a group his individuality was lost. He was at one with Emerson in his opposition to the social communities which, inspired by the doctrines of Fourier,[38] had begun to spring up in New England. "I said

[38] It is important to observe what little success the social movements of that day were able to secure. Their absence of success was certainly not due to their lack of numerousness. It was the individualistic tendency of

that I suspected any enterprise," he remarked to his friend Bellew, "in which two were engaged together." Certainly there could have been no more extreme declaration of the individualistic creed than is to be found in those words. Yet they were more natural on Thoreau's lips than on those of any of his contemporaries, for while the spirit manifest in them was implicit in the doctrines of the whole individualist school, none of his friends or literary compatriots tested their meaning in practice. Thoreau did. A man who could note that "to-day I earned seventy-five cents heaving manure out of a pen," and was willing to undertake and did undertake any number of other humble tasks in order that he might live intellectually "free and uncommitted," that in his in-dividual solitude he might weave for himself a "silken web or chrysalis" from which he might eventually "burst forth a more perfect creature"—such a man had a greater right to speak of self-reliance and self-dependence and individual freedom than those who, despite their doctrines, preferred the comforts of social life to the hardships of individual iso-lation. If Thoreau was wrong in pursuing the life he did, it was because the doctrine he adopted was based upon a social error. Man is a social animal and cannot live in individual isolation. Individual man at times can, but man as a whole cannot. Even on the frontier the theory of self-reliance and self-dependence broke down; it was only by means of social co-operation that communities could be organized and cities built. If the West preserved more of individual independence than the East, it was because of the differences in environ-

the day, and the fallacy in their social logic, which caused their downfall. Owen's colony in New Harmony and Brook Farm were only two of the many colonies which were organized at that time. After the publication of Albert Brisbane's *Social Destiny of Man* (1840) Fourierism became the new vogue with a certain section of the American public. Fourier forums, Fourier journals, Fourier colonies were formed in various parts of the country. In New York, Pennsylvania, Ohio, Massachusetts, New Jersey, Indiana, Illinois, Michigan, and Wisconsin these Fourier colonies spread. Some of them were short-lived, although a number of them endured from two to thirteen years. For a time *The New York Tribune* gave over a whole column to the Fourier idea. (Cf. John McMaster: *History of the People of the United States*: New York, 1916: Vol. VII, p. 145.)

ment which we stressed in an earlier paragraph, because the communities and the cities were similar and the form of social life was less conducive to stratification and rigification. Once the question of a strength arose, however, the issue became social. The strength of the frontier in politics, for example, was seen when it banded itself together almost in mass and literally forced Jackson into the White House; or when again, as in the case of Van Buren, it allied its interests with those of the petty bourgeoisie in the East, and perpetuated thus something of the control of national politics which it had originally secured with the election of Jackson. But Thoreau, like Emerson, was not interested in individualism when it assumed a political form. He was not interested in individualists who organized themselves socially in order to defend their individual freedom. He believed in the pure individual, the transcendental individual, the individual who lived alone and aloof from the group. His conception of individualism was satisfactory for himself but not for the world. In other words, his conception of individualism was too philosophically pure to be of any practical value. Fitting as a pattern for his own life, it was not suitable as a pattern for the life of individuals as a whole. But Thoreau did not appreciate that contradiction. He condemned mankind for not understanding the wisdom of his way of life, oblivious to the fact that if mankind pursued that way it would have ended in its destruction. In his contention that "the gregariousness of men is their most contemptible and discouraging aspect," he showed how completely ignorant he was of the fact that it was that very gregariousness which made it possible for men to progress, and without which society could never have evolved and the human mind never have advanced. What he did, in simple, was to carry his individualist philosophy to such an extreme that his mind became closed to the importance of those social realities upon which civilization has been built. "What men call social virtues, good fellowship," he stated, "is commonly but the virtue of pigs in a litter, which lie close together to keep each other warm." In the light of such statements, it was natural enough for him to be convinced that "God does not sympathize with the popular movements,"[39] and that "there is but little virtue in the action of masses of men."[40] We cannot stress too strongly here how much more deeply these men were influenced by the frontier force than they were by the impact of their immediate environment. In truth, practically all the revolt which they expressed in their works can be definitely traced to the westward influence. Wherever, as in the case of Emerson, we discover reactionary tendencies, defense of the large property-owners against the small, we can in almost

[39]Undoubtedly a considerable part of Thoreau's contempt for men in the mass, or for man as a whole, was personal in origin as well as social. While the cultural tendency was social, the transformation which it experienced in Thoreau's mind was peculiarly personal. Any individual who could write that nature was "more human than any single man or woman can be," and who, as Hawthorne said of him, "prided himself on coming nearer the heart of a pine-tree than any other human being" (Mark Van Doren: *Henry David Thoreau:* Boston, 1916. p. 30), certainly revealed abnormal characteristics, possibly of a sexual nature, which unquestionably played a rôle in shaping the direction of his life as well as his thought. Unfortunately it is impossible in this book to enter into an analysis of the psychological complexes involved in the lives of many American authors, for such analyses would carry us far afield from the purpose of this study. My aim is to show as far as possible the relationship between literature and culture, tracing in what ways American literature expressed American culture, and pointing out in conclusion what forces in American culture to-day are changing American literature. The natural stress in such a study must be upon tendencies rather than upon individuals, but it should not be thought that because of that stress I would deny the importance of individual factors in literary expression. That individual factors are less important than cultural forces I have no hesitation in stating at once. But the theory that individual factors should be completely ignored is without rational justification.

[40]It is significant to point out that Thoreau's essay on *Civil Disobedience,* from which this last quotation was taken, has provided inspiration for many men. Gandhi, for example, has claimed that it has been his moral guide ever since he first came upon it at the beginning of his career in South Africa. In fact, in his trip to England last year for the Round Table Conference, a copy of this essay of Thoreau was the only book he carried with him. It is easy to see how Thoreau came to inspire him. Such words as these in the essay were exactly what Gandhi sought:
"I think we should be men first, and subjects afterward. . . .
"How does it become a man to behave towards the American government to-day? I answer, that he cannot without disgrace be associated with it. . . .
"The authority of government . . . can have no pure right over my person and property but what I concede to it."

all instances recognize their Eastern origin. Though the East
had become more sympathetic toward art at that time than
it had been in the seventeenth century, its way of life had
continued to be too imitative of English patterns to provide
the inspiration necessary to creative art. A wealthy class had
grown up and had begun to manifest an interest in art, as
we have seen, but its interest was mainly content with copies of English styles and little concerned with the creation
of native ones. While the frontier was the first cultural force
that tended to liberate our literature from its colonial heritage, it was not the early frontiers which effected that manu-
mission. The early frontiers, as we shall show in the subsequent section of this chapter, were too unstable to encourage
intellectual revolt and too inchoate to establish a new tradition. The initial frontiers were too constantly in a stage of
break-up, centrifugal forces triumphing over centripetal, to
create a cultural nucleus. Wherever social organization is so
fluid, so somersaulting in time and place, it is difficult for tradition to grow and deepen. At first, in fact, as we shall see, the
tendency was to imitate instead of to create, and it was only
later, when camps changed into communities, and communities were transformed from growing towns into expanding
cities, that a western pattern was able to emerge.

Even Melville, who laid his Walden in the far-away seas,
was not unaffected by the frontier force. "Melville, always
facing West," as Constance Rourke described him, was indirectly influenced by the same western movement which electrified the minds of Emerson, Thoreau, and Whitman. In
the last analysis, these men were drawn toward the West as
a means of escaping the industrialism of the East. While
Thoreau rhapsodized over the music of telegraph wires,[41] he
loathed the railroad, and the sight of industry in action—as

[41]Thoreau's description of the telegraph wires reveals as much of the
spirit of his age as of himself. "The telegraph harp again. . . . It was as
the sound of a far-off glorious life, a supernal life which came down to
us, and vibrated the lattice work of this life of ours. . . . It stings my ear
with everlasting truth. It allies Concord to Athens, and both to Elysium.
It always intoxicates me, makes me sane, reverses my views of things. I
am pledged to it."

also did most of his contemporaries. Industrialism was rapidly converting New England into a vast octopus of factories and mills. In order to escape that octopus Thoreau moved to Walden—and Melville, by necessity rather than by choice, to Typee.[42] In Typee, where he was held in captivity for a time he found a civilization which was freed of the commercial cunning of his own land, freed from the monetary madness which was the obsession of his people. But it was not the philosophy of *Typee* which, as Duyckinck has related, "made a reputation for its author in a day."[43] It was partly the appeal of the Pacific region, which was beginning to loom large then in the imagination of the country, and the romance of the new place and people, that attracted the public to the book. After all the South Seas constituted part of the Pacific pattern; they belonged to the possibilities of the New America and not the old. But even *Typee,* free as it was of lascivious description and allusion, had to be expurgated in its second edition. Few things were more revealing of the absurd middle-class moral temper of the time than the excisions which had to be made from *Typee* to suit the censor.[44] *Typee* represented the revolt of an individual who hated the corruption of his own civilization, who saw through its shams and hypocrisies, and yet knew no other way of dealing with it than to flee. The more serious, the more significant task of changing that civilization, staying with it to transform it, did not inspire him. Like Thoreau, he preferred to desert it, to build his fantasies where he could be free of it. All his novels, including his masterpiece *Moby-Dick,* in which, in symbolic form, our whole capitalist society was indicted, advanced no further in its solution. Nevertheless,

[42] Lewis Mumford: *Herman Melville:* New York, 1929: p. 68. Although, in my opinion Mr. Mumford makes Melville into a more significant author than he really is, and reads a good deal of himself into Melville's work, his life of Melville provides an inspiring picture of the man and his work.

[43] E. A. and G. L. Duyckinck: *Cyclopædia of American Literature:* New York, 1856: Vol. II, p. 673.

[44] Meade Minnigerode: *Some Personal Letters of Herman Melville:* New York, 1922: pp. 25–27.

Melville escaped more of the influence of the middle-class ideology of his day than did any of his contemporaries, and, enchanted by the primitive felicity of Typee, fell upon a purer and remoter vision. But it was a vision of the past, unfortunately, and not a vision of the future.

In terms of America, however, Melville, like Emerson, looked to the West for the coming of the new race—the native, the representative American race. It was the America of the East, of New England, that had repelled him and driven him from its shores. Critical as he was of the "happiness boys" who had arisen in the West at that time, the romancers and the humorists, he, nevertheless, did not surrender his faith.

It was interest in the possibility of that new western pattern which intrigued the mind of Emerson, and made him assert, as we previously noted, that "America begins with the Alleghanies." It was the impact of that western force which saved the leading literati of that day from complete intellectual subservience to English influence. At no time in our history was the struggle against the colonial complex carried on with such determined vigor and intensity. Even the excited nativists of the Revolutionary period had not been more extreme. Scarcely an American litterateur of the time but was not stirred by the impulse to be American. Bryant, Willis, Cooper, Thoreau, Whitman, and even Poe, joined with Emerson in his clamor for an American literature. Nevertheless, powerful as was this protest, it did not, as we pointed out in the first chapter, achieve its end. The very fact that "no American publisher (would) meddle with an American work," as Hawthorne stated, "seldom if by a known writer, and never if by a new one—unless at the writer's risk"[45] tended unconsciously if not consciously to make the American writer adhere to the old patterns instead of striving after the new. As a consequence, eager as the writers of that day were to become American, they remained in their crea-

[45]Quoted from Newton Arvin's admirable study *Hawthorne:* Boston, 1929: p. 32.

tive work British to the end. They could not establish a contact between their critical convictions and their creative art. The poetry of Bryant, Emerson, Longfellow, Lowell, and the novels of Cooper and Hawthorne, were scarcely less English in spirit than the work of their British contemporaries. Indeed, the only Easterner among them all that broke through the English cultural blockade was Whitman, who without hyperbole can be described as the first American poet. How dearly he paid for his independence we shall see in the next few pages.

Hawthorne, despite the fact that he has been described by Louis Bromfield as "the most subtly American"[46] of our nineteenth-century writers, was far less American than most critics have been inclined to believe. While *The Scarlet Letter* undoubtedly dealt with an American theme, and was saturated in the Puritan background of an earlier century, its rhythm was as much English as it was American. Its shadowy, ghost-like characters did not spring life-like from the American soil, did not communicate the flesh and blood of the American environment. It certainly marked no definite break with the English tradition in the sense that the works of Whitman and Twain did—or those of Anderson, Lewis and Hemingway do to-day. In fact, Hawthorne was one of the few writers of his time who participated little if at all in the cry for Americanness which characterized his age, and living in such comparative solitude as he did he was not even stirred by the impact of the frontier. At best, he had little of the sansculotte about him. In 1854, he complained that "our Government grows more intolerable every day. I wish it might be changed to a monarchy."[47] While in England he observed that he felt "more at home and familiar there than even in Boston, or in old Salem itself."[48] "If I

---

[46] Essay by Louis Bromfield on *Hawthorne* in *American Writers on American Literature*. Edited by John Macy: New York, 1931: p. 97.
[47] Quoted from Newton Arvin: *Hawthorne:* Boston, 1929: p. 226.
[48] Ibid., p. 230.

were rich enough," he added, "I doubt whether I should ever leave it (England) for a permanent residence elsewhere." Although at times Hawthorne's affection for England wavered, his admiration for the English tradition remained steadfast throughout his life. He was not moved by the possibilities of the "barbarous" West; he could not see an American pattern emerging there in its new sunrise of impulse. Emerson's advocacy of Americanness did not interest him. Representing in his own philosophy the ideology of the conservative upper bourgeoisie of the time, he scorned Emerson as *"that everlasting rejector of all that is and seeker for he knows not what."*[49] This man, then, whom Emerson in turn described as having no insides,[50] depicted a Puritan-Yankee world that was as unreal as it was exquisite. No one could deny Hawthorne's exquisiteness, his genius at securing mystical and magic effects; no one could question his superb artistry as a stylist, his ability to make words suggest more than they said, and to lift themselves by their own limbs, as it were, above the horizon of fact into that of fancy. But get into reality they could not. Indeed, notwithstanding the background of most of his novels and stories, the reality of America was blotted out of his mind. He lived close to himself but not close to the country in which he was born and nurtured. He was almost like an alien living in its midst. The only part of it which interested him was its past. Its future did not concern him at all.

When we turn to Whitman, however, it is like moving from a world of dead things into one that is exuberantly, volcanically alive. Hawthorne's was a beautiful dead world, a crepuscular realm where everything real lost its reality, one in which shadows shaped themselves into gorgeous silhouettes, and figures were made of spirit instead of clay; Whitman's was a live world, one in which the daylight constantly shone, and where people were made of flesh and blood, and energy throbbed through every artery of impulse. An extrovert to the finger-tips, Whitman demanded a real world in which everything palpitated with life, and more life. Force was to Hawthorne of all things the most loathesome; to Whitman force was life.

And it was Whitman's privilege to become the first genuine force in the creation of an American art.

It is only fair at this point, however, to admit that part of Whitman's achievement was unquestionably due to the force of Emerson. While Emerson in his poetry never attained the Americanness which he believed our literature should express, his vision of the West, his declamations upon the necessity of turning our eyes to the frontier instead of to Europe, his advocacy of native patterns, however crude, instead of foreign ones, endowed him with the power of a prophet. If he did not succeed in introducing Americanness into his own art, he at least succeeded in hastening the day when that Americanness could be realized. In the case of Whitman alone, in bringing him out, as it were, and helping him find himself, his influence was of a most creative variety. "I was simmering, simmering, simmering," Whitman wrote; "Emerson brought me to boil." In fact, Emerson did more than make Whitman boil! Without knowing who Whitman was, he recognized in *Leaves of Grass* the moment he read it those aspects of original Americanness for which it was later extolled. Emerson's enthusiastic praise of the volume was especially significant in the light of the cold reception which it received on the part of the American press at that time. If nothing else, Emerson's reaction proved that his interest in literary Americanness was more than skin-deep curiosity, for when faced with a piece of work as singularly American as *Leaves of Grass* he did not allow its rough, native qualities, with their barbaric newness, to blind his appreciation of its poetic excellence. Furthermore, his reaction was all the more praiseworthy when we remember that his own verse was in a style as unAmerican as Whitman's was American. His letter to Whitman at the time, in view of all that has occurred since, possesses a unique significance:

Dear Sir:

I am not blind to the worth of the wonderful gift of *Leaves of Grass*. I find it *the most extraordinary piece of wit and wisdom that America has yet contributed*. I am very happy in reading it, as great power makes us happy. It meets the demand I am always making of what seems the sterile and stingy Nature, as if too much handiwork or too much lymph in the temperament were making our Western wits fat and mean. I give you joy of your free and brave thought. I have great joy in it. I find incomparable things, said incomparably well, as they must be. I find the courage of treatment which so delights us, and which large perception only can inspire.

I greet you at the beginning of a great career, which yet must have had a long foreground somewhere, for such a start. I rubbed my eyes a little, to see if this sunbeam were no illusion; but the solid sense of the book is a sober certainty. It has the best merits—namely, of fortifying and encouraging.

I did not know, until I last night saw the book advertised in a newspaper, that I could trust the name as real and available for a post-office.

I wish to see my benefactor, and have felt much like striking my tasks, and visiting New York to pay you my respects.

R. W. EMERSON. (Italics mine.)

But Emerson did not stop there. Anxious that the book receive the recognition that he believed it deserved, he sent it on to Carlyle, describing it in a letter which announced its coming as "a nondescript monster which yet has terrible eyes and buffalo strength . . . *and (is) indisputably American.*" (Italics mine.)

Whitman's Americanness in verse was as distinctly a product of the frontier as were Emerson's doctrines of self-reliance and self-dependence, or Thoreau's contempt for authority and the state. There was nothing New Englandish or Mid-Atlantic about Whitman's approach, nothing derivative of England or any other part of Europe. Whitman not only condemned European influence and advocated our complete emancipation from the colonial complex, as did Emerson, but, more important still, he effected that emancipation in his art. His lines:

"Pass'd! Pass'd! for us, forever pass'd, that once so mighty world,
    now void, inanimate, phantom world,
Embroider'd, dazzling, foreign world, with all its gorgeous legends,
    myths,
Its kings and castles proud, its priests and warlike lords and courtly
    dames,
Pass'd to its charnel vault, coffin'd with crown and armor on,
Blazon'd with Shakespeare's purple page,
And dirged with Tennyson's sweet sad rhyme"——

not only celebrated what he believed was the passing of European influence from our shores and the freedom which had become ours with that passing, but what is more significant, they fulfilled that freedom in style as well as in content. The brash, defiant, magnificent independence of Whitman's verse, its contempt for conventional patterns, its passion for pyrotechnical design, its exaggerated and extravagant individuality, its undisciplined intensities, its amorphousness, its rhythmical abandon, were all products of the frontier force. Whitman above all others of his time absorbed that force, and, charged by its electrical compulsion, converted it into verbal dynamics. No poet since Langland had ventured such freedom of verse form or hazarded such newness of poetical pattern. The anapestic and dactylic revolt of the English romantic school had been scarcely a revolt at all when compared with that of Whitman. Whitman transformed the individualistic revolt of the frontier into poetic form. Langland's verse freedoms had been an outgrowth mainly of the Lollardistic revolt of his time,[51] expressive of the vigorous individualistic spirit of the lower middle class in England in the fourteenth century; Whitman's poetic revolt was an outcropping of the frontier force, voicing the violent individualistic spirit of the petty bour-

[51] Thomas Cuming Hall: *The Religious Background of American Culture*: Boston, 1930: p. 231.

geoisie, which, freed in the West of the encumbering presence of feudal restrictions and the oppressive hand of the
upper bourgeoisie, broke down almost every barrier of restraint that civilization had placed upon the individual. It
was that individualism run rampant, tearing up the very
roots of the social impulse, which Whitman caught on wing,
as it were, and infused into his poetry. It was that American
individualism, which was without parallel in any other part
of the world, and which made the individual contemptuous
of the past and worshipful of the new, that Whitman expressed in his reaction against the old poetic forms and his
advocacy of the new. The traditions of poetry meant nothing
to Whitman—no more than did the traditions of the state to
the frontiersman. The only thing that mattered was the individual—in literature as well as in life. In his inscription to
Leaves of Grass Whitman gave that attitude dynamic form:

Small is the theme of the following Chant, yet the greatest—
namely, One's Self—that wondrous thing, a simple, separate person.

Again in another place and also in many other places, Whitman declared:

Nor do I understand who there can be more wonderful than myself.

But this individual conceit, this exaggerated egotism, this
arrogance of personality, must not be interpreted in terms of
its face value, that is, as a personal weakness of the author,
an eccentricity of genius. It was far more than that. That a
personal element was involved in it would be ridiculous to
deny, but the personal element was unquestionably sec-
ondary to the environmental. Egotistic as Whitman undoubtedly was, for there is plenty of evidence to prove
that he possessed that trait in abundance, it was an egotism
which he absorbed from the environment rather than created
in himself. His American contemporaries were scarcely less
egotistic in spirit. The very extremities of Whitman's ego-

tism, its blind naïveté, its anti-intellectual character, testified to pioneer origins. The frontiersman who set himself up as a final authority, who despised the wisdom of savants, who looked upon himself as the equal of all men, provided the prototype from which Whitman's great "I" was derived.

Whitman's attitude toward literature revealed how true that relationship was in actual practice. His contempt for style, convention, form, was an intrinsic part of that whole psychology. "I have not only not bothered much about style, form, art, etc.," he wrote, "but confess to more or less apathy (I believe I have sometimes caught myself in decided aversion) toward them throughout, asking nothing of them but negative advantages—that they should never impede me, and never under any circumstances, or for their own purposes only, assume any mastery over me." Whitman's genius lay in putting theory into practice. Like Thoreau in the physical world, Whitman in the literary world unhesitatingly followed his theories to their ultimate conclusions. Having no reverence for the past, and little concern for the prejudices of the present, he not only made no genuflections to the literary traditions of his predecessors or contemporaries, but insisted upon expressing himself, his individuality, at all costs, literary criteria notwithstanding. It was in consequence of that logic that he frequently protested against his works being adjudged as "literature"—as also did his disciples, especially Doctor Bucke.[52] His poetry above all was the expression of a man, an individual, unique, exuberant man, who valued that expression because it got a man onto paper, got a man into words, and who cared nothing about the rules and regulations which the literary man was supposed to observe in the composition of his art. It was individuality in which he was interested and not the devices of artistic form.[53] Everything must bend and give way before

[52] Mr. Furness has declared also that Whitman's "purpose as he perceived it . . . was at bottom a religious rather than a literary one." Cf. *Walt Whitman's Workshop: A Collection of Unpublished Manuscripts.* Edited by Clifton J. Furness: Cambridge, 1928.

[53] While critics discussed and debated the problem of form in Whitman's

the advance of individual impulse. The individual is supreme—let tradition beware. Such was his message. Such was
his challenge to the world of his day.

This message, this challenge, could have come from no
other country but America, could have flowed from the pen
of no other poet but an American. But it was not the America of New England speaking, not the America of the Mid-
Atlantic states, not the America of the South. It was the
America of the West, the America which had already become the driving force of the continent. It was the America
where men believed they were free, where individualism was
supreme. It was the America which had already begun to eat
its way into the America of the East, the America which
had captured the imagination of Emerson and thrilled the
intelligences of so many of the literary men in Boston and
New York and Philadelphia. It was the America where
democracy, spelt with a capital, had become a reality, a living, pulsing, inspiring reality. It was not in the South where
slavery prevailed that democracy lived; it was not in the
North where commerce and industry had monopolized the
state that democracy had arisen; it was only in the West
where the oppressed masses of the East, and the mot-
ley-minded, land-hungry immigrants from Europe had
plunged, that democracy had taken form and acquired size.
It was that West which had become the moving spiritual
force of the era that provided Whitman with his great inspiration, that made him the poet of individuality, the poet
of self-reliance, and, as he described himself, the "Bard of
America and Bard of democracy."

It certainly cannot be said that the source of Whitman's

verse, and one of the most recent and interesting of such discussions has
resulted in showing that after 1855—before that he had employed rime
in the manner of the conventional poet—Whitman definitely resorted
to epanaphora and epanalepsis in order to get certain of his poetic effects
(Autrey Nell Wiley: "Reiterative Devices in *Leaves of Grass.*" *American
Literature*, Vol. I, No. 2, May, 1929, pp. 161–170) there can be little
doubt that those rhetorical devices were seldom used by Whitman as
part of a conscious design or pattern but rather as a spontaneous part of
his theme.

and Emerson's doctrines can be traced to the former's journey through the West in 1849, or the latter's contacts with the West in his twenty years of lecturing there. Unquestionably both men were definitely influenced by what happened to them in the West, but it was the impact of the West as a spiritual reality rather than its immediate impression as a personal experience, that determined the direction of their ideas and the character of their principles. The spiritual challenge of the West swept down upon the whole of America, awakening potentialities of impulse which had been untapped before. It was to that challenge that Emerson and Whitman responded. While their personal experiences in the West may have added meaning and fervor to their response, their influence was conditional and not causal. In fact, Emerson wrote many of his most stirring essays, reflecting the rising power of the West, long before he ventured into the frontier territories. No doubt Whitman's experiences in the West were of a more intimate variety than those of Emerson. Working his way as he did, crossing the Alleghanies, steamboating down the Ohio and Mississippi rivers, locating himself in New Orleans as a newspaper editor, and finally returning through the Great Lakes and Niagara, Whitman experienced much of the West in its sprawling immensity and magnificence. At least the sight and smell of the vast expanses, the presence of sky-sweeping forest areas as yet untamed by man, the vision of new towns and cities lifting their faces out of the surrounding wildernesses, and the contact with the people in those towns and cities, must have afforded him part of the inspiration of *Leaves of Grass*.

In his thirty-fifth year Whitman decided to "strike up the songs for a new World." Those new songs, which he dedicated himself to create, must be democratic. The West, which had come to stand for democracy in its purest form, must be in them. The plain man must constitute their essence, their throbbing pulse. "Literature strictly considered has never recognized the People," he maintained "and, whatever may be said, does not (do so) to-day. . . . The great poems, Shakespeare included,—are poisonous to the idea of the pride and dignity of the common people, the life-blood of Democracy. The models of our literature, as we got it from other lands, ultramarine, have had their birth in courts, and basked and grown in castle sunshine; all smells of princes' favours. Of workers of a certain sort, we have, indeed, plenty, contributing after their kind; many elegant, many learned, all complacent. But, touched by the national test, or tried by the standards of Democratic personality, they wither to ashes. I say I have not seen a single writer, artist, lecturer, or what not, that has confronted the voiceless, but ever erect and active, pervading, underlying will and typic aspiration of the land, in a spirit kindred to itself."[54] But who, in Whitman's opinion, were those common people who represented the "life-blood of Democracy"? They were not the New England industrialists, the New York merchants, the Southern planters—they were the lowly car-conductors, the humble steeple-jacks, the hard-working farmers, the bridge-builders, the time-keepers, the road-makers, the shop-keepers, the sailors, the firemen, the policemen, the men in the backwoods as well as the men in the cities. It was those lowly types that he extolled. "There is that indescribable freshness and unconsciousness about an illiterate person," he declared in his Preface to the first edition of *Leaves of Grass*, "that humbles and mocks the power of the noblest expressive genius." It was not the North, not the South, which gave these men their chance, their democratic opportunity. It was only the West, as Whitman realized, that provided that possibility, "Radical, true, far-scoped, and thorough-going Democracy may expect . . . great things from the West" he wrote in *The Brooklyn Eagle*. "The hardy denizens of these regions, where common wants and the cheapness of the land level conventionalism (that poison to the Democratic vitality) begin at the roots of

[54] Quoted from John Addington Symonds: *Walt Whitman: A Study*: London, 1893: p. 123.

things—at first principles—and scorn the doctrines founded on mere precedent and imitation. There is something refreshing even in the extremes, the faults, of Western character. Neither need the political or social fabrics expect half as much harm from those untutored impulses, as from the staled and artificialized influence which enters too much into politics amid richer (not really richer either) and older-settled sections." In his poem *Pioneers, O Pioneers!* he hailed the "Western youths" whom he saw "tramping with the foremost" taking up the task of progress which "the older races . . . beyond the seas" had wearied of if not deserted. It was in the West, then, which he described as "the great heart and trunk of America" that this nation was to be spiritually reborn.

It was the democratic way of life which the West opened up for all men who would hazard its perils that would save America from becoming a stereotyped copy of Europe. It was that America, which had it in it to become "the race of races," that America with its vastness of size and energy, its freshness of vision and response, which Whitman recognized as the source of our creative impulse. "Our genius is Democratic and modern" he asserted, "I demand races of orbic bards, with unconditional, uncompromising sway. Come forth, sweet democratic despots of the West." He realized how imitative our culture was at the time, how unAmerican, despite the hullabaloo which was to be heard on every side in favor of things American, a hullabaloo created in considerable part by many who in their own works expressed the same imitative tendencies which in their criticisms they affected to despise. Whitman was the first American writer to escape the domination of the colonial complex because he not only talked about the importance of our cultural emancipation but actually turned for inspiration to the only part of America where that emancipation could be attained. He tempered his style to fit the new American substance. While Emerson continued to fashion his sentences in the manner of an American Carlyle, shaping them in keeping with the English tradition, anxious to violate no canons of style or taste, Whitman went to the roots of the matter, saw that the America which confronted him, the West that stretched out endlessly before the eye of traveller and pioneer, demanded a new tradition, a new pattern, and then set about with his own pen to realize that newness in his own verse. The old canons of style and taste, which Thoreau as well as Emerson respected and observed in their prose and verse, were "grown not for America," Whitman maintained, "but rather for her foes, the feudal and the old." It was the roughness, the crudity, the spontaneity of American life as it was lived in the prairies, on the farms, in villages, in cities, the fluidity, the fascinating diversity, the newness, the democracy, that Whitman sought to capture in his poetry and communicate to the world. The old rhymes, metres, and stanzas would not do for this new substance. They had become staled by the old cultures which they represented. They had to be broken with as one would break with a disease. The "barbaric yawp" was better far than the precise refinements of English verse, filled as it was with the "thin sentiment of parlours, parasols, piano-songs, tinkling rhymes, the five-hundredth importation, or whimpering or crying about something, (and) chasing one absorbed conceit after another." The spontaneity of the country could only be captured in spontaneous verse, verse which was freed of the conventions and inhibitions of the established tradition of the time."

Professor Carpenter's attempt to show that Whitman's employment of free verse was directly derivative of the influence of Ossian is exceedingly ingenious and not without an element of truth. There can be no question as to the fact that Whitman admired Ossian or little doubt, when one has compared the verse of the two poets, that Whitman was influenced by McPherson's technique. At the same time, Whitman in no sense imitated Ossian. At best Ossian may have suggested to Whitman the possibilities of translating poetic sentiments into rhythmic prose, and of making rhythmic prose into a freer and finer form of poetry. One thing is certain, however, and that is that regardless of how deeply Whitman may have been unconsciously influenced by Ossian, he converted the rhythm and spirit of Ossian, as Professor Carpenter points out, *"into an entirely new type of poetry."* (Italics are mine.) (Frederick I. Carpenter: *The Vogue of Ossian in America: American Literature*, Vol. II, No. 4, January, 1931, pp. 405–417.) And it was that *newness* which was what was most significant in Whitman's poetry.

It was the pursuit of that belief, and its successful translation into actual verse, that made Whitman into the first American poet, no, more, the first American writer, to escape the bondage of the colonial complex. It was the influence of the frontier force which provided him with that belief, and inspired him with its challenge.

But America, as we endeavored to show in the first chapter, was not prepared for that emancipation. Its economic status and cultural advance had not yet reached the point where it was able to divorce itself from its maternal tradition. It still preferred things English to things American, its protests to the contrary notwithstanding. Consequently, when Whitman confronted it with its first American product he met with attack and rebuff on almost every side. The frontier force which he reflected was still looked upon askance by most of the minds in the East. In the eyes of many the West was as an illegitimate part of the country, a combination of the *hoi polloi* of many nations and tongues. Even Emerson, as we have seen, did not cherish the sight of the frontier in action. The national consciousness which it was beginning to create in a deep-rooted sense of the word had not yet taken hold of the East or come to dominate the country as a whole. America was still too definitely divided into Americas for it to come to look upon itself as a unified whole. While it was not until after the Civil War that the differences between those Americas began to dissolve—in a vestigial sense the differences remain even to-day though their strength has been sapped out by the process of industrialization which more and more has tended to weld the country into a unified economic unit—it was not until the Spanish-American War that the country as a whole became national-minded and interested in a national tradition. Not until then did Whitman, as was stated before, win the national recognition and respect that is his to-day.

Although individuals in various places became enthusiastic about Whitman's work shortly after its appearance, the general reaction to it was negative—an indignant negative. The English critic, Edward Dowden, to be sure, as a young man seized upon Whitman's *Leaves of Grass*, and hailed it in *The Westminster Review*[55] as "the poetry of democracy." In addition, Dowden showed in his article that previous to the appearance of Whitman no genuinely native work had appeared in American literature. Rossetti, to be sure, defended Whitman too, and managed to have *Leaves of Grass* published in England, but only after he secured Whitman's permission to delete "any poem, though otherwise fine and unobjectionable, which contains any of his extreme crudities of expression in the way of *indecency*." (Italics mine.) Robert Buchanan exceeded all the other English critics, however, in his enthusiasm for Whitman's greatness, and became what may be called the first Whitmanite. Describing Whitman's style as his "greatest contribution to knowledge," he extended his enthusiasm to such a point that he wrote that "some day it will be among Tennyson's highest honours that he was once named kindly and appreciatively by Whitman." Even Swinburne was excited about Whitman for a while and lauded his poem *A Voice from the Sea* as "the most lovely and wonderful thing I have read for years and years."[56] Later on, however, his reaction cooled and he became more

[55] Dowden's article shared the fate of many appreciations of Whitman. It was first turned down by *The MacMillan Magazine*, and then after being accepted and set in type by *The Contemporary Review* was at the last moment again refused. Dowden then "sent the article as a gift to *The Westminster Review*, in which it appeared, July, 1871." (Harold Blodgett: *Whitman and Dowden. American Literature*, Vol. I, No. 2, May, 1929, p. 171.)

[56] W. B. Cairns: *Swinburne's Opinion of Whitman. American Literature*, Vol. III, No. 2, May, 1931, p. 126.

critical and at last even condemnatory in his judgment of him. Then also, there was John Addington Symonds who claimed that "*Leaves of Grass* which I first read at the age of twenty-five, influenced me more perhaps than any other book has done, except the Bible; more than Plato, more than Goethe."[57] But even in England these reactions were singular. George Eliot regretted not having deleted a quotation from Walt Whitman which she had inserted in *Daniel Deronda* lest it "might be taken as a sign of special admiration, which I am far from feeling."[58] Even as late as March 18, 1876, *The Saturday Review*, in a slashing article on Whitman, commented on the absurd extravagance and shameless obscenity" of Whitman's verse and further observed that it was "very glad indeed to hear that his writings are unsaleable, and that no respectable publisher or editor in America will give him countenance by printing his contributions."[59]

In America, as *The Saturday Review* noted with gratification, Whitman's fate was extremely tragic. While Emerson had displayed an early appreciation of Whitman's genius, and Thoreau—despite the fact that in one place he had said that *Leaves of Grass* "(was) as if the beasts spake"—had revealed something of an understanding of Whitman's importance when he had declared, "He is Democracy," few others had taken their stand.[60] Messrs. Fowler and

[57]John Addington Symonds: *Walt Whitman: A Study:* London, 1893: p. 41.

[58]Kennedy: *The Fight of a Book for the World:* West Yarmouth, Mass., 1926: p. 37.

[59]Quoted from the article reprinted in Albert Mordell's *Notorious Literary Attacks:* New York, 1926: p. 215.

[60]Professor Kenneth B. Murdock has recently unearthed a poem of Charles Eliot Norton (cf., *A Leaf of Grass from Shady Hill:* With a review of Walt Whitman's *Leaves of Grass.* Edited by Kenneth Murdock: Cambridge, Mass., 1928) and also a review of *Leaves of Grass* by Norton, in both of which Norton revealed an appreciation of Whitman which was remarkably advanced for his time. While Norton in his review condemned Whitman's grossness of speech, at the same time he praised the "epic directness" of his poetry, and extolled his "original perception of nature." Norton's poem, which appeared anonymously in *Putnam's Magazine*, was written in direct response to the inspiration of *Leaves of Grass.*
    A letter of Lowell, which appears in the volume, is interesting as revealing the opposite, the more common, reaction to Whitman.

Wells, in whose Phrenological Cabinet[61] *Leaves of Grass* was early put on sale, soon withdrew their support of the book. Many bookstores throughout the country, once the knowledge of the volume had spread, refused to handle the book at all. Wanamaker in particular flatly forbade having a copy of the book in his store.[62] John Greenleaf Whittier threw his copy of *Leaves of Grass* into the fire. Later on, when the neglect of Whitman by the American public had reduced him almost to beggary and it was necessary to appeal to the American literati for enough money to purchase a horse and buggy for him, Whittier, who was one of those to whom the appeal was made, wrote the following letter to *The Boston Transcript* in order to prevent the public from thinking that he in any way endorsed the verse of the distressed poet:

TO "THE BOSTON TRANSCRIPT"

A WORD OF EXPLANATION

To the Editor of *The Transcript:*

I suppose it is a necessary consequence of one's notoriety of any kind to have all his words and acts regarded as public property and subjected to exaggeration and misrepresentation. Ordinarily one does not find it of much use to complain of this; but there are cases where it seems a matter of duty to make an explanation. A friend recently informed me that Walt Whitman of Newark, N. J., was in straitened circumstances, disabled and paralytic, and that an effort was being made to procure for him the means of exercise in the open air. I did not know him personally, and had but very slight knowledge of his writings, which while indicating a certain virile vigor and originality, seemed to me often indefensible from a moral point of view.

But I had heard of his assiduous labors as a nurse in Union hospitals, and had read his tender tribute to the memory of President

---

[61] In an amazingly illuminating article, *Walt Whitman and his Chart of Bumps* (*American Literature*, Vol. II, No. 4, January, 1931, pp. 350–384), Mr. Edward Hungerford traces Whitman's interest in phrenology, shows that he was convinced that phrenology was a sound science, and then deals in detail with the part which phrenology played in Whitman's poetry and in his conceptions of a "perfect Human Being." Unfortunately, in this study, it is impossible to deal with many of the interesting implications which are suggested by Mr. Hungerford's article.

[62] Horace Traubel: *With Walt Whitman in Camden:* Boston, 1905: p. 98.

Lincoln, and with no idea of its being made a matter of publicity, gave my mite for the object to which my attention was called, stating at the same time my feeling in regard to some portions of Whitman's writings, and my wish for his own as well as the public's sake, for their expurgation. I should be extremely sorry to have a simple act of humanity on my part towards a suffering man regarded as sanctioning or excusing anything in his writings of an evil tendency.

With no wish to sit in judgment upon other, and making all charitable allowance possible for differences in temperament, education, and association, I must confess to a strong dislike to what is sometimes called the sensual school of literature and art. My friend Dr. Holmes, who was also a contributor, wishes me to say that his gift, like my own, was solely an act of kindness to a disabled author, implying no approval whatever of his writings.

JOHN G. WHITTIER.[63]

Danvers, Mass.

Whittier's letter, recording Holmes' reaction to Whitman in addition to his own, is an important document in our literary history, revealing as it does the New England reaction to literature at the time—the literature of the country as a whole as well as that of Whitman. But not only Whittier and Holmes shared that reaction. Lowell's letter to Norton had revealed the same reaction. The magazines shared it; the publishers shared it; the public shared it. As the article in *The Saturday Review* indicated, Whitman was hemmed in on every side by an American public which would not recognize him:

"The real truth," says an American journal, which has taken up the subject apparently in the interest of Whitman, "is that, with the exception of a very few readers, Whitman's poems in their public reception have fallen still-born in this country (America). They have met and are met to-day, with the determined denial, disgust, and scorn of orthodox American authors, publishers, and editors, and in a pecuniary and worldly sense have certainly wrecked the life of their author. . . . Repeated attempts to secure a small income by writing for the magazines during his illness have been utter

[63]*Whittier Correspondence—1830–1892.* Edited by John Albree (1911): pp. 242–243. The letter finally was not sent. I am indebted to Mr. Albert Mordell, who is now writing a life of Whittier, for the discovery of this letter.

failures. *The Atlantic* will not touch him. His offerings to *Scribner* are returned with insulting notes; *The Galaxy* the same. *Harper's* did print a couple of his pieces two years ago, but imperative orders from headquarters have stopped anything further. All the established American poets studiously ignore Whitman."

When Robert Buchanan came to America in 1885 he found that all that *The Saturday Review* had reported was true. "Whitman is simply outlawed" he confessed with dismay. "In a land of millionaires, in a land of which he will one day be known as the chief literary glory, he is almost utterly neglected. . . . The literary class fights shy of him."[64] Sick at the sight of a Boston which ignored Whitman, he wrote a poem in *The Academy* lamenting the poet's plight, in which the following lines, dedicated to Whitman, appeared:

> "How I conjure thee, best of Bards
> Scatter thy wisdom Bostonwards!
> Tell Howells, who with fingers taper
> Measures the matron and the maid,
> God never meant him for a draper. . . .

Later on, at the close of the century, he repeated his experience in these words:

I inquired about Walt Whitman, and they volubly assured me that Lowell and Holmes and Longfellow were still alive.

Now why was it that in the twentieth century the whole reaction toward Whitman changed? Many critics have accounted for the change in terms of morals.[65] The advanced morals, the freer morals, of the twentieth century, have made it possible for Americans to respond to Whitman without compunction. Without question, there is an element of truth in that contention, and yet it is far from the whole

[64] Harold Blodgett: *Whitman and Buchanan: American Literature*, Vol. II, No. 2, May, 1930, pp. 138–139. The two other quotations from Buchanan that follow are also from this article.

[65] Henry Seidel Canby: *Classic Americans:* New York, 1931: p. 343. Dr. Canby does not base his whole explanation on that thesis, but he points out its importance as a factor.

truth. Sensuous as was Whitman's poetry, it was never lewd, as were many of Burns' Epistles, and never immoral and salacious as were many of the poems of Byron. Although it did exalt the body electric, it was scarcely more fleshly, in terms of the times, than the poetry of Rossetti. Even Swinburne's poems had not been free of the "fleshy taint," and one of his volumes, *Poems and Ballads,* had been condemned and burned.[66] Yet Burns, Byron, Swinburne, and Rossetti were always esteemed as poets even in America, much though they may have been disesteemed as men, or as the authors of certain unfortunate verses. Buchanan, for that matter, who in *The Contemporary Review* had attacked the Rossetti school as "fleshy,"[67] had declared that though he had discovered "fifty lines of a thoroughly indecent kind" in *Leaves of Grass* he was convinced that Whitman's poetry as a whole proved that he was "a most mystic and least fleshly person." And Buchanan, who in many ways was the most prudish of men, was correct. All one needed to do was to turn to any of the Elizabethans to discover diction that far surpassed Whitman's in frankness of utterance on the sexual side. More than that, Whitman himself personally attacked even the freedom of morality which had begun to grow in his day, sneered at the "contemptible lucubrations of the Free Love Convention" which was held at Utica, and was convinced that benefit might be derived from giving publicity to the convention, for they, "as evidences of the fanaticism and folly of irreligion, go far to correct one's tendency toward scepticism."[68] Even in discussions of his *Calamus* poems, Whitman sturdily and fiercely denied their homosexuality, and rebuked John Addington Symonds for suggesting the possibility of that interpretation.[69]

[66]Cf. the author's *Sex Expression in Literature:* New York, 1926: p. 252.
[67]Ibid., p. 250.
[68]Emory Holloway: *The Uncollected Poetry and Prose of Walt Whitman:* New York, 1928: Vol. II, pp. 8–9 (footnote).
[69]The problem of Whitman's alleged homosexuality does not particularly concern us here, although it is worthwhile making note of the fact that abundant evidences do suggest its possibility. The most striking evidence, I think, is to be found in the change which he made in his

Even if Whitman was an intermediate type, he cannot be accused of having consciously abetted the cause of homosexuality, for he took special pains to prove to his friends and the public that he was an assured heterosexual. In that particular alone, as well as in his constant stress, in post Civil War days, upon the importance of the spiritual factor in life,

poem, *Once I Passed Through a Populous City*. In his notebooks, where the poem was originally written, these lines appeared:

"But now of all that city I remember only the man who wandered with
  me there, for love of me,
Day by day, and night by night, we were together,
All else has long been forgotten by me—I remember,
I say, only one rude and ignorant man who,
  When I departed, long and long held me by the hand, with silent lip,
  sad and tremulous."

When this poem was given out for publication Whitman changed it in such a way as to make the man in the poem seem a woman. (Ibid., p. 102.) Other tendencies of Whitman, particularly his boast of having six illegitimate children, a boast which there is no evidence to justify, and which several of his biographers are convinced was founded upon fiction rather than upon fact, would seem also to indicate an anxiety on his part to cover up a possible homosexual proclivity. Also the fact that as far as can be discovered Whitman had very little to do with women, in fact, definitely avoided them upon many occasions, would tend to strengthen that hypothesis. Even his friendship with Peter Doyle, who stated that "woman in that sense (the sexual sense) never came into his head," revealed a distinct homosexual inclination, judging from what we know of the correspondence which took place between them. Indeed, the Doyle episode is very difficult to explain except as a homosexual deviation. Edouard Bertz, of course, was convinced that Whitman was a homosexual as also was W. L. Rivers who maintained that "in almost everything except outward form he (Whitman) was a woman." Bertz cited the following poem as indicative of Whitman's pederastic tendency—the poem, by the way, appeared in the 1860 edition of *Leaves of Grass*, but was omitted by Whitman in all later editions:

"Sullen and suffering hours! O, I am ashamed—but it is useless—I am
  what I am!
Hours of my torment—I wonder if other men ever have the like, out of
  the like feelings?
Is there even one other like me—distracted—his friend his lover lost to
  him?
Is he too as I am now? Does he still rise in the morning dejected, thinking who is lost to him? and at night, awaking, think who is lost?
Does he too harbor his friendship silent and endless? harbor his anguish
  and passion?"

Guillaume Apollinaire believed likewise that Whitman was an intermediate. (Cf. *A Whitman Controversy,* being letters published in *Mercure de France*, 1913–1914.)

he served as a defender of established morality rather than as its assailant.

No, it was not the sexual element alone in Whitman's poetry which made it impossible for America to appreciate him in the nineteenth century. Did not Emerson appreciate him? And was not Emerson squeamish enough about morality? Did not Dowden in England esteem him to the end of his days although he believed in the moral outlook? The sexual factor explains something of the difficulty but by no means all. The main difficulty was in Whitman's Americanness, his revolt against the English tradition, his disrespect for the refinement of upper-class culture, and the consequent crudities and roughnesses, which, characteristic of American life at that time, reflected themselves in the style as well as content of his verse. Whitman was a cultural iconoclast. He believed in that democracy in literature which all his contemporaries except Emerson—and Emerson only in theory —stoutly opposed. Their faith, influenced by the colonial complex, was founded upon the upper middle class tradition which prevailed in English art. The counterpart of Jefferson and Jackson in literature, Whitman had little chance of winning the support of many of the upper bourgeois critics in the East. His petty bourgeois philosophy, elevating the common man to a position of equality with his betters, even exalting him above them at times, might suit the tastes of the Jacksonians but not those of the successful and wealthy middle class. If the poetic departure marked by his verse signified anything American to them, which in general it did not, it represented that part of America which they looked down upon with contempt. In brief, Whitman's "barbaric yawp" impressed them, victimized still by the colonial complex, as an unpardonable violation of poetic tradition, the poetic tradition of the mother country.

In the twentieth century when America became national-minded in the imperialistic sense of the word, and the attitude of inferiority which was associated with the colonial complex broke down and was replaced by a growing con-

fidence in the significance of our own culture, as independent
of that of England or Europe, the prejudice against Whitman disappeared. The twentieth-century enthusiasts, who
took up Whitman and proclaimed his doctrines, it is illuminating to observe, were far more interested in his Americanness, his individualism, and his gospel of freedom, than in
his sex candor and challenge. He was a rediscovery for them
not because he represented a point of view toward sex that
had been in advance of the generation in which he had lived,
but because, to quote the words of Mr. Van Wyck Brooks,
he "precipitated the American character." In a short span of
years he became known in various camps as the creator of the
American tongue, the father of free verse and the inspiration of American cultural independence. In a deep-rooted
sense, it was their fear of the American character, their fear
of what Whitman had called the American totality, far more
than their fear of his sex ethics, that blinded the New England group, for example, to Whitman's significance. Because
of that colonial-mindedness Longfellow and Whittier and
Holmes could not realize—as did Waldo Frank and Lewis
Mumford in the next century—that they represented the
old and the imitative in American culture, whereas Whitman
represented the new and the native. "Cultural America in
1900," as Mr. Frank has noted, "was an untracked wilderness but dimly blazed by the heroic ax of Whitman."

But the twentieth century in its enthusiasm for Whitman
not only exaggerated his significance—his significance was
great enough as it was—but it also misinterpreted the direction of his doctrine. In the excitement of the first two
decades of the century, for example, radical youths seized
upon Whitman as the prophet of social revolution, and defended him as the spiritual leader of the proletariat. No less
a youth than John Dos Passos, then in his twentieth year,
the same year in which he graduated from Harvard, raised
the challenge: "Shall we pick up the glove Walt Whitman
threw at the feet of posterity?"[70] Since that time Dos Passos

[70]John Dos Passos: *Against American Literature: New Republic*, October 14, 1916.

has reversed his position, and instead of continuing a Whitmanite has become a revolutionary. But such has not been the fate of most of the Whitmanites, many of whom still think of him in that revolutionary rôle. He was a great progressive force in terms of his day but not in terms of to-day. Whitman was not a believer in social revolution and was not a fugleman of the proletariat. He was just as much a petty bourgeois individualist in social philosophy, just as much a believer in private property, as were most of his contemporaries. His conception of democracy was individualistic and not social. "In it," as he wrote, "I include emperors, lords, kingdoms, as well as presidents, workmen, republics." His concept of individual man was ego-centric to the extreme. His accent upon the American totality, America en-masse, was the accent not of a socialist or a communist but of an individualist. "I will effuse egotism and show it underlying all," he wrote, expressing as he did the fundamental spirit of his philosophy. He was as excited as Emerson by the evidences of economic prosperity in the West, thrilled by the promise of cheap land which might over-night be turned into a goldmine, an oil-well, or perhaps a new city. Even his love of the lowly was not nearly so comprehensive as is usually thought. In that very love the petty bourgeois character of his philosophy obtruded. It was not the laborer he loved, but the white laborer. With all his affirmations of the Kosmos, all his zest for the eternal in the humblest of things, he could not include the Negro within the scope of his affections. The Negro to him, a piece of property, did not constitute part of his Democracy. Resenting the activities of the Abolitionists, whom he described as "a few foolish and red-hot fanatics," he attacked them upon frequent occasions and painted a terrible picture of the influence of the Negro upon democracy:

As if we had not strained the voting and digestive calibre of American Democracy to the utmost for the last fifty years *with the millions of ignorant foreigners, we have now infused a powerful percentage of blacks, with about as much intellectual calibre (in the mass) as so many baboons.* (Italics mine.)

Even while he objected to slavery in the West, for example, where he wanted the states to be free, he saw no reason why it should not exist in "Cuba and the Brazils." But worse than that are his special observations on the Negro as a race and on the character of slavery as a whole:

> Would we then defend the slave trade? No; we would merely remind the reader that, in a large view of the case, the change is not one for the worse, to the victims of the trade. The blacks, mulattoes, etc., either in the Northern or Southern States might bear in mind that had their forefathers remained in Africa, and their birth occurred there, they would now be roaming Krumen, or Ashanteemen, wild, filthy, paganistic—not residents of a land of light, and bearing their share, to some extent, in all its civilizations.
>
> *It is also to be remembered that no race ever can remain slaves if they have it in them to become free. Why do the slave ships go to Africa only?* . . .
>
> For the Brazils, for Cuba, and it may be for some of the Southern States of this Confederacy, the infusion of slaves and the prevalent use of their labor are not objectionable on politico-economic grounds. *Slaves are there because they must be—when the time arrives for them not to be proper there, they will leave.* (Italics mine.)

Indeed, not only did Whitman in the case of the Negro fail to measure up to the mark of humanity for which he has always been so extravagantly credited, but, more revealing still, he never reached that point of illumination which Thoreau did when he recognized that slavery, in another form, was present in the North as well as in the South, for as the latter said subjection exists "wherever men are bought and sold, wherever a man allows himself to be made a mere thing or tool" whether as a wage-slave or a bond-slave.

Notwithstanding the ardor of his advocates, and the visionary enthusiasms of many of his interpreters, Whitman is a prophet of the past and not of the future. His individualism, his ego-infusing spirit, his romantic conception of democracy in which he could be the poet of both "the slaves and the master of slaves" and in which emperors could fit as well as workmen, belong to the nineteenth century and not to the twentieth. Glowing as was the promise of his individualistic utopia in the nineteenth century, its glow to-day, in a world in which individualism has become a myth, has lost its lustre, and burnt down into a depressing yellow. The workers of to-day could not turn to his doctrines for inspiration. The idea of a world proletariat, which has become the worker's inspiration in the twentieth century, "would have been" as Henry Seidel Canby correctly remarked "repugnant to him" . . . (for) "his joyous individualism has no part in the programme of those who in Russia now exalt the common man as a proletarian whose end is that equality of opportunity with which Whitman began." But not only in the U. S. S. R. is individualism dead. It is dead also in our industrialized society with its centralized controls, its horizontal and vertical trusts, its monopolies and cartels, its robotized workers and ruined farmers,—and its absence of a frontier. No, Whitman's message is not for this day. It belonged to a different America and grew out of a different scene. Those who take it up to-day do so in hopeless protest against the America that is with us, believing that through its challenge they can save the country from its present economic destiny. But their hope is as foolish and futile as that of the romantic Southerners who still believe in the possible restoration of old Dixie.

Nevertheless, we must remember that however critically we may view to-day the attitudes of Emerson, Thoreau, and Whitman, they represented a progressive force in their own day. They were necessary and forward-looking expressions of their own environment. Their philosophy at that time was a positive one; it is only to-day that it has become a negative one. In the nineteenth century, it was a challenge spurring men to action, driving them across the face of the continent, carrying with them the energy of a new age. It was only after that continent had been conquered, and that age had passed, that this philosophy lost its positive meaning. To-day, faced as we are by a different age, it is nothing more than a hollow echo of a dead past.

IV

Now that we have dealt with the influence of the frontier force upon the literature of the East, let us turn to the frontier regions themselves and consider the literature that burgeoned forth there. In the first place, let us keep in mind the fact that the western frontier was in a constant state of flux from the middle of the eighteenth century until practically the end of the nineteenth. During the first hundred and fifty years which it took the frontier to reach the Appalachians its influence upon the country as a whole as well as its advance as a cultural entity was comparatively slight; during the next fifty years, when it surmounted the mountain barrier and surged on to the Mississippi, its progress became more rapid and its influence more profound; during the succeeding fifty years, however, when, sped on by the railroad, its movement became almost electric, it changed character so rapidly that the rest of the country could scarcely catch up with its momentum. It was only during the last two stages, particularly the last, that the frontier itself became a cultural force, influencing the literary outlook of the nation.

From the very beginning frontier literature revealed a strong predilection for the religious. As we showed in the second section of this chapter, the individualism of the frontier farmers found its most dynamic form of cultural expression in religion. Religion, in truth, was their only cultural bond. "Most persons in the West read very little upon any subject but elections," wrote James H. Perkins, one of the best commentators on frontier life, "but of those who do, the majority, we believe, are readers upon religion."[71]

[71] R. L. Rusk: *The Literature of the Middle-Western Frontier*: New York, 1926: p. 314. For the student in the field, it is needless to add that Rusk's study is the most excellent and exhaustive that has been done in this connection. While I am extremely indebted to Doctor Rusk for many references and clues in this section of this chapter, in order to trace certain tendencies which I consider of extreme significance in frontier literature I found it necessary to go directly to many of the frontier magazines and the frontier books themselves for certain corroborative materials.

Indeed, the same petty bourgeois religiosity which early pervaded New England became dominant in the West once the trail-blazing days were succeeded by those of community settlement and construction, and much of the literature that arose was inspired by religious necessity. Only the geography of the region, the remoteness of centres of influence, and the difficulties of instituting controls, prevented the religious forces from overwhelming the western frontier as successfully as they had the New England. The volume which appeared as early as 1816, *A New Kentucky Compostion of Hymns and Spiritual Songs; together with a Few Odes, Poems, Elegies, etc.*, written largely by a certain William Downs, was typical of the religious literature that began to flourish. Among the hymns and songs interspersed in the book were many that revealed Downs as a poet not less dour than his New England predecessor, Michael Wigglesworth. In fact the following lines from the *New Kentucky Composition* could just as easily have constituted part of *The Day of Doom:*

> "The rocks shall melt with fervent heat,
> And world pass off with noise so great,
> In flames they and their works shall burn,
> While sinners down to hell shall turn.
>
> Sinners enwrapt in flames shall mourn,
> With devils howl! with devils burn;
> But saints shall mount beyond the void,
> Leave flames behind and dwell with God."[72]

Downs, it is true, revealed, in much of his verse, a revivalistic turn which was not characteristic of the poetry of Wigglesworth, a difference reflecting the disparities in character and culture between the New England and the Western frontiers, but in general sentiment the two writers were the same. Other volumes of similar character were common in many parts of the West. While "there is nothing of the old Puritan spirit beyond the mountains," *The Hesperian or*

[72]Ibid., p. 314

Western Monthly Magazine observed, "yet we are convinced that there is a strong disposition there to hear, think, and speak upon theological and moral matters," and thereupon added that "the characteristic of the literature popular in the West is either religious teaching or exciting narrative."[73]

It was not long, however, before the religious emphasis was succeeded by the moral, and frontier literature became an adventure in the didactic. William D. Gallagher, who was the editor of *The Western Literary Journal and Monthly Review* which was published in Cincinnati in 1836, and who was one of the leading frontier writers of his period, heralded the advance of the moral sentiment in Western literature as marking a great cultural advance:

Never before was there a literature like this—so pervaded by the beautiful and the true—so informed of the inner life of man—so responsive to the harmonious chords of the eternal spirit. It is preeminently the literature of Humanity—speaking to and from the common heart, as never spake the literature of the past age. Leaving fabled gods and goddesses to wage, as they list, their wars of rapine and lust, and revenge; leaving scarcely less fabled heroes to dare the strife of ocean and escape from the seductive evils of imaginary Valepsos as they may; leaving adventurous bards and lecherous princes to shift for themselves, as best they can, among the awful shades and circling fires of the Inferno; it seeks its themes in the world about us and carries to the doubting mind, the agonized heart, and the crushed spirit the words of truth and consolation, and hope. No home of man is so high or so low, but it will pass the threshold and deliver its message of good.[74]

Magazine after magazine stressed the same ideal. *The Western Literary Magazine and Journal of Education, Science, Arts and Morals* declared in the introduction to its first volume that it had aimed "to furnish a Journal to whose introduction to the parlor arch or social fireside no parent however fastidious can object . . . (and) to displace as

[73] Issue of November, 1839, p. 435.
[74] William D. Gallagher: *Progress in the Northwest*: Cincinnati, 1850: p. 58.

much as possible such a literature, the direct influence of which is to undermine the foundation of all that is exalted and noble and praiseworthy in either character or institutions."[75] *The Hesperian* had previously discoursed upon "the demoralizing effects of Smollett's and Fielding's novels," described them as "poisonous and seductive works," and declared that such fictions in the West were "rapidly being displaced by novels and other works of fiction of a much more wholesome and healthy character."[76] *The Cincinnati Literary Gazette* took the same stand toward the works of Fielding and Smollett. "We do not share in the regrets that many feel for the comparative neglect of our old standard novelists, particularly Fielding and Smollett," that magazine announced, "(for) the genius and talent displayed by these authors when united with the looseness of morals and the vulgar pictures of vice represented by them have an unfavorable tendency."[77] Even after the middle west frontier became more stabilized, its moral outlook did not change. As late as 1882, the western magazine, *The Criterion*, derided those humorists and wits, including Mark Twain, who at times descended to the salacious:

Coarseness, especially, is a serious defect often noticed in humorous writing. Ludicrous speeches or stories contained characters whose conversation was frequently ribald and indecent, in which pure sentiment and the noble and romantic elements in human nature were often ridiculed and belittled in such a way that the unreflecting reader became ashamed that he had ever entertained any thought beyond those of the most practical and commonplace order. Of course, sickish sentimentality and much hypocrisy are common in every community, and the humorist who makes them a target for his ridicule does the public good service, but his influence is pernicious if he falls into the habit of carelessly deriding really pure and lofty sentiments with coarse jests and quips.[78]

What we have represented here in this attitude is the same petty bourgeois psychology which prevailed in the East,

[75] Published in Columbus, 1831.
[76] Issue of August, 1838, p. 298.   [77] Issue of February 14, 1824.
[78] *The Criterion*, St. Louis, August 12, 1882, p. 12.

first in religious and then in moral form. Despite the wild and rugged character of the environment, despite the rapacious appetites for exploitation and plunder which that environment encouraged, despite the utilitarian emphasis demanded by that environment, which, in the opinion of Timothy Flint, made "the people too busy, too much occupied in making farms and speculations to think of literature"[79]— despite all those handicaps, once the frontier elbowed its way forward, leaving cities behind it as it advanced, it began to assume all the petty bourgeois characteristics which had predominated in the East. While the boatmen, the scouts, the Indian fighters, the gamblers, the tavern-keepers, who pressed onward as the frontier-fringe swayed farther and farther to the west, preparing the way for the cowboys, the gold-seekers, the train robbers, retained their picturesqueness of type until the frontier annihilated itself, the growing cities they left behind them rapidly divorced themselves of their presence and influence. It was in the thinly settled parts of the West, in the small towns and primitive settlements, that those types continued to lend color—and chaos—to the environment. *Indeed, the early energy of the West was spent in replacing unstable types by stable.* The fact that the West remained for a long while a territory of small towns and settlements, however, prevented the stabilizing force of the cities from exercising much influence upon the rest of the country. Consequently, while the cities swiftly took on all the aspects of petty bourgeois civilization, the outlying territories preserved the more primitive characteristics of the early pioneer environment. Western culture, to be sure, in its maturer forms, grew up in the cities and not in the settlements, although it must be admitted that the life in the border regions undoubtedly influenced the cultural forms which sprang up in the urban centres.

Lexington, for example, which in the beginning of the

[79]Timothy Flint: *Recollections of the Last Ten Years in the Valley of the Mississippi*: Boston, 1826: p. 185.

nineteenth century was known as the "Athens of the West," acquired all the characteristics of a small petty bourgeois metropolis—for that was what being a metropolis meant in those days when Chicago was still nothing more than a promising lake town of as yet uninspiring proportions. Before 1820 Lexington was the centre of western culture. All the early literary life in the West circled about it and disseminated from it. Publishing houses arose in Lexington printing and selling magazines and pamphlets as well as books. The first newspaper in the West was published in Lexington as far back as 1787. The University of Transylvania, attracting numerous scholars of note, helped strengthen the cultural position of the city. Even the theatre got an early start in Lexington and, notwithstanding the attacks of the religious elements, managed to make headway there. Before the end of the first quarter of the century, however, as economic power shifted from Kentucky to Ohio, Cincinnati superseded Lexington as the cultural hub of the West. Within a short span of years, Cincinnati became a creative force in the intellectual life of the western states. By 1840 its presses printed seven newspapers every week and, including textbooks, over half a million books every year. The theatre flourished even better there than in Lexington. A number of theatres were opened in fairly rapid succession; and Shakespearian plays were staged as well as those medleys of melodrama and farce which so quickly won popular acclaim in western cities. But not even Cincinnati could monopolize the cultural strength of the West. Louisville soon vied with it as a theatre centre, and St. Louis surpassed it as a philosophic force in the West; it became a philosophic power in the nation.

Beginning with the appearance of *The Missouri Gazette* in 1808, St. Louis slowly began to rise in cultural stature, but it was not until long after with the foundation of the St. Louis school of philosophers and the publication of the first metaphysical journal to be printed in America, *The Journal of Speculative Philosophy*, that its position was assured. The St. Louis school, headed by Harris, Brockmeyer, and Snider, is important not only in terms of its own environment, but also in terms of its influence upon New England thought of that day. Afforded its poetic force by Brockmeyer, a Hegelian-inspired Thoreau of the West, and its logical challenge by Harris, a Yankee who discovered in the Absolute an escape from confusion, this philosophic school, which was convinced that Hegel had outmoded Kant, brought Alcott to the West and made Emerson into the sage of the frontier. Indirectly this St. Louis school influenced the course of Transcendentalism in the East, and provided a point of conjunction between the thought of the two regions.[80] The cosmopolitan character of the city as a whole, which included a strong German and French element as well as an English, was undoubtedly an encouraging factor in the development of the school. Curiously enough, this idealistic school aimed to be most American in the application of its logic, and Harris went out of his way in an attempt to interpret the nature of American life in terms of the Hegelian dialectic. Individualism and the state were considered in their historical rôles, as theses, anti-theses, and syntheses, but always in the light of the American differential. At all events St. Louis became the philosophic centre of the West, and through its magazine, which introduced Fichte and Hegel to American readers for the first time,[81] it came to influence such diverse Eastern thinkers as Josiah Royce and William James.

By the time the theatre struck the West in the nineteenth century, the religious prejudice against it in the North had turned into moral protest, and in many cities the theatre, in ethical disguise, had actually made progress. In the West the same petty bourgeois objections to the theatre arose as had sprung up in the East, but because of the expansiveness of the territory and the intractable aspects of the en-

[80] Woodbridge Riley: *American Thought* (Second Edition): New York, 1923: p. 240.
[81] Ibid., p. 247.

vironment those objections had seldom been able to be enforced. In Lexington the matter of the immoral influence of the stage had been debated by the students in Transylvania University and a little later the same debate was renewed in Cincinnati. When a new theatre was erected in Cincinnati in 1819 Mr. Drake, the manager, promised to preserve it against the invasion of impure influences and immoral plays.[82] Prizes were offered in many cities for the best defense of the stage. In Detroit and St. Louis and in most of the larger western cities the controversy over the theatre became an important issue. The theatre advanced, nevertheless, despite its enemies, for its enemies were not in the same advantageous position they had been in in the North and could not successfully call a halt to that which they opposed. Besides, isolated as the western cities were from contact with other centres of culture, and unrelieved as was their life by the diversities of activity and amusement which had developed in the East, the theatre was able to establish itself with more ease in the West than in the North. Moreover, in many river towns where the primitive conditions of life had not cultivated the so-called refinements of petty bourgeois civilization, the theatre was welcomed with boisterous enthusiasm. No debates interfered with its arrival there. Indeed, it was in order to meet the demand for theatric performances that the "show-boat" was devised. William Chapman, who was, perhaps, the first show-boat producer, constructed his "floating playhouse," as it was then called, to supply the river-towns with a stage which they could not otherwise afford.[83] This show-boat, which in most cases was nothing more than an old scow upon which an improvised house had been erected, with wooden benches to seat the spectators, and with a muslin-curtained stage set off by candles to divide the audience from the actors, ploughed its way up and down the Ohio and the

[82] R. L. Rusk: *The Literature of the Middle-Western Frontier*: New York: Vol. I, p. 434.
[83] Walter Long: *A Sociological Criticism of the American Drama*: *The Modern Quarterly*, Vol. II, No. 4, p. 272.

Mississippi, playing in town after town with increasing success. In time, it is true, the show-boat disappeared, but it was only after the towns had grown wealthy enough to build their own theatres.

As early as 1814, Drake, aided by the actor, Usher, built a crude theatre in Pittsburgh, and staged there Tobin's *The Honeymoon,* a popular comedy of the time. The success of their group was immediate. Later they churned their way down the Ohio to Frankfort, Kentucky, where their Pittsburgh success was duplicated. Different companies visited other cities, and in several cases, particularly in that of the town of Natchez, they were importuned to visit individual towns at the special request of the citizens. Very soon various towns throughout the Mid-West built playhouses by popular subscriptions.[84] By 1835, for instance, New Orleans had constructed a theatre superior to any in America. About the same time St. Louis erected a theatre which cost $65,000 to construct. Chicago, which advanced with enormous strides in the fifties, built in 1857 an even more imposing theatre than the one in St. Louis. Following the gold-rush, theatres sprang up with unparalleled swiftness in San Francisco, and it was not long before the theatre became an established institution in that city.[85]

Although the West, as we have just seen, responded with such fresh enthusiasm to the theatre, it was the East which originally brought the theatre to the West, and not the West which created it out of its own necessity. The early appearance of the theatre in the West resulted from the spirit of speculation on the part of Eastern actors and producers.

[84] Ibid., p. 271.

[85] In these running comments on the growth of the theatre in western communities, it is worthwhile noting the extreme interest in the theatre which the Mormons manifested. Appreciating the educational value of the stage, Brigham Young and other Mormon prophets early converted the theatre into an established institution. In 1861, they began the construction of the Salt Lake Theatre which involved an expenditure of over one hundred thousand dollars. While at first only religious plays were staged, it was not long before the religious barriers were removed, and the Salt Lake Theatre became a centre for all manner of significant theatrical performances.

The promise of the West, as we have noted, had already begun to flood the East with Niagara-like intensity, and actors and producers, laden with the plays of Shakespeare, Massinger, Fletcher and Kotzebue, ventured into the new country with something of the same speculative zeal that characterized the spirit of the pioneers. They deserted the East because the conditions that prevailed there did not allow them enough opportunity to attain prestige and wealth. The West promised them better conditions, and if it did not assure them of prestige it did guarantee them wealth. In this case at least the spirit of speculation was beneficial instead of disastrous in its cultural consequences.

As a result of its isolation, and because of the conflict in economic interests which soon grew up between the two regions, the West very soon developed a feeling of hostility for the East, which often translated itself in its literature in the form of contempt. The North in particular was resented by the frontiersmen, and it was not long before the Yankee became a symbol of stigma in the Ohio and Mississippi country. As Timothy Flint recorded in his *Recollections of the Last Ten Years in the Valley of the Mississippi*, everywhere in the state of Ohio the Yankee was held in scorn. "Everywhere in this state," he observed, "fine stories about Yankee tricks, and Yankee finesse (prevail). . . . I might relate a score of Yankee tricks that different people assured us had been played off on them. I will only relate, that whenever we stopped at night and requested lodgings, we were constantly asked if we were Yankees, and when we answered we were, we constantly saw a lengthening visage. The common reply of the boatmen to those who ask them what is there lading is 'Pit-cone indigo, wooden nutmegs, straw baskets and Yankee notions.' "[86] Unquestionably part of that reaction by way of reciprocity sprang out of the New Englander's contempt for the frontiersman, a contempt which turned into bitterness in the early part of the nine-

[86] Timothy Flint: *Recollections of the Last Ten Years in the Valley of the Mississippi:* p. 32.

teenth century when the working class in the North had been rendered unstable and undependable by the steady migration of workers to the West. In the main, however, the hostility was an outgrowth of the feeling of independence which the back-country inspired, the sense of democratic equality which had developed and which made the citizens of the West scornful of the cultural airs and arrogances that the East assumed—the petty bourgeois scorn and hatred for the enamel and veneer of the upper bourgeois way of life.

As a matter of fact, one of the most striking ways in which the West asserted its frontier spirit in literature was in its defiance of the cultural conventions of Boston and London. For a considerable time, to be certain, English and even New England writers were popular on the frontier, and early frontier authors accepted them as their models. James Hall, for example, was an open disciple of Scott, and even followed Cooper, who in turn had copied Scott, in certain of his models. In poetry Thomas Pierce exalted Pope, Milton, and Thomson, and Timothy Flint extolled Mrs. Hemans and Thomas Moore. M'Clung admitted his debt to Cooper in his novel, *Camden: A Tale of the South.* Burns' poetry was openly imitated for a time in various magazines in the West. Indeed, most of the early frontier prose and verse was imitative in character, imitative in fact in a most stilted and artificial manner.[87] But this period of imitation was not very long-lived. The conditions of the environment were in too definite a conspiracy against it. Even during the period of imitation, the spirit of revolt had set in with determined intensity. Magazines and newspapers declaimed against it and clamored for the development of a western culture. It was not an extension of New England or Southern culture that they desired, but a culture native to their own soil, sprung out of their own environment, a spontaneous product of western interests and western

[87] W. H. Venable: *Beginnings of Literary Culture in the Ohio Valley:* Cincinnati, 1891: p. 271.

ideals. Even in church hymns this insistence was manifest. The author of *The Columbian Harmonist* asserted that his volume contained materials "particularly adapted to the different Churches in the Western Country,"[88] stressing thus as early as 1816 the concept of regional loyalty. In other books the same declaration appeared. James Hall's *The Western Reader* was described by him as "a work of Western origin and manufacture."[89] Another volume, *The Federabian or United States Lessons: Intended to Promote Learning and a Knowledge of Republican Principles, in the Minds of Our Youth*, made an explicit defense of "our National Literature," but by national it really meant Western. "In this work" its author, Henry Houseworth, announced, "fewer extracts from British authors will be inserted than is usual in our school books, because it is considered they are not suited to our republican institutions."[90] When Samuel Wilson in 1802 brought out a new issue of his volume on grammar he entitled it the *Kentucky English Grammar*. The M'Guffey *Readers*,[91] emphasizing as they did the moral motif in all their selections, made their direct appeal to regional enthusiasts. If we turn to the magazines proper, we shall discover the Western spirit predominant in the vast majority of them. The early aim of *The Western Messenger*, which, by the way, was concerned with religion as well as literature, was to encourage Western writers and the growth of a Western literature. It was only after it failed in that pur-

[88] R. L. Rusk: *The Literature of the Middle Western Frontier*: New York: Vol. I, p. 316.

[89] Ibid., Vol. I, p. 266.   [90] Ibid., Vol. I, pp. 266–267.

[91] As Professor Schlesinger suggests in his excellent essay on *American History and American Literary History* (cf. Foerster's *Reinterpretation of American Literature*, p. 163), "the activities of Wm. H. M'Guffey . . . did more to influence the general literary tastes and standards of the period than the soft effulgent rays of the entire Cambridge-Concord constellation. Even in this year of our Lord there are more M'Guffey clubs in the United States than Browning Societies." Although Professor Schlesinger is correct in his emphasis, it must be remembered that important as M'Guffey's influence was, it was in the West far more than in the East that its presence was felt. Besides it must not be forgotten that with all his piety and didacticism, M'Guffey was scarcely more moral in his stress than were Longfellow, Whittier, or Emerson in the East.

pose that it turned toward Eastern and European writers for its materials. Other Western magazines, however, held fast to their regional convictions. *The Western Literary Magazine and Journal,* for example, manifestly declared that "we have counted the cost, and now we are ready to say, 'The West must have its own literature, and not rely wholly on foreign product for the necessary supply. She owes it to the world . . . that the principles of equality on which our nation professes to be based, may still be further vindicated before the universe.' "[92] *The Western Monthly Magazine* became even violent in its defense of Western independence in literature. "Why should not we be renowned," it asked, "for arts as well as arms—for literature as well as for liberty? Shall we leave it to the sons of New England to clothe our descendants in their manufactures, supply their firesides with comfort and teach them the rudiments of science?" In another place the editor of the same magazine observed that "situated in the bosom of the West . . . the true American spirit exists in its purity," and then, proceeding to inveigh against the impure influences of foreign sources, added that "for the pure within of native minds pining for support and action, they substitute the dross that reaches us beyond the Atlantic."[93] Later on the same magazine became even more vehement in its denunciations of foreign influences:

How tamely do we submit to the domination of the British Press! While we shrink from the contamination of their cash and cotton goods, neither of which could do us any great harm, with what apathetic indifference do we see their books distributed throughout the whole extent of our republic, and exercising a silent but powerful influence on the morals and taste of the country![94]

The Hesperian denounced the same foreign influences in even more vitriolic fashion:

And here I cannot refrain from remarking that nearly all our fashionable schools for the education of the wealthy classes of soci-

[92]*Western Literary Magazine and Journal,* Columbus, Ohio, 1831, p. 48.
[93]*Western Monthly Magazine,* August, 1834, p. 429.
[94]Quoted from W. B. Cairns: *American Literature from 1815–1833:* Madison, 1898: p. 28.

ety and all the literary periodicals I have read with a few exceptions, have an anti-American tendency. Indeed such is the rage for foreign manners, and foreign fashions and foreign tongues, that your barber shaves you according to the fashion latest from London or Paris, your lady's milliner dresses her out with a Victorian bonnet! and the dandies begin to curse their grooms, and the madames to scold their husbands, in French, while good old patriotic *Yankee Doodle* and *Hail Columbia*, give way to the Italian air and Polish waltz.

Our common school education should be patriotic and to be patriotic it must be American in character. Yes, it should be *American* in its character, even at the risk of being homely. The association between the tune and the ballad is not stronger than that between the sentiment and language of a nation.[95]

In an earlier issue of that magazine, a reviewer had remarked, in attack upon *The Token* (a souvenir magazine), that he considered the fact that it was "mostly European grain and not American grain" to be the most serious indictment to be charged against it.[96] *The Cincinnati Literary Gazette* belabored Irving for allowing his interests in foreign countries to overweigh those for America.[97] In fact, we can turn to almost any magazine of the time and find abundant signs of revolt against both the colonial complex and the New England domination of Western culture. The West was determined to stand upon its own legs, without the support of "foreigners" and Yankees. "People east of the Alleghanies," *The Hesperian* claimed, "appear to have the most imperfect ideas of the stage of society in the Mississippi Valley, and to be singularly ignorant of the great and rapid strides which their countrymen here are making, in the refinements and luxuries, as well as the substantial necessaries of civilization. And what would *The New York Star* think," the article went on to add with increasing pride, "if we were to tell it that we of the Ohio capital can within any four or five days summon to our presence, from the handsome villages and young cities which dot the earth within the distance

[95]*The Hesperian*, March, 1839, p. 341.
[96]*The Cincinnati Literary Gazette*, October 16, 1824: article entitled *From the Portfolio of a Backwoodsman.*
[97]Ibid., February, 1839, p. 326.

of fifty miles around us, half a score of large and excellent
'musical bands,' whose instruments are the costliest and the
best which the New York market can supply."[98]

It was this sectional loyalty naïve and pathetic though it
was at first, this dedication to itself, as it were, this confidence
in its own potentialities, which helped prepare the way for
the rise and growth of Western realism and humor, and the
appearance of a native American pattern. The East, as we
have seen, had staged a sturdy fight against the colonial complex, but to little avail. Only Whitman, who had been carried away by the force of the West and who had been swept
on by the impact of that force to make his innovations in
verse harmonics, had managed to escape its influence. Emerson, Bryant, Lowell,[99] Holmes, Longfellow, continued to
the end of their days to imitate English patterns in their
creative art.[100] They developed no American pattern; of that
we can be overwhelmingly positive. In the West, on the
other hand, where a new democratic way of life had developed which was antagonistic to the way of life in England,
and where, in addition, contacts with the mother country
were so removed that they could not be very binding, the
emergence of an American pattern was almost inevitable. In
many cases the early Western writers who imitated English
styles and patterns, of whom Timothy Flint was an example,
were Easterners who had come to look upon the West as a
natural extension of the East. Few of the Western writers
who were born in the West, and who were native to its culture, adopted such styles in their work. The nature of the
environment in which they lived militated against their
adoption and perpetuation. Even those Eastern writers, the
humorists in particular, who, later on, came to write for the

[98] *The Hesperian*, March, 1839, p. 341.
[99] In one instance, in his *Biglow Papers*, Lowell came close to breaking
with the English tradition. The instance proved all too singular, however, for almost all the rest of his poetry was in the imitative sphere.
[100] Even the influence of German and Italian literature upon Longfellow could not save his work from becoming a lineal representative of
Victorianism in America.

West, adopted the simple realistic matter-of-fact style that the Westerners—and in time the whole country—enjoyed.

The West was not a place for belles-lettres in the old sense of the word. The meeting place and melting pot of polyglot hordes, who swarmed like hungry animals over the face of the earth that lay before them, the West had no need for culture as a refined conception. What culture the West did need sprang up from the soil, a kind of vagabond product, taking form in myth and legend. The Timothy Flints and James Halls did not interpret that West; they merely described it, noted its external characteristics, painted its surfaces. It was the Davy Crocketts and the Mike Finks who caught up within themselves and communicated the intractably chaotic spirit of the West.[101] It was in such personages, the tall tales that were woven about them and spun out into extravagant and conflicting legends, one more fantastic than another, that the early West lived, and not in the works of its official authors. Davy Crockett's cocksure contempt for culture, his pride in his illiteracy, and his claim that it got him further than the "booklarnin" gentry, were typical of the early frontier psychology.[102] It was not the psychology which dominated in Lexington, say, or Cincinnati, where a petty bourgeois gentry had grown up, but the psychology of the populace, the psychology which wrote itself into the folklore and which differentiated the Western spirit from the Eastern. Into that psychology the figure of the boatman inevitably crept; legends sprang up about him, and the picture of him singing as he sailed or paddled his way down rivers or up stream, made him into a romantic personage, intriguing to child as well as adult. (Mark Twain turned to him as a symbol of strength upon more than one occasion.) Negroes lyrical with spontaneous song and rhythm enriched the Mississippi coun-

---

[101]Constance O'Rourke in her volume, *American Humor*, has provided a fine, stirring picture of that aspect of the American temper.

[102]When Crockett was elected to United States Congress, representing a constituency of one hundred thousand people, he could not read, and scarcely knew how to sign his name. (Crockett's Autobiography. Quoted from John S. C. Abbott: *David Crockett*: New Hampshire, 1874: p. 253.)

try with their childlike gaieties and enthusiasms. Irish reels and jigs became popular patterns wherever they spread. The game of snuffing a candle with a ball, as Audubon recorded,[103] became a popular pastime among the Kentuckians who considered rifling a great art. Dancing, story-telling, burlesque, everything that was ebullient, fascinated the early frontiersman and entered into his folk-culture.

It was out of that background, that what has become known as American humor arose. Almost all our early humorists either constituted part of that background or at least wrote in response to it. Western humor was perhaps the first genuinely American contribution to our culture. Springing out of the new rhythm of life which the West had created, it captured an element of the American tempo which had eluded the Bryants, the Emersons, and the Thoreaus. The very smell and sting of the country was in it, the largeness, the crudeness, the paradoxical simplicity and diversity of it. The optimism bred in that country, the only country at that time which held forth promise to the oppressed millions of the earth and which made the common man into a hero, penetrated into that humor and endowed it with almost epic exaggeration. American humor became a snapshot reflection of the American soul. Its broad, farcical, slapstick character was an unequivocally native product. It was the only kind of humor which could have meaning to the plain-speaking, simple-minded, polyglot populations that inhabited the West. Into its fun-loving, uproarious, rollicking spirit raced the naïve, exuberant enthusiasms of the land-thrilled populace of the day. It was the humor of a people who believed in the future, who saw the earth before them and felt it was theirs, and who, secure in themselves, abandoned themselves to the comic spirit in all its extremes of the burlesque and the grotesque. Humor such as that was unknown elsewhere in the world. French humor was unlike it; German humor bore no resemblance to it; English humor was made of very dif-

[103]J. J. Audubon: *Delineations of American Scenery and Character:* Edition New York, 1926: p. 61.

ferent stuff; and Russian humor was descended from a different stock. If one would turn for a moment to the humor
of pre-Revolutionary Russia and compare it with the humor
of nineteenth-century America, or even the humor of America of to-day, for the earlier pattern has persisted down into
the present, one would discover at once the difference which
I have stressed. Compare the humor of Averchenko, the
leading Russian humorist of the last century, or that of Teffy,
whom Mirsky considers a more native humorist, with that of
Artemus Ward, one of the leading American humorists of
the same century, and the contrast will be at once patent. The
humor of Averchenko, like that of Russian humor in general, even that of the peasants, was sharp, and cruel, and not
without an undertone of the tragic in its expression. The humor of Ward, on the other hand, was light and risible, and
even at its most satiric it never lost its underlying comic
appeal. In the case of Russia the spirit of the country under
the Czars, the suffering that the people endured under their
rulership, the absence of any semblance of freedom or any
glimpse of promise, robbed the country of the comic spirit
and prevented its humor from adopting a more carefree and
joyous tone. If we turn to English humor and compare it
with American, another type of contrast will present itself.
English humor has carried down with it something of the
subtle wit of the aristocratic tradition; American humor, on
the contrary, derivative of a humble background of petty
bourgeois farmers and merchants and El Dorado-seekers of
the West, has nothing of that subtlety about it but is blunt,
boisterous, and burlesque in manner and substance. It is not
difficult to understand, therefore, why the Englishman sneers
at American humor, and why the American is convinced that
the Englishman lacks a sense of humor. In *How to Tell a
Story* Mark Twain dealt with this difference as it manifested
itself in fiction. "The humorous story is American," Twain
pointed out; "the comic story is English, the witty story is
French." In a word, the difference is one of *subtlety*. To
Twain, however, bred in the frontier tradition, and contemp-

tuous of the refinements and subtleties of English and French art, the American story was superior to the others. With a naïveté characteristic of the Western outlook, he described the humorous story as "strictly a work of art, high and delicate art," and dismissed the English and French types by declaring that "no art is necessary in telling the comic and witty story, anybody can do it."

Before the first half of the nineteenth century had passed, American humor had come to constitute part of the American rhythm. When Royall Tyler in *The Contrast* had used the Yankee as a butt for comic jest, American humor was still in the embryo. By the time Davy Crockett died in the third decade of the next century, however, American humor had managed to root itself into almost every aspect of American life. Politics became permeated with it; no political speaker dared address an audience without interspersing his speech with humorous anecdotes. Part of Lincoln's success as a speaker was due to his skill as a story-teller. Even frontier clergymen were wont to sprinkle their sermons with humorous stories and allusions. And conversation in shop, tavern, and open field became rich with humorous jokes and fictions. Magazines responded to the tendency, and "Fun Jottings" and "Joke Corners" became a familiar part of their contents.[104] By 1880 there was scarcely a newspaper which did not have a humorous section or column. Toward the close of the century, Bret Harte, in an article in *Cornhill Magazine* (July, 1899), summarized in a most effective manner the whole development:

While the American literary imagination was still under the influence of English tradition, an unexpected factor was developing to diminish its power. It was *Humor*—of a quality as distinct and original as the country and civilization in which it was developed. It was at first noticeable in the anecdote "story," and after the fashion of such beginnings, was orally transmitted. It was common in the barrooms, the gatherings in "country stores," and finally at public

[104] Frank Luther Mott: *A History of American Magazines, 1741–1850*: New York, 1930: p. 424.

meetings in the mouths of "stump orators." Arguments were clinched and political principles illustrated by a "funny story." It invaded even the camp meetings and pulpit. It at last received the currency of the public Press. But wherever met it was so distinctly original and novel, so individual and characteristic, that it was at once known and appreciated abroad as "an American story." Crude at first, it received a literary polish in the Press, but its dominant quality remained. It was concise and condensed, yet suggestive. It was delightfully extravagant —or a miracle of under-statement. It voiced not only the dialect, but the habits of thought of a people or locality. It gave new interest to slang. From a paragraph of a dozen lines it grew into half a column, but always retaining its conciseness and felicity of statement. It was a foe to prolixity of any kind, it admitted no fine writing nor affectation of style. It went directly to the point. It was burdened by no conscientiousness; it was often irreverent; it was devoid of all moral responsibility—but it was original! By degrees it developed character with its incident, often, in a few lines, gave a striking photograph of a community or a section, but always reached its conclusion without an unnecessary word. It became—and still exists as— an essential feature of newspaper literature. It was the parent of the American short story.[105]

The humorists who arose in response to this development and who accelerated its growth, Artemus Ward, Petroleum V. Nasby, Seba Smith, Bill Nye, Josh Billings and a score of others, extending even down until to-day with Will Rogers, introduced into American literature a native slant and a realistic challenge.[106] Notwithstanding their extravagances and exaggerations, their slapstick gestures and verbal burlesques, these men, especially in their political satires and strictures, did more to destroy the romantic tradition than did any of their more dignified literary contemporaries. Their misspellings, their phonetic spellings, their contempt for all conventional spellings, were characteristic of the frontiersman's scorn for book-learning and European culture. Outlandish as were the stories of these humorists, preposterous as were

[105]Quoted from T. Edgar Pemberton's *Bret Harte:* London, 1900: pp. 160–162.
[106]Walter Blair: *Burlesques in Nineteenth Century American Humor: American Literature:* Vol. II, No. 3, p. 243; and D. A. Dondore: *The Prairie and the Making of Middle America:* Cedar Rapids, 1926: p. 238.

their fictions, nonsensical as were their allusions, there was a realistic twist about many of them which made the people think as well as laugh. While Stedman, voicing the sentiment of the New England literati who were emulative still of the English tradition, deplored the fact that the whole country had been deluged by the cheap humor of the West, and warned his contemporaries that literature had little hope in the face of "the present horrible *degeneracy* in public taste,"[107] it was this very humor, this so-called *degeneracy*, indigenous to the core, which was to lead to the production of one of the first significant writers in America to flow out of the native tradition.

That writer was none other than the humorist: Mark Twain.

While Walt Whitman should be described as the first American poet, Mark Twain must be credited with being the first American prose writer of any importance. Both men were products of the frontier force, which as we have shown in earlier sections of this chapter, was not something that was confined to its own region; it was a force that swept abroad in the land; gathering energy from its source, it arose like an intellectual typhoon, spiralling this way and that as it acquired momentum, and scattering itself in a myriad fragments as it spread. Even Europe felt its impact. Chateaubriand responded to it, and wrote his novel, *Atala,* in reaction to its magnificence; the European masses responded in an intenser fashion, picked up their belongings, abandoned the countries of their birth, and, spellbound by the promise it held forth, were drawn by its suction into the centre of its influence. Few American writers of the day were not shaken by its presence. Only Whitman, however, in the East, as we previously pointed out, absorbed the fulness of its impact, and, overwhelmed by the magnitude of its power and the magnificence of its promise, transmuted it into poetic form. Twain, on the other hand, did not have to absorb its impact;

---

[107] Walter Blair: *The Popularity of Nineteenth Century American Humorists: American Literature:* May, 1931: Vol. III, No. 2, p. 180.

its impact was part of his native heritage; it lived in his spiritual bloodstream. With him its influence was not derivative but fundamental. He expressed it in his person, exhaled it in his words, voiced it in his philosophy. In short, he became its dynamic symbol in literature.

Beginning as a pure frontier product, reeling off in his prose all the spontaneity of that region, its hilarious gaieties and irresponsible enthusiasms, he ended in the East as a convinced pessimist and a dyspeptic philosopher not less desperate in his despairs than Leopardi. In a way, he was the Charlie Chaplin of American literature. Ever eager, especially in his latter days, to be a Hamlet, he was forced to remain a Falstaff. There were, thus, two Mark Twains and not one, and those who have tried to interpret the contradictions in his character have tripped up very often by their failure to see that this dichotomy in his personality had as much to do with the environment as with the immediate conflict of his soul. The youthful Mark Twain, the Mark Twain of the West, the avatar of the frontier, who loved pilots, and miners, and the common run of people, who felt himself part of the region he described, and who in humorous form gave life to those people and to that region—that Mark Twain was an optimist, a lover of life, a devotee of the soil and of the country which he cherished with such childish pride. The other Mark Twain, the older Mark Twain, the Mark Twain of the East, the Mark Twain who was successful, had lost that optimism and zest, had lost the faith of his youth. The America that he saw growing up about him was not the America of his dream. The promise of the frontier had begun to grow stale. The era of the trusty boatmen had vanished. Industry had overcome the nation, and subdued the land and those who had once controlled it. Before he wrote *What Is Man* and *The Mysterious Stranger*, America had already "snatched the Philippines," as he remarked in an article, and "stained the flag." Indeed, there was little left of the America which he once loved. Nothing expressed his disillusionment more completely than his conversation with Tchaikoffsky, the Russian revolutionist, who appealed to him to address a mass meeting.

I told him what I believed to be true: that our Christianity which we have always been so proud of—not to say so vain of—is now nothing but a shell, a sham, a hypocrisy; that we have lost our ancient sympathy with oppressed peoples struggling for life and liberty; that when we are not coldly indifferent to such things we sneer at them, and that the sneer is about the only expression the newspapers and the nation deal in with regard to such things; that his mass meeting would not be attended by people entitled to call themselves representative Americans, even if they may call themselves Americans at all; that his audiences will be composed of foreigners who have suffered so recently that they have not yet had time to become Americanized and have their hearts turned to stones in their breasts; that these audiences will be drawn from the ranks of the poor, not those of the rich; that they will give and give freely, but they will give from their poverty and the money result will not be large. I said that when our windy and flamboyant President conceived the idea a year ago of advertising himself to the world as the New Angel of Peace, and set himself the task of bringing about the peace between Russia and Japan and had the misfortune to accomplish his misbegotten purpose, no one in all this nation except Doctor Seaman and myself uttered a public protest against this folly of follies. That at that time I believed that that fatal peace had postponed the Russian nation's imminent liberation from its age-long chains indefinitely—probably for centuries; that I believed at that time that Roosevelt had given the Russian revolution its death-blow and that I am of that opinion yet.[108]

Carking psychological conflicts and heart-shaking tragedies too had come upon Twain, and embittered his personal outlook. To have remained the same man, then, to have retained the same philosophy, through all those vicissitudes of change, would have been impossible for any but the most insensitive personality.

The Mark Twain we are interested in, however, the Mark Twain who is important to American literature, is the early Mark Twain, the Mark Twain who was the author of *Innocents Abroad*, *The Gilded Age*, and *Huckleberry Finn*, and

[108] Mark Twain: *Autobiography*: Vol. II, pp. 292–293.

not the older Mark Twain, the Mark Twain who was the author of *What Is Man* and *The Mysterious Stranger*. *What Is Man*, for example, voicing the disenchantment of spirit that overcame him toward the end of his life, is a revealing philosophic exercise but nothing more. Its literary significance is infinitesimal. *Huckleberry Finn*, on the other hand, expressing the philosophy of his earlier life, and carrying within it the seeds of his own experience and the spirit of his native environment, is a significant fiction. Indeed, its literary importance has increased instead of decreased with the years.[109] Representing the younger Mark Twain who meant more to American literature than the older, and representing the America which at that time was the most American, *Huckleberry Finn* stands out not only as Twain's best work but also as one of the few *American* classics.

While Mark Twain had less difficulty in attaining recognition in America than Walt Whitman, it was not until the twentieth century, when the colonial complex broke down in the rising tide of nationalistic impulse, that he became appreciated for what he really was. In the nineteenth century he was viewed as a "funny man," a superb humorist, a literary burlesquer. Acclaimed far and wide for his fun-making proclivities, for his skill in evoking laughter, he was seldom considered in a serious vein, as an artistic genius or a literary force. When he mounted a platform, people began to laugh before he started to speak. Nothing that he said was taken seriously. Although William Dean Howells, possibly because of his own mid-western rearing, early appreciated the significance of Twain's literary genius, there were few others in the East who esteemed it at its true value. It was Howells, in fact, who said to Twain: "You have already written the longed-for Great American Romance, though nobody seems to know it—and you will do it again. *What stupendous fame*

[109] Because its hero lied and swore, *Huckleberry Finn* was forbidden in the public library at Concord, Mass., when it was first published. Sixteen years after its appearance, it was ejected from the Denver library, and barely escaped a similar fate in the Brooklyn Public Library as late as 1905. (Ibid., Vol. II, p. 333.)

you would have if you were only a foreigner!"[110] Henry L. Mencken described excellently Twain's fate in the nineteenth century when he observed that "with only his books to recommend him, (Twain) would probably have passed into obscurity in middle age; it was in the character of a public entertainer, not unrelated to Coxey, Dr. Mary Walker and Citizen George Francis Train, that he wooed and won the country. The official criticism of the land denied him any solid literary virtue to the day of his death."[111] Only in the twentieth century was Twain's fame esteemed at its real worth. Van Wyck Brooks found Twain significant enough to write one of his best books about him: *The Ordeal of Mark Twain*, and Waldo Frank was moved to call Huckleberry Finn "the American epic hero," and to declare that "the soul of Mark Twain was great."[112]

The Americanness of Twain was scorned in the nineteenth century just as that of Whitman was scorned. In the case of Twain there was no sexual candor to be feared or shunned, for, as Twain has recorded, his wife edited every line he wrote and removed from his work every passage that bordered on the salacious.[113] The main objection to his work was that it was not in the English tradition. It was American in its humor, American in its slang idiom, American in its frontier spirit. In every way it violated the canons of good taste which England had established. It hugged close to the soil of its native land instead of to that of the mother coun-

[110]Clara Clemens: *My Father Mark Twain*: New York, 1931: p. 102.

[111]Henry L. Mencken: *Prejudices, Second Series*, essay on the "National Letters": pp. 52, 53.

[112]Waldo Frank: *Our America*: New York, 1919: p. 38.

[113]Twain's own description of this supervision is interesting in this connection, revealing as it does the deplorable effect it had upon the candor and strength of his work: "She would sit on the porch at the farm and read aloud, with her pencil in her hand, and the children would keep an alert and suspicious eye upon her right along, for the belief was well grounded in them that whenever she came across a particularly satisfactory passage she would strike it out. Their suspicions were well founded. The passages which were so satisfactory to them always had an element of strength in them which sorely needed modification or expurgation, and was always sure to get it at their mother's hand." (Mark Twain: *Autobiography*: New York, 1924: pp. 89, 90.)

try. It expressed the barbarous, inchoate, spontaneous spirit of the American people instead of the refined, elegant, dignified spirit of the English literary code.

Innocents Abroad, which sold over thirty-one thousand copies within the first six months of its publication, was, perhaps, the first *American* work of prose to appear in this country. Few books have voiced the spirit of the frontier, which represented at that time the only part of the country where the colonial complex did not predominate, as clearly and as challengingly as *Innocents Abroad.* Like Whitman, Twain sensed in democracy, democracy in the frontier form, the distinguished characteristic of America. But it was not democracy that stopped at the ballot. It was democracy that ran through the whole course of life, permeating economics as well as politics, art as well as science. When he went abroad he poked fun at European art and culture, satirized the masters, preferred copies of the masterpieces to the originals, and sneered at the fake idolatry of the old which dominated European civilization. He preferred the new, the American. And yet his contempt was not based on the sheer prejudice of the barbarian. His opposition to European art was founded upon his democratic bias. "We visited the Louvre," he wrote, ". . . and looked at its miles of paintings by the old masters. Some of them were beautiful, but at the same time *they carried such evidences about them of the cringing spirit of those great men that we found small pleasure in examining them. Their nauseous adulation of princely patrons was more prominent to me and chained my attention more surely than the charms of color and expression which are claimed to be in the pictures.* Gratitude for kindness is well, but it seems to me that some of those artists carried it so far that it ceased to be gratitude, and became worship. If there is a plausible excuse for the worship of men, then by all means let us forgive Rubens and his brethren."[114] In another place, he continued in the same vein but with added bitterness. "And who painted these things? Why Titian, Tintoretto, Paul Vero-

[114] Mark Train: *Innocents Abroad:* pp. 87–88.

nese, Raphael—none other than the world's idols, the old masters."

"Andrea del Sarto glorified his princes in pictures that must save them forever from the oblivion they merited, and they let him starve. Served him right. Raphael pictured such infernal villains as Catherine and Marie de Medici seated in heaven and conversing familiarly with the Virgin Mary and the angels (to say nothing of higher personages), and yet my friends abuse me because I am a little prejudiced against the old masters—because I fail sometimes to see the beauty that is in their productions. I cannot help but see it, now and then, but I keep on protesting against the grovelling spirit that could persuade those masters to prostitute their noble talents to the adulation of such monsters as the French, Venetian, and Florentine princes of two and three hundred years ago, all the same . . .

"I am told that the old masters had to do these shameful things for bread, the princes and potentates being the only patrons of art. If a grandly gifted man may drag his pride and his manhood in the dirt for bread rather than starve with the nobility that is in him untainted, the excuse is a valid one. It would excuse theft in Washingtons and Wellingtons, and unchastity in women as well."[115]

What are these moral judgments of art but the pure product of the ideology of the frontier? The frontier with its petty bourgeois psychology believed in the free man, the freedom of individual man from the tyranny of aristocrats as well as plutocrats. It believed in itself, as we have said, it believed in its own principles and potentialities. It did not want to be tied on to Europe. It refused to be over-awed by an adoration of the old. It was at one with Mark Twain in his remarks upon European people and places; it shared his dislike for tapestries and his scorn for venerated sites and vistas. Its spirit spoke in Twain's carping description of the Arno as "a great historical creek with four feet of water in the channel and some scows floating around." Only an Amer-

[115] Ibid., p. 175.

ican, too, could have made Twain's famous reflection upon the Grand Duomo of Florence—"a vast pile that has been sapping the purses of her citizens for five hundred years, and is not nearly finished yet."

Innocents Abroad, then, was not the result of a sudden outburst of distemper by an American who was at once irritated and amused by the European things he saw. It was an individual outgrowth of a whole social philosophy. Back in earlier days, when he was associated with *The Californian*, the literary journal which Charles Henry Webb had established and with which Bret Harte was connected for a time, Twain had begun the work which later found more coherent form in *Innocents Abroad*. In his first pieces in *The Californian*, he had started making fun of art, had ridiculed the opera, and had even gone so far as to satirize science.[116] And, above everything else, in all his writing there he had early revealed his preference for the language of the people to the language of the dictionary. Indeed, in true frontier style, he had shown, in an imaginary discussion with a miner, the folly and futility of dictionary-diction as an instrument of human communication.

In *The Gilded Age*, which Twain wrote in collaboration with Warner, he turned his attention immediately to America, and launched a vigorous attack upon the political corruption in the nation. Twain's picture of how Congress was controlled, and how votes were bought and sold, combined with his ironic preface celebrating the achievements of our "ideal commonwealth," made his volume into one of the most challenging of the time. From beginning to end it stung with satire. "We send many missionaries to lift up the benighted races of other lands," the authors dryly observed, "how much cheaper and better it would be if those people could only come here and drink of our civilization at its fountain-head." *The Gilded Age* was one of the earliest and best embodiments of the petty bourgeois philosophy of the

[116] *Sketches of the Sixties*, by Bret Harte and Mark Twain, being forgotten material now collected for the first time from *The Californian*, 1864–1867: San Francisco, 1926: pp. 131, 151.

frontiersman in his struggle against the corrupting influence of the class in power. In fact, *The Gilded Age* was the precursor of those many attacks upon the exercise of power, which were to be made by the novelists and politicians of later generations. It anticipated in its way the novels of Frank Norris and Herbert Quick and the political protests of William Jennings Bryan and Robert M. La Follette. Its humor was of that biting, realistic variety which stabbed at the same time that it entertained. In *The Gilded Age* appeared evidences of that bitterness which later on was to dominate Twain's philosophy. The situation which Twain attacked in that book, however, was soon to become hopeless of cure, for within little more than a decade the West was to be controlled by the railroads and enslaved by the financial forces of the East.

At no time, except perhaps when he became so obsequious over the Oxford degree that was bestowed upon him, did Twain desert his forthright petty bourgeois point of view; at no time did he "sell out" his philosophy to the upper bourgeoisie of the East. In the twentieth century, if he had lived until our day, it is even likely that he might have joined in with Dreiser and taken a communistic stand. But living when he did, when all of America, even its labor movement, was dominated by a petty bourgeois instead of a proletarian psychology, the petty bourgeois position was the most advanced one of his type could take. To such as Twain it often seemed the stand of the revolutionary. In *Roughing It* he sarcastically condemned the American practice of not mining "the silver ourselves by the sweat of our brows and the labor of our hands, but to *sell* the ledges to the dull slaves of toil and let them do the mining." He was always enthusiastic about the French Revolution, and even defended the Terror without hesitation. His condemnation in *Life on the Mississippi* of the influence of Sir Walter Scott upon the South was of the same petty bourgeois strain:[117]

[117] But even Twain's deference to petty bourgeois morality, a defense which as we have seen was most injurious to his work, could not make him stomach Oliver Goldsmith's *Vicar of Wakefield*. In *Following the Equator*

Then comes Sir Walter Scott with his enchantments, and by his single might checks this wave of progress, and even turns it back; sets the world in love with dreams and phantoms; with decayed and degraded systems of government; with the silliness and emptiness, sham grandeurs, and sham chivalries of a brainless and worthless long vanished society.

Twain at least sought to make his philosophy inclusive. He tied up his art with his politics. "I have never tried in even one single instance to help cultivate the cultivated classes," he wrote in defense of his treatment of the English upper classes in *A Yankee at the Court of King Arthur*, "I was not equipped for it, either by native gifts or training. And I never had any ambition in that direction, but always hunted for bigger game—the masses." Even in *Huckleberry Finn*, the virtues extolled are those of the petty bourgeois frontiersman. Huck is a western lad, embodying the independent, dare-devil spirit of the region, a rapscallion type contemptuous of rules and regulations, scornful of Sunday-school and even of civilization—scornful of everything but himself and what he regards as right. Huck, an epic embodiment of the frontier in knee-pants, sticks by himself in defiance of what others think, in defiance even of institutions and all the moral paraphernalia of the conventional world.[118]

It was the triumph of Northern capitalism in the Civil War which determined the destiny of America during the rest of the nineteenth century, and which still determines it to-day. The Civil War was a progressive war, and those liberal historians who belittle its significance fail entirely to understand its historical content. Like the Revolutionary

he commented in this manner on that book: "Also, to be fair, there is another word of praise due to this ship's library: it contains no copy of the *Vicar of Wakefield*, that strange menagerie of complacent hypocrites and idiots, of theatrical cheap-john heroes and heroines, who are always showing off, of bad people who are not interesting, and good people who are fatiguing. A singular book. Not a sincere line in it, and not a character that invites respect; a book which is one long waste-pipe discharge of goody goody puerilities and dreary moralities; a book which is full of pathos which revolts and humor which grieves the heart."

[118] Even Mark Twain's perturbation over whether he should permit Huck to mutter the word "hell" could not destroy the genuineness of Huck's personality.

War, the Civil War marked another step in advance in the solidification of the country as a whole. "Where can you find an American so pedantic, so absolutely idiotic," wrote Lenin, "as to deny the revolutionary and progressive significance of the American Civil War of 1860–65?" Marx, even earlier than Lenin, had stressed the social importance of the Civil War in terms of its historical content. Few of our historians have yet realized the challenging significance of the Civil War force, with the Abolitionist movement, led by Garrison, Whittier, and Wendell Phillips, as its precursor, and the Reconstruction movement, led at first by Thaddeus Stevens and Sumner, as its aftermath. Instead of appreciating the progressive idealism of Garrison and Sumner, our historians have spent most of their energy dealing with the corruption of the Thermidorian era which followed.

The Abolitionist movement represented one of the most significant progressive forces in the pre-Civil War era. Its influence among many American writers was direct and decisive. Beginning in 1826 with John Quincy Adams' sonnet in which the following lines appeared:

> Who but shall learn that freedom is the prize
> Man still is bound to rescue or maintain;
> That nature's God commands the slave to rise,
> And on th' oppressor's head to break his chain.
> Roll, years of promise, rapidly roll round,
> Till not a slave shall on this earth be found.

American men of letters took up the challenge to slavery, and addressed an increasing part of their energies to its destruction. While Whittier and Lowell assumed the lead in that challenge, and are best remembered for it, scores of obscure and forgotten literati contributed their talents in unstinted devotion to the cause. Long before Adams' poem, of course, there were writers who had attacked slavery— writers in the South as well as in the North. In fact, anti-slavery societies were organized in the South in the eighteenth century, at a time when slavery was not the profitable institution it became after the invention of the cotton-gin. It was the northern writers, however, who led the fight. At the beginning of the nineteenth century, the northern writers stood alone. In the South practically every writer at that time, overwhelmed by the impact of his environment, had become an apologist for slavery. In the North, on the other hand, spurred on by the intensifying conflict between the two environments, anti-slavery writers multiplied. In earlier days Cotton Mather, Samuel Sewall, John Woolman, and later on John Trumbull, Timothy Dwight, Mrs. Morton, Susanna Rowson, William Dunlap, Philip Freneau, and Robert Montgomery Bird began the attack; it was John Greenleaf Whittier, James Russell Lowell, and Wendell Phillips, however, who converted it into a resounding challenge.

Like most movements in their inception the Abolitionist movement grew out of a small nucleus. When Benjamin Lundy began to publish *The Genius of Universal Emancipation,* he had but six subscribers. Garrison did not have many more when he started *The Liberator.* Lowell's lines, descriptive of those men, are historically if not poetically unforgettable:

> They were men, who dared to be
> In the right with two or three.

But these men, aided by a movement that multiplied on all sides, became so formidable that they at once inspired and terrified a large part of the nation. A reward of $5,000 was offered by the State of Georgia for the body of Garrison. Abolitionists were tabooed and persecuted, outlawed in business, excluded from "respectable" society, satirized in the press, and classified as insane fanatics. Even Emerson, who was not deeply stirred by the cause of emancipation—the only time he was moved at all was when he learned of the murder of Lovejoy and when the Fugitive Slave Law was passed—was not very friendly to the Abolitionists or their work. "Those who are urging with utmost ardor what are called the greatest benefits to mankind, are narrow, self-pleasing, conceited men," Emerson said of the Abolitionists, "and affect us as the insane do." It was Doctor Holmes, as Chapman pointed out in his book on Garrison, who declared that "it would have taken a long time to get rid of slavery if some of Emerson's teachings in that lecture had been accepted as the whole gospel of liberty."

If the Abolitionist movement did not achieve the creation of great literature, it did more to inspire the literati with social purpose than any other force of its day. It made men like Thomas Wentworth Higginson participate in an attack on the Court House in Boston in an effort to rescue the fugitive slave, Anthony Burns; it made Wendell Phillips demand the use of force in order to free the nation from slavery; it drove Theodore Parker to challenge all Americans to arise and save their "brother man"; it inflamed Thoreau to such a point that he declared that "if there is any hell more unprincipled than our rulers and our people, I feel curious to visit it. . . . If we would save our lives, we must fight for them"; it spurred Lowell to write *The Biglow Papers,* which constituted a direct attack upon the Mexican War, a war waged, as Lowell declared, for the spread of slavery throughout the farther sections of the Union; and it moved Whittier to write many of his most vigorous poems, and after the Civil War was over to pen one of the few fine poems which stands to his credit, *Laus Deo.* Even Longfellow was stirred sufficiently by the social fact to express his sympathy for the slave, and to point a warning finger toward the South lest it fail to heed the awful fate which it might bring upon itself. Garrison's vigorous attack upon Christianity for aiding the cause of slavery was not surpassed by Whittier's merciless tirade against the Christian church in his poem, *A Sabbath Scene.* His words:

> Then down with pulpit, down with priest,
> And give us Nature's teaching!

continue still to have appeal and meaning. Change the situation from bond-slavery to wage-slavery, and the words have an immediately contemporary pertinence.

As Doctor Lorenzo Dow Turner has shown in his valuable study, *Anti-Slavery Sentiment in American Literature,* there were scores of writers, many popular in their time but now forgotten, who allied themselves with the Abolitionists. The one, however, who did more than any other to arouse sentiment in favor of emancipation was Harriet Beecher Stowe. Less of an artist than Whittier and Lowell, she was able, by virtue of the simplicity and sentimentality of her appeal, to win the wider response of the populace. It was its literary vices rather than its virtues which made *Uncle Tom's Cabin* such a phenomenal success. Appearing in magazine form a year after the passage of the Fugitive Slave Act, it crystallized in its challenge all the tumultuous sentiment of opposition which had sprung up at the time. Even Emerson, as we have noted, had become stirred by the crisis created by the enactment of the Act. The North was waiting for just such a book. It might even be said, judged by its success abroad, that all the world outside of the South was waiting for just such a book. Uncle Tom became a symbol of slavery in action. People talked of Uncle Tom in a more intimate sense than they ever did about Dickens' characters. He became a familiar reference wherever slavery was discussed. The novel was dramatized by nine different authors, including Mrs. Stowe herself. But Mrs. Stowe did not stop her anti-slavery activities with this one novel. In 1855 she published another novel, *Dred,* and in 1859 still another, *The Minister's Wooing,* both of which dealt with the slavery question in a condemnatory fashion, the former directly and the latter indirectly. Neither of these novels, however, attained the popular fame of *Uncle Tom's Cabin.*

Once the Civil War was over, the social energy invested in the Abolitionist movement dissipated itself into ineffectual channels. Holmes and Whittier celebrated the victory of the North with poems of triumph—triumph not of might but of virtue. A few years later, however, both of these men, content with the destruction of bond-slavery but undisturbed by the tragic presence of wage-slavery, became social reactionaries. Only Wendell Phillips, realizing that the eradication of bond-slavery was but one step in social advance, insisted upon carrying the fight for emancipation to the workers' front. Phillips alone of all the Abolitionists turned radical, and saw that it was wage-slavery which next had to be eradicated.

The Civil War settled the question of national supremacy, which had vexed the course of the nation since the end of the eighteenth century. It set into motion those processes which were to give to the country for the first time in its history the semblance of a united whole. By the end of the century those processes had already developed sufficient momentum to create a consciousness of national identity. This unity, it is true, was not the outgrowth of voluntary co-operation on the part of the nation as a whole, but was the result of industrial conquest on the part of the industrial and financial forces in the East. It was Northern capitalism which forced the rest of the nation to march in step with its own programme of progress. If the two Americas which had existed in the East before the Civil War were not immediately fused into one America, one thing was accomplished; the remnant of the other America, the South, was no longer able to play a decisive rôle in national policy or to interfere with the advance of Northern capitalism. Moreover, the introduction of industry into the South marked the beginning of the process of unification, and if industry at the present time has not yet secured control of the Southern scene, it will be only a matter of time before the present controls of the petty bourgeoisie are disestablished by the rising power of the industrial bourgeoisie. While the conquest of the West did not involve a Civil War, its execution was scarcely less brutal and harrowing—and what is worse, its justification was founded upon an even greater lie. Through control of the means of transportation and finance, it was able to exploit the farmers and workers of the West, and reduce them to a condition of economic slavery, at the same time that it was able to spread its power beyond its national borders, and, by war, cunning, and chicanery, subdue the West Indies, the Philippines, and the lower Americas.

The Northern conquest of the West, which meant the conquest of the petty bourgeois forces of the West by the upper bourgeois forces of the North, constitutes one of the most horrible and vicious chapters in American history. It was through the railroad that the conquest was begun. Before the Civil War, railroad lines had been laid out, but the problem of states' rights had prevented most of those plans from being put into execution. Trans-continental railroads needed a united country to encourage their growth. Once the Civil War was concluded, however, and Northern capitalists were free to stretch their exploitive fingers from one end of the nation to the other, the whole country was tracked with railroad lines, extending from the Atlantic to the Pacific. The passage of railway bills became a common occurrence in Congress. One railroad after another was chartered by the national government—the Union Pacific, the Central Pacific, the Atlantic and Pacific, the Texas Pacific, the Great Northern and many others. The government, which supported, and was part of, the whole development, very often gave the railroads free lands and granted them loan-subsidies. In short, it did everything within its power to stimulate railroad enterprise. But the railroad capitalists were not content with lining the country with railroad systems. What they had to do was to populate that country, fill it with farmers, encourage business undertakings, stir up new towns and cities, begin booms—or otherwise the railroads would be a failure, for there would be no freight to carry and no passengers to transport. Then began, in answer to that need, a campaign for population such as has never been seen elsewhere in the world. Railroad capital invested stupendous resources in that campaign. It performed the function of a state in recruiting immigrants for the community. It despatched its agents all over Europe in an attempt to woo the inhabitants from their native lands. It published its advertising pamphlets in every important language and had its agents distribute them widely over Europe. Steamship and railroad officials in various European countries co-operated in this distribution. Every type of appeal, however lurid, was employed by the companies. Pictures of American prosperity, of poor peasants who had become suddenly rich immediately after they had come to America, of shopkeepers who had become manufacturers and mayors of western towns, provided the main inspiration of this literature. In other cases, America was painted as the land of freedom and democracy where the European masses could escape the oppression which they had experienced in their homelands. Fake letters from settlers were invented, describing the beauties of the West and the unbounding riches which were in store there for all who came in search of them. Nature was depicted as ideal for farming, in fact for every form of occupation. College professors were even induced to prove that there was sufficient rainfall west of the Missouri to provide for ideal agriculture.[119] Once the immigrants had been brought to America, the struggle to locate them near respective railroad sites began. It was at that point that the keen competition between the different companies became most vicious. Whole trainloads of Swedes, Norwegians, Germans, Poles, Bohemians, were stolen by the agent of one company from another, and sometimes re-stolen, and shifted off in different directions from those in which they had originally started. This type of guerilla warfare between the companies, in which the helpless immigrants were the ones who suffered, continued until the free lands were exhausted and the frontier was closed.

But the railroad capitalists were not interested only in European settlers. They spent as much if not more of their energies in endeavoring to persuade the American populace to move westward. They propagandized the East with their pamphlets and brochures, stressing the superior advantages of the West over the East from the point of view of health as well as wealth. They offered special reductions of fare to

[119]John D. Hicks: *The Populist Revolt:* Minneapolis, 1931: p. 11. In the early part of his book, Doctor Hicks gives an excellent account, to which I am considerably indebted, of this whole development.

all who wished to visit the West, and survey the possibilities of settling there. Where families were involved, even greater reductions, with particular privileges, were allowed. In fact, everything which would encourage the Easterner to go West, and the farther west the better, was utilized by the companies. With the aid of the Homestead Act, which had been passed in 1862, and the Timber Culture Act, which followed eleven years later, the free land which the settler needed in most cases was there for him to secure. What the railroads had to do was to persuade him to go after it. And in that effort they were most successful. Between 1870 and 1880, for example, the population of Nebraska leaped from 122,-993 to 452,402, that of the Dakota Territory from 14,181 to 135,177, that of Kansas from 364,399 to 996,096. In the eighties the great booms arose, and artificial towns were made over night and natural towns were magnified far beyond their economic capacity. Lands were mortgaged far beyond their real worth, and real-estate values in general soared into fabulous figures. But then, in 1887, the drouths came, and the reaction set in. The boom burst, panic followed, and before another decade had passed the artificial towns had disappeared, and the natural ones had been reduced in size, and thousands of ruined farmers and bankrupt business men and real estate speculators had started back East.

The railroad capitalists, in the meanwhile, had profited enormously by this growth of the West, and little by little had enslaved the very farmers that they had formerly induced to settle in the new territories. By establishing exorbitant freight charges, they were able to exploit the farmer at the point of exchange, and make him into a vassal of Eastern capital. "The consolidation and combination of railroad capital . . . in maintaining an oppressive and tyrannical transportation system (demands) instant, vigorous and increasing action on the part of the producers"—such was the challenge of the Farmers Alliance men in the Northwest in 1880.[120] But the challenge was of little avail. While the

[120]Ibid., pp. 147, 148.

farmers did not surrender the fight, but actually carried it into the field of political revolt, they were beaten down finally by the forces of the East, which in the twentieth century got a strangle-hold upon the nation.

It was that change in the American scene, signified by the closing of the frontier and the disappearance of the freedom and autonomy of the West, resulting in the exploitation of the farmers by the forces of finance, that altered the character of Western literature, and destroyed the optimism inspired by the early frontier force. The pessimism that followed wrote itself deeply into the spirit of the nation. It was reflected as definitely in the changed philosophy of Mark Twain as in the fiction of Hamlin Garland and Frank Norris. While it would be absurd to deny that certain personal factors in Twain's life affected the pessimism of his later years, it would be equally preposterous to assert that the change in American life which we have just noted had little to do with its growth. In his younger days Twain had been an ardent democrat; indeed, he had accepted democracy not as a political form but as a living faith. He had extolled things American because they were democratic instead of aristocratic in character. When abroad he had constantly rained down attacks upon the Europeans, and with a frontier flourish, had seldom failed to announce his Americanism upon every possible occasion. Once that democracy had been destroyed, however, and the nation had fallen into the hands of the bankers and industrialists, his petty bourgeois enthusiasm turned into bitterness. The imperialistic development of the country after the Spanish American War aroused his instantaneous antagonism. When President Roosevelt wired General Wood and congratulated him on his victory in the Philippines, Mark Twain denounced the whole business in words which still carry with them the ring of challenge:

His whole utterance is merely a convention. Not a word of what he said came out of his heart. He knew perfectly well that to pen six hundred helpless and weaponless savages in a hole like rats in a trap and massacre them in detail during the stretch of a day and a half, from a safe position on the heights above, was no brilliant feat of arms—and would not have been a brilliant feat of arms even if Christian America, represented by its salaried soldiers, had shot them down with bibles and the Golden Rule instead of bullets. He knew perfectly well that our uniformed assassins had *not* upheld the honor of the American flag, but had done as they have been doing continuously for eight years in the Philippines—that is to say, they had dishonored it.

Twain's denunciation was not that of a radical who disbelieved in private property as an institution and who saw in the conquest of the Philippines as in all imperialistic conquest the inevitable development of the property-impulse; it was, on the other hand, the protest of a petty bourgeois who believed in private property as an institution and who was loath to see the private property rights of smaller nations infringed upon or usurped by larger nations, even when the larger nation was his own country. The pessimism that overtook Twain, then, was not the pessimism of a mind which loathed the capitalistic character of his civilization, and saw in it the source of most of the evils of his time. It was pessimism, on the other hand, of an individual who deplored the growth of large capital at the expense of small capital, and resented the ensuing suffering which resulted when large capitalists, organizing themselves into the dictators of the nation, pressed the small capitalists to the wall, and, as in the case of the farmers in the West and the Filipinos in the East, employed every form of exploitation and force in order to extend their power. A close witness of all this change in capitalistic enterprise, it is no wonder that his latter-day philosophy became colored by a despair which made him distrustful of both life and man. Not only did he live to see the disappearance of practically all the vestiges of petty bourgeois democracy which he had cherished, but he also came to know man in his worst, that is his most acquisitive, form. Sensitive as he was to such change, it was almost inevitable for one of his temperament to become convinced "that of all creatures that were made (man) is the most detestable," and to observe that "in all the list he is the only creature that has a nasty mind."[121] But all this disillusionment as to the nature of man was bound up inextricably with his disillusionment with social institutions and concepts. The old truths of the frontier became lies to him in the twentieth century, when the West had become a place of slavery instead of freedom. "There are certain sweet-smelling, sugar-coated lies current in the world," Twain wrote in his *Autobiography*, "which all politic-men have apparently tacitly conspired together to support and perpetuate. One of these is that there is such a thing in the world as independence; independence of thought, independence of opinion, independence of action. . . . Another is, that there is such a thing in the world as toleration. . . . Out of these trunk-lies spring many branch ones: to wit, the lie that not all men are slaves; . . . that I am I, and you are you; that we are units, individuals, and have natures of our own, instead of being the tail-end of a tapeworm eternity of ancestors back and back and back—to our source in the monkeys, with this so-called individuality of ours a decayed and rancid mush of inherited instincts and teachings derived atom by atom, stench by stench, from the entire line of that sorry column, and not so much new and original matter in it as you could balance on a needle-point and examine under a microscope."[122] This contempt for man, this confession of despair at the human race, expressed with almost Nietzschean vigor and forthrightness, revealed not only the pessimism which had eaten its way into Twain's mind but also the pessimism which had begun to overwhelm the age. Frank Norris absorbed it, and, as we shall see in the next chapter, Theodore Dreiser became a victim of it as well as Mark Twain.

Years before Twain wrote those words in his *Autobiography*, indeed, years before he conceived of *What is Man*, romanticism had been succeeded by realism on the frontier.

[121] Mark Twain: *Autobiography*: New York, 1924: Vol. II, p. 7.
[122] Ibid., Vol. II, pp. 8–10.

Bret Harte, it should be remembered, despite his entire realities of pioneer life, had hovered much closer to the romantic tradition than to the realistic. In his fiction as well as in his verse he was far more imitative than original. Even his best stories, *Luck of Roaring Camp* and *Outcasts of Poker Flat,* had little of the America, that is the frontier, rhythm in them. The Americanness of the humorists, whom Harte wrote so well about years later in England, he was unable to capture in his own work. Even the naturalness of dialogue which Mark Twain achieved, he was never able to acquire. While it is true that, as Julian Hawthorne pointed out, he never "contributed (a) lovable or respectable woman to literature," he seldom failed to resort to the didactic to cover up the sins of his characters. The West to Harte was more like a romantic venture than a realistic invasion. "I regard the story of the Argonauts of '49," he averred in one of his lectures, "as quaint as that of the Greek adventurers; a kind of crusade without a cross, an exodus without a prophet."[123] Great as Harte's vogue was in the seventies, it did not continue for a long period. The writers who succeeded him in influence were more interested in realistic fact than in melodramatic episode.

One of the first of those realists was Edward Eggleston, who, like many of the western authors, did most of his writing in the East, where he had settled in his early thirties. A circuit rider for the Methodist Church for several years in the West, Eggleston continued his ministerial career in the East for a while, became the rector of a non-sectarian church in Brooklyn, but finally gave up religion altogether and adopted the outlook of the sceptic.[124] Eggleston, to be exact, was not a realist in the modern sense of the word; certainly he did not go as far as the later realists, especially not the twentieth-century ones. But, as he has informed us and as his novels testify, he did make a serious effort to face

[123] Bret Harte: *The Argonauts of '49:* p. 1.
[124] George Gary Eggleston: *The First of the Hoosiers:* Philadelphia, 1903: p. 121. It was George Eggleston, Edward Eggleston's brother, who called the latter the "First of the Hoosiers." (Ibid., p. 13.)

the facts of western life, and paint them without attempting
to distort their forms or heighten their colors. Part of his
failure to achieve greater distinction in his fiction was undoubtedly due to his inexorable fidelity to fact as he saw it.
When Eggleston became editor of *Hearth and Home,* he
literally had to fight the entire board of control of the magazine in order to introduce fiction into its pages, so much at
that time was it disesteemed in the West.[125] When *The
Hoosier Schoolmaster* appeared in it, Eggleston was warned
by one of his ecclesiastical friends that he doubted "if true
consecration is compatible with the literary work you are
doing."[126] But Eggleston continued his work nonetheless,
and later on, when he went East, he succeeded Theodore
Tilton as editor of *The New York Independent.* Eggleston
had been Tilton's subordinate until Tilton was discharged
for writing his startling editorial on Love, Marriage, and
Divorce, in which he advocated divorce.[127] In later life,
Eggleston planned an extended *History of Life in the
United States,* but after twenty years' research only managed
to complete two volumes of the series. Even in his historical
work, Eggleston attempted to adhere as faithfully to reality
as he did in his fiction.

Whatever his failures were, Eggleston deserves credit for
being one of the first of the frontier writers to oppose the
romantic conception of the West which had been foisted
upon America and the world by the writers in the East, in
particular by Cooper and Simms. "It used to be a matter of
no little jealousy with us, I remember," Eggleston noted in
the preface to the first edition of his novel, *The Hoosier
Schoolmaster,* "that the manner, customs, thoughts, and feelings of New England country people filled so large a place
in books, while our life, not less interesting, not less romantic,
and certainly not less filled with humorous and grotesque

[125]Ibid., p. 295.
[126]Ibid., p. 308. At that time, it should be remembered, as G. C. Eggleston notes: "No Methodist church in Southern Indiana allowed any
musical instrument at its services." (P. 111.)
[127]Ibid., p. 325.

material, had no place in literature. It was as though we were shut out of good society. And, with the single exception of Alice Carey, perhaps, our Western writers did not dare speak of the West otherwise than as the unreal world to which Cooper's lively imagination had given birth." Eggleston's words indicated the change that had already come over Western literature. The early pioneer West was beginning to fade. The new West, invaded by the railroad, had become a less romantic place. This new West with its bumptious prides and patriotisms, its soil-stinging earthiness, its strong-arm eloquence and danger-defying logic, had to face an environment which was being changed faster than it was able to go, and by forces which were beyond its control. Eastern finance in the form of iron and steel was swiftly binding it hand and foot.

No American writer depicted that change as faithfully and as successfully as Hamlin Garland. Eggleston was affected by it, but he dealt very little with it. Garland was not only affected by it, but was a distinct product of it, and wrote of it with an intimacy which no other American writer save Howe has surpassed. What Garland's fiction lacked in structural and æsthetic excellence, it compensated for in social significance. Not content with realism, which struck him often as a form of literary compromise, he determined to be a "veritist." The truth about life must be told at all costs. Truth was more important than charm, content more significant than form. In stories such as *The Lion's Paw* and *The Return of the Private*, or in his novel *The Rose of Dutcher's Cooley*, it was the *facts* of Western life which concerned him more than the technique of translating those facts into literary fictions. In his volume, *Crumbling Idols*, he announced and outlined his veritistic theory which was to encourage "a literature, not of books, but of life." Like E. W. Howe, who, in his book, *The Story of a Country Town*, had preceded him in the realistic genre, Garland was more interested in the world of social fact than in the world of literary imagination.

A pure product of the frontier force, Garland expressed in his younger years all the optimism, the democratic faith, the self-reliant ideal, which were characteristic of his frontier contemporaries and those who were influenced by the logic of the West. In his thirty-fourth year, in the same volume which we cited before, *Crumbling Idols,* he declared, with an exuberance for which the West was noted throughout the nineteenth century, that "henceforth, when men of the Old World speak of America, they will not think of Boston and New York and Philadelphia, they will mean Chicago and the Mississippi Valley. . . . The schools of book-poets (the Eastern group, Whittier, Longfellow, Holmes, Lowell) is losing power. The rise of Chicago as a literary and art centre is a question only of time and of a very short time; . . . Henceforth St. Louis, New Orleans, Atlanta, Denver, San Francisco, Cincinnati, St. Paul, and Minneapolis, and a dozen more interior cities are to be reckoned with." His objection to the New England school was only one form of his uncompromising hostility for the colonial complex. He recognized in Longfellow, Whittier, Lowell, and Holmes the persistence of European imitation instead of the presence of native originality. In his preface to the same book, he maintained that "American art to be enduring and worthy must be original and creative, not imitative." And again, in another place, he asserted, voicing the individualistic spirit of the West, "I do not advocate an exchange of masters, but a freedom from masters. I defend the right of the modern to create in the image of life and not in the image of any master, living or dead." What he sought to do was to make America aware of the fact that the West was the one part of the country which possessed the spirit of originality, the one part of the nation in which a native impulse inhered. Garland's words, when re-read to-day, bring back to us a consciousness of how profound an influence the colonial complex continued to exercise over our literary life far down into the nineteenth century. "The history of American literature," Garland wrote, "is the history of provincialism slowly becoming less all-pervasive—the history of the slow development of a distinctive utterance. By provincialism I mean dependence upon a mother country for models of art production. . . . *Our colonial writers, and our writers from 1800 to 1860, had too little to do with the life of the American people, and too much concern with British critics.* . . . It has kept us timidly imitating the great writers of a nation far separated from us naturally in its social and literary ideals."[128] (Italics mine.) In his essay on *Literary Centres,* Garland pointed out that the East regarded itself as English, and therefore imitated English styles and patterns. The West, on the other hand, he contended, did not derive from England, but rather from Teutonic lands, and would "not be dominated by the English idea." "About 1885, at the time when I began to write of the Middle West," Garland noted in his recent book, *Roadside Meetings,*[129] . . . "so far as the pages of the literary magazines of that year were concerned, Wisconsin, Minnesota, and Iowa did not exist. Not a picture, not a single story or poem, not even a reference to these states could I discover in ten thousand pages of print. . . . England was depicted, and Palestine and Egypt, but not one word of the prairies of Illinois or the hills and lakes of Wisconsin could I find. . . . They were eager for the plains of Araby and the Vale of Cashmere, but the prairies of Iowa had no allurement." Even as late as 1885, as Garland observed, the colonial complex continued to fetter the mind of the East, and inspire the literati there to turn to England for materials instead of to their own country. Garland's championing of Whitman against the indifference if not hostility of the New England group was a product of this same attitude, this Western attitude as opposed to the Eastern, another manifestation of the connection between the frontier mood and the growth of Americanness in our prose and verse. Indeed, Garland's defense of Whitman is especially significant in this particular, for while he disagreed with the Bostonians in

[128] Hamlin Garland: *Crumbling Idols:* Chicago, 1894: pp. 1–8.
[129] Hamlin Garland: *Roadside Meetings:* New York, 1930: p. 119.

their imitation of foreign models, he agreed with them completely in their moral attitude. The veritist, he announced, "is tired of war and diseased sexualism. . . . Illicit love is the most hackneyed theme in the world." He was at one with Whittier and Longfellow and Lowell in opposing immorality in literature. And yet he could write Whitman and compliment him on "the transcendent power of *Leaves of Grass*" and call him "a great teacher," while the overwhelming majority of the New England literati considered *Leaves of Grass* little more than a composite of literary barbarisms and crudities, an insulting violation of the poetic tradition. If the sexual element had provided the main source of objection to Whitman, if Whitman had been as immoral a poet as many of the Bostonians avowed, Garland would have been as ardent an opponent of his verse as were Holmes and Whittier. The sexual element in Whitman's verse did not bother Garland, who found in his "elemental lines" something spiritually satisfying; it was the New England and Mid-Atlantic writers, who were still colonial-minded, and therefore unable to appreciate the Americanness of Whitman's verse, who affected to be repelled by the "sensuality" of his philosophy. Interestingly enough, Tennyson, who was the most moral of poets but who was not handicapped by the influence of a colonial complex, experienced no such repulsion in reading Whitman's verse.

Garland came closer to portraying the spirit of the frontier in his autobiographical works, however, than in his fiction. Beginning with his *A Son of the Middle Border*, which appeared in 1917, and continuing in *A Daughter of the Middle Border*, *Trail-Makers of the Middle Border*, and *Back Trailers*, he told the story of the Garland family from the time of their emigration West toward the middle of the last century to their return East in the twentieth century. While Garland's autobiographical writing like his fiction is without æsthetic distinction, it is so rich in intimate detail and historical insight that it is very likely that the picture which it has provided of the frontier background will endure. Tell-

ing us as he did in *Roadside Meetings,* that "Horace Greeley's *Go West, Young Man, Go West,* had been the marching orders under which the Garlands and McClintocks and
all their neighbors had been moving for forty years," he has
related in his various autobiographical narratives the experiences of that family and the fate of his soul. Above all, his
work has been consistently realistic—that is at least within
the province of what he has considered realism. The frontier
he described was not the frontier of romance, but the frontier
of defeat. As in his stories in *Main Travelled Roads,* the
hardness of the farmer's life in the West, the oppression of
the land laws, the vicious successes of the speculators, stand
out in his autobiographical works and give them their realistic—or veritistic—challenge. In his description of Richard,
in *Trail-Makers of the Middle Border,* Garland has caught
successfully the petty bourgeois psychology of the young
frontiersman:

> Like the youth in the city who from his garret hears the roar of
> vast enterprises and imaginatively shares them, so this young Yankee,
> working for wages on a raft, imagined himself a part of the up-
> building of a great state, and was happy in the belief. In all this he
> was typical of his generation.

But that psychology did not survive. The idealism of that
generation turned into the disillusionment of the next. The
father who had started out full of hope and heroism found
himself desolate of spirit a few decades later. Land taxes
weighed down upon him and made his life into a constant
struggle to meet them. The old pioneer days when he had
been "so patriotic, so confident, so sanguine of the country's
future" had passed. In their stead had come the days of
despair and defeat. "He had come a long way from the
buoyant faith of '66," Garland wrote in description of his
father's later years, "and the change in him was typical of the
change in the West in America."

The note which Garland sounded has been echoed and

reechoed in almost all the literature of the West in recent generations. The condition of the farmer, caught tighter and tighter in the web of Eastern finance, has grown progressively worse from year to year. With the exception of Joaquin Miller, who in *Overland in a Covered Wagon,* wrote the most vivid and telling story of the life of the pioneers on their westward journey through Oregon and California, practically all the Western writers have been concerned with the passing of the frontier and the tragedy that has followed.

Miller, like most of the frontier writers, had difficulty in winning recognition in the East. His first book, which after debate finally appeared in England under the title of *Songs of the Sierras,* was refused by every American publisher. As Julian Hawthorne, then living in London, said: "The English recognized him before we did, and valued him more highly and justly."[130] In America, with the colonial complex operative, a western talent such as Miller's had even less chance of acceptance than Whitman's. Attacked in America as an impostor, a wife-deserter, and a faker, he was hailed as a genuine American poet by Dante Gabriel Rossetti and many other English critics, and numbered among his English acquaintances such renowned persons as Swinburne, Tennyson, William Morris, Browning, and even Gladstone and Queen Victoria.[131] Inferior in æsthetic value as his verses undoubtedly were, they were scarcely much worse than the greater part of the poetry of Whittier and Lowell which passed as canonized verse in its day. While a few of his poems caught something of the rhythm which Whitman had captured, the majority of them fell into the conventional tradition. Remembered mainly as the romantic American who strutted down Piccadilly, sombrero-crowned, with an open red shirt, scarf and sash, which, combined with his shockingly long hair and beard, made him into one of those picturesque types which seem to step out of a picture, he really

---

[130] Harr Wagner: *Joaquin Miller and His Other Self:* San Francisco, 1929: p. 69.
[131] Ibid., p. 81.

deserved more credit than he has received for his depiction of frontier life in *Overland in a Covered Wagon* and also for the influence which he exerted on Europe in acquainting it, however extravagantly, with the spirit of the West. Describing an earlier day, and a different part of the frontier, the part which was the last to escape the domination which had overtaken Garland's middle border, Miller was, perhaps, the last of the frontier writers to preserve something of the old romantic attitude, the old optimistic spirit, in his delineation of the West. "And what noble pioneers!" he wrote in apostrophic vein, "poor enough they were, most of them, as were we all at first, but they were all industrious, honest as a rule, and as steady as oak; devout people, who always insisted upon building a church and schoolhouse, however humble, the first thing."[132] But Miller at best lived the life of a fascinating eccentric, peregrinating about the world, and then removing himself from the sphere of things when he returned to his native country; he was seldom close to the soil or to the people in the sense that Garland was or Twain. All too often also his poetry revealed little that was native and became nothing more than a cheap echo of Byron and Swinburne. Unfortunately, in much of his poetry as well as his personality there strutted the spirit of the charlatan.

If English writers were content with Miller's picture of the frontier, American writers at the time were not. As early as 1879 in *The Duke of Stockbridge* Edward Bellamy had depicted the conflict between the agricultural and financial interests which manifested itself in Shays' rebellion. Although *The Duke of Stockbridge* was a romance, laid back a hundred years in the American past, its challenge was just as immediate at the time it was written as during the time it described. Nine years later in *Looking Backward*, Bellamy outlined the contours of an imaginary Utopia which won the interest of a considerable part of America at the time. This Utopia was not based on Marxian lines, with the proletariat

[132] Joaquin Miller: *Overland in a Country Wagon*: Edition, New York, 1930: Edited by Sidney G. Firman: p. 92.

as the source of power, but was a romantic retreat, holding more appeal for the unfortunate and defeated petty bourgeois elements of that day than for the workers. Indeed, Bellamy's book was not written from the point of view of the worker but from that of the middle class, and it was to the lower middle-class elements in our society that it made its widest appeal. Bellamy societies, organized in response to the appeal of his doctrine, sprang up in divers sections of the country. Even a newspaper, *The Nationalist,* was founded in defense of the Bellamy ideal. In his later volume *Equality,* Bellamy dealt in even more detail with the private property motivation and its consequences in social life, particularly in thwarting the realization of that equality which democracy promised. Not only was economic citizenship as necessary as political citizenship, but industry had to be collectivized and the profit motif removed before society could be made truly social and equality actually established. Bellamy marked one of the earliest departures from the individualistic philosophy of the American petty bourgeoisie, and yet even the spirit of his doctrine, the basis of its appeal, as we stated above, was founded upon logic that was more attractive to the lower middle class than to the uncrystallized proletariat. Bellamy eschewed appeal to class as signifying pettiness of outlook. He wished to appeal to all of society, to be above class concepts and differentiations. Even religion was to have a place in his Utopia which was to be "the realization of God's ideal of (the race)."[133] Bellamy was much closer to the tradition of the Utopian socialists, the Fourierists and the Owenites of the early part of the century, than to the scientific Marxian socialists, who did not make any real headway in America until the twentieth century. In a way too, the doctrines of Bellamy, like the illations of Ramsay MacDonald in the twentieth century, obscured the class issues at stake, and tended to confuse rather than to clarify the logic of social progress.

[133] Edward Bellamy: *Looking Backward:* Boston and New York, 1887: Edition used, 1929: p. 272.

But Bellamy's attacks upon the predatory influence of industry and finance, attacks as implicit in *Looking Backward* as in *The Duke of Stockbridge,* were translated more successfully into literature by Frank Norris in his novels *The Octopus* and *The Pit.* While Norris lacked the social vision of Bellamy, he possessed artistic gifts which were immeasurably greater than those of Bellamy. At the time Norris wrote the frontier had not only closed in on itself, but the railroad magnates had already driven the farmers into a state of economic slavery. The conflict, as Norris saw it, was between the ranch and the railroad. The railroad, that vast, earth-swallowing Octopus, with its cyclopean eye driving through the dark, symbolized the defeat of the individual, the conquest of the farmer, and the victory of the age of steam and steel. Not even the organization of the Farmers' Alliance and the creation of the Populist party were able to stem the tide of defeat. In *The Pit,* the second novel in Norris' trilogy on Wheat—the third novel was never written—the scene shifted to the wheat exchange where the lives and fortunes of farmers were gambled away by the brokerage speculators. Norris' vision of wheat as the great staff of life, the soil incarnate, as it were, which has imbued his character Vanamee in *The Octopus,* with an understanding of the meaning of creation, represented, perhaps, the last poetic outgrowth of the frontier force. Already in *The Pit* that poetry has passed. And, save as we shall see in the next chapter in a few of the novels of Willa Cather, it never returned.

But Norris' western novels did more than sing the "swan song" of the frontier, as Miss Hazard ably expressed it; they marked off the beginning of a new mood in our literature. In not only *The Octopus* and *The Pit,* but also in *McTeague* and *Vandover and the Brute,* Norris gave early voice to the defeatist mood which has pervaded American literature since his day. The optimism which had resounded over the country in response to the early rhythm of the West, bursting forth in a cry to action which Emerson and Whitman had taken up and proclaimed, broke down in Norris' fiction into pessimism and despair.

It was Norris who taught us that tragedy was abroad in the land. While Eggleston had abandoned the youthful optimism of his predecessors, the spirit of despair had never predominated in his works. Even the youthful Garland in *Crumbling Idols* had retained something of the previous optimism. It was only later that the defeatist mood overwhelmed him. E. W. Howe, we must remember, in his novel *The Story of a Country Town* had anticipated Norris's mood, but Howe represented the tragedy of the frontier like one, who, overwhelmed by the tragedy himself, had lost the vigor to protest. All that he could do was to become cynical. In the intervening forty-seven years that elapsed between the publication of *The Story of a Country Town* and *Plain People*, he contributed little of importance to our literature. Few writers, it should be noted here, have revealed as well as Howe the petty bourgeois philosophy of the West. "Of all the games worth a candle," Howe wrote in *Plain People*, "success is the first." Despite the tragic turn of the years, which has left the West defeated and despoiled, Howe still believes in the competitive way of life of the early frontiersmen—and the Rotarians of to-day. "Men hustling to do better than the competitors they hate have done more for the world," Howe averred, "than the great souls who dream of universal love . . . (for) the men in pursuit of money make less trouble than the big idealists with their experiments."[134] Again,—convinced still that all is well in the worst of systems, he has declared that "our present competitive system is as necessary, as firmly founded in experience, as our system of eating three meals a day." Even the optimism of earlier days has not spent itself with him, for upon no other ground could one explain the folly of committing such words as these to paper:

We moan about those enjoying Special Privilege. There is no such thing in the United States, except the special privilege we all

[134] E. W. Howe: *Plain People*: New York, 1929: p. 304.

enjoy as Americans over the people of other countries. We moan also about an oppressive Plutocracy. There is no such thing in this country except that we are all Plutocrats as compared with the average citizens in other countries.

The least profitable profession in the world is that of a thief. There never was one who made a success at it. He cannot marry unless he marries a woman who is not at all particular; he can't build a home, know the joys of honest friendship; *he cannot be elected county treasurer, to the legislature, to congress, or to the presidency, as may an honest man.* (Italics mine.)

But, if nothing else, Howe has stripped American individualism of its philosophic pretense, its ornament of disguise, and exposed it as it really is, as a savage, cut-throat philosophy of men and women who have never learned to dream.

Significant as Howe was as a frontier novelist, for it can be said without exaggeration that *A Story of a Country Town* was one of the most realistic and revealing of western novels, he cannot be described as a literary force. Frank Norris can. In all his novels Norris evidenced the growth of that despair which was overtaking European literature as well as American, a despair which sprang out of the realization of the impotency of the individual in the face of elemental forces. In Europe that despair had grown out of somewhat different conditions, and had set in at an earlier date. In America it arose out of definite social changes which transformed the whole philosophy of the American people, converting its optimism into pessimism, and replacing its comic tradition by a tragic one. The defeat of the petty bourgeois farmers of the West, which meant the defeat of the last vestiges of individual freedom in the nation, spelt the end of an epoch in our historical development. The industrial and financial forces in the nation had conquered. The agrarian ones were definitely subdued. In the industrialized nation which had evolved, the place of the individual was to become less and less conspicuous and creative. Norris sensed in the defeat of the farmers the defeat of a civilization—a civilization which, with its frontier forests and prairies, and its rich wheat-giving soil, had afforded an opportunity for the individual which industry would never tolerate. Henceforth, the individual would be at the mercy of forces and not be a creative force in itself. The Octopus would be the victor and not the individual. In *McTeague* as well as in *The Octopus* and *The Pit*, the characters, Trina and McTeague, were buffeted about like corks in a current. In *Vandover and the Brute*, which it has been suggested revealed something of Norris' own dilemma, and which was not published for a number of years after his death, the individual was made into the victim of a mania, lycophobia, and shown to be helpless before its personal depredations. Already the voluntaristic beliefs of the first part of the nineteenth century had given way to the deterministic. The day when man made his own environment was over. The time when men believed all one had to do was to "hitch (his) wagon to a star" had disappeared. The time had now come when it could be declared that man was made by his environment, not the environment by him. It was that truth which Norris, the first of our realistic writers to turn deterministic, made bold to announce and defend. While Zola, a disciple of the deterministic science of his day, undoubtedly influenced Norris in that direction, there can be but little question, as the themes of his novels testify, that it was the change in the American environment which was far more important in shaping his philosophy.

Norris at bottom was a fighter, and he fought his way clear of most of the vestiges of the romantic tradition which had survived. Like Garland, although he would never have used the term, he was a veritist at heart. He has been called by many a naturalist, but he was not. "I never truckled; I never took off the hat to Fashion, and held it out for pennies," he wrote in *The Responsibilities of the Novelist*. "By God, I told them the truth. They liked it or they didn't like it. What had that to do with me? I told them the truth." But the fact of the matter was he did not tell them the truth, or at least not all the truth. Like all the western writers, those native to the West as well as those influenced by the West[135] —in fact, we might as well say like all the American writers of the nineteenth century—he never told the truth about sex. He told the truth about the sordidness of life, its brutality, its misery. He never hesitated to assail a social evil, never stopped short of trying to right a wrong. His novels were "naked truths," as one of his admirers described them, in every sense but the sexual. The sexual candor of Zola he never attempted. He was too clearly a product of the petty bourgeois environment in which he had lived to rise above the middle-class prejudice against sex in literature. His characters, unlike those of Howells, might not live moral lives, it is true, but the psychological consideration of the nature of their immorality, or even the nature of their morality, he never ventured to include within the province of his concern.

But Norris was not singular in that respect. Frontier literature from the very beginning, as we have pointed out, had been a *moral* literature. Norris merely continued in the same tradition. Twain, as we have noted, allowed his wife to censor his books lest they express any immoral sentiments or suggestions. Bret Harte had never violated the bourgeois sexual code in his fiction. Eggleston had avoided any approach to such an intimate theme. Even E. W. Howe had not invaded it. And Hamlin Garland, who preferred veritism to realism because the latter did not tell enough of the truth, was even more emphatic in his opposition to the introduction of sex into literature. The new literature of the West which he wished to see would depict life, "not love life." . . . If the past celebrated lust and greed and love of power, the future will celebrate continence and humility and altruism. Measured by our standard, the writers of "The Restoration" were artificial in manner and vile in thought. They smell always of the bawdy house and their dramas sicken us with

[135] Whitman here was somewhat of an exception, although even Whitman's approach to the matter of sex was very different from that characteristic of the twentieth century.

the odor of filth through which their writers reeled the night before." Veritism, in other words, could be built upon an interpretation of life in which sex did not intrude, save as "the wholesome love of honest men for honest women."

These western writers were not the precursors of that revolt against middle-class morality which took place in twentieth-century literature. True to the frontier type, they held on to its petty bourgeois morality to the end. If their attitude had prevailed, we could have had no Dreiser, no Anderson, no Hemingway. But new developments were occurring in American civilization making it impossible for that attitude to predominate. The notion that one could tell the whole truth about life without consideration of the sexual impulse became so altered, that, in the excitement of change, the new age almost came to believe that the whole truth about life revolved about the sexual impulse. Both attitudes, the products of exaggerations and extremes, are bound to pass as our present chaos crystallizes into a new order. Sex will then be seen to be an important part of life, but not, the Freudians to the contrary notwithstanding, the whole of life.

CHAPTER VI

FROM SECTIONALISM TO NATIONALISM

By the end of the nineteenth century a new America had been born. The industrial energy of the nation which had been let loose after the Civil War had welded America together into a new unit. A new national psychology had been created that had begun to unify the nation. The doctrine of states' rights had receded into the background, and aside from affording conversational threat for the aged veterans of the Confederacy, had lost its meaning in the new scene. As the industrialists and financiers came more and more to control politics, individual states came to think of themselves as parts of the national unit instead of as separate units in themselves. The upper bourgeoisie, in the financial and the industrial world, had saddled itself so successfully upon the country that it had been able to endow it with an artificial unity such as had never been seen before in the nation. Even the momentary unity which had been attained at the time of the Revolutionary War had been weak in comparison. With the coming of the Columbian Exposition held in Chicago in 1893 that unity realized itself in a chorus of national enthusiasm. The Exposition, which attracted world-wide attention, and which brought people from every state in the Union to witness its wonders, filled America with an overflowing sense of pride in its own achievements. Chicago became a meeting place for Americans all over the country. Men and women came to it almost as to a Western Mecca, to see with their own eyes the icons of the new age. "Chicago," wrote Henry Adams, "was the first expression of American thought as a unity."

At the same time that this inner change was going on within the nation, the pressure for outer expansion developed with swift intensity. New battleships were built, and the Navy as a whole was reconstructed. Early in the decade, a difficulty with Chile cropped up almost leading to a war. Two years later, after instituting a fake revolution in Hawaii, an attempt was made to annex the Islands to the United States. Only the obstinacy of President Cleveland prevented the Hawaiian Treaty from going into effect. Roosevelt at the time had written to Lodge that he did "wish that our Republicans would go in avowedly to annex Hawaii."[1] Not very much later Brazil crossed our path and a conflict nearly ensued. In the meanwhile, talk of annexing Cuba, which the plantation aristocrats had steadily advocated before the Civil War, became rife, and when revolt broke loose in the island the financiers and industrialists realized that the opportunity had arrived at last for turning that talk into action. The Spanish American War which resulted shortly thereafter, and which closed with the conversion of the United States from a nation into an empire, was not the outgrowth of a sudden situation, then, but the culmination of a definite line of policy which had developed during the whole decade previous. Since that war America has become the new Roman Empire of the West. Little that is on this continent has not been tarnished by her Midas touch. Venezuela, Colombia, Honduras, Nicaragua, Haiti, Guatemala, Mexico—all, one after another, have been swallowed into her economic maw. Dollar-diplomacy has triumphed as the most advanced form of imperialism technique.

It was the Spanish American War which opened up this new era in our history. Before that war "the national mind," as Mr. Millis noted, "appears to have been uncomfortably divided between a glorious optimism and an inferiority complex."[2] In our cultural life that inferiority complex had expressed itself, as we have shown, in the form of the colonial complex. Once America became a major nation, a

---

[1] Quoted from Walter Millis: *The Martial Spirit:* New York, 1931: p. 25. Mr. Millis has described this period in illuminating detail, and I am indebted to him for several references in this connection.

[2] Ibid., p. 4.

first-rate power, however, that sense of inferiority began to disappear and the colonial complex ceased to exercise its disastrous influence upon our cultural existence. Our life, in other words, began to take on a magnitude of its own, and to acquire that confidence in itself which it hitherto had lacked. Within a decade the American rhythm which had appeared first in response to the frontier force developed into a national rhythm which expressed itself throughout the length and breadth of our literature.

But the interest in things American, American art, American folklore, American antiques, American language, and American literature, developing with such velocity in the twentieth century and translating itself into new and native forms, did not grow up as a patriotic apostrophe to the new imperialistic ruling class. On the other hand, as we shall see, this ruling class was even less interested in art than were those of the eighteenth and nineteenth centuries, and the new American literature which sprang up was hostile rather than sympathetic toward its aspirations. What that ruling class succeeded in doing, however, was not in winning allies to its sides but in welding the country into a national unit and infusing it with a national consciousness. It was able to serve that function, as we pointed out before, because it had industry and finance at its command. So long as the country was more agrarian than industrial such national consciousness was impossible to create, the relationship between the two forms of production being too antagonistic in their conflict of interests. Before the end of the century, however, industry had won the battle and America had become an industrial nation. The rise of industry had already reached a point of national concentration. Early in the twentieth century a writer in *The Nation* (May 16, 1907) noted that "the tendency toward industrial concentration is thus pronounced all along the line. The five years under consideration (1900–1905) bear witness to it in the most positive manner." The agrarian forces, to be certain, did not surrender easily, and, for that matter, continued to fight throughout the twentieth century, but it was a losing fight. The creation of the Interstate Commerce Commission in 1887 to supervise the railroads, and the passage of the Sherman anti-trust act in 1890 were among the last victories of the petty bourgeois agrarian forces in their struggle against the economic dictatorship of upper bourgeoisie. With the passage of the McKinley tariff act in 1890—"protective in every paragraph," as McKinley announced, "and American in every line and word"[3]—the power-politics of the Republican party, the representative of the industrial and financial interests, became the dominant force in the nation. The age of trusts and monopolies began, and there was nothing on the horizon to halt its advance. Even the passage of restrictive laws was of no avail. "The outburst of trust promotion in 1899–1901," *The Nation* observed, "was one of the most notable events in our entire economic history. In a night, as it were, industrial combinations sprang up on every side. Exactly half the trusts enumerated in the census were floated within the eighteen months prior to June 30, 1900."[4] Not even the election of the Democratic party in 1912 and again in 1916 was able to stem the march of the industrio-financial oligarchy. By that time the power of the oligarchy was so strong that no political party was able to interrupt its destiny. The differences between the Republican and Democratic parties consequently became more and more meaningless except as political fictions. So much alike, in fact, had the two parties become by the end of the World War that La Follette in 1924 found it necessary to organize a new party in order to give expression to the dying protests of the oppressed petty bourgeois elements in the population.

The nationalism, therefore, which industry had brought into being diffused itself over the nation as a whole, extending from its political periphery to its cultural centre. At last America was knit together into a reasonably compact and

[3]Ibid., p. 7.
[4]*The Nation*, May 16, 1907. Article entitled: *The Trusts and Industrial Concentration:* p. 448.

united economic pattern. The main conflicts in the nation henceforth would be industrial and not agrarian. The day of the North, and the South, and the West as separate cultural entities was over—over at least except for the diehards. Whatever differences persisted would tend to become recessive instead of progressive. From one end of the country to the other industry was standardizing ways of labor, ways of education, ways of thought, ways of life.

As the ruling class became more imperialistic, and made its power felt throughout the world, the sense of inferiority bred by the colonial complex began to lose its cultural hold upon the psychology of the nation. The East which Hamlin Garland had described as English in 1884 abandoned that Englishness early in the twentieth century. In time only the Irving Babbitts and Paul Elmer Mores remained as last vestiges of the English tradition. The conversion of Sherman from the academic, English tradition to the realistic, American one marked an important stage in that intellectual transition. Where before his conversion Sherman, like More, had held himself aloof from the mainstream of contemporary American literature, after his conversion he went out of his way, almost with a childish enthusiasm for the new and the native, to welcome the rising school of American writers. The wealth which had come with the new America had created a kind of cocksure independence, a belligerent braggadocio which penetrated into the core of the nation. The time had come when America could *afford* to speak out. The day when *The Atlantic Monthly* was the final authority for American intellectuals was dead. Higginson's words that on his lecture tours "it was so strange to dip down in these little Western towns and find an audience all ready and always readers of *The Atlantic,* so glad to see me," belonged to a past age. Even the time when *Harper's* within a short span of years ran "three novels of Dickens, four of Thackeray's, one of Bulwer, two of George Eliot's, six of Trollope's"[5] had vanished. New magazines had arisen and the old

[5]Algernon Tassin: *The Magazine in America:* New York, 1916: p. 241.

magazines had to change their character, that is become more American, in order to survive. Publishing houses also had to give audience to the new tendency. The time had come when the American public could—and would—buy the books of young American authors. The day when Mr. Dana Estes remarked, in an address before a Committee of Congress on the need for copyright, that "for two years past, though I belong to a publishing house (Estes and Lauriat) which emits nearly $1,000,000 worth of books per year, I have absolutely refused to entertain the idea of publishing an American manuscript (because) it is impossible to make the books of most American authors pay"[6] —that day too had disappeared. The day had come in the twentieth century when American publishers were no longer going to make their money on English books but on American ones. As a nation America became interested in American things, naïvely and childishly proud of American things. Even the crudities of America, the barbarities, no longer repelled. American antiques became a new vogue, displacing European antiques in importance of appeal. Even American music evoked a new sense of loyalty on the part of many of the critics. "The sense of inferiority . . . and timid dependence upon Europe" from which American music had suffered in the past already had begun to disappear, Mr. Daniel Gregory Mason has contended, and a new and promising group of American composers had arisen. Even American speech which was neglected and scorned in the past came in for belated recognition, and in addition to Professor Krapp's and H. L. Mencken's studies in that field a new magazine, *American Speech,* was founded with Louise Pound, one of America's most distinguished philologists, as editor. *American Speech* was followed a little later by another magazine, *American Literature,* edited by Jay B. Hubbell, who in the Foreword to that magazine pointed out that *"within the last few years* American scholars have awakened to the fact that our literary history supplies a rich and comparatively un-

[6]Ibid., p. 369.

worked field." (Italics mine.) American folklore of every variety began to engage the interest of artists, scholars and collectors. American folk art, Mr. Holger Cahill declared, in a recent article in *The American Mercury*, "makes one of the most fascinating chapters in the history of the arts of design in the United States."[7] Indian folklore too came in for an increasing and almost worshipful share of appreciation, and things Negroid, the Spirituals, the blues, and jazz, literally took the nation by storm. Besides the interest in things American as part of a national tradition, a national synthesis, as it were, there has recently developed an interest in things sectional and regional. This latter interest, afflicted as it undoubtedly has been—and is—with a blind-alley zeal for the immediate, is an inevitable reflection of this new and more intense interest in America which has arisen in this century. At the same time, it represents, in the form it has taken, a cultural lag in the social process. There is good reason, therefore, why Ruth Suckow should regret that "now, at the very moment when the nation begins to be seen in its full stature, the backward movement is in swing again," for in a sense these new emphases upon regionalism and sectionalism belong to the past and not to the future. They signify a sectional lag and not a national advance. They show that the cultural unification of the country is still far from complete. They indicate a reintensification of that concern for American things which the frontier had tended to encourage in the nineteenth century, a groping for those elements in the American environment which might communicate a native tradition. Out of that tradition, as we have observed, Mark Twain arose, and that long stream of humorists who contributed to our culture so much that was genuinely and significantly American. Unfortunately, that movement has now spent its energy; the frontier force in itself is dead. Consequently, these efforts of the "new regionalists," indicative as they are of the renewed search for Americanness in our culture, are pursuing paths which will tend to produce to-day a

[7] *American Mercury*, September, 1931, Vol. XXIV, No. 93, p. 46.

literature that is sophomorically "different" in a local sense instead of æsthetically original in a national sense.[8] While there is a certain truth in Mr. McWilliams' observation that

despite its extravagant ambitions and occasional lapses in sense, regionalism has made Americans stand on their own legs. A quarter of a century ago it was an easy task to establish a critical reputation in this country merely by quoting foreign names in public places— Strindberg, Nietzsche, d'Annunzio, etc. The works of the late James Gibbons Huneker read to-day like a catalogue of moribund foreign names, æstheticisms, traditions,

the essential falsity in the outlook of the new regionalists will militate against their legs striding very far in advance. Although there is no objection to their absorbing the spirit of their regions, the climate, the customs, the folklore, and the speech, the problems that face American literature to-day go deeper than those factors. It is no longer possible, as Mr. Tate has advocated, to "return to the provinces, to the small self-contained centres of life," for our literary inspiration. The so-called self-contained centres of life are no longer self-contained but are already bound up with the vast nexus of our civilization. The airplane, the railroad, the automobile, the newspaper syndicate, the radio, and all the other

[8]An outgrowth of the new national psychology which we have described, these regional movements began early in the twentieth century in response to the changes in the environment which then occurred. As Carey McWilliams points out in his excellent survey of this movement in his University of Washington Chapbook, *The New Regionalism*, "the Southwest led the way in the development of regional culture." (P. 8.) The Texas Folk-Lore Society was organized in 1909; thereafter numerous other societies were formed and a score or more regional magazines established. Among the latter were such diverse publications as *The Southwest Review, Folk-Say, Laughing Horse, Morada, Prairie Schooner, The Midland, Hesperian, Bozart, The Grinnell Review, The Frontier, Ozark Life, Pasque Petals*. (Of *Pasque Petals*, Dr. O. W. Coursey, author of *The Literature of South Dakota*, declared: "It publishes the poetry of South Dakotans only; but once a South Dakotan, always a South Dakotan." P. 13.) Other statements of the new regionalists have been even more silly and bumptious. In addition to Mr. McWilliams' study, Mary Austin, Ruth Suckow, Genevieve Taggard, and Allen Tate have given attention to the movement. The October–December, 1931, issue of *The Sewanee Review* published a symposium on Regionalism.

varied developments of our technological civilization, in large part have destroyed already those self-contained centres and made them into minor replicas of other centres in different parts of the country. Main Street has become very much the same in almost every part of the nation.

II

But the imperialistic advance of the upper bourgeoisie, once it had captured the political and economic power of the nation, was accompanied by inevitable conflicts and contradictions. While industry made it possible for it to begin to weld the country into a national unit, it was able to do so only at the expense of driving the petty bourgeoisie to the wall and creating a multiplying proletariat. In fact, growing out of the conditions it created, in the agrarian zones as well as in the industrial, it precipitated a crisis in American life which has already changed the cast of American character.

In the first place, as we have seen, it drove the petty bourgeois forces to the defensive, and by weakening their economic position practically destroyed their political power. By subtle propaganda—high tariffs bring prosperity, etc.— it actually won the allegiance of a considerable part of the working class who were misled by the idea that expanding industries would redound to their benefit and provide them "with full dinner pails." So successful was its propaganda that had it not been for the split in its party in 1912—Wilson drew 2,000,000 less votes than Taft and Roosevelt combined, and even less for that matter than Bryan had secured upon previous occasions—the Republicans undoubtedly would have maintained uninterrupted control of the government from the end of the nineteenth century to the present. The petty bourgeoisie—made up of farmers in revolt against exploitation by the railroads, shopkeepers, small manufacturers, shippers, and traders, and all the commercial and in-

dustrial in-betweeners who were oppressed by the large capitalists—fared worse and worse from year to year as large industry and finance undersold and underpaid it, robbed it in
the open market, and by combines and monopolies crippled
and paralyzed it when it was not actually destroyed in the
struggle for survival. Its political position had not shifted
greatly since 1892, when it was expressed in the platform
of the People's party, to 1912, when Wilson expressed it
in the platform of the Democratic party. In general, the
petty bourgeoisie was "on the side of individualism as
against Socialism," as Professor Merriam summed up its
stand, "(for) democracy as against plutocracy; and on the
side of collectivism where necessary to curb monopoly or
unfair competition . . . but not for the type of collectivism
implied in the labor theory and ideal of industry adminis-
tered by the standardized union association of men, in which
all stood upon the same level of production and compensation regardless of individual differences in capacity . . .
(for) a progressive income tax, but not for a single tax on
land; for an inheritance tax to prevent swollen fortunes, but
not for common ownership of capital."[9] But the America
which had come into being had left few loopholes in which
to satisfy the demands of the petty bourgeoisie. The individualism which it exalted, in keeping with the economic interests of its life, was being edged out and gradually extin-
guished by the industrial forces at work in the nation. The
trusts and monopolies, with their vertical and horizontal
ramifications, their syndicates and chain-stores, were driving
the petty bourgeoisie to inescapable defeat, forcing it either
into bankruptcy or a poverty-stricken existence. The banks,
controlled by the large depositors, the financiers, and not by
the petty depositors, encouraging large enterprise instead of
small—with power over the government, and often over
the industrialists themselves, which represents one of the
most glaring contradictions in the superstructure of capitalist economy—abetted the same process. Both these forces in

[9]Charles A. Merriam: *American Political Ideas, 1865-1917:* p. 20.

turn were destroying the philosophy of entrepreneurship[10] which had dominated the nation since its inception—in fact, since the first colonists had landed upon its shores.

With the disappearance of the philosophy of entrepreneurship, the individualistic ideology of the petty bourgeoisie began to lose its pertinence and challenge in the new economic scene. As early as 1912, Allen Kline, in an article in *The Forum*, stressed the importance of "the breaking down of (the) basic philosophy of individualism"[11] in America. The individual entrepreneur found himself more and more helpless before the power of big business which could manufacture goods cheaper and sell it at a lower price than he could, and which, by virtue of its control of the state, could protect itself against any opposition that threatened. Big business no longer believed in the competitive logic of early middle-class economics; it had learned the wisdom of trustified industry which abolished competition—except between the trusts. By proving that it could undersell the petty bourgeoisie at every point, it destroyed the very principle upon which the ideology of the latter was founded, namely, the competitive. Regretting this state of affairs, *The Nation* magazine, with forthright petty bourgeois vehemence, decried the fact that "a few great corporations not only control nearly all the work done, but dictate the technical methods to be followed," and then added that "*the absence of competition works the same harm to engineering that it does to any other pursuit.*" (Italics mine.)[12] In terms of the state the indus-

---

[10]With the coming large-scale enterprise, swamping and suppressing that of small scale, the capital necessary to undertake new enterprise mounted in such proportions that it soon became well-nigh impossible for the unwealthy individual to undertake a fresh venture—unless he sold out his main interests to those who provided the capital. Even in agrarian regions, farmlands fell into the hands of mortgage men and large financiers, the cost of land increased to a more and more prohibitive point. The small capitalist thus, that is the petty bourgeois, was crushed on every side by an economic system which totally disregarded what he considered his legitimate rights and demands.

[11]*The Forum*, August, 1912. Article entitled *Party Principles and Industrial Development*, p. 27.

[12]*The Nation*, January 10, 1907, Vol. 84, No. 2167.

trial and financial bourgeoisie was definitely plutocratic instead of democratic, and in the process of its rule it unhesitatingly did away with many of the democratic rights and liberties which the petty bourgeoisie had endeavored to perpetuate ever since the days of Jefferson. The so-called loss of individual liberty,[13] which has been the subject of so much consideration in our generation, resulted from the defeat of the petty bourgeois forces in our civilization.

In the last analysis, the conflict between the upper and lower bourgeoisies in the twentieth century revolved, in a practical as well as philosophical sense, about the problem of individualism. In the latter part of the nineteenth century it was the individualism of the petty bourgeois farmers, which found its political expression in the Populist movement, that was paramount. The Populist movement was practically dead, however, by the end of the century, and the farmer's cause died with it. The farmers, of course, have continued to protest from time to time but at no period since the defeat of the Populist movement have they been able to create a formidable opposition to the forces of Wall Street which they recognize as their enemy but which they have not yet learned how to fight. In the twentieth century the individualistic challenge arose in the cities. Then it was the petty bourgeois groups in the urban centres who led the opposition, with the agrarian forces playing second rôle. The rights of the individual were being eliminated. The individuality of individual man was being crushed by an industrial system which respected him only as a number. The petty bourgeois independence which he had cherished was being destroyed by a way of life which was hostile to its presence. Characteristically enough, *The Nation*, with its petty bourgeois liberal outlook, recognized that fact at once. "The railway has in its territory a practical monopoly," it observed in its issue of January 17, 1907, "and thus an enormous power over the fortunes, the happiness and even the

[13]Cf. Ernest Sutherland Bates: *This Land of Liberty*: New York, 1930: for the best discussion of this theme.

lives of individuals. It is no more legitimate for a railway than for an aristocracy to lay intolerable burdens on the individual. So with other corporations. There must be some limit to their powers of action, *or the individual would be helpless.* Harriman and Wall Street with its fifty odd millions from the Union Pacific treasury . . . is the feudal lord of our ancient régime, crushing the individual by an irresistible weight." But the protests of *The Nation,* and of other magazines and groups, were of little avail. The position of the individual became worse instead of better with every increasing year, and the principle of individualism in reality became little more than a nineteenth-century fiction, meaningful particularly to politicians who continued to exploit the concept in order to deceive the masses, who had not yet advanced beyond the nineteenth-century tradition.[14]

That petty bourgeois revolt, expressing itself in literary form in the muckraking movement, reached an early peak about 1910, and in the rise of the Progressives, conspicuous in the election of 1912, blossomed forth with melodramatic violence. 1912, indeed, was the critical year for the whole movement. It marked the last stand of the petty bourgeoisie. After that, the petty bourgeois forces continued to challenge the ruling order, but their challenge had lost its vigor. La Follette's feeble revolt in 1924 revealed how weak its forces had become within the span of little more than a decade. In 1912, however, those forces arose with the might of a blind dying Samson, threatening to overthrow the temples of the new Philistines. Frightened by the alarming strength of Roosevelt and Wilson, both of whom bid fair to represent the cause of the downtrodden lower middle class, the Republican party itself made genuflections to the enemy in hopes of winning part of its support. It was Wilson, to be sure, who best represented the interests of the petty bourgeoisie, and whose doctrine of The New Freedom came to represent its philosophy in its most modern form.[15] Roose-

[14]*The Nation,* January 17, 1907, p. 51.
[15]Charles A. Beard and Mary Beard: *The Rise of American Civilization:* New York, 1927: Vol. II, p. 606.

velt, nevertheless, captured part of Wilson's programme with his petty bourgeois denunciations of big finance and his forthright attacks upon the trusts. Both Wilson and Roosevelt made the individualistic issue into a cardinal point in their platforms; the individualistic rights of the small business man must be protected against the anti-individualistic tendencies of big business; the individualistic rights of the farmer must not be trampled upon by the anti-individualistic power of the banks and the railroads. In other words, the individual entrepreneur must be preserved; America must remain a country of small business men, a country in which the petty bourgeoisie would constitute the solid framework of society. They did not want a state run by a group of financiers and industrialists on the top, with the rest of the population rendered helpless by their power. In short, they did not want the anti-individualistic, anti-democratic upper bourgeoisie to constitute the ruling class; they wanted the individualistic, democracy-seeking, petty bourgeoisie to constitute that ruling class.

But neither the election of Wilson, nor his re-election, as we have noted, was able to stem the advance of the upper bourgeoisie in the economic field, nor prevent it from wielding power even when its political representatives were not in office.[16] The rationalization of industry which developed with such intensity immediately after the World War, plus the overwhelming supremacy of power which the bankers secured in the world market, resulting in Wall Street's becoming the dictator of international finance, crippled the petty bourgeoisie beyond repair. The structure of modern industry has robbed its individualistic doctrine of meaning —and reduced its concept of individualism into a nineteenth-century recollection. But more than that, new contradictions in the economic order have converted its programme of de-

[16]As Peter McArthur pointed out in a revealing article on *The Science of Political Corruption*, "the little bosses were bought up by the magnates of business life and the big bosses who carried out their will came into being. . . . Politics became an essential part of big business." (*The Forum*, January, 1912, p. 32.)

mocracy into a futile fiction, and cleared the road for the perpetuation of the industrio-financial dictatorship. Even in 1912 the failure of the democratic programme of the petty bourgeoisie had begun to make itself apparent on many sides. Article after article in the magazines emphasized its failure. "Principle has been replaced by Capital in the name of the people," an editorial in *The Forum* noted, "the plutocrats govern."[17]

The retrogression of the petty bourgeois forces in our nation will undoubtedly mark the beginning of a new stage in our civilization. As the impotency of the petty bourgeois ideology becomes more apparent, a definitely crystallized proletarian ideology will be able to arise and take its place as the challenging adversary of the prevailing oligarchy. The development of industry and finance, as we pointed out in a previous paragraph, has not only undermined the position of the petty bourgeoisie but it has also created an ever-expanding and ever-more-exploited proletariat. Moreover, the harder the upper bourgeoisie presses the petty bourgeoisie, the more members of the latter class are driven off into the proletariat. In the past, the conflict of forces in America has been mainly between the upper bourgeoisie and the petty bourgeoisie. While the struggle between the proletariat and the bourgeoisie existed throughout most of the nineteenth century, it was obscured by the fact that in political outlook as well as in economic logic the American proletariat in large part tended to adopt the ideology of the petty bourgeoisie.[18] The proletariat was wage-conscious but not class-conscious. From the very beginning of the nineteenth century signs of class-consciousness had manifested themselves on the part of various groups of proletarians, but it was not until after the Civil War that those groups began to identify themselves with any national plan or programme. Indeed, from the time when the cordwainers were indicted

[17]*The Forum*, August, 1912, p. 244.
[18]Anthony Bimba: *The History of the American Workingclass*: New York, 1927: p. 192.

in 1806 for conspiracy for banding themselves together in an attempt to raise their wages[19] and the Irish dock workers in 1836 "rioted for higher wages"[20] to the great railroad strike of 1877, the American workers had revealed an abundance of fight but little capacity for carrying that fight in extended or united form across the face of the nation. The rise of the Knights of Labor in the eighties—it had been organized as a secret order in 1869—had signified the beginning of a national labor organization. But even the Knights of Labor, notwithstanding the class-conscious utterances of certain of its members, was far more petty bourgeois than proletarian in its ideology. Its aim was "to create a healthy public opinion on the subject of labor (the only creator of values or capital) and the justice of it receiving a full, just share of the values of capital it has created." In connection with the class struggle, for example, it declared that: "we shall with all our strength, support laws made to harmonize the interests of labor and capital, for labor alone gives life and value to capital, and also those laws which tend to lighten the exhaustiveness of toil."[21] It was not until 1892, when the Socialist Labor party, a class-conscious organization, entered the national election for the first time, that a proletarian ideology began to show any signs of synthesis. But even then the signs were slight. The total vote gathered by the party was little over 20,000. The vast majority of the workers, as we have stressed throughout this analysis, was still petty-bourgeois-minded and, therefore, voted for the petty bourgeois programme of the People's party. In other words, the great flare of class-conscious protest which the anarcho-syndicalists had stirred up in the Mid-West in the eighties, particularly in Chicago, had died down five years after its leaders had been executed for alleged connection with the throwing of the Haymarket bomb. It was not until the twentieth century that

[19]James Oneal: *The Workers in American History*: New York, 1921: p. 160.
[20]Louis Adamic: *Dynamite*: New York, 1931: p. 6.
[21]Documentary History, etc.: Vol. X, pp. 23–24. Quoted from Anthony Bimba's *History of the American Workingclass*: New York, 1927: p. 174.

an organized class consciousness grew up among the workers. The so-called official labor movement, however, the American Federation of Labor, which had displaced the Knights of Labor from its position of leadership among the American workers, evinced few deviations from the petty bourgeois ideology. At first its leader, Samuel Gompers, had mouthed a few phrases about the need for a class-conscious proletariat, but long before his death he had repudiated his earlier words and converted his organization into a petty bourgeois appendage of the existing order. By the third decade in the century it had become an open agency of the ruling class; its bureaucratic officialdom had become so cowardly and corrupt that it suppressed strikes and upon more than one occasion clearly sold out the cause of the workers to the employers. It was in different sections of the labor movement that evidences of a growing class consciousness had begun to arise. With the organization of the Industrial Workers of the World in 1905, that class consciousness manifested itself with challenging clarity. Its preamble declared that "the working class and the employing class have nothing in common. . . . Between these two classes a struggle must go on until all the toilers come together on the political, as well as the industrial field, and take and hold that which they produce by their labor through an economic organization of the working class, without affiliation with any political party."[22] Although the I. W. W. became a menacing thorn in the side of the employers, and actually won a number of temporary successes, it never grew as rapidly as the petty bourgeois unions in the American Federation of Labor. The A. F. of L. outstripped it in growth even during its period of greatest success. The psychology of the vast majority of the workers was still too petty bourgeois for them to join a revolutionary organization. Other organizations, however, such as the Amalgamated Clothing Workers of America, re-

[22]Later on, in the DeLeon split in 1908, at its fourth convention, it abandoned all recourse to political action, and, becoming anarcho-syndicalist in emphasis, it flung its whole stress upon the industrial field.

vealed definite signs of class consciousness in their organization. In the political field, the Socialist party, which had been organized in 1901, and which had replaced the Socialist Labor party as the political leader of the masses, grew rapidly and before the World War had begun it had over 90,000 members. In the election of 1904 it polled over 400,000 votes and in 1912 approximately a million.[23] For a time, the Socialist party was active in the unions, stirring up class consciousness among them, and even threatening to destroy the Gompers leadership. Later on, however, its influence waned, and after the split of the party in 1919, it ceased to play an important rôle in trade-union activity. The organization of the Communist party in 1919—at first two Communist parties were created, the Communist Labor party and the Communist party, and it was not until two years later that they were united[24]—by the left-wing members of the Socialist party who split from the old organization, marked the appearance of a new and dynamic class-conscious group on the American scene. Since that time the Communists have boldly carried revolutionary proletarian doctrine into the trade-union field, and for a time their efforts met with considerable success in a number of unions. Later on, however, with ejection meted out to them on every side by the A. F. of L. and weakened still more by the expulsion of two factions within their own organization their contacts with the organ-

[23] While most of the petty bourgeoisie was alarmed by this growth in the Socialist movement, a section of that class began to feel more sympathy for the workers than for the upper bourgeoisie. After all, the workers were far less an enemy than was big business. In many magazine articles of the time that sympathy found direct voice. "Our industries are not democratic," declared *The Outlook*, "they are autocratic. They are carried on by the few in control over the many, and by the few largely for the benefit of the few." (June 10, 1911, p. 284.)

[24] In 1921, the executive committee of the Communist Party in union with other left-wing elements, created the Workers Party of America. The Communist Party itself at that time had been forced to operate underground and it was not until June 7, 1923, that it found it feasible to dissolve its underground organization, and openly identify itself with the Workers Party of America which then became the official name of the Communist Party of America, and the American branch of the Communist International. (Bimba: p. 317.)

ized labor movement became less intimate and decisive. Since the depression of 1929, however, the Communists have succeeded in increasing the spread of their propaganda among the workers, and with indefatigable zeal have striven to instill them with a proletarian ideology in place of their petty bourgeois one.

If the large majority of the workers, notwithstanding the extremity of the depression and their own deprivation, still remain petty bourgeois in their outlook, it is only because the American tradition of petty bourgeois individualism and independence has rooted itself so deeply in their minds that the new conditions of life have not yet been able to break down its defenses. Although the frontier has been closed for over four decades now, and the opportunities for individual advance in terms of the land as well as business have been reduced to an uninspiring minimum, the worker continues to think of himself as an individual instead of as a member of a class. Enamored still with the illusion of individual success and the belief that he is a potential capitalist, the American worker has not yet discarded the nineteenth-century tradition. The official labor movement, with its corrupt petty bourgeois leadership, has tended to perpetuate rather than to destroy that illusion. The conditions of twentieth-century American life, nevertheless, are rapidly preparing the way for the disappearance of that false conviction. The defeat of the petty bourgeoisie on the economic and political fronts is expediting that change. The rationalization of industry in turn is aiding its acceleration. In fact, in the light of the development of American industry and the obvious defeat of the petty bourgeoisie, it can be said without undue hazard that the third decade of this century should chalk off a new epoch in the history of the American working class, signified by a definite change in its ideology.

In summary, then, twentieth-century America began with the rise to power of the industrial financial bourgeoisie, and the retreat of the petty bourgeoisie to the background. In politics as well as in economics, the position of the petty bourgeoisie has become more and more helpless. In addition, a proletarian ideology has begun to grow in America, and if as yet it is only in the embryo, the nature of the environment bids fair to make it into the new and most challenging enemy of the ruling class. In time it will succeed the petty bourgeoisie in political and economic importance, and carve out a new destiny for itself—and the nation.

III

Now that we have considered the social forces which have determined the character of twentieth-century America, let us turn to the literature of the century and show how it reflected their influence.

The inevitable figure to begin with is William Dean Howells. Howells represented better than any one else in his generation an intellectual bridge between the West and the East, the frontier force and the coastal. Born in the West, in Ohio to be exact, in 1837, Howells was appointed as consul to Venice while still in his twenties—he won the appointment as a result of a campaign biography he had written of Lincoln—and settled in the East as soon as he returned to America. There he functioned first in Boston, and then in New York as a dominant literary figure until his death. Because of his early contacts with the West, Howells was better able to understand and to interpret the literature of that region than were his New England contemporaries. His early and enthusiastic appreciation of the literary significance of Mark Twain, at a time when the East looked upon Twain as a "funny man," a literary clown, was an evidence of that deeper understanding and wider insight. "His books . . . express a familiar and almost universal quality of the American mind," Howells wrote in eulogy of Twain's work, "(for) they faithfully portray a phase of American life."[25] He was one of the first, if not the first, to recognize the promise of Garland's work, and to advise him "Whatever

[25]Mildred Howells: *Life and Letters of William Dean Howells:* New York, 1928: p. 390.

you do, keep to the West."[26] Indeed, he never lost sight of the West, and until the end of his life he carried over in his critical outlook a considerable part of its ideology.

In a precise sense, Howells belonged far more to the West than to the East. There was a conflict in him, to be sure, that was never finally resolved. At one time he could declare, in implicit defense of his own fiction, that "the more smiling aspects of life are the more American," while at another he could become so aroused by the contradictions in American life that he could apodictically maintain that "wherever there is competition there will be the oppression of the weak by the stronger,"[27] and even translate his feelings into action and write a letter to the Governor of Illinois in defense of the victims of the Haymarket frame-up. The former observation was a carry-over from the Western optimism of his early days, the optimism of the frontier, the West that was still in its expanding stage, still predicative of promise. The social pessimism which expressed itself in the latter tendency, and which overtook him later, was influenced to a degree by the works of Edward Bellamy, particularly *Looking Backward*, and those of Tolstoi, but more so by the events which in the eighties converted the West from a place of hope to a place of horror.[28] His interest in the Haymarket situation indicated the beginning of his social outlook. The engineers' strike which followed in 1888, and the Homestead strike which occurred in 1892, won his immediate consideration, and even found a place in his novels. In fact, the terrifying class struggles of his day played a definite part in shaping the character of his fiction for a number of years. In such novels as *Annie Kilburn, A Hazard of New Fortunes, The Quality of Mercy*, and *The World of Chance*, the industrial conflicts of his day found distinct voice. In *A Traveller from*

[26]Garland: *Roadside Meetings*, op. cit., p. 60.
[27]Garland: *Roadside Meetings*, op. cit., p. 63.
[28]Cf. Walter Fuller Taylor: on the *Origin of Howells' Interest in Economic Reform: American Literature*, Vol. II, No. 1, March, 1930. This is a striking article dealing with the influence of the industrial order upon Howells' fiction.

Altruria, which was a whimsical extension of *Looking Backward,* he ventured to depict a world in which the evils of modern industrialism would disappear. *Through the Eye of a Needle,* which was a sequel to *The Traveller from Altruria,* enlarges upon the same theme in a rural instead of an urban vein. Even the single-tax idea which had risen into prominence at the time, absorbing the interest of his friend Garland, discovered a place in two of his novels. All in all, Howells was more alive to the social issues of the day than was any other American novelist, and living as he did between two worlds, the West and the East, he was able to see more of the underlying implications which determined each than could most of the literary men of his time.

Howells' adoption of realism as a literary philosophy was a distant outgrowth of the frontier force. His conviction, which he stated with vigor upon more than one occasion but which received its best expression in *Criticism and Fiction,* namely, that "the arts must become democratic," was a direct derivative of the frontier-inspired logic of Whitman and Twain. Like his predecessors who were concerned with the creation of a native art, an art which smelt of the earth instead of the lamp, Howells realized that that art must grow out of the people, that it must embody the "common beauty, (the) common grandeur," which were characteristic of America and not the romantic beauty which was indigenous to Europe. Howells carried the fight for realism into the very citadel of the enemy: New England. At the time when Howells waged his fiercest fight for the realistic outlook, American literature as a whole, especially in the East, was still afflicted with the colonial complex. Howells was grievously aware of that fact, and like Emerson and Whitman in an earlier generation he devoted his energies to the extermination of its influence. In 1893, for example, in an article in *The Forum,* Hamilton W. Mabie showed that the two most widely read books in America at the time were *David Copperfield* and *Ivanhoe,* with *The Scarlet Letter, Uncle Tom's Cabin,* and *Ben Hur* ranking below them in popularity of appeal.[29] As late as July, 1897, in an article on the *Modern American Mood* which was published in *Harper's New Monthly Magazine,* Howells noted that "in letters we are but too meekly attentive to what they say of us over there, and in the arts, our study of European methods and movements has been so diligent that it would be hard to find anything distinctly American in many of our paintings, statuary, and edifices. We even take seriously the comments of French travellers upon our life, and our richer people conform strictly as they can to the social usages of the English aristocracy."[30] In another place Howells even admitted that many of the Western writers had not freed themselves from the overawing influence of the colonial complex. "We even felt that we failed in so far as we expressed something native quite in our own way," he wrote, "the literary theories we accepted were New England theories, the criticism we valued was New England criticism, or, more strictly speaking, Boston theories, Boston criticism. . . . Literature in Boston, indeed, was so respectable, and often of so high a lineage, that to be a poet was not only to be good society, but almost to be good family."[31] The realism which Howells advocated was intended as an attack upon that respectability—an escape from the colonial complex which had throttled the creative impulse in the East and made it lamely imitative. For a long time Howells' attacks were resented, and his own realistic fiction was condemned by Eastern critics.[32] But Howells fought on nevertheless, with undiminished zeal, defending the work of such young realists as Frank Norris, Harold Frederick, Stephen Crane and Hamlin Garland. While his own fiction never achieved the realistic intensity and revelation which characterized the realism of the later twentieth-

[29]Herbert Edwards: *Howells and the Controversy over Realism in American Fiction: American Literature,* Vol. III, No. 3, November, 1931, p. 244.
[30]P. 200.
[31]William Dean Howells: *Literary Friends and Acquaintances:* New York, 1900: pp. 115, 145.
[32]Herbert Edwards: op. cit., pp. 240–243.

century school, his influence as a critic undoubtedly prepared the way for the rise of that school and for the appearance of a literature that was less imitative and more native in character.

But Howells' realism, characterized by himself as "reticent realism," was caught up by the same contradictions which marred his social perspective. Constantly trying to live in two worlds, a world of democratic vision, made up of humble people and humble things, a world that was born of the West, and a world of genteel decorum and Brahminical dignity, made up of men and women who prized comfort above convictions, a world that was born of the East, he was never able to extricate himself long enough from either world to clarify his own position and conclusions. While he was far in advance of his literary associates in accepting radical propositions that they violently repudiated, he almost invariably expressed his radicalism in such a way that it became innocuous. This was just as true in the field of literature as in that of politics. In both fields he was what might be called a parlor sansculotte. He never carried his realism beyond the point of "reticence" nor his radicalism very far beyond the point of propriety.[33] Indeed, his active radicalism was comparatively short-lived. As early as July 27, 1896, he confessed in a letter to a friend that he was "rather quiescent in (his) social thinking now."[34]

In his fiction, for example, notwithstanding his eagerness

---

[33] His stand in the Chicago Anarchist case marked the only time when his radicalism assumed any heroic proportions—and even then his letter to the Governor of Illinois and the one he sent to the *New York Tribune* were more mild than vigorous in their tone. His remarks on the Homestead strike (Mildred Howells, op. cit., Vol. II, p. 25), in which he declared that the strikers were "Playing a lawless part, and that they must be made to give up the Carnegie property," were scarcely phrased in a way that would have very seriously frightened Whittier who had refused to write a letter to the Governor of Illinois in behalf of the Haymarket victims. Even Howells' opposition to the Extradition Treaty with Russia, and his ardent praise of Henry D. Lloyd's attack upon Standard Oil in his book, *Wealth Against Commonwealth* (ibid., pp. 35 and 54), were not voiced in such a manner as to awaken any revolutionary response.

[34] Mildred Howells, op. cit., p. 70.

to be faithful to fact, he never deviated from the bourgeois moral code, never ventured to admit the presence of the sexual factor in life. The men and women in his novels live as if sex never intruded upon them, never tormented them, never stirred them to any emotion except that of marital love.[35] In practically all his many novels, Howells safely avoided the problem of sexual immorality, and when, as in *A Modern Instance,* one of his characters, Hannah Morrison, failed to pursue a pure path, he simply banished her from the narrative. In no instance was Howells' treatment of the sexual impulse realistic. His realism was confined to outer things; it never reached those inner portions of personality, those frontiers of self, where conflicts of impulse intensify and torture. Only the realism of exterior things, actions, events, episodes, concerned him. Even that exterior realism, as we have noted, stopped short of the intimate. It portrayed only those exterior things which did not violate the moral emphasis of the day. In a word, it was not candid realism, but "reticent" realism.

The same middle-class compunctions which prohibited Howells from becoming a genuine realist, in the sense that Dreiser, Anderson, Lewis and Hemingway were to become not long afterwards, also prevented him from becoming a genuine radical. To the end he never quite got beyond his petty bourgeois ideology. From time to time he betrayed the weakness in his radical approach. Like so many would-be radicals who cling unconsciously to the petty bourgeois ideology, Howells was ever eager to appeal to the public for jus-

---

[35] In actual life Howells revealed the same short-sighted prejudice. In connection with Mrs. Stowe's publication of the life of Lady Byron, in which she exposed Byron's love for Augusta, Howells, in a letter to his father, delivered the following attack upon the English poet, revealing by his words the tenor of his moral outlook:

"The world needed to know just how base and filthy and mean Byron was, in order that all glamor should be forever removed from his literature, and the taint of it should be communicated *only to those who love sensual things,* and no more pure young souls should suffer from him through their sympathy with the *supposed* generous and noble traits in his character." (Italics mine.) (Mildred Howells, op. cit., Vol. I, p. 150.)

tice, to place the worker's case before the world. He never realized that it was only to the proletariat, as the Marxians have shown, that such an appeal, in the last analysis, could have meaning. It was their interests which were at stake and not those of the world. He continued to believe that the cause of the workers could be solved by the ballot. In a letter to his father which he wrote immediately after Berkman's attempt to kill Frick, he declared in that naïve fashion characteristic of those who have not been able to shed their petty bourgeois psychology: "In one thing the labor side is wrong. It has the majority of votes, and can vote the laws it wants, and it won't, but prefers to break the laws we share. This must come to an end, and probably will soon."[36] In *A Traveller from Altruria*, the same fallacy appears. "Why how preposterous they (the workers) are when you come to look at it," one of the characters states, obviously expressing the author's own views, "They can make any law they want, but they prefer to break such laws as we have. If they chose, it would take only a few years to transform our government into the likeness of anything they wanted." At no time did Howells realize that a ruling class would never surrender its power and property except by force. In characteristic style he retained the home as "the very heart of the Altrurian system" and arranged it so that "in Altruria every man is a gentleman, and every woman a lady."

Nevertheless, Howells must be credited with having advanced farther along social lines than any of the literati of his time, and even though he did retain a considerable part of the petty bourgeois ideology of his period, in the field of realism as well as of radicalism he helped break the ground for the rise of that realistic movement which has dominated American literature throughout this century and for the coming of the muckraker's movement which was to precipitate in the person of Upton Sinclair the appearance of the first signs of radical culture in this country.

The change which had come over American life, resulting

[36] Mildred Howells, op. cit., Vol. II, p. 26.

from the conditions described in the first two sections of this chapter, revealed itself in vivid form in the periodical literature of the time. Magazine after magazine disclosed an increasing awareness of the new national consciousness which had grown up in the nation. The bumptious contempt for art and childlike exaltation of action which had characterized a considerable part of the nineteenth-century psychology had already disappeared. It would have been hard to find a writer in the twentieth century who would have declared, as did a writer in *Appleton's Journal* in the previous century, that "as a means of culture, art is overrated; as an elevating force it is misunderstood. . . . It is overlooked that art-loving peoples are apt to become sensuous and effeminate; it is forgotten that solely by robust virtues and not by our sensibilities and emotions can we win the crown of real greatness."[37] In the new century the tendency was to exaggerate the significance of art rather than to underestimate it. Toward the end of the previous century, as the nationalistic spirit of the country had intensified, Whitman had begun to be appreciated. In an article which appeared in *The Bookman* in January, 1898, De Wolfe Howe asserted that "the things which most open-minded readers of Whitman can accept and rejoice in are his large enthusiasm for mankind, especially in 'These States,' *whose national spirit he utters as no one else has done.*" (Italics mine.)[38] The article, which in the main was remarkably appreciative in spirit, at the same time was not free from an element of the apologetic. Whitman still was an unaccepted poet in his own country. Nevertheless, his Americanness was beginning to be understood and esteemed. As the next century advanced, however, the appreciation of things genuinely American increased, and Whitman won his now established place as a truly American poet. In fact, before the first decade of the century had elapsed, American art became the great vogue. *The Nation*

---

[37]*Appleton's Journal*, New York, January 30, 1875. Editor's Table, p. 148.
[38]*The Bookman*, January, 1898, p. 437.

addressed itself to an attack upon Fannie Bloomfield Zeisler, one of the extraordinary pianistic talents of that day, because she played a serenade of Rachmaninoff instead of one of the pieces of Edward McDowell, who, it declared, "has written much better pieces than that *Serenade*—who, in fact, has written better piano music than any Russian living, and any dead Russian for that matter, except Rubenstein—should not Edward McDowell be played by American pianists?"[39] *The Nation's* review of Parker's opera *Mona* was written in the same vein; "In Mr. Parker's opera (*Mona*) one listens in vain for a note distinctly American," it stated. "His going back two thousand years need not have prevented the composer from writing a genuinely American opera."[40] In another place, *The Nation* became even more nationalistically confident in its evaluation of American painting:

> Beautiful painting is hardly any longer attempted save in America. It is not merely that the finest things here from the great Sargent to the great Thayer, hanging opposite each other, to small pictures in unregarded corners are by Americans; it is that a love for the art itself, for beauty of workmanship, beauty of color or beauty of tone or line or arrangement seems almost wholly extinct in the European schools. . . . But every canvas that reaches real distinction, every picture that gives one pleasure in the highest degree from its perception of some form of beauty in nature or its intrinsic quality of a work of art, will be found to bear an American name.[41]

In an article which was published in *Scribner's* exactly a year later Louis Howland stressed those influences toward consolidation that were active in the nation, and which were making for a national culture:

> Fortunately many influences are at work to bind the nation together. We all know there are. The very tendency of the time is towards consolidation. A true and deep unity does exist even now underneath all differences. And how superficial and trivial those differences are as compared with those which characterize the peo-

[39]*The Nation*, January 31, 1907, p. 113.
[40]Ibid., March 21, 1912, p. 246.   [41]Ibid., April 18, 1907, p. 113.

ple of different sections in even so small a country as England.
. . . Many of us do not think nationally, but when in the history
of the world did the ordinary average man think nationally? We
ought not to make too much of this defect. Whitman is right, for
there is "a curious and absolute fusion steadily annealing, com-
pacting, identifying all."[42]

It is important to observe his eulogistic reference to Whitman. By 1908, Whitman had already become sufficiently accepted to be quoted as a man of vision. Although Howland
did not realize that it was industry which had begun to fulfil
Whitman's belief, he was perfectly conscious of the fact that
the process of consolidation was afoot, and that it was that
process which was to provide America with the possibilities of
a native culture. Eight years later, that process had advanced
so far that R. J. Coady, in an article on *American Art* which
appeared in his own magazine *Soil*, felt impelled to declare with overwhelming confidence that "there is an American art. Young, robust, energetic, naïve, immature, daring
and big-spirited. Active in every conceivable field. . . . It is
not a refined granulation nor a delicate disease—it is not an
ism. It is not an illustration to a theory, it is an expression of
life—a complicated life—American life. . . . It has grown
naturally, healthfully, beautifully. It has grown out of the
soil and through the race and will continue to grow. It will
grow and mature and add a new unit to Art."[43] But this interest in, and exaltation of, things American did not stop
with the fine arts. Even the dime novel became extolled as
a valuable American product. In another article in the same
issue of *Soil*, Adam Hull Shirk defended the dime novel as
worthy of "an important place in the development of the
literature in this country." Dime novels, he claimed, "are
typically American. The characters grow out of our local environment; the actions result from social laws, ordinances,

---

[42]*Scribner's*, April, 1908. Article entitled: *Provincial or National*, by
Louis Howland: p. 455.
[43]*Soil* (A Magazine of Art), New York, December, 1916, Vol. I, No.
I, p. 3.

and customs. The situations could not happen anywhere else."[44] Such exaggerations, however, became common on every side, and in the excitement of the discovery of an American national consciousness many minds, sober as well as sentimental, were stirred into a variety of irrational response. Fortunately, minds like those of Van Wyck Brooks and Waldo Frank, caught in the whirl of that excitement, did not lose their equilibrium. While Brooks realized that the twentieth century marked "the beginning of our true national existence," he insisted with characteristic tenacity that what American writers had to learn was that they were at the starting-point of their development and not at its fulfillment.[45] If they began at the ground and worked up they might construct an organic culture which would result in a great national fruition, Brooks contended, but if they started at the peaks and tried to fly forward they would only end up with broken wings and bruised bodies.

But side by side with this growing national consciousness which infected the age, there raced the struggle between the upper and the lower bourgeoisie which penetrated into that national consciousness and darkened its spirit. The optimism which characterized the rise of national consciousness in England during Elizabeth's time was not present in this twentieth-century insurgence of a national tradition in America. Pessimism instead of optimism was its predominant note. The exuberant and expansive spirit which characterized Elizabethan poetry and drama in the sixteenth century did not pervade the American spirit in the twentieth century. The American writers who rediscovered America in the

[44]Ibid. *The Dime Novel as Literature*: pp. 39–43. Interestingly enough, the author, even as late as 1916, clings to the petty bourgeois attitude toward sex in his defense of these cheap fictions. "They are not immoral," he averred, "they are not trash. There is nothing hectic, nothing degenerate, nothing decadent about them. They seek to implant no creeds beyond honesty and decency. Their God is strength, readiness in emergency, action. They never halt, never grow over-sentimental, nor do they dabble in sex problems."

[45]*The Seven Arts*, New York, April, 1917, Vol. I, No. 5: *The Culture of Industrialism*, p. 665.

twentieth century were not enthusiastic about the country that faced them, of which they were a part. They did not write apostrophes to its greatness, or dedicate epics to its future. They lacked the patriotic confidence of Emerson, the nationalistic faith of Whitman. Indeed, one of the most interesting contradictions of the period was the fact that while its writers became imbued with a nationalistic consciousness, they did not become instilled with a patriotic faith—or at least the vast majority of them did not. It was the passing of that America which Emerson and Whitman believed in, which kept these new writers of the petty bourgeois America of the nineteenth century from adopting a patriotic outlook. The America which they confronted was an America in which the tradition of individual freedom was in the process of being lost. The upper bourgeoisie had already sapped the strength out of the petty bourgeoisie, and stultified the principles upon which the petty bourgeois ideology of the nineteenth century had been founded.

Twenty-five years before the close of the nineteenth century, a writer in *Appleton's Journal* had declared that "the few in most things have the upper hand of the many. It is the interest of a few manufacturers and not the interests of the whole people that rules and governs our tariffs. It is the interest of the few and not the many that guides the government of our cities."[46] By the beginning of the twentieth century that protest had risen into a social issue. The new magazines, representing the cause of the petty bourgeoisie, took it up; the new writers, products of the same ideology, addressed themselves to its defense. The cities became the new centre of attack. *McClure's Magazine* led the journalistic onslaught.[47] *Everybody's Magazine*, a close second, became filled with the same protest, and in article after article assailed the conditions of American life which had brought the century to such a pass. Before the end of the

[46] *Appleton's Journal*, March 20, 1875, p. 372.
[47] According to Lincoln Steffens the first muckraking article, entitled *Tweed Days in St. Louis*, appeared in *McClure's Magazine* in October, 1902.

first decade of the century those protests had risen into a movement which, deriving its title from Roosevelt, soon became known as the "muckraking movement." The revelations of the muckrakers, Lincoln Steffens, Ray Stannard Baker, Ida Tarbell, David Graham Phillips, Upton Sinclair, and others, played an important part in the attacks which the petty bourgeoisie lodged against the upper bourgeoisie in the election of 1912.

"We have not 'as good a government as we deserve' but we have as good a government as money can buy," in an article in *Everybody's Magazine*, Percy Stickney Grant avowed. "Government by corporation influences is impossible," Grant continued, reflecting in every word the growing opposition of the petty bourgeoisie. "It must reduce itself to a battle between giants who shelter themselves behind the patriotic devices of great parties while the people perish."[48] "It was the rich," Grant was convinced, "who were responsible for 'New York' vice." But the rich had not only corrupted the cities by their corporational control; they had ruined the country also by their predatory economics. "The American farmer unless he has large capital at his command, is discontented, more and more so, with manual toil," another writer in *Everybody's* pointed out. "Time was when a greater part of migration from the farms was a symptom of thrift, but now a great deal of it is the result of despair."[49] Other writers were even more forthright in their condemnation. In an article on *The Railroads and the People*, which appeared in *Everybody's* in the same year, Harold I. Cleveland attacked the railroad corporations for the ruin that they had brought upon the country, that is, upon the petty bourgeois farmers and business men:

Brutality—downright, unwarranted, criminally short sighted brutality—characterized the creation and completion as well as much of the management since of the railroads of the Northwest. The indictment is not presented in a spirit of narrow-mindedness.

[48]*Everybody's Magazine*, New York, November, 1901, p. 506.
[49]Ibid., April, 1901, p. 410.

In many particulars the operation of the railway land grants were brutally unfair. In the indictment also are the discriminations in freight and passenger tariffs, the special privileges granted corporations as against private individuals, the extermination of industries which chanced to cross railway will, the arbitrary suppression of human instincts in employees, the deliberate creation of powerful legislative lobbies, the ruthless swinging of rights of way thru public and private property—all these brutalities of a type now roundly denounced by the entire English speaking world when repeated in China by Belgian and German railway interests. Yet the Chinaman has not endured much more in the last two years from corporation thick headedness than has the real builder of the Northwest during the last sixty years—the man behind the plow.[50]

The Nation joined in with the same petty bourgeois forces of opposition and warned its readers that "unless either the current be changed or the tariff speedily revised, we may confidently expect to see monopoly working out the destiny even more overwhelmingly in the future."[51] In another article the same magazine declared that "monopoly, to be sure, will work its deadening effects in a profession as fatally as in trade or manufacture."[52] Practically no American magazine was uncognizant of how intense the struggle had become between the petty bourgeois and the upper bourgeois forces in the nation. *Scribner's* devoted a great deal of attention to the issue. *The Habit of Getting Rich,* an article which appeared in its February, 1906, number, expressed with almost perfect fidelity the spirit of the petty bourgeois protest of the time:

We don't mind how rich a few of the neighbors get, provided the rest of us have a fair share. We Americans are not an envious people. Opportunity has been too free here for that. . . . *But when it appears that some of the neighbors are getting together such inordinate and preposterous accumulations of wealth as threaten to diminish in important measure the mass wealth that the rest of us may try for,* then we begin to knit our brows. If the great money makers seem to be playing their games with such success *that threaten*

[50]Ibid., August, 1901: p. 241.
[51]*The Nation*, May 16, 1907, p. 448.
[52]Ibid., January 10, 1907, p. 24.

to deny reasonable opportunities to play our little games, we shall begin to have serious views about unrestricted money-making being made a habit.

That is what is happening now in our country. . . . These fortunes that grow larger year by year begin to daunt us. To build up one often seems truly a bad habit; an ill service that the builder does to his country, his neighbors, his descendants and himself. We wish the fashion for constructing them would pass.[53] (Italics mine.)

In *The Bookman* eight years earlier, the author of the *Bookman's Table* had warned the public of the dangers which would ensue with the growth of a plutocracy. "When oligarchies became suddenly rich they became demoralized," the writer stated. "The temptations and opportunities are much more widespread. Our middle classes are becoming debauched and materialized."[54] Frederick C. Howe revealed the whole temper of the period when, in an article in *Scribner's* on *The American and British City*, he described the change which had come over the American spirit as a result of the passing of the petty bourgeois tradition. "More recently a reaction has come over us," Howe averred. "There is a note of depression, of pessimism in our talk. The condition of our cities, the corruption of our states, the decadence of Congress, the ascendency of privileged interests in our Senate, has destroyed our complacency. From a condition of childish belief in the talisman of democracy we have passed in a few years' time to a state of mind bordering upon despondency before the colossal lust that confronts us. A very large number of people see only failure in our institutions. They are oppressed by the apparent impotence of popular government to find a way out."[55] *The Forum*, in its editorial notes, maintained that "this is not a civilized country. . . . It is a monetized country. . . . The Senate will answer nothing, defend nothing . . . owning or owned by the corporations and predatory political machines."[56] But this protest remained petty bourgeois to the

[53] *Scribner's*, February, 1906, p. 252.
[54] *The Bookman*, October, 1898, p. 168.
[55] *Scribner's*, January, 1907, p. 113.   [56] *The Forum*, May, 1912.

end. It was just as much concerned with the protection of private property as was the logic of the upper bourgeoisie, only it wished to protect the private property of the small capitalists against the depredations of the large. *The Nation* at the time summed up the whole attitude with precision, when it stated that "government in the United States as elsewhere has often been too indifferent to public welfare,[57] that social classes themselves the inevitable outcome of competition, have too often been mutually hostile;—must be admitted. *The panacea of socialism is indeed rejected* but the tremendous problem of the government to the mass is still unsolved. We are still compelled to think that imperfect as the performance has been thus far, the practical sphere of government, in a democracy, is neutral rather than paternal; and that when a government has insured for its people individual liberty in industry and politics; equal rights in law, security for person and property—it must leave each man to work out his own salvation."[58] (Italics mine.)

The rise of the muckrakers, as we suggested in a preceding paragraph, was a direct outgrowth of the desperate form which the conflict between the petty bourgeoisie and the upper bourgeoisie had taken at the turn of the century. The "clean-up" campaign which the muckrakers instigated was a direct attempt to expose the nefarious rôle which the corporations and trusts played in our moral and political life. America was being corrupted by big business; its political life was being ruined by a plutocracy; its moral life was being debauched by wealthy classes which had degenerated as completely as the Roman aristocracy at the end of the

---

[57]It is important to bear in mind that whenever reference is made to "public welfare," it is not the welfare of the workers which is meant or included in the reference, except to the degree that the workers represent the petty bourgeois psychology, but the welfare of the petty bourgeoisie which has constituted ideologically what has been known as the American public. Wherever the workers' cause has been involved, as in the case of strikes, the petty bourgeoisie, when it has been implicated, as in the administrations of Wilson, has fought it as bitterly as it has fought the tactics of the upper bourgeoisie.

[58]*The Nation*, March 14, 1907, p. 248.

empire. In *The Shame of Cities,* Lincoln Steffens[59] exposed the corruption of urban government, mincing nothing in his attacks upon the evils he uncovered. In his *Autobiography* Steffens recounts in detail the rise and fall of the whole muckraking movement. At first he believed the evil was due to the presence of dishonest men in the offices of power, but later on he became convinced that it was the nature of the economic system that produced the evil, and therefore concluded that wherever "business is dominant, business men must and will corrupt a government which can pass laws to hinder or help business."[60] Steffens was the shrewdest of the muckrakers and saw at that time what has come to pass since, that "if this process goes on this American republic of ours will be a government that represents the organized evils of a privileged class (big business)."[61] In an article of his in *Everybody's Magazine,* in September, 1910, he showed that the "boss of all bosses" was "J. P. Morgan." But Steffens was only one of a multitude of muckrakers. Ida Tarbell exposed the operations of the oil trust; Ray Stannard Baker exposed the machinations of the beef trust; David Graham Phillips, in *The Treason of the Senate,* exposed the corruption of that body; Upton Sinclair, in *The Jungle,* exposed the truth about the meat-packing industry and its criminal disregard for the public's health, and in *The Moneychangers* exposed the facts about Wall Street. Roosevelt was instrumental in having the Pure Food Act passed in order to cure the food evil which Sinclair had exposed. The greater evil, the conditions of life which the workers had to endure, and

---

[59]Amusingly and naïvely enough, a certain professor of history, ignorant apparently of the class conflict going on in America at the time, said to Steffens: "The muckrakers dominated a period of the history of the United States. Muckraking was a movement the origin of which will some day be a subject of historical inquiry. You were the first of the muckrakers. If you will tell now how you happened to start muckraking not only will you contribute to our knowledge of an important chapter of American history; you may throw light upon the rise and the run of social movements." (Lincoln Steffens: *Autobiography:* New York, 1931: p. 357.)

[60]Ibid., p. 417.   [61]Ibid., p. 413.

which Sinclair had described in such realistic and revealing style, he was not concerned with at all. As Sinclair said, he aimed at the brain but only succeeded in hitting the belly of the public. Exposures sprang up everywhere, crowding into newspapers, magazines, and books. There promised to be no end of them.

But then, in a few years, they stopped. Muckraking lost its flair. Suddenly the magazines forsook their interest in it. The new decade had decided to become dignified. Ray Stannard Baker, who had adopted the pseudonym of David Grayson in order to save his more quiet work from association with his muckraking excavations, soon retired from the scene and wrote under his pseudonym alone.[62] It was better that Ray Stannard Baker die and David Grayson live. The upper bourgeoisie had brought its pressure to bear upon the editors of the magazines,[63] and with the financial resources at its command, it could not be defied. "Big business rallied and organized itself and the Wall Street bankers got to work," as Upton Sinclair described in *Money Writes*, with the result that "every magazine in the United States that was publishing any statements injurious to big business was either bought up or driven into bankruptcy, and the muckraking era passed into unwritten history. The public was told that it, the public, had become disgusted with the excesses of the muckrakers; and the public believed that, just as it had formerly believed the muckrakers. . . . It was obvious enough that the 'excesses' had been committed by those who made the muck, not by those who raked it; and the fact stands on record that out of the hundreds of exposures published, and hundreds of thousands of single facts stated, not one was ever disproved in a court of law."[64] Not until several years after the World War was another muckraking magazine, *Plain Talk*, able to arise and survive for about half a

[62] Fred L. Patee: *The New American Literature:* New York, 1930: pp. 157, 158.
[63] V. L. Parrington: *Main Currents in American Thought:* New York, 1927: Vol. III, p. 407.
[64] Upton Sinclair: *Money Writes:* New York, 1927: p. 25.

decade. But even that magazine, edited by G. D. Eaton, who was really more interested in books than in social life, found it hard to continue in the face of constant opposition. After Eaton's death, the magazine became a more hardhitting muckraking affair under the editorship of Walter Liggett,[65] but when the company that controlled it became insolvent, it was found impossible to secure a purchaser for the magazine.[66] Despite a circulation which had increased steadily in the last year of its existence, the pressure of big business, operating through its refusal to advertise in its pages, indirectly discouraged the enthusiasm of possible purchasers. *Plain Talk,* in the twenties, was the black sheep among American periodicals. The other magazines had long before learned to be good sheep, or at least if they were not good they had learned not to be nasty. The new wisdom which they had adopted instructed them in the virtue of always being gentlemen, never raising their voices, never demonstrating vehement emotions, and, above all, even if a Teapot Dome affair were involved, of never descending to the childish practice of employing harsh names or truth-stinging adjectives.

But this upper bourgeoisie which had put a quietus upon the muckraking magazines, had already acquired sufficient wealth in the twentieth century to constitute a pseudo-aristocracy. Earlier in the century, at the same time that the petty bourgeois muckrakers were creating such a social hullabaloo in the nation, this upper bourgeoisie began to develop a cultural outlook upon life that was considerably different from that of its forefathers. As the industrial and financial structure of the nation advanced, this upper bourgeoisie lost almost all its immediate contact with the sources of its income. It became a class of absentee owners. It had closeness neither

---

[65]Since the death of *Plain Talk*, Mr. Liggett has continued his courageous muckraking career, as a free lance. His recent life of Hoover, forthright in its attacks from beginning to end, marks his latest exploit in the muckraking genre.

[66]The new *Plain Talk* that has recently appeared bears practically no relationship to its literary namesake.

with the land, nor, in many cases, with any specific enterprise. Its closeness was with capital in its accumulated form, and with the variety of enterprises in which its money was invested. In most cases it began to live in places remote from where its capital was invested, and in many cases, except in terms of the market values involved, knew little of the nature or operation of the enterprises with which it was financially connected. And above all, if it knew little, its children knew less of the actual origins of its wealth. Every semblance of intimacy with the productive process, which its nineteenth-century forefathers had known, it had sacrificed. Accretion of wealth was no longer dependent upon expenditures of energy in behalf of its acquisition, or sacrifice of time in search of its further discovery. Carnegie could offer to buy off a war, the one that was imminent for a time between the United States and Venezuela, with his wealth. Henry Ford could undertake to send a Peace Ship to Europe in an attempt to bring the European combatants to terms. In other words, its wealth had become so great, that it now could afford to become interested in other aspects of life besides the purely economic. Almost inevitably, like a new revelation, culture came into its ken. It began to realize that culture also had its rewards, even though they might not be recorded in Bradstreet form. And so the American collectors began their art-plundering invasion of Europe, and in the homeland American museums, American galleries, American libraries, and American foundations were created to perpetuate the glory of the new patrons of art and learning.

Even before this pseudo-aristocratic middle class began to patronize the arts and sciences in such extensive form, American magazines had not been neglectful of its promise. The same magazines which gave voice to the critical outlook which prevailed during the muckraking decade, had not closed their pages to appreciations of the cultural interests of the plutocracy. At the beginning of the century, in its section on Chronicle and Comment, *The Bookman* had advised its readers to "take a common sense and philosophical view of our plutocratic fellow-citizens who are trying to crystallize themselves into a distinct and separate caste." The article then continued:

Of course, their immediate aims and aspirations are wholly personal to themselves, but *incidentally they are doing a great deal for the country*. Their money erects magnificent buildings, which are to our people a much needed lesson in architecture; it establishes art collections and brings to the country many of the exquisite treasures which Europe has possessed. The donors import to our national ensemble a decorative element in their sumptuousness, their imported luxury and the ornamental accessories of their life.

Instead of attempting to deter our plutocrats in their efforts to become aristocrats, one should rather help them along and prevent them from making those breaks which arise from an imperfect knowledge of their models.

Most of us haven't money enough to do the things which they do, but that is no reason for being envious or uncharitable.[67]

In another article in the same issue of *The Bookman* the upper bourgeoisie were defended in even more ardent style:

There is no doubt that there exists a very widespread and very ominous undercurrent of resentment against the evils that have sprung directly from the accumulation of capital in the hands of singularly able but thoroughly unscrupulous men. This feeling of resentment exists not only among the very poor, but it extends to a very large and very influential portion of the American people. Intelligent people freely recognize that the union of capital is not only necessary but desirable. Without it most of the great enterprises of which our country is so proud could never have been carried to success. . . .

The inimical feeling which exists and which is loosely described as antagonism to the trusts does not spring from envy of the rich. It does not at all resemble the hatred which the proletarian of Europe cherishes for the rich bourgeois. No one who is imbued with the American tradition feels dislike for the very wealthy man. Americans, in fact, rather admire those who have made great sums of money, and they admire them because the money bears witness to certain qualities that are needed to make money, thrift, perseverance, energy, sagacity, judgment.[68]

[67]November, 1900, p. 210.   [68]Ibid., p. 228.

By the end of the first decade of the century American magazines had already acquired the habit of making obeisances
to the new patrons of art and wisdom. The upper bourgeoisie had diverged from the multitude, *Scribner's* pointed
out, "due to the formation of tastes which the multitude did
not share or understand, tastes luxurious, it is true, but often
refined."[69] Admitting, as the writer did, that "there was a
feverish anxiety to establish a substantial distinction between
the rich and the non-rich," he defended it by showing that
"its expression is in the closely guarded 'cottages' of Newport, in lieu of the monstrous Saratoga hotels of the fifties.
It tends to the creation by the rich of a 'monde' of their own
with fairly defined and narrow limits." It was that same
nouveau riche aristocracy that soon began to cultivate the
anti-democratic concept of the "civilized minority," exalting
itself and those who shared its newly acquired vision as the
elite of the race. The rest of society became the canaille of
humankind, the "uncultured majority." At first the arti-
ficiality of the distinction was obvious. Before long, however,
its advocates came to look upon themselves as the *biologically
select,* the products of finer clay. The common clay which
Whitman had exalted, the democracy of all, binding the
lowest with the highest, exalting the infinitesimal along with
the infinite, it dismissed as false doctrine. Even the idea of
educating the mass of mankind into an appreciation of life
on its more cultural levels it scorned as impractical because
impossible. It agreed with the writer who had declared in
The Bookman near the close of the nineteenth century that
"culture is not a product of democracy. But we have gone on
offering the doubtful blessing of free education, and the air
is full of the gabble of the imperfectly educated."[70]

With the coming of this leisure-class element within the
upper middle class the moral emphasis of that class was
replaced by the æsthetic. In the beginning, even in the nine-

[69]*Scribner's*, September, 1909, p. 378.
[70]*The Bookman*, November, 1895: article entitled *The Criticism of Life:*
p. 203.

ties, it was the "art for art's sake" attitude, taken over from England at the time, which it began to cultivate. "The theory which is known as 'art for art's sake' has long been preached to deaf ears," H. B. Watson had observed in an article in *The Bookman*, as early as November, 1895, "but the ears are opening," he added, "and in whatever regard it is held in lay minds there seems little doubt but it will inspire and persuade writers of the future."[71] Since that time, to be sure, the æsthetic shibboleth has gone through various permutations, and while the art for art sakers have disappeared as a group, if not as individuals, their philosophy clings to a host of attitudes which are still defended. But it is not their attitude which is dominant any longer, but a derivative of it, namely, the "above the battle" attitude, the detached objective attitude, the Olympian attitude, which finds its supreme embodiment in the artist who looks upon the world of things as vain show, who sees man as petty and movements as pettier, and who refuses to allow his philosophic vision to be distorted by participation in their change and chaos.

Let us trace how this Olympian, "above the battle" philosophy got an intellectual hold upon our generation. That the attempt to be above the battle is evidence of a defense mechanism can scarcely be doubted. Only those who belong to the ruling class, in other words, only those who had already won the battle and acquired the spoils, could afford to be above the battle. Fiction which was propagandistic, that is, fiction which continued to participate in the battle, it naturally cultivated a distaste for, and eschewed. Fiction which was above the battle, that is fiction which was concerned only with the so-called absolutes and eternals, with the ultimate emotions and the perennial tragedies, but which offered no solutions, no panaceas—it was such fiction that won its adoration. "It is possible that we are growing a bit tired of the novel with a purpose," *The Nation* declared in its issue of April 18, 1912, reflecting that change in the process of con-

[71] *The Bookman*, November, 1895: article entitled *Living Critics*: p. 186.

summation, and then added in a carping vein that the "American novelist, like the American playwright, has listened to the counsel which urged him to look for his materials in problems of the nation and the day."[72] The new aim was to escape social reality and to exalt individual emotionality. In short, this new ideology, like that of all leisure classes, sought to cultivate literature as a form of escape—escape either from boredom or from its own limitations of self and soul. Hence, the contempt with which this class looks upon the virtues of its fathers and mothers—and as Gilbert and Sullivan so well put it—of its sisters and its cousins and its aunts. No one has embodied this contempt so well as George Bernard Shaw who has made just that kind of mockery of middle-class virtues which this new leisure class has so extolled. The lower middle class, which still clings to middle-class virtues and which worries about the kinks in its Ford cars and is ignorant of the value of original Rembrandts or first editions of Rabelais, does not know Shaw at all, or at best is acquainted with him only as a name, with no understanding whatsoever of his works. The little reading it does, and in America it is very little, is confined to the Henry van Dykes, the Booth Tarkingtons, the Warwick Deepings on the upper levels, and to the Harold Bell Wrights, the Rex Beaches, and the Somers Roches on the lower levels, with the corner drug store as a still lower retreat. It is not this lower middle class which determines literary values to-day, but this leisure class outgrowth of the upper middle class. American critics no longer have to fight for the recognition of George Bernard Shaw or even James Joyce. This new leisure class accepts them eagerly, purchases their books, and gloats over their satires and excoriations. Even the eccentricities of Joyce, little understood though they may be, become all the more precious because so confined in their appeal. Had this development of the upper bourgeoisie, resulting in the creation of a leisure class, not arisen, American magazines would still be dominated to-day by the moral-ridden formulas of the nine-

[72] P. 384.

teenth-century middle class. Our critics to-day do not demand moral stress in our literature, nor do they clamor for purity and righteousness as did their predecessors, for the influence of this leisure class has broken down the cultural barriers which had been erected and upheld for over two centuries by the petty bourgeoisie.

This ideology, then, is that of a leisure class which is clearly able to live on its inheritance, develop a contempt for work, and a disregard for money, and has begun to find time to "civilize" itself, as Clive Bell has phrased it, in the *Art of Living*. It was the influence of that leisure class which made possible what Henry L. Mencken as well as Clive Bell has exalted as the "civilized minority." Of course, it should not be thought that this civilized minority is entirely confined to the leisure class to which we have just referred. As we stated before, it is simply this leisure class which, by virtue of the change in the middle class itself, has come to dominate literary fashion. As is always the case, many members of the lower classes tend to ape the manners and attitudes of the upper, and when, as is the condition to-day, the current literary ideology becomes an "above the battle" one, fitting so perfectly the philosophy of this leisure class, and for that matter of most leisure classes, eager aspirants from the lower classes at once become excitedly anxious to feel themselves part of that "civilized minority." Thus it is that school teachers who wish to be different and pharmacy clerks who are ambitious of intellectual distinction adopt this "above the battle" ideology and, scornful thus of their colleagues and employers, find a substitute satisfaction in their intellectual kinship with the literary and philosophic almighties. This "above the battle" audience, therefore, is more a vertical than a horizontal affair, however horizontal may have been its origin.

In literature this attitude of cultural superiority exercised a devastating influence. Whereas in the nineteenth century authors aimed to write for the people, however much they may have failed in the attempt, in the twentieth century they began to write for the "civilized minority," thereby severing their relationship with the social whole. This was not only true of writers who adopted the ideology of the upper bourgeoisie, but it also began to become increasingly true of many writers who had been imbued with the petty bourgeois tradition. The petty bourgeois tradition had never eschewed the novel of propaganda, never forsaken the novel of social or moral purpose. But the petty bourgeois tradition was dying in the literary field as well as in the economic and political, and while throughout the next two decades men like Herrick, Sinclair, and Dreiser continued to express it in varying forms, the rest of American literature began to succumb to the "above the battle" ideology of the upper bourgeoisie—who could afford to be "above the battle," since they were the all but enthroned masters of the state.

Another factor in the development of the upper bourgeois ideology in the twentieth century was in the sphere of morality. As the wealth of the upper bourgeoisie grew, its interest in morality waned. Of course, being a bourgeoisie, an upper bourgeoisie which had arisen from a petty bourgeoisie, and living in a nation which to a large extent still swore by petty bourgeois standards, it could not afford to scorn morality in the way that European aristocracies had done. In fact, not until this day, has it ever failed to advocate morality for the masses, petty bourgeois as well as proletarian. At the same time its wealthier way of life inclined it to be less and less moral. The middle-class morality which its forefathers practiced, and which it was taught, could no longer discipline it. Divorce rent its family apart, and sexual license ate into the spirit of its moral life, rotting it at the root. Newspapers became crowded with the story of its scandals; its amours provided thrills for the underlings who were ever eager to know the truth about how the four hundred lived. Court records, in the form of divorce suits, alienation of affection cases, and all that intricacy of conflict which violates the secrecy of the domestic sphere, became public property through the agency of the press. The so-called "loose-living" of the upper set became the common knowledge of the populace. Upton Sinclair dedicated his novel, *The Metropolis*, to the task of exposing the loose and licentious character of its life. Other novelists took up the same cue, and finally Cornelius Vanderbilt himself, a member of the upper set, told the truth about his own class in *Reno*. Even to-day this form of exposition has not ceased, for the lower middle class mind of America is always willing to become horrified and morally indignant whenever it hears of a violation of its moral code. One of the latest expositions of this variety was Mr. Gifford's book, *Caviare for Breakfast*, which appeared last year, and which purported to recount Mr. Gifford's personal experiences among the plutocrats whom he met and associated with as the tutor to their children. While Mr. Gifford advanced nothing new in his study, he did manage to give a more revealing picture of the inner lives of certain members of the plutocracy than have most novelists who in the main have described the upper set from more limited and less intimate contact.

This deterioration in the moral life of the upper bourgeoisie had a profound effect upon the psychology of the nation. Heretofore, the upper bourgeoisie had attempted to perpetuate the moral habits of its forefathers. If it had not succeeded in living as strait-laced a moral existence as say John Adams or James Madison, it certainly had not adopted the loose manner of living which characterized its behavior in the twentieth century. Above all, when individual members of its class did err they did not allow their peccadillos to become the property of the public. If a financier or industrialist in the nineteenth century had a mistress as well as a wife, he did not tend, except under most extraordinary circumstances, to do what a number of our plutocrats almost inevitably do to-day—as in the case of a well-known newspaper man and a famous movie-actress—namely, make the fact known to the world by gestures and actions that are unmistakably obvious and intentioned. Deviations from the middle class credo were concealed in the nineteenth century; in the twentieth century they were shamelessly flaunted before the public eye. In fact, as newspaper accounts and court records show, many members of the upper bourgeoisie in this century have boasted of their mistresses with the same type of bravado that the English aristocrats did during the reign of Charles II. As a result of this change in the moral character of the ruling class, the only class which has carried on the fight for the preservation of middle class ethics has been the petty bourgeoisie. Just as wealth so often tends to disintegrate the finest moral fibre, the lack of wealth so often tends to preserve it. If the American plutocrats had been forced to continue to work for the wealth they accumulated, in other words, had they been kept close to the grindstone of production, they would have disadhered from the middle class code with much less frequency. The transformation of America from an agrarian to an industrial nation, accompanied by the ensuing change of the country from a nation into an empire, with the consequent enhancement of imperialistic enterprise, flooded the land with too much wealth for it to remain in its old state, or for the class which secured the vast bulk of that wealth to retain its old character.

In the nineteenth century, the upper bourgeoisie in New York as well as the Brahminical tribe of upper bourgeoisie in Boston defended the moral tradition of the middle class with almost as much ardor as the petty bourgeoisie in the West. In short, its wealth had not become great enough to corrupt its morale. In the twentieth century, that defense was left almost entirely in the hands of the petty bourgeoisie. The campaign for moral censorship which was marked by the rise of Comstock and which has aroused so much conflict in the twentieth century, has been almost wholly petty bourgeois in origin. In the nineteenth century such censorship was unnecessary. The upper bourgeoisie was at one with the petty bourgeoisie in demanding morality in literature, and every American author from Irving, Bryant, Emerson, Thoreau, and Hawthorne to Longfellow, Whittier, Lowell, Holmes,

Twain, and Howells observed it with a fidelity that could not be questioned. In the twentieth century, however, when the morality of the ruling class began to break down, those defenses weakened, and within a short time the literature of the country began to reveal evidences of revolt against the middle class standard of literary values. It was then that the petty bourgeoisie arose to the occasion, as it were, and warned the populace to what depths of degradation our literature had begun to sink, and by means of censorship boards and vice committees, threatened to save the minds of children and adolescents (who seldom read American books but turned usually to Boccaccio or Rabelais or Shakespeare for sexual candor) as well as adults from such pollution. For over a decade this battle raged with increasing ferocity.

It was Mr. John S. Sumner, the successor to Anthony Comstock, who, as secretary to the New York Society for the Suppression of Vice, provided the leading defense for the perpetuation of petty bourgeois virtue in literature. Within the span of a few years the Society took action against a score of books. Dreiser's *The Genius* was only one of the outstanding novels of the day that it attacked. In fact *The Genius* was condemned also by the Vice Society of Cincinnati, which discovered that the novel contained seventy-five lewd passages and seventeen profane. F. L. Rose, secretary of the Western Society for the Suppression of Vice, asserted that "we have succeeded in having it removed from possibly every book store in the city." All plates, copies and sheets of *Jurgen* were seized on January 14, 1920, and it was not until two years later that the ban on the novel was lifted. Other novels, representing several literatures such as *Women in Love, Casanova's Homecoming, Jude the Obscure, The Damnation of Theron Ware, Hagar, Homosapiens, Trilby, Suzan Lenox,* were assailed also. Various authors, among them Bliss Perry, Booth Tarkington, H. W. Boynton and Henry van Dyke, declared themselves in favor of the censorship. It was Hamlin Garland however, faithful to the petty bourgeois tradition to the very end, who summed up this protest better than any one else in the following words:

> Among the younger writers I sense a quality akin to the jazz band, the modern dance, and the moving picture, and while I am willing to grant that each generation must have its chance to state itself in its own way, I find myself revolted by an over-insistence of sex themes and by a kind of sad ego-mania in these writers. Their characters whine and complain and shirk. As poets they are obsessed with their own petty concerns. As novelists they have small sense of humor or proportion, and for the most part they are lacking in sound craftsmanship. After reading a few of them I am filled with disgust of their futility, and I return to Howells with a sense of getting back to broad culture, sanity, humor and good workmanship.

But victory was no more possible for the petty bourgeoisie in the literary field than in the economic or political. Just as the consolidation of industry and the centralization of capital had destroyed its vigor on the economic front, and lent strength to the industrio-financial oligarchy, the enormous growth of cities in the East, with the consequent decline of religion and the power of the churches, made it impossible for the petty bourgeoisie to extend its control very far beyond the borders of its immediate influence. This was emphatically true in Eastern cities, especially New York. In the South, to be sure, where, as we pointed out in the third chapter, the petty bourgeoisie still rule, this condition of latitude does not prevail. In Savannah, for example, as I have just learned, several courageous persons interested in the little theatre movement managed at great hazard to stage Eugene O'Neill's play, *Anna Christie*. Undoubtedly, if such ventures were repeated with sufficient frequency, they would be irrevocably outlawed. Even in Los Angeles as late as February, 1926, O'Neill's drama, *Desire Under the Elms*, was attacked, and the actors were seized by the police on the charge of having presented a play dangerous to the morals of the American people. The actors were detained under arrest until four-thirty the next morning, their finger-prints having been taken as a precaution against their escape, and were not allowed to go at liberty until a bail of eight hundred and fifty dollars had been provided. After deliberating for almost nine hours, the jury was unable to come to an agreement. Eight were for conviction, four for acquittal. As a result the play was able to continue, and, at the risk of demoralizing the whole community, it ran on for over ten weeks. But the vigor of that opposition has already waned. With the rapid downfall of the petty bourgeoisie in the economic sphere the petty bourgeois ideology has lost its power in the larger communities where big business, with its creation of a new group of workers in the engineer, the expert, the manager, the efficiency man, and with its regimentation of industry and commerce, has brought into being a world which is not at all identified with the logic of the petty bourgeoisie.

Another force which helped shatter the defense of the petty bourgeoisie in the field of literature was the so-called sexual revolution which developed with intensity during the decade that followed the World War. The economic emancipation of woman which was expedited by the war, the spread of birth-control information, the popularity of sex literature, the sweeping interest in sexual experimentation which became prevalent during that decade—all these were further testimony of the breakdown of the petty bourgeois defenses in the moral field, for the girls and boys who created what Judge Ben Lindsey called "the revolt of modern youth," and effected what other writers have described as "the sexual revolution,"[73] were boys and girls in the main from petty bourgeois environments. No doubt, the younger generation of the upper bourgeoisie had preceded these petty bourgeois youths in the sphere of sexual revolt, but it was not until these members of the less wealthy classes extended that revolt down through the lower ranks of society that it began to assume proportions which awakened the community to its

[73]Cf. Lindsey: *Revolt of Modern Youth:* New York. Calverton: *Bankruptcy of Marriage:* New York.

presence. By the end of the twenties there could be no doubt
about the fact that the old morality had lost its influence
upon the minds of the younger generation, which by that
time not only did not cling to the moral-minded bourgeois
literature of the nineteenth century but avidly read—or at
least those among them who were interested in literature
read—Sherwood Anderson, D. H. Lawrence, Ernest Hemingway, and in many cases even James Joyce.

After three hundred years of dominancy, then, the dictatorship of the bourgeoisie in the moral field was broken
down at last. In literature as well as in life its code was no
longer binding, no longer the cultural compulsive which
made young and old regard it as absolute. In brief, its moral
tradition had become effete. The upper bourgeoisie no longer
revered it, and the petty bourgeoisie, rendered impotent by
the crushing tentacles of big business and industrial capitalism, and lacking in the urban centres the religious support
which science had undermined, was unable to wage a vigorous fight for its preservation. Unfortunately, no other
ideology had arisen to take its place—the proletarian ideology
had not yet wedged its way far enough into the mind of the
masses to have developed into a cultural force—and nothing
but an era of moral chaos followed. Faced everywhere with
the breakdown of the moral defenses of the bourgeois order,
American youth, unable to see a way out, has continued to
falter and flounder about in a vortex of moral confusion.
But just as disorder always precedes the appearance of a
new order, the present chaos can be looked upon as nothing
more than a transitionary stage in the social process, the
necessary period through which minds, freed of the old,
must pass before they can adapt themselves to the new.

IV

The one figure in twentieth-century American literature
who represents better than any one else a composite of the
forces active in this country during those years is Theodore

Dreiser. Born in the West, and early imbued with its individualistic tradition, Dreiser, as a young man, migrated to the East, where he was confronted with a new civilization. Before setting forth for the East, however, he spent four years in Chicago, St. Louis, and Pittsburgh, where he worked as a reporter. In those Western cities he came face to face with industrialism in full blast, but it was not until he arrived in New York that the full measure of American civilization made its impact upon him. In that city, after carking tribulations and failures, involving hackwriting and hackeditorship, he finally began to find himself in terms of that civilization. With that blundering, bull-dog tenacity which has always been characteristic of him, he held on to what he had found, namely a philosophy of civilization which several other American writers, particularly Frank Norris and Stephen Crane, had begun to find and work out in their fictions, and fought for it through the years when those other writers had long since died and for the time being at least had been partly forgotten.

The philosophy, if such it may be called, which Dreiser had discovered was that of realism. Now realism, as we endeavored to show in the chapter on the frontier force, was a late growth in American literature. Afflicted by the colonial complex, the East would have nothing to do with it, and the West turned to it in fiction only when the conditions of life there provoked its appearance. Beginning with Eggleston and extending to Howells, the realistic movement made slow headway in the nineteenth century. It was not until the twentieth century, as the conditions of life all over the country conspired against the perpetuation of the romantic outlook, broke the spinal tie of the colonial complex and made America face the spectacle of a civilization which was rapidly destroying every tradition which it had cherished, that the realistic movement could become the dominant movement of the day. It was Theodore Dreiser, seeing and sensing that change which had come over the nation, who came to stand as the great exponent of that movement in the twentieth

century. Strange as it may seem, Dreiser was the legitimate
—or shall we say, in the light of Howells' moral outlook,
illegitimate?—successor to Howells. Howells had fought for
the realistic approach long before Dreiser had come upon
the literary scene, and, as we have seen, had even turned his
attention toward the labor movement which the rest of the
literati had ignored.[74] But Howells, victimized by the bourgeois moral code, had never been able to advance the movement beyond the stage of "reticent," that is halfway, or
muffled, realism. Dreiser destroyed the reticence and replaced
it with candor. He can be called, therefore, the father of
candid realism (or what many critics prefer to call naturalism) in American literature. And yet Dreiser's candor never
went any further than the individual. He never ventured
into the field of social candor—or at least he has not done
so until now, although his recent conversion to Communism
may predicate a change in his development—as did Upton
Sinclair. In fact, he never turned his attention to the labor
movement as did Howells in several novels, the young
Ernest Poole in *The Harbor*, and Sherwood Anderson in
Marching Men. But the labor movement, the masses, belong
to another phase of realism, social realism, which neither
Howells nor Poole nor Anderson understood although their
interest in the field is of historical value.

Dreiser's realism, viewed in the light of to-day, then, is
an individualistic realism. Influenced though he was by Balzac and Zola, his realism is fundamentally American in spirit
and character. Indeed, Dreiser is one of the first of the
American novelists to reveal a freedom from the colonial
complex. His very crudeness, if you will, is American. He
was not concerned with English critics or English styles, but
went his way as if England never existed. He was saturated
with the American environment, and expressed it in whatever he wrote. He was one of the first writers, following

[74]Of course, there were a few American writers who had not evaded the
theme. John Hay's novel, *Bread Winners*, had dealt with the labor movement, but in an unsympathetic vein. Howells at least was sympathetic
in his approach. Bellamy, too, had been sympathetic.

Whitman and Twain, who embodied within his works something of the American rhythm. Nothing foreign, unless it be a trace of Balzac or Zola, dictated the nature or substance of his works. Like Twain, he was born in the Mid-West, grew up in the Mid-West, and while later on he discarded the impulses and aspirations he had originally imbibed, there, he has never tired of writing of it as his autobiographical words abundantly record. He belongs to the tradition of Walt Whitman and Mark Twain and not to that of Washington Irving and Nathaniel Hawthorne.

It was in revolt against the middle-class moral code that Dreiser's individualistic realism made its most marked advance. But Dreiser did not carry his revolt at once to its logical extreme. For a while, he clung to an element of the petty bourgeois outlook, as *Sister Carrie* attested. Indeed even in *The Genius,* as its finale reveals, he had not yet forsaken the petty bourgeois literary dictum. After all, he had been reared in a petty bourgeois environment, and while he had early deserted its religious ideology its economic and political ideology remained with him until very late in life. The chapter headings alone of *Sister Carrie* show how much he was still influenced by the moral outlook of the older generation. Such chapter headings as these illustrate how closely tied he still was to the bourgeois code: In Elf Land Disporting: The Grim World Without; Without the Walled City; The Slope of the Years; The Kingdom of Greatness; The Pilgrim Adream; When Waters Engulf Us We Reach for a Star; The Lure of the Material; Beauty Speaks for Itself. But not only the chapter headings disclose that closeness with the old outlook; one need but read the book at random and one will alight upon passage after passage that betrays the same affiliation. The third paragraph in the novel dealing with the temptations of the city, the ninth chapter which contains the description of the quiet loveliness of the petty bourgeois home as contrasted with the unhappy frigidity of the home of Hurstwood, the man of wealth, and finally the last paragraph wishing Carrie well in her dream of happiness which she will never feel—each in its way reveals the persistence of the old motif, the old petty bourgeois sentimentality, which was so ubiquitous in nineteenth-century American fiction. It was only later that Dreiser escaped the larger part of that influence and learned to face the individual as a whole without the intrusion of moral considerations or compunctions. Then it was that he depicted the sex life of the individual in detail, closing his eyes to none of his impulses or actions. The characters he dealt with from the beginning, however, were not the nice people one would meet at a Howells dinner party or social gathering, but people who were less nice but more real. In general, they were, like Carrie Meeber and Jennie Gerhardt, people of humbler station, who had to struggle against the adversities of life instead of enjoy its comforts. The America which Dreiser saw was a sordid America, and he betrayed no hesitation in describing that sordidness in terms of its environment and its people.[75] Almost inevitably the fate of his characters was tragic. In no instance were they inspired by noble motives of romantic ideals. They were of the earth, and they carried the impact of the earth about with them, with the mud clinging to their heels. From Jennie Gerhardt to Eugene Witla, from George Hurstwood to Frank Cowperwood, from Isidor Berchansky to Clyde Griffiths, evil conflicted with good, weakness with strength, the bitter with the sweet, with defeat in one form or another the ineluctable victor. Everywhere in Dreiser's fiction, life has lost its lustre and promise and become gray and futile.

While unquestionably Dreiser was influenced by the scientific spirit of his age, and was stirred by the deterministic doctrine which had gained a significant place in European thought of that period, leaving its impress upon the fiction

[75]As early as 1917, Mr. Mencken in an article entitled *The Dreiser Bugaboo'* (cf. *Seven Arts*, August, 1917, pp. 507–517) showed how completely Dreiser was disregarded by the critics of the old genre and how many of the more modern-minded critics fought his work because of its sordidness and naturalism.

of the day, especially that of Zola, it is to America and not to Europe that we must look for the basis of his philosophy of despair. Dreiser, like Twain, had started forth with the optimism characteristic of the spirit of the early frontier. In later years, describing his youthful reaction to his native environment, he declared that "to me it seemed that all the spirit of rural America, its idealism, its dreams, the passion of a Brown, the courage and patience and sadness of a Lincoln, the dreams and courage of a Lee or a Jackson were all here." But Pittsburgh put an end to all that. Pittsburgh, where he saw the blast furnaces, and witnessed men like human ingots become lost in the molten process of making steel, came to stand as a symbol for him of industrialism in action. "The very soil," he wrote, referring again to the western country, "smacked of American idealism and faith, a fixedness in sentimental and purely imaginative American tradition in which I, alas, could not share—I had seen Pittsburgh." While scientific doctrine might contend that man's behavior is determined by forces over which he has no individual control, one had but to observe the rise of industrial America to realize that truth without reference to scientific doctrine at all. Dreiser realized it at once, intuitively if not rationally. Forces had become stronger than men. Things had become stronger than wills.

In Dreiser, then, is embodied that whole conflict of the individual with his environment which had begun to consume the age. Before long he became aware of what had happened to the western country in which he was born, and conscious also of what had occurred in the cities. In both places the individual was being crushed, in the one instance the petty bourgeois agrarian and in the other the petty bourgeois urbanite. And, what was worse, there seemed to be no way out. It was the despair of that situation, the helplessness of the individualistic-minded petty bourgeois, that Dreiser expressed in his fiction. The petty bourgeois individualist had no way to turn. He was snared in a trap. For Dreiser that trap became the world which governed with a merciless hand the destiny of the individual. Even the individual who rose to power, the titan, the financier, was bound eventually to be swept to defeat. No matter how he turned, he was certain to be caught. Strong men as well as weak men were forced to bow before this new Nemesis. Tragedy stood over all, a steel scythe that cut across the face of the country, sparing nothing in its sweep.

While Dreiser may have understood little of what was happening to the petty bourgeoisie, he was fully aware of what was occurring to the individual. He recognized clearly enough that American civilization in the twentieth century had sounded the death-knell of American civilization of the nineteenth century. If he did not realize that the passing of the individualistic American tradition of the nineteenth century meant the defeat of the cause of the petty bourgeoisie, he did appreciate the fact that the cause of the individual had been sacrificed to the success of the machine. And since he saw no escape, there was nothing to do but, like a Nietzchean yea-sayer, to surrender to its tragedy. Only in the last year, or perhaps two years, has he discovered a way out. That way, which he has voiced in his recent book, *Tragic America*, is communism. During all the years that preceded, however, when he wrote his most significant novels and autobiographical narratives, that way was closed to him. Lacking faith in the future only the tragedy of the present could permeate his works. With his new faith in communism, however, it is possible that his future fiction may undergo a change in spirit which hitherto it has never revealed.

But the individualistic conflict did not reflect itself only in the novel. With the rise of the Progressive movement which, as we have noted, reached a peak in the election of 1912, and which marked a culminating point in the expression of the individualistic philosophy of the petty bourgeoisie, all America became stirred by the individualistic issue. Roosevelt's attack upon the trusts, Wilson's defense of the rights of the small capitalist were all aimed against the monster of industrialism, represented in political form by the Republican party, the agent of the upper bourgeoisie. They were all dedicated to a defense of the individual against the crushing power of the corporations and the trusts. This vast insurgence of individualistic impulse, a kind of swan-song, as it were, of the whole individualistic movement, broke loose in the poetry of the period in the form of the free-verse revolt.

It was a matter of more than historical coincidence that Harriet Monroe's magazine, *Poetry*, was founded in 1912, the year when the individualistic movement was making its boldest and last great fight in the political and economic field. The free-verse genre, to be sure, developed in Europe long before it arrived in America, although, as we shall see, it took a different turn here from that which it assumed in Europe. It was in the symbolist movement in France that the first revolt against conventional forms occurred, and in the tangential offshoots of that movement, the cubism of Apollinaire, the "fantasism" of Dèrème, the unamism of Romains, the dadaism of Tzara, and the semi-sur-realism of Breton, it attained its most individualistic extremes. The individualistic conflict in Europe acquired a corner-driven despair long before it did in America, where it was not until the end of the nineteenth century that the individualistic philosophy went down in defeat. From the very beginning Miss Monroe's magazine became a meeting place for the poetic intransigeants of the day. A little later, Margaret Anderson's magazine, *The Little Review*, abetted the same intransigeants in prose as well as in poetry. Early in its career, *Poetry* printed the imagistic verse of H. D., and several defenses of Imagism by Ezra Pound, and shortly thereafter its pages became filled with the free verse of various American poets who agreed with the Imagists in their declaration that "we fight for it (free verse) as for a principle of liberty," although they were not content to accept all of the other five fundamentals in the Imagist credo. Inspired by the individualistic flare-up of the time, these poets discovered in

free verse a medium in which they could express a part of
their individuality that the older, more restricting and conventional forms of verse had thwarted. They believed that
it was necessary to create new rhythms to express the new
moods of the age. They were convinced, to quote the mani-
festo of the Imagists again, that "the individuality of a poet
may often be better expressed in free verse than in conventional forms." In brief, like the petty bourgeois individualists in the economic and political sphere, they were determined that nothing should be permitted to stand in the way
of the expression of individuality in the poetic sphere. In
time, as the movement advanced and civilization became
more crushing, isolating the individual artist further and
further from the group, individuality became everything
and tradition nothing. A decade later, in the Proclamation of
the *transition* group—a group made up largely of American
expatriates who had found Paris a better place to survive in
than New York—the individualistic revolt reached such a
point of extremity that it was definitely stated that "the
writer expresses; he does not communicate."[76]

Although it was largely through the efforts of the Imagist
group, especially those of Amy Lowell, that the new poetry
movement won acceptance in America, it was not the Imagist
poets who advanced that movement in terms of the national
perspective. In fact, none of the Imagists came very close to
America in the content or character of his work. It was such
poets as Robert Frost, Vachel Lindsay, Carl Sandburg, and
Edgar Lee Masters, who responded to that movement in
terms of the rising national consciousness of the time. They
shot forth like corks suddenly spurted out of a current,
carrying the swiftness of that current with them in their
flight. If that flight was short-lived, it was only because the

[76] For those interested in the further discussion of this tendency, the
reader is referred to Vol. V, No. 3, of *The Modern Quarterly* (pp. 273–323),
wherein a whole symposium is devoted to the theme. Max Eastman in
The Literary Mind (New York, 1931) also devoted considerable space to
the topic. His essay on *The Cult of Unintelligibility* deals with the more
absurd aspects of the movement.

individualistic revolt it reflected was making a dying flight instead of a new-born one.

The one poet who was an immediate forerunner of the 1912 revolt was Edwin Arlington Robinson. Prior to Robinson's appearance on the American scene in 1896, with his first volume of poems, *The Torrent and the Night Before,* poetry in this country had lost the place of significance which it had possessed earlier in the century. Minor poets such as Moody, Hovey, and Cawein had sprung up but they had added little of significance to American literature. Three years after the publication of Robinson's first volume, Edwin Markham created a stir with the appearance of his poem *The Man with the Hoe,* but the stir did not last, for Markham's poetic talent was of too thin an order to sustain itself over the years. Even *The Man with the Hoe* was more significant from a social point of view than a literary. It revealed little skill of structure, and its diction lacked that imaginative quality which is the necessary test of poetic art. It was because Robinson possessed that skill and imagination that his work endured. Received in comparative silence at first, Robinson's work did not secure the appreciation it so much deserved until the second decade in the twentieth century when its significance as a native contribution to American literature was recognized at last. Robinson was the first poet after Whitman to capture something of the American rhythm.[77] If in much of his later work he has wandered from the realm of reality, losing himself in the fogs of the supernatural and the mystical, his earlier work clung close to the earth, to the Yankee soil from which it was sprung. *The Children of the Night, Captain Craig,* and *The Man Against*

[77]Constance Rourke's words in this connection are worthy of note: "That haunting sense of English standards which had taken so many obsessive forms in an early day both in and out of the realm of literature had by no means died by the latter end of the century: small groups of minor writers were still appearing who sought to imitate English writers; American literature was still, at the most hopeful, regarded as a province of English literature. . . . His (Robinson's) poetry could never be mistaken for English poetry by any sensitive reader; the tone, the idiom, the latent sound of the voice are American." (Op. cit., p. 273.)

the Sky, were autochthonous creations, reflecting in their subdued and cerebral way the spirit of the New England country in which their author was born. They extend, in a more original and brilliant fashion, those earlier approaches to something resembling Americanness which were suggested in such poems of Whittier as *Skipper Ireson's Ride* and *Snowbound.* Robinson has expressed in his poetry the same mood of disillusion and despair which has predominated in the fiction of Dreiser and that of the whole realistic school. His Tilbury folk are a sad, desolate, barren lot, without the inspiration of hope or dream. Even his version of the Arthurian legends ends upon a note of despair. But Robinson's despair, or pessimism if you prefer, which at times, with a Khayyamesque gesture, bids man to "live and laugh" despite the tragedy which faces him, was a product of New England and not of the West. The West, even democracy, has never troubled Robinson. Only New England has worried him. The passing of the old New England, the New England of his fathers, when life was unscarred by industrialism in its present, most vicious form, and men and women moved with more ease and command upon the earth—it was that passing, the passing again of an individualistic culture, which made him see life in terms of unending gloom.

The poets who came after Robinson, although at the same time his contemporaries, did not attempt to dissipate that gloom. Instead, ranging from Masters to Jeffers, they lent it a thicker and darker hue. In this particular, Robert Frost might be cited as a partial exception, for while he certainly never struck a continued optimistic note, he never permitted his general grimness of outlook or sombreness of spirit to prevent him upon occasion, especially as in his volume, *West-Running Brook,* from venturing into fields of brighter prospect. Edgar Lee Masters and Carl Sandburg, however, let little of the sun into their works. It was the spiritual darkness which had come upon America, crucified by the consequences of industrialism, that haunted them, and that fired them with poetic challenge. *The Spoon River Anthology* retold, in tombstone monologue, what had happened to the frontier which had once inspired Walt Whitman and Mark Twain with hope and vision. *Chicago Poems* and *Smoke and Steel* revealed what industry had done to life—and the individual. Together they related the tragedy of American life in town and city, on the farm and in the factory.

With the appearance of Masters' volume *The Spoon River Anthology* in 1915 and Sandburg's *Chicago Poems,* in 1916, preceded as both volumes were by James Oppenheim's *Songs for the New Age,* Vachel Lindsay's *The Congo and Other Poems,* and Robert Frost's *North of Boston,* American poetry can be said to have definitely severed itself from all trace of the colonial complex. These new poets spoke the language of the people, the language of the American people and not of the English critics; it was a simple language, crude often, bare of artificial ornament, but vigorously natural and native. This new poetry was rooted in the American soil, and cared only for the American soil. If not contemptuous of English influence, it was thoroughly indifferent to it. The free-verse movement released opportunities for the development of new patterns, new cadences, the crashing through of belligerent individuality, which made it all the easier for this new school to break away from the old patterns, the outworn conventions, which had been sanctified by the English tradition. At last an American poet, Walt Whitman, the precursor of the modern free-verse movement, became the source of poetic inspiration. The free-verse movement made it possible for these poets to advance much further than Robinson in their achievement of native independence in literary outlook and expression. By 1917, as Louis Untermeyer declared, this "new poetry was ranked as America's first national art."[78]

If the vitality of that movement died within the next decade it was not because the native elements in it provided insufficient impetus for its inspiration. The native elements

[78] Louis Untermeyer: *Modern American Poetry:* New York, 1930: Fourth Revised Edition. Preface, p. 16.

survived even after its individualistic spirit was abandoned. The return to the English tradition could never recur. The colonial complex, with the sense of inferiority it communicated, had lost its grip upon the nation. It was not the native aspect of the movement that died, then, but the individualistic energy, derivative of the petty bourgeois revolt, which had endowed it with vigor. The twenties saw the end of that last spurt of individualistic energy which inspired the poetic revolt of the teens. The petty bourgeoisie at last was crushed on every front. The face of rugged individualism could hardly conceal any longer the ghostlike visage that trembled behind its verbal masque.

V

Just as the twentieth century witnessed the decay of the petty bourgeois forces in the city, it also saw those same forces undergo an even more swift defeat in the town and country. The fight which the Western farmers and townsmen had put up toward the end of the nineteenth century, as we have shown, disappeared in the twentieth. With the conquest of the West by the industrialists and the financiers of the East, all sign of fighting energy went out of the petty bourgeois elements in the West. Like Hamlin Garland, those who could, and who still had the power, returned East, while the vast majority who stayed saw the land which had once inspired them, and its products which had once given them promise of unceasing wealth, slip away into the hands of those who in many cases never saw that land and never came into contact with its productive forces. As the twentieth century advanced, and conditions grew worse instead of better, the literature of social protest, with its undertone of pessimism, changed into a literature of desolation, with an undertone of despair. Extending from Hamlin Garland and Frank Norris to Willa Cather and Ruth Suckow, that desolation has deepened, turning into stinging satire in the novels of Sinclair Lewis.

The one, and last literary figure who was able to retain something of the energy and vigor of the frontier force, was Jack London. With the passing of London, the frontier force had expended the last trace of its literary energy. Since London's death it has given birth only to satire and despair. Part of London's enormous energy, retentive through the years, even until his death, was undoubtedly due to the fact that, unlike Garland and Norris, he did not stop short with the petty bourgeois ideology of individualism but advanced to the collective philosophy of socialism. Had he stopped where most of his contemporaries did, and taken his stand upon an individualistic base, notwithstanding the personal energy he possessed, in all likelihood he would have been driven into the camp of the pessimists. The conditions of the country would have demanded it. Instead, convinced as he became that socialism and not individualism was the philosophy that America, that the world, should adopt, he was able to escape in part that spiritual *cul de sac* in which most of his contemporaries were caught.

A child of the working class, London did not have to acquaint himself with proletarian life in order to understand its miseries and horrors. He did not have to listen to the polemics of soap-boxers in order to realize that a civilization which reduced men and women to such levels of degradation should not be permitted to survive. As a newspaper boy, a factory worker, a stoker, a jute-mill slave, and an international hobo he saw enough of the world in its manifold ramifications to know how the vast majority of the people lived. His early experience with Coxey's Army taught him the fallacy of petty bourgeois individualism as a philosophy of life. At first like many romantic youths infected with wanderlust, he had envisioned himself as one of Nietzsche's "blond beasts," but after his experiences with workers, and his appreciation of what they suffered, he realized the error in his romantic attitude. "I think it is apparent that my rampant individualism was pretty effectively hammered out of me," he wrote, "and something else as effectively ham-

mered in. But, just as I had been an individualist without
knowing it, I was now a Socialist without knowing it." At
first he had been a believer in war, in Anglo-Saxon superiority, in the biological inferiority of women, and in the power
of might making right; once his ideology changed, however,
those "blond-beast" convictions disappeared, and he became
an anti-militarist, an internationalist, a feminist, and an advocate of a proletarian revolution, in which right instead of
might would triumph. Once he had read into the literature
of Socialism and had become convinced of the correctness of
his new outlook, he took an active part in the Socialist Labor
party, and later joined the Socialist party, of which he remained a member until a few months before his death when
he resigned from it "because of its lack of fire and fight, and
its loss of emphasis on the class struggle."

While London became a socialist early in life, his literary
work proved that he never finally resolved the conflict within
himself between the individualistic and the socialistic impulse. Until late in life he was frequently attacked by the
radical press for the "blond beast" motivation which continued to express itself in almost all his stories of adventure.
In those stories, however, ranging from the Far North to the
South Seas, he made his richest contributions to the literature
of action. In a way, to be sure, it was even a literature of
escape, but it was not the escape of delicate, fuzzy souls to
the imaginary realm of Poictesme but the escape of virile
men who were vital parts of their environment.[79] Later on,
it is true, when he wrote exclusively for money, turning out
four books a year, his fiction became tawdry and shallow. By
that time the man whose first literary efforts were in the

---

[79] It is interesting to note Lenin's reaction to certain of London's fiction. Krupskaya has this revealing note on Lenin's response to two of
London's narratives: "Two days before his (Lenin's) death I read to him
in the evening a tale of Jack London, *Love of Life*—it is still lying on the
table in his room. It was a very fine story. In a wilderness of ice, where
no human being had set foot, a sick man, dying of hunger, is making for
the harbor of a big river. His strength is giving out, he cannot walk but
keeps slipping, and beside him there slides a wolf—also dying of hunger.
There is a fight between them; the man wins. Half dead, half demented,

field of poetry, and who always wished to turn to it again, had been irrevocably buried. Unquestionably there was a primitive restlessness in the man himself which could not be changed by any philosophy, and which manifested itself with almost autobiographic fidelity in much of his fiction, particularly, to be sure, in *Martin Eden*. The struggle in part, as Upton Sinclair has described it, was between "self-discipline versus self-indulgence, asceticism versus self-expression."[80] It should not be forgotten, however, that London himself, while he admitted the contradiction that lived within him, frequently endeavored to defend the nature of his fictions from a socialist point of view. *Martin Eden*, London contended in a letter to Upton Sinclair, "is an attack upon individualism."[81] The suicide of the protagonist was intended to represent the death of the "blond beast." His defense of *The Sea Wolf* was similar. Those novels did not represent the "glorification of the red-blooded superman," Upton Sinclair contended, ". . . . (but) rather a demonstration of the fact that the all-conquering superman . . . dies at the age of forty." Defeat and not victory was meted out to the "blond beasts."

However one may wish to interpret that side of London's character and work, there was another side to him and his writing which was not open to misinterpretation. That side was his definitely social side which was voiced in *The People of the Abyss;* in his essays which appeared in two volumes, the first entitled *The War of the Classes,* published in 1905, and the second called *Revolution and Other Essays,*

he reaches his goal. That tale greatly pleased Ilyich. Next day he asked me to read him more Jack London. But London's strong pieces of work are mixed with extraordinarily weak ones. The next tale happened to be of quite another type—saturated with bourgeois morals. Some captain promises the owner of a ship laden with corn to dispose of it at a good price: he sacrifices his life merely in order to keep his word. Ilyich smiled and dismissed it with a wave of the hand." (Nadezhda K. Krupskaya: *Memories of Lenin:* New York, 1930: p. 209.)

[80] Upton Sinclair: *About Jack London: The Masses,* Vol. X, Nos. 1 and 2, November and December, 1917. Issue Nos. 77 and 78.

[81] Jack London: *Essays of Revolt.* Collected and edited with an Introduction by Leonard D. Abbott: New York, 1926: p. 4.

which appeared in 1910. *The People of the Abyss* related his experiences in the London slums where he buried himself as a worker, living with the downtrodden in the midst of all their misery and starvation. "Saturday night I was out all night with the homeless ones," he wrote to Anna Strunsky Walling,[82] "walking the streets in the bitter rain, and, drenched to the skin, wondering when dawn would come. . . . I returned to my rooms Sunday evening, after thirty-six hours' continuous work and a short one-night's sleep. To-day I have composed, typed and revised 4,000 words (*People of the Abyss*) and over; I have just finished. It is one in the morning. I am worn out and exhausted and my nerves are blunted with what I have seen and the suffering it has cost me." In his novel, *The Iron Heel,* and in his story, *The Dream of Debs,* his radicalism assumed even more challenging form than in *The People of the Abyss.*

In the Preface to *The War of the Classes,* London endeavored to trace something of his own career as a socialist and the career of the *Socialist* party at the time:

When I was a youngster I was looked upon as a weird sort of creature, because, forsooth, I was a socialist. Reporters from local papers interviewed me, and the interviews, when published, were pathological studies of a strange and abnormal specimen of man. At that time because I made a stand in my native town for municipal ownership of public utilities, I was branded a "red-shirt," a "dynamiter," and an "anarchist"; and really decent fellows, who liked me very well, drew the line at my appearing in public with their sisters.

But the times changed. There came a day when I heard, in my native town, a Republican mayor publicly proclaim that "municipal ownership was a fixed American policy." And that day I found myself picking up in the world. No longer did the pathologist study me, while the really decent fellows did not mind in the least the propinquity of myself and their sisters in the public eye.

.   .   .   .

And then came the day when my socialism grew respectable,—

[82]Anna Strunsky Walling: *Memoirs of Jack London: The Masses,* Vol. IX, No. 9, Issue No. 73, July, 1917, p. 16.

still a vagary of youth, it was held, but romantically respectable. . . . It was not I that changed, but the community. In fact, my socialistic views grew solider and more pronounced. I repeat, it was the community that changed, and to my chagrin I discovered that the community changed to such purpose that it was not above stealing my thunder. The community branded me a "red-shirt" because I stood for municipal ownership; a little later it applauded its mayor when he proclaimed municipal ownership to be a fixed American policy. He stole my thunder, and the community applauded the theft. And to-day the community is able to come around and give me points on municipal ownership.

What happened to me has been in no wise different from what has happened to the socialist movement as a whole in the United States. In the bourgeois mind socialism has changed from a terrible disease to a youthful vagary, and later on had its thunder stolen by the two old parties,—socialism, like a meek and thrifty working-man, being exploited became respectable.[83]

Wherever he went London never ceased to pride himself upon being a proletarian. In a speech which he delivered before a socialist meeting in Los Angeles in 1905, he rebuked the chairman for describing him as a scholar and philosopher, and avowed:

Before people had given me any of these titles with which the chairman so lavishly credits me, I was working in a cannery, a pickle factory, was a sailor before the mast, and spent months at a time looking for work in the ranks of the unemployed; and it is the proletarian side of my life that I revere the most, and to which I will cling as long as I live.[84]

After the presidential election of 1904, when the growth of the socialist vote was nothing short of phenomenal, and *The Chicago Chronicle*, *The Brooklyn Daily Eagle*, and *The Chicago New World* declared that socialism was at our very doors, London was convinced that what we had to do was to prepare for the revolution. "The revolution is here now," he told the students whom he addressed in various universi-

[83]Jack London: *The War of the Classes*: New York, 1905: Preface, pp. v-ix.
[84]Jack London: *Essays of Revolt*: p. 5, from Foreword.

ties from coast to coast. "Stop it who can." *The Iron Heel*
was his answer in fiction.

After London no other Western writer carried on his
challenge. Lindsay caught something of his vision, but then
lost it in a mirage of words. His affection for the land blinded him to what was happening elsewhere in the nation, and
prevented him from recognizing what was to be done.[85]
Sandburg adopted London's challenge for a while, but forsook it later when success came his way. He lacked London's
strength of conviction. London deviated too at times, as in
his brief liaison with the oil industry, and in his sentimental
observations about Hawaii, but he always returned to his
radical stand in the end. Alone of all the native Western
writers, and in his fashion, despite his tendencies to romanticism, he was as indigenous as Twain, he saw a way out.
Ruth Suckow did not; Sherwood Anderson did not; Willa
Cather did not; Sinclair Lewis did not. They lacked either
the courage or the vision, or perhaps both, to see what had
to be done. They remained petty bourgeois in their philosophy, while London became socialistic in his approach. That
his socialism was muddled at times, and contradicted often
in the tenor of much of his fiction, is to be regretted, but such
defects are inconsiderable when compared with the significance of his stand as a whole, and the effect of it upon the
country and the world.

In the novels of Willa Cather and Ruth Suckow there is
nothing of London's positive spirit. Challenge has been replaced by lamentation. Antonia, it is true, grows as intimately
out of the soil as a tree or a flower. Alexandria finds her ecstasy in the earth instead of in the artificial and vicarious devices of art. Yet, as Miss Cather reveals in her later novels,

---

[85]Gorham Munson in *Destinations* expressed Lindsay's philosophy very
well when he said that Lindsay aimed to make Beauty and Democracy
synonymous, with the Church standing above sanctifying their union.
"The neighborhood spirit (localism) serving God and Art and Democracy, is the force that shall create a rebirth for which the metropolis is
sterile." It was in such words that Mr. Munson aptly described Lindsay's
philosophy. (*Destinations:* New York, 1928: p. 67.)

A Lost Lady and *The Professor's House,* all this devotion is to a lost cause. The old ideals of the country have been ruined and nothing remains but the desolation that follows defeat. Ruth Suckow's *Country People* is a literary testimony to what has occurred. Her characters are dull, drab people, unimaginative as robots. It is those country people, who are typical of the new generation of "country people," that represent what has happened to our agrarian civilization. It is the more aspiring but not more enticing small-town cousins of those "country people" that Sinclair Lewis in *Main Street* has satirized with such success.

Perhaps the most arresting member of this whole tribe of literary Jeremiahs is Sherwood Anderson. Anderson and Lewis represent, as Van Wyck Brooks would have put it, America's coming of age in fiction. Better even than Dreiser they signify the arrival of a native American tradition. Their work is exclusively American. Their stories and novels are unmistakable products of the American environment; there is nothing of England, nothing of the English tradition, living in them. Anderson spoke the truth when he said: "The dust of my civilization was in my soul."

Deserting his job in a moment of self-discovery, Anderson decided his spiritual survival depended upon his escaping the atmosphere of commerce. Like John Webster in *Many Marriages,* he discovered that life possessed creative possibilities which the petty bourgeoisie denied. Groping about in Chicago, stimulated by his early contacts with Margaret Anderson and her group, and spurred on by the rising literature of the day, he set to work on his fiction with renewed enthusiasm. Beginning with his first novel, *Windy McPherson's Son,* and extending to his recent book *Hello Towns,*[86] Anderson has continued to deal with the same theme which has

[86]His most recent book, *Perhaps Women* (New York, 1931), falls into a different category and need not be discussed here, except to say that it sentimentally bewails once more the effect of machinery upon men, and augurs that modern man is becoming more and more impotent in the face of the machines and that we shall "have to turn the American world over to women" (p. 139), in order to save the race.

occupied the attention of Western writers for the last few generations, namely, the change which has come over the West with the coming of industrialism. In a way, Anderson's reaction to the theme has been unique. As realistic in places as Garland and Norris, although never as objective in his depiction of the passing of the old America, he has dealt with the more wistful side of that tragedy instead of the more gruesome. His treatment of the character of his father, who appears in several of his books, has been most typical of that tendency. In addition, Anderson's characters tend to become more introspective than the characters of other Western writers, they more often turn inward instead of outward in their revolt, and seek escape in revolutions within the individual instead of within the outer world. Psychologically that type of emphasis represented the last attempt of the individual to save his individualism in a world that harassed it in whatever direction he turned. It was a type of emphasis which soon became characteristic of the period.

"For this book of chants," Anderson wrote in the Preface to his volume of poems, *Mid-American Chants*, "I ask that it be allowed to stand stark against the background of my own place and generation. Honest Americans will not demand beauty that is not yet native to our cities and fields." Such also is the plea that can be made for all his fiction. It stands out stark against its background; it is part of that background; its characters are extensions of that background or of himself who in turn is but another extension of it. It has in it the crude poetry and the sprawling chaos of that background. Its rhythm is the rhythm of that America which it interprets. It has all the uncertainty of that rhythm, all the stumbling cadences which constitute its verbal structure— all the futility of spirit which has crept into its tempo with the coming of the new century.

What Anderson has done, in a singular and significant way, has been to describe in his novels and stories and autobiographical works the change which came over the Mid-West towns between the time when "the tired berry pickers walked

home from the fields in the dust of the roads swinging their
dinner pails . . . (and) the old men lit their pipes and sat
gossiping along the curbing at the edge of the sidewalk on
Main Street," when "the people were to each other like
members of a great family," and the time when industry arrived, that "new force that was being born into American
life . . . the new force (that) stirred and aroused the people, (that) was meant to seal men together, to wipe out national lines, to walk under seas and fly through the air, to
change the entire face of the world in which men lived." Anderson, as his words show, realized what few American writers at that time did, that it was industry which was welding
the country into a national unit, and creating a national consciousness. His novel, *Poor White*, traced in moving detail
that vast change which industry created. His autobiographic
narrative *A Storyteller's Story*, which stands next to *Winesburg, Ohio*, as his most significant work, deals with that same
change in more intimate if less intense fashion. All his short
stories reflect it in one way or another, revealing as they do
what has happened to small-town characters and aspirations.

Although Anderson was one of the first American novelists to write with sympathy and understanding of the proletariat—his second novel, *Marching Men*, dedicated to
"American Workingmen," was an attempt to study proletarian life and envision the rise of the workers in their in-
vincible march upon the citadel of capitalism—he never escaped the petty bourgeois ideology of his fathers.[87] He never
reached the point, or at least has not so far, which London
reached when he shed himself of his petty bourgeois heritage, or even the point which Dreiser has advanced to to-day
with his adoption of communism as a social solution. To this
very day he still remains isolated from the proletarian ideology and its revolutionary logic. His isolation, however, is not

[87] In an article entitled, *Sherwood Anderson's Confusion*, Joseph Freeman
has shown with admirable clarity the nature of the petty bourgeois
ideology embodied in Anderson's philosophy. (*New Masses*, Vol. IV, No.
9, February, 1929, p. 6.)

that of unsympathizer. It is not that of a Hergesheimer or a Cabell, for whom the labor movement is something which belongs to another world. Upon more than one occasion he has manifestly declared himself in favor of labor in its struggle against capital. In the recent Danville strike, for example, he delivered an address before the strikers which will not be forgotten.

Notwithstanding his sympathies with labor, Anderson has visualized life all too frequently in terms of a golden age which never existed, an age when the artisan and not the mechanic dominated, and when life flowed with a fulness that our industrial civilization has destroyed. Like the petty bourgeois farmer who loved the crude implements to which he was accustomed and loathed the new implements that machinery had created, Anderson has extolled the old and rejected the new. He has been convinced that with the replacement of hands by machines, a glory went out of the earth. The closeness of hands to materials, the creative feeling inspired by that contact, has haunted him throughout his life and constituted an ever-recurring motif in his fiction. As he has often said, he has believed that culture must grow up "growing as culture must always grow—through the hands of workmen. . . . In their fingers the beginning of that love of surface, of the sensual love of materials, without which no true civilization can ever be born." He has constantly lamented the extinction of that culture, with its manual charm and inspiration. Unlike Masters, Anderson has felt nothing but sympathy for his characters, and the tragic fate which has befallen them. Nothing of bitterness has crept into the pages of *Winesburg, Ohio, The Triumph of The Egg,* or *Horses and Men.* The flare of satire and the whip of irony have been absent from his delineation. Only an aching nostalgia for that dead world when hands and hearts worked as one has pervaded his work and sapped it dry of hope.

Only recently, Anderson has begun to alter his outlook. Under the impact of new developments in the nation in the twenties, he has begun to rid himself of part of his hatred for the machine. In one of his latest poems, *Machine Song: Automobile,* he has written:

> I am sick of my old self that protested against the machine. I am sick of that self in me, that self in me, that self in me, that would not live in my own age.
>
> I myself rejected the machine, I scorned it, I swore at it. It is destroying my life and the lives of all of the men of my time, I said. I was a fool. How did I know it would serve me like this?

There is almost a kind of puerile naïveté about this confession, and yet it is not unlike the naïveté that is characteristic of most of his work. There is a disarming honesty about it that is taking, yet which is combined with a childish confusion which prevents that honesty from getting at grips with deeper significances. But Anderson at least is trying to escape from the morass of his age, even though often when he most earnestly endeavors to find a new orientation, as in his latest book, he becomes more lost in its chaos. In another passage of the same poem, from which we quoted in the foregoing paragraph, he reveals a reaction to the individualistic theme which is interesting as an indication of a new awareness on his part of what is happening to the age and the individualism which he and his forefathers once believed in:

> "In my own age,
> In my own age,
> In my own age,
> Individuality gone,
> Let it go.
>
> Who am I that I should survive?
> Let it go.
> Let it go.
> Steady with the hand. Give thyself, man."

Whatever else one may wish to say about those stanzas, which scarcely constitute very lofty verse, it is obvious that they represent a far cry from the individualistic philosophy of Emerson and Whitman.

When we turn to a writer such as Sinclair Lewis, we are confronted by an individual whose work is just as indigenous as that of Anderson, and yet whose reaction to the Western theme is satiric instead of regretful. While Anderson's fiction is anachronistic in background, Lewis' is overwhelmingly contemporary. *Main Street* and *Babbitt* relate, in satiric style, what has happened to the West, to the former frontier regions once populated by pioneer types fresh with inexhaustible energy and optimism. Better than any other novelist of his time, Lewis has reflected that change in terms of human detail as well as social totality. In *Elmer Gantry* he has traced with slightly less success the evolution of the preacher type which the West brought into being, and who in "revivalist" clothes has continued to exploit the demand for theatricality on the part of the hysterically religious. If in *Elmer Gantry* Lewis deviated a bit from type in order to limn a specific individual, in *Main Street* and *Babbitt* he was as faithful as a photographer to his materials.

The people that Lewis has dealt with have been middle-class people, the lower middle class, or as in *Babbitt*, the middle middle class. The problems that harass them are the same problems which we have discussed in the preceding pages of this chapter. Caught as that class is between the imminent pressures of big business, on the one hand, and its corollary, mass production, on the other, a vice which tightens its grip every day, this class has been forced to wriggle now this way, now that, in order to find some form of personal escape. Chain stores, standardized manufacture, in fact the whole scheme of modern production, as we have shown, have minimized the part that the individual can play in that process. It is that new reality which has destroyed the complacency of the petty bourgeoisie and corrupted its faith. It is this new reality which has made the petty bourgeoisie restless and recalcitrant. And thus, to elude something of this difficulty, the Carol Kennicotts turn for a moment to experimentations, seeking in culture an outlet for what they can no longer find in life, and even testing out sex as a possible solution for their dilemmas. Babbitt ventured into even newer fields and contrives even newer theories, but the Kennicotts as well as the Babbitts return to the fold in the end, and like the children in Maeterlinck's *Blue Bird*, they find the strange more hostile than the familiar, and realize that if happiness is to be had at all it must be at home, amidst the things they have known, rather than elsewhere amidst things which are alien. A complete satire would not have acceded to such a capitulation, but what we must bear in mind is that Lewis' sympathy for these characters is far greater than his detestation of them. Even in *Arrowsmith*, where no such capitulation occurs, we have the hero, like a nineteenth-century prophet, retreating into the wilderness to escape those aspects of civilization which threaten to corrupt his scientific work and vision—a gesture as futile as that of Carol Kennicott or George F. Babbitt. The escape of *Dodsworth* is equally negative. In the main, most of Lewis' characters, even in his earlier novels, face and solve the same problems only with different variations. *Our Mr. Wren*, for example, is a simplified edition of *Main Street*. Istra Nash adumbrates Carol Kennicott in a number of ways, and in her oft-quoted sentence: "When a person is Free, you know, he is never free to be anything but Free," they are identical.

Unfortunately, Lewis' whole approach to the American scene—and as we have stressed throughout this book, it is the nature of the author's approach to society in large part which determines the interpretation and direction of his materials, the elements which he stresses and the factors which he ignores—has been from the petty bourgeois point of view. The most American of American writers, Lewis himself has confessed that he is far more in sympathy with the characters he has ridiculed than his critics have recognized. "Actually, I like the Babbitts, the Doctor Pickerbaughs, the Will Kennicotts, and even the Elmer Gantrys, rather better than any one on earth," he admitted in an article in *The Nation* several years ago.[88] "They are good fellows," he added,

[88]*Mr. Lorimer and Me: The Nation*, July 25, 1928.

"they laugh—really laugh." That is one of the main reasons why Lewis has been so eminently successful in depicting these types. Beneath all the satire, ridicule, and attack, a steady undercurrent of sympathy on the part of the author for the characters thus portrayed is always present, a sympathy more obvious at certain times than at others, but it must be admitted, never obtrusive. His concept of the so-called good life, of Utopia in other words, coincides all too well with the ideals of his characters, their unexciting insipidities of taste, their unadventurous quest for the domain of the delightful and the convenient. Commenting upon Mr. Lorimer's Utopia, Lewis reveals this in a most unpremeditated way:

> Now, Mr. Lorimer's Utopia, I fancy, would consist of a world of delightful and miraculously convenient little homes; of people competent in their jobs; and for vacation, the Canadian wilds, the South Sea Islands with dinner in Paris. *I don't know that I can in any way improve on this Utopian vision.* Matter of fact, I don't believe my Utopia would vastly differ from that of Mr. George Lorimer of *The Saturday Evening Post.* (Italics mine.)

Before the twentieth century, as we have seen, Europe refused to give American literature serious consideration. There were isolated critics who had written approvingly of various American writers, Emerson, Hawthorne, Thoreau, but as a whole American literature was neglected if not scorned. At the end of the World War, however, that attitude consciously began to change. What with half the Western world in debt to America, literary tribute was as much in order as fiscal. America at last had made a dent in European life that deepened with every advancing year. What is more, Europe to-day is in the process of being Americanized. With such developments afoot, it was natural that a tendency to accept American literature along with American capital would arise. In all likelihood, the selection of Sinclair Lewis as the Nobel Prize Winner in Literature was determined in large part by that process—how else, except on the basis of caprice, can we explain the choice of Lewis instead of Gorki, Gide, Galsworthy, Thomas Mann, or Barbusse?

If we turn back to Lewis' work once more, we must admit without hesitation that he has caught something of America in it which no one else has ever done with such astonishing success. His work is American to the core. Its style, its dialogue, its rhythm are native. In a minor sense he has written the saga of the American petty bourgeoisie of the small towns and upstart cities of the West. His character creations live. We can recognize his characters just as we can recognize individuals from their photographs. In a word, they are photographs but not portraits. They live without, but not very deeply within. In the main, with the exception of Arrowsmith, they are shallow, stupid, uninspiring people, lacking in the very creative energy which is necessary to drive an artist on to his best work. They are the expression of a dying class, a class that has lost its firmness of fibre, its strength of morale. Once a source of great energy, this class to-day has withered at the root, like a desiccated plant, and expended the energy it once nourished. It seeks now for the cultures of other groups and classes because it no longer has a culture of its own.

VI

Side by side with this development of a native literature, expressed in poetry by Robinson, Frost, Sandburg, Lindsay, and Masters, in fiction by Dreiser, Anderson, Lewis, and Hemingway, and in the drama by Eugene O'Neill, Paul Green, and Lynn Riggs, there grew up a dynamic interest in the literary possibilities of the indigenous materials provided by the Indian, the cowboy, and the Negro.

The concern for the Indian which Cooper and Longfellow had shown had been of a romantic order; when they wrote about him they limned him in their image instead of his own. Longfellow's approach, for instance, was so unindigenous that he turned to Finland for the poetic measure in which *Hiawatha* was composed. With the coming of the twentieth century, however, and the interest in American things which sprang up with the rising national consciousness, the Indian became exalted as an important factor in the native equation. Indian poetry, Indian mythology, and Indian folklore were studied for their native significance. While in the nineteenth century anthropologists like Morgan, Cushing, and Schoolcraft, from whom Longfellow drew his factual materials, had studied the cultural life of the Indian, it was only in the twentieth century that his artistic contributions to culture became a matter of interest and challenge. While John G. Neihardt's *The Song of the Indian Wars* signified an important advance over the Longfellow approach, it still did not make a very serious attempt to catch the Indian rhythm. Early in the century, however, Mary Austin had begun her studies of Indian rhythm, and before many years had passed she had made marked progress with her "Amerindian airs." Cronyn's anthology of American Indian verse had helped make the public more aware of the importance of the aboriginal contributions of the Red-man, but it was Mary Austin more than any other who continued to foster the interest in Indian materials and to show that they constituted the basis of what she has called the "American rhythm." In her book, *The American Rhythm,* she brought together a significant collection of Amerindian Songs, "re-expressed from the originals," prefaced by a lengthy discussion of the origin and meaning of Indian poetry in terms of American life. While her theory is open to many criticisms and emendations, there is about it a freshness and originality which has not been adequately appreciated. Her attempt to show that American free verse, in precisely the sense that it is different from European free verse, as exemplified in the poetry of Whitman, Sandburg, Lindsay, and Masters, is derivative of the aboriginal rhythm, has an element of truth about it although it is far from the whole truth. The Indians sang, in their own poetic way, she declared, "in precisely the forms that were later to become native to the region of Spoon River, the Land of Little Rain, and the country of the Cornhuskers." While we may doubt the causal connection which she has suggested, since the geographic fact is much less of a determinant than the cultural, there can be no question about the fact that the Amerind form is much closer to the *vers-libre* mold than to the classical. In that respect Indian poetry is genuinely unique. Its rhythms are different from those of other primitive peoples —and by virtue of disparities in cultural level, very different from those of the ancient Jews and Greeks upon whose rhythmic models most European verse has been based. But the contention that American poetry in the future, as it becomes more native, will be built upon those Amerind rhythms is scarcely less than fantastic.

In this pursuit of nativeness, the cowboy has fared even better than the Indian. Long before scholars and artists became interested in the cowboy, the American cinema had exalted him as a romantic figure and made him attractive to audiences in almost every part of the world. So successful was the cinema in this propaganda that many Europeans came to think of America as an extended wild-west show, with the cowboy as the inevitable hero and the Indian as the equally inescapable villain. In 1908, however, the serious study of the cowboy commenced, and cowboy lore began to take on literary dimensions. John Avery Lomax, with a zeal scarcely less persevering than that of the ballad-hunting Percy, set forth upon the task of scouring the country in search of cowboy songs and ballads. Few clues, however obscure, escaped his notice. At length in 1911, after practically a three years' quest for material, he published his volume: *Cowboy Songs and Other Frontier Ballads.* Eight years later he brought out a collection of cowboy poetry: *Songs of the Cattle Trail and Cow Camp.* Since Lomax began his work other enthusiasts have entered the field, until to-day with N. Howard Thorp's *Songs of the Cowboys,* Margaret Larkin's *Singing Cowboy,* Charles J. Finger's *Frontier Ballads,* and Carl Sandburg's *The American Songbag,* few of the old cowboy songs remain uncollected.[89] The Texas Folk-Lore Society too has been exceptionally diligent in forwarding this work, and has rescued more than one native song from oblivion. The most famous of the cowboy songs is the one entitled *The Dying Cowboy*, sometimes called, *O Bury Me Not on the Lone Prairie*.

" 'O, Bury me not on the lone prairie,'
These words came low and mournfully
From the pallid lips of a youth who lay
On his dying bed at the close of day.

He had wailed in pain till o'er his brow
Death's shadows fast were gathering now;
He thought of his home and his loved one nigh
As the cowboys gathered to see him die.

'O bury me not on the lone prairie
Where the wild cayotes will howl o'er me,
In a narrow grave just six by three,
O bury me not on the lone prairie.

'In fancy I listen to the well-known words
Of the free, wild winds and the song of the birds;
I think of home and the cottage in the bower
And the scenes I loved in my childhood's hour.

'It matters not, I've oft been told,
Where the body lies when the heart grows cold;
Yet grant, O grant this wish to me,
O bury me not on the lone prairie.

.   .   .   .

'O bury me not on the lone prairie
Where the wild cayotes will howl o'er me,
Where the buzzard beats and the wind goes free,
O bury me not on the lone prairie.

[89] The Finger and Sandburg volumes, of course, are not specifically cowboy collections as are the others, but they contain enough cowboy songs in them to make them a relevant reference.

'O bury me not,' and his voice failed there,
But we took no heed of his dying prayer;
In a narrow grave just six by three
We buried him there on the lone prairie.

Where the dew-drops glow and the butterflies rest,
And the flowers bloom o'er the prairie's crest;
Where the wild cayote and the winds sport free
On a wet saddle blanket lay a cowboy-ee.

.   .   .   .

O we buried him there on the lone prairie
Where the wild rose blooms and the wind blows free,
O his pale young face nevermore to see,—
For we buried him there on the lone prairie.

Yes, we buried him there on the lone prairie
Where the owl all night hoots mournfully,
And the blizzard beats and the winds blow free
O'er his lowly grave on the lone prairie.

And the cowboys now as they roam the plain,—
For they marked the spot where his bones were lain,—
Fling a handful of roses o'er his grave,
With a prayer to Him who his soul will save.

'O bury me not on the lone prairie
Where the wolves can howl and growl o'er me;
Fling a handful of roses o'er my grave
With a prayer to Him who my soul will save.' "[90]

This song, as J. Frank Dobie has shown, was derived from a popular song, entitled, *The Ocean Burial*, written by W. H. Saunders about 1850.[91] What the cowboys did was to translate the old song into their own familiar idiom, add a chorus to it and provide it with a new setting. Other cowboy songs

[90]*The Southwest in Literature:* edited by Mabel Major and Rebecca Smith: New York, 1929: p. 61.
[91]Leonidas Warren Payne, Jr.: *A Survey of Texas Literature:* Chicago, 1928: p. 40.

which best succeed in preserving something of the spirit of cowboy life are *The Cowboy's Dream, Whoopee Ti Yi Yo, Git Along Little Dogies, Old Paint,* and *The Texas Cowboy.* These cowboy songs and ballads belong as definitely and natively to American literature as the old English ballads belong to English literature, and as Lynn Riggs has shown in his play *Green Grow the Lilacs* they can be used to excellent effect in the theatre.[92]

But more important than either the Indian or the cowboy literature which has been recovered, and added to the native stock of our tradition, is the growth of Negro literature which has made a far greater contribution to American culture. The contributions of the Negro to American culture are as indigenous to our soil as the legendary cowboy or gold-seeking frontiersman. In fact, I think it can be said without exaggeration, that they constitute a large part of whatever claim America can make to originality in its cultural history. In song, the Negro spirituals and the Negro blues; in tradition, Negro folk-lore; and in music, Negro jazz—these three represent the Negro contribution to American culture. Unfortunately, despite the excellent work of Miss Austin, Indian culture has been so largely exterminated, that it is hardly able to challenge that of the Negro. When Dvořák sought to find an inspiration in the American environment for his New World Symphony, he inevitably turned to the Negro. The Negro in his simple, unsophisticated way has developed out of the American milieu a form of expression, a mood, a literary genre, a folk tradition, that are distinctly and undeniably American. At a time when most of America, at least in its literary forms and tendencies, was victimized by the colonial complex, and imitated foreign models, the

---

[92]Those who have written about the cowboy, in certain cases cowboys themselves, including such diverse writers as Charlie Siringo, Andy Adams, Emerson Hough, and Will James, have helped dispel the myth about the cowboy which has been created by the cheap wild-west magazines and the cinema. Perhaps the best book on this whole field, as J. Frank Dobie suggests, is Andy Adams' *The Log of a Cowboy,* a narrative of the old trail days, which was published in 1903.

Negro was developing a native and original culture of his own creation. The social background of Negro life in itself was sufficient to inspire an art of no ordinary character. Indeed, the very fact that the Negro, by the nature of his environment, was deprived of education, prevented his art from ever becoming purely imitative. Even where he adopted the white man's substance, as in the case of religion, he never adopted his forms. He gave to whatever he took a new style and a new interpretation. In truth, he made it practically into a new thing. There were no ancient conventions, no bourgeois codes, that he, in his untutored zeal, felt duty-bound to respect, and no age-old traditions that instructed him, perforce, as to what was art and what was not. He could express his soul, as it were, without concern for grammar or the eye of the carping critic. As a result, his art is, as is all art that springs from the people, an artless art, and in that sense is the most genuine art of the world. While the white man has gone to Europe for his models, and is seeking still European approval of his artistic endeavors, the Negro in his art forms has never gone beyond America for his background and has never sought the acclaim of any culture other than his own. This is particularly true of those forms of Negro art that come directly from the people. It is, of course, not so true of a poet such as Phyllis Wheatley or of the numerous Negro poets and artists of to-day, who in more ways than one have followed the traditions of their white contemporaries rather than extended and perfected the original art forms of their race. Of course, in the eighteenth century when Phyllis Wheatley wrote, those Negro art forms were scarcely more than embryonic. To-day, on the other hand, their existence has become a commonplace to the white writer as well as to the black.

In a subtle way, Negro art and literature in America have had an economic origin. All that is original in Negro folklore, or singular in the Negro spirituals and blues, can be traced to the economic institution of slavery and its influence upon the Negro soul. The Negro lived in America as a slave for over 240 years. He was forced by the system of slavery into habits of life and forms of behavior that inevitably drove him in the direction of emotional escape and religious delirium. Existence offered him nothing to hope for but endless labor and pain. Life was a continuous crucifixion. The earth became a place of evil. As a downtrodden and suppressed race he had nothing to discover within himself that insured emancipation or escape. His revolts had all proved ineffectual. Inevitably he turned toward the white man for the materials of his "underdog" logic. He accepted and absorbed the ideas of the ruling class, as do most subordinate groups and classes, until they became a part of his reaction. The white man's paradise suddenly became a consuming aspiration. He became enamored of it as of a holy vision. His belief in it became a ferocious faith. Its other-worldly aspect only lent it a richer enchantment. There were no realistic categories to thwart or limit its undimensioned beauty and magnificence. The scarcities of this world had no meaning in the infinite plenitude of the next. Gold could be had for the asking, and everything was as dream would have it in a land beyond the sun.

It was as an expression of this consecrated other-worldly ardor that the Negro spirituals came into being and grew into form. There is more, far more, than the ordinary Christian zeal embodied in them. These spirituals are not mere religious hymns written or recited to sweeten the service or improve the ritual. They are the aching, poignant cry of an entire people. Jesus to the Negro is no simple religious saviour, worshiped on Sundays and forgotten during the week. He is the incarnation of the suffering soul of a race. In such a spiritual as *Crucifixion*, one finds this spirit manifest:

> "They crucified my Lord,
>   an' He never said a mumbalin' word;
>   They crucified my Lord,
>   an' He never said a mumbalin' word;
>   Not a word, not a word, not a word.

> They nailed Him to the tree,
> an' He never said a mumbalin' word;
> They nailed Him to the tree,
> an' He never said a mumbalin' word;
> Not a word, not a word, not a word.
>
> They pierced Him in the side,
> an' He never said a mumbalin' word;
> They pierced Him in the side,
> an' He never said a mumbalin' word;
> Not a word, not a word, not a word.
>
> The blood came twinklin' down,
> an' He never said a mumbalin' word;
> The blood came twinklin' down,
> an' He never said a mumbalin' word;
> Not a word, not a word, not a word.
>
> He bowed His head an' died,
> an' He never said a mumbalin' word;
> He bowed His head an' died,
> an' He never said a mumbalin' word;
> Not a word, not a word, not a word."

Or in such a spiritual as *Swing Low Sweet Chariot,* we discover the other-worldly motif in fine, moving form:

> "Swing low sweet chariot,
> Comin' for to carry me home,
> Swing low sweet chariot,
> Comin' for to carry me home,
> O swing low sweet chariot,
> Comin' for to carry me home.
>
> I looked over Jordan, and what did I see,
> Comin' for to carry me home,
> A band of angels comin' after me,
> Comin' for to carry me home;
> If you get a dere befo' I do,
> Comin' for to carry me home,
> Tell all my friends I'm comin' too
> Comin' for to carry me home.

> O swing low sweet chariot,
> Comin' for to carry me home,
> Swing low sweet chariot,
> Comin' for to carry me home,
> Comin' for to carry me home."

When we turn to the blues and the labor songs, the economic connection is more obvious. Here we have folklore in poetic form, springing spontaneously from the simple everyday life of an oppressed people. The blues have a primitive kinship with the old ballads that is strikingly curious upon close comparison. While the rhyme scheme employed in the blues is often less clever and arresting than that found in the ballads, the incremental repetitions are not less effective, and the simple, quick descriptions are often as fine in this form as the other. The labor songs, growing up as part of the workaday rhythms of daily toil, have a swing about them that is irresistibly infectious. The musical swing of the hammer, its sweeping rise and fall, is communicated, for instance, with rhythmic power in the song entitled *John Henry:*

> "Dis is de hammer
> Killed John Henry,
> Killed him dead, killed him dead,
> Busted de brains all outer my pardner
> In his head, yes, in his head."

And in the familiar levee song, we meet with another not less enticing rhythm:

> "Where wuz your sweet mamma
> When de boat went down?
> On de deck, Babe,
> Hollerin' Alabama Bound."

The Negro has retained unquestionably in his art a certain primitivism that is remarkably refreshing in contrast to the stilted affectations of the more cultured styles and conceptions. We come closer to life with these primitivisms, feel beauty in its more genuine and intimate and less artificial and cerebral forms.

These primitivisms of the Negro are a singular evolution of our American environment. In describing them as primitive, we do not mean that they are savage in origin, or that the instincts of savagery linger in them, but that they are untutored in form and unsophisticated in content, and in these aspects are more primitive than civilized in character. The art of primitive peoples is often the very opposite in spirit to that of the American Negro. The art, for instance, of the African Negro is entirely without that exuberance which is so emphatically dominant in the art-expression of the American Negro. African art is rigid, economical of energy, and almost classic in its discipline. The exuberance of sentiment, the spirited denial of discipline, and the contempt for the conventional, that are so conspicuous in the art of the American Negro, are direct outgrowths of the nature of his life in this country.

In jazz this vital and overwhelming exuberance of the American Negro reaches its apex in physical dynamics. If the origin of jazz is not entirely Negroid—that its fundamental form is derivative of Negro rhythms no longer can be disputed—its development of attitude and expression in America has certainly been chiefly advanced by the Negro. While the spirituals represent the religious escape of the Negro, the jazz rhythms vivify his mundane abandon. To-day this mundane abandon has become a universal craving on the part of youth in Europe as well as in America. Since the war, the dance has become a mania. It is the mad, delirious dance of men and women who have had to seize upon something as a vicarious outlet for their crazed emotions. They have not wanted old opiates that induced sleep and the delusion of a sweet stillness of things and silence. They have not sought the escape which an artificial lassitude brings to minds tormented with worry and pain. They have demanded an escape that is active, dynamic, electrical, an escape that exhilarates, and brings restfulness only from exhaustion. Jazz has provided that escape in increasing measure as its jubilant antics and rhythms have become madder and madder in their tu-

mult of release. To the Negro the riotous rhythms that constitute jazz are but an active translation of the impulsive
extravagance of his life. Whether a difference in the calcium
factor in bone structure or conjunction, accounting for an ex-
ceptional muscular resiliency, or a difference in terms of an
entirely environmental disparity, be used to explain the
Negro's superior response to jazz, his supremacy in this new
departure in music remains uncontested. Jazz, Stokowski
contends, "has effected a profound change in musical outlook." In this change, Stokowski adds:

> The Negro musicians of America are playing a great part. . . .
> They have an open mind, and unbiased outlook. They are causing
> new blood to flow in the veins of music. The jazz players make
> their instruments do entirely new things, things finished musicians
> are taught to avoid. They are path-finders into new realms.

Jazz reflects something of the essential irresponsibility, or
rather the irresponsible enthusiasms and ecstasies, that under-
lie Negro life here in America, and which give to Negro art
such singular distinction in verve and spontaneity. While
jazz in its inferior forms is a vulgar removal from the idea
of the exquisite which prevailed in music before our day, it
nevertheless has the virtue of great originality and the vigor
of deep challenge. In a very significant sense, indeed, it remains as the only original contribution to music that has
been made by America.

If the spirit of jazz is captured almost to a point of precision in these lines from *Runnin' Wild:*

> "Runnin' wild; lost control,
> Runnin' wild, mighty bold,
> Feelin' gay and reckless too,
> Carefree all the time; never blue
> Always goin' I don't know where,
> Always showin' that I don't care,
> Don't love nobody, it ain't worth while
> All alone; runnin' wild,"

it would be a serious and most reprehensible exaggeration to
maintain that it is this mood which permeates all Negro art

in America. In fact, much of contemporary Negro poetry is as far removed in spirit from the jazz motif as the poetry of John Milton is from that of T. S. Eliot. There is, indeed, an over-seriousness, even an affected dignity in the work of many Negro poets. This tendency to an artificial loftiness of utterance, verging often upon the pompous, is more marked in the work of the Negro writers of the nineteenth century than of the twentieth. In many cases education removed the Negro writer further from his people, and inclined his work in the direction of imitating the artificial standards of other groups rather than of advancing and perfecting those of his own. As a result a certain naturalness and fine vigor of style were lost. While the tendency has not disappeared, a reaction has already set in against it, and to-day Negro writers have begun to develop a more candid approach.

It is important to note that it was not until the twentieth century that the significance of the Negro contributions to art were recognized by the white public. Although the spirituals belong far back into the nineteenth century, white America did not become conscious of their importance until the twentieth century. In fact, it was only after the World War that they began to win the wide popularity in America which they now command. In England, for example, where the prejudice against the Negro was absent, the Negro spirituals were sung with fervor and enthusiasm in the nineteenth century by the people of various classes. In America, however, it was not until the development of a national consciousness, and the consequent interest in things native, that the Negro's contributions to art were taken with any seriousness. It was only then that his spirituals and blues were rewarded with the appreciation and esteem that they deserved.

About the same time that the spirituals and blues came into vogue, a new school of Negro writers arose. Unfortunately, this new school, despite its innovations in technique and its challenge of spirit, remained racial in its emphasis. In one sense, however, it made a significant advance. In the poetry of Langston Hughes, for instance, there is a freshness

even in artifice which was absent in the poetry of individual
Negro poets in the nineteenth century. Even Paul Dunbar,
who was the leading Negro poet prior to our own day,
avoided the affectations and conceits of his contemporaries
only in his poems of dialect. In the verse of such writers as
Albert A. Whitman, Mrs. Harper, George Moses Horton,
James Madison Bell, Joseph Seaman Cotter and James
David Corrothers this literary fallacy is unpleasantly conspicuous. They aspired to the stately, when they should have
aimed at the simple. Their poetry, as a consequence, was
hopelessly inept and sentimental. It is only with the present
day, and the emergence of the contemporary school of Negro poets, led by such figures as Langston Hughes, Countee
Cullen, Jean Toomer, and Claude McKay, that this type of
verse has been condemned with scorn.

If the recent developments in Negro literature cannot be
characterized as a renaissance, they certainly must be noted
as marking off a new stage in the literary history of a people. Without question the work of Jean Toomer, Rudolph
Fisher, Burghardt Du Bois, and Walter White in fiction;
Langston Hughes, Countee Cullen and Claude McKay in
verse; and Abram L. Harris, Alain Locke, Franklin Frazier,
James Weldon Johnson, Charles S. Johnson, and George
Schuyler in the essay, has been distinguished by fine in-
telligence and advancing artistic vision. Surely at no other
period, and certainly never in so short a time, have so many
Negro writers of genuine talent appeared. If among these
writers, no great artist or great thinker has so far evolved,
there is no reason for despair. The great achievement of
Roland Hayes on the concert stage, and of Paul Robeson in
the theatre, gives promise at least of similar success in the
literary art in the future. The appearance of these numerous
artists and the growth of this newer spirit on the part of the
Negro, is really not so much a rebirth in the sense of a renaissance, as it is the hastening of an old birth which had formerly been retarded in its growth and evolution.

Steadily the trend in this new Negro literature has developed in favor of the vigorous instead of the exquisite. Challenge has become more significant than charm. The submissive acquiescences of the Booker T. Washington attitude and era have now become contemptuously anachronistic. The sentimental cry of a nineteenth-century poet such as Corrothers:

> "To be a Negro in a day like this—
> Alas, Lord God, what evil have we done"

has been superseded by the charging defiance of a twentieth-century poet such as McKay:

> "If we must die—let it not be like hogs
> Hunted and penned in an inglorious spot,
> While round us bark the mad and hungry dogs,
> Making their mock at our accursed lot.
>
> If we must die—oh, let us nobly die,
> So that our precious blood may not be shed
> In vain; then even the monsters we defy
> Shall be constrained to honor as though dead!
>
> Oh, Kinsmen! We must meet the common foe;
> Though far outnumbered, let us still be brave,
> And for their thousand blows deal one death-blow!
> What though before us lies the open grave?
> Like men we'll face the murderous, cowardly pack,
> Pressed to the wall, dying, but—fighting back!"

The admission of inferiority which was implicit in so much of the earlier verse, the supplicatory note which ran like a lugubrious echo through so many of its stanzas, has been supplanted by an attitude of superiority and independence on the part of such poets as Countee Cullen, Langston Hughes, and Gwendolyn Bennett.

In Cullen's lines:

> "My love is dark as yours is fair,
> Yet lovelier I hold her
> Than listless maids with pallid hair,
> And blood that's thin and colder . . ."

one discovers this attitude expressed with exquisite conviction. In Gwendolyn Bennett's stanza:

> "I love you for your brownness
> And the rounded darkness of your breast;
> I love you for the breaking sadness in your voice,
> And shadows where your wayward eye-lids rest . . ."

we are confronted with it again in definite form. Hughes gives to this same attitude a touch of African aspiration:

> "We should have a land of trees,
>   Bowed down with chattering parrots
>   Brilliant as the day,
>   And not this land where birds are gray. . . ."

George Schuyler in prose has given this same attitude a sharp, ironic turn. His clean-cut, biting style, inevitably in keeping with his theme and purpose, is at times superb. He meets his materials with a directness that compels by its vigor. His writing is never sentimental; rather it has a hard, metallic brilliance that convinces without endeavoring to caress. In *Our Greatest Gift to America,* which deals in satiric form with the Negro's position in this country, Schuyler's criticism is acute and devastating.

As the radicalism of the Negro has become more assertive and aggressive, a new attitude has begun to reveal itself in his fiction. There has been a marked tendency in the past, except in stories of dialect, for Negro writers, following the middle-class pattern, to centre their attention upon the more enlightened and prosperous members of the race. In *Fire in the Flint,* for instance, Walter White has chosen a doctor for his protagonist; in *There Is Confusion,* Jessie Fauset has featured a dancer as her star; in *Quicksand,* Nella Larsen has selected a school teacher for her main character; and in *The Dark Princess,* Du Bois has made an aristocratic woman into his heroine. To-day in the novels of Rudolph Fisher and Claude McKay the class of characters has shifted. In

The Walls of Jericho and *Home to Harlem* the main characters are proletarian types, piano-movers and stevedores, who are endowed with little education and less culture. The lives of these lower types are seen to be as fascinating and dramatic as those of the upper. In fact, a certain native drama is revealed in the lives of these colored folk that is absent in the lives of most white people in the same class of society. This added drama flows from the freer and more irresponsibly spontaneous way in which these black men live. In time no doubt these proletarian types will occupy an increasingly larger part in the Negro literary scene.

Vigorous as this literary revolt of the contemporary Negro writer has been, it is only to-day with the changing philosophy of Langston Hughes and the advancing challenge of Eugene Gordon that a proletarian element has begun to pervade it. A number of years ago Claude McKay had advocated the proletarian approach, but after he left America his interest in that approach waned. Hitherto, with the single exception of McKay, its protest had been exclusively racial, and in an ideological sense it had taken over in considerable part the petty bourgeois philosophy of the white man. This absorption of the white man's ideology was due to the rise of the so-called new Negro, the emergence of a clearly defined Negro bourgeoisie, and the development of the belief that the Negro could find himself as an individual in American civilization. Among what E. Franklin Frazer has called La Bourgeoisie Noire[93] that belief still remains, although in recent years with the defeat of individualism as a philosophy, it has lost its former challenge, and Negro writers are tending to divorce themselves from it more and more. Langston Hughes' play *Scottsboro Limited,* which appeared in the November, 1931, issue of *The New Masses,* has indicated something of that advance, and several of the stirring articles of Eugene Gordon published in recent months, especially one entitled *Black Capitalists in America,* have

[93]*The Modern Quarterly,* November–February, 1928–1929, Vol. V, No. 1, pp. 78–84.

furthered the revolutionary outlook on the part of the contemporary Negro.

VII

Arresting and spectacular as these advances have been in the development of a native literature, their significance has been overshadowed by the growth of another movement, the proletarian movement, which has sprung up in the last two decades of this century. As the struggle between the upper bourgeoisie and the petty bourgeoisie intensified, expelling more and more of the latter into the proletariat, and robbing the proletariat of more and more of its petty bourgeois psychology, the proletarian ideology, which had begun to express itself on the economic and political field in the last quarter of the nineteenth century, finally achieved literary consciousness. It was in the pages of the magazine, *The Masses,* that that consciousness first attained literary focus. While Howells had descanted often upon the evils of competition and had argued for a social system based upon co-operation, and had even declared himself a socialist, he had never attained anything resembling a proletarian consciousness, nor ever understood anything concerning the meaning of a proletarian ideology. In fact, Bellamy had been less removed than Howells from the proletarian point of view, even though he had never conceived of its full dimensions, as we have seen, nor realized the direction of the class struggle in a Marxian sense of the word. Not until the appearance of *The Masses* did the proletarian ideology, in its embryonic literary form, begin to assume any semblance of order or direction.

It was through the editorial guidance of Max Eastman, ably assisted by Floyd Dell and John Reed, that *The Masses* came to exercise a dynamic influence upon the younger generation of its day. It is difficult for us at the present time to appreciate the important rôle that *The Masses* played during its career, especially in the teens, for the issues it once faced have so altered since the war, and most of its former editors and associates have drifted away from the movement they once afforded such momentum, and left the banner of revolt which they raised to be carried on by others. "A revolutionary and not a reform magazine," as it declared, it took up its defense of a radical position at a time when *Soil* was still enamored of single-taxism, and *Seven Arts* was still trying to find itself in terms of the American scene. While a radical magazine such as *The International Socialist Review* had approached the cultural problem from a Marxian point of view, it had not included the field of creative literature within its domain. Moreover, *The Masses* did not set out to be original or erudite in a scholarly way, as did *The Socialist Review*, but to be original in a journalistic way, boldly declaring that in addition to being a revolutionary magazine it was also "a Magazine with a sense of Humor and no Respect for the Respectable; Frank; Arrogant, Impertinent; Searching for the True Causes; a Magazine Directed against Rigidity and Dogma wherever it is found; Printing what is too Naked or True for a Money-Making Press; a Magazine whose final Policy is to do as it Pleases and Conciliate Nobody, not even its Readers—A Free Magazine."

It must be admitted, however, that while *The Masses* advocated a proletarian viewpoint, and in the main consistently defended a revolutionary position in its editorials, its literary output on the whole fell far short of its aim. Its editors, particularly Max Eastman, were too much infatuated with the art-forms of the period to encourage with sufficient zeal the composition of poetry and fiction of a revolutionary cast. In large part it was this artificial dichotomy between the real world and the art-world which kept the creative side of *The Masses* from becoming as revolutionary as was its critical. In issue after issue, when even the crisis of war was at stake, revolutionary editorials and stinging articles quick with dynamite would be followed by poetry or sketches of the most sentimental and syrupy strain. In the June, 1917, issue, for example, when the country had already been plunged into the maelstrom of war, and John Reed in an article on *The Great Illusion* declared that what we must fight was Capitalism and not the Central Powers, there also appeared poems, three of them on the same page as Reed's article, entitled: *Gypsy Song, I Know, Transition, April Night,* and *The Happy Rain,* each one vying with the other in sentimentality. If the fiction was not as lackadaiscal as the poetry, it certainly cannot be said to have been very revolutionary. In one field, however, its creative contents matched its critical, namely, in that of the cartoon. Boardman Robinson, Bob Minor, Art Young, George Bellows, and a dozen others lent a vigor to the magazine with their drawings that even its best editorials and articles could not surpass. To this day no other American magazine has ever succeeded in assembling within its pages the work of such an array of artists who had something to say and who knew how to say it.

Part of the failure of *The Masses* to realize a revolutionary aim in its poetry and fiction was due to the nature of the time and to the character of its audience as well as to the attitude of its editor. After all, it must be remembered that *The Masses* was not read by the proletariat. However revolutionary its purpose, it was the non-revolutionary petty bourgeois elements in the population which constituted its chief reading public. Even its contributors, aside from its editors, were not revolutionary in the main, but iconoclastic intellectuals who were in revolt against specific aspects of society rather than against its structure as a whole. As a result the magazine was never able to acquire that revolutionary unity in outlook which *The New Masses,* by way of contrast, has managed to achieve.

But *The Masses* which was founded originally in 1911, with Thomas Seltzer as editor,—in 1912 Piet Vleg succeeded Seltzer—and was taken over by the Eastman group in 1913, belonged to a different period in American history from *The New Masses.* The Bolshevik Revolution had intervened. In the teens revolutionary interest on the part of the intellectuals of the time was due more to the struggle between the petty bourgeoisie and the upper bourgeoisie than to the struggle between the bourgeoisie and the proletariat, however acute the latter struggle had become. The protest of most of the writers for *The Masses* was a back-wash of the muck-rakers' movement of the first decade of the century. Like Upton Sinclair they had seen the muck of America, had witnessed, with horror and disgust, the tactics and technique of the new imperialism, but instead of remaining iconoclasts, as did the muckrakers of the time, they pursued the line of Upton Sinclair and became revolutionists. Nevertheless, their revolutionary propaganda was addressed far more directly to the petty bourgeois liberals than to the masses. Even *The Masses* boast that it was a "free" magazine smacked much more of the petty bourgeois clamor for freedom at the time, freedom in art, in literature, in sex, in politics, than it did of the proletarian needs of the period.

But such was the spirit of the time, such was the best that could be done at that period. And notwithstanding its failures from a revolutionary point of view, *The Masses* performed an indispensable function in stirring up ferment among the American intellectuals and literati of its day, and in breaking the ground for a more critical formulation of the proletarian position. While Eastman, for instance, did not realize the direction which radical literature was going to take—nothing proved that better than his *Enjoyment of Poetry,* which was more reactionary than revolutionary in its argument—he did supply the intellectual backbone that was needed for those young writers who were just beginning to seek a new orientation for their hitherto incoherent protests. Eastman made *The Masses* a meeting-place for the discontented intellectuals of the decade, and from the point of view of recent American literature there was no more productive meeting-place that could have been provided, for in the pages of *The Masses,* and later on in *The Liberator,* appeared the early work of Eugene O'Neill, Witter Bynner, Louis Untermeyer, Arturo Giovannitti, Carl Sandburg, Edgar Lee Masters, Ernest Hemingway, Edmund Wilson, Sherwood Anderson, John Dos Passos, John Howard Lawson, and a host of other writers who have been conspicuous in the American literary scene ever since. If *The Masses* did not succeed in making many of these men revolutionists, it did manage to give their protest something of social direction at the time, and in other cases it did manage to revolutionize their minds. "I suppose that the most unique and important feature of the old *Masses*," Max Eastman has asserted, "was that while maintaining an editorial policy essentially Marxian it drew into its pages the work of wide circles of the intelligentzia who had revolutionary feeling, but no understanding of such a policy and very little conception what it was all about. In this way, for instance, John Reed, who graduated from Harvard as an anarchist, the spiritual child of Lincoln Steffens, was drawn into the scientific proletarian movement."[94] Such was the function of the magazine, and insofar as it fulfilled that function it played a more important part in shaping the character of American literature of that day, and of much of American literature which was to follow, than did any other periodical of that time, or than did most of the vast bulk of books which were published during the same decade.

The most important work in *The Masses*, as we previously stated, appeared in the form of editorials and articles, especially those by Max Eastman and John Reed, editorials and articles which at the time of the war in particular stood bravely by their radical convictions when the rest of America was surrendering to the tide of war-impulse which had swept over the country.[95] Despite the significance of that

---

[94]From a letter of Max Eastman to Ely Estorick, May 13, 1931. Mr. Estorick is now working on a book, *The Birth of Proletarian Literature.*

[95]At the time when Upton Sinclair declared that "this war must be fought until there has been a thorough and complete democratization of the governments of Germany and Austria and I say that any agitation for peace which does not include this demand is, whether it realizes it or not, a pro-German agitation" (*The Masses*, September, 1917), when the anarchist, Benjamin R. Tucker, "favored war to the limit" and when John Dewey defended conscription as national expedient, and *The New Republic* demanded that diplomatic relations with Germany should be broken at once, and urged that "the Navy should be mobilized . . . (and) terms and conditions of our entrance into the war should be discussed and announced." (*The Masses* editorial: April, 1917, Vol. IX, No. 6, Issue No. 70, p. 8.)

work, we should not let it blot out the remembrance of many of the literary products of the magazine, particularly the satires of Charles Erskine Scott Wood, later combined into the volume *Heavenly Discourse,* and the poems of Arturo Giovannitti. If Giovannitti was not a great poet, he gave all the promise in those days of future greatness which, unfortunately, was not fulfilled. While in the same magazine Max Eastman with catlike felicity was writing innocuous poems about "Seashore," "Hours," and "The Lovely Bather," and Untermeyer was apostrophizing "Wind and Flame," Arturo Giovannitti was dedicating himself to the task of creating poetry of a more vigorous social order. In *When the Cock Crows,*[96] a poem inspired by the lynching of Frank Little, Giovannitti achieved a degree of poetic power which no other poet of the time, with perhaps the exception of Sandburg at his best, was able to rival.

When *The Masses,* under the pressure of the war-environment, turned into *The Liberator,* at which time John Reed, who later was to die in Soviet Russia and be buried in the Kremlin, resigned from the editorial staff, much of the uncompromising vigor and zeal of the old magazine was lost. *The Liberator* attempted to carry on the same fight which *The Masses* had upheld, and in its way it kept alive what it could of the old impulse. The audience to which *The Masses* had appealed, however, was dispersed, and even where it still remained in contact with the magazine its interests had become so divided that it was no longer willing to follow the old leadership. Moreover, in conjunction with the new development of the times, the leaders themselves had lost the art to lead. Nevertheless, *The Liberator* did publish some important proletarian material, and in its increasingly limited way furthered the proletarian cause. Perhaps the most significant work it published was Floyd Dell's series of

[96]*The Masses,* October, 1917, Vol. IX, No. 12, Issue No. 76, pp. 18–20. Unfortunately, Genevieve Taggard failed to include this poem in her otherwise excellent collection of Masses-Liberator poetry: *May Days.* (New York, 1925.)

essays on *Literature and the Machine Age*. Those essays marked the first appearance in the United States of social criticism, projected from a radical point of view. In those essays, Dell, who had been deeply influenced by Eastman, ventured far in advance of the latter in his interpretation of literature as a reflection of social forces.

Since the demise of *The Liberator* in 1924, when it was combined with the *Soviet Russia Pictorial* and *Labor Herald*, the three magazines appearing under the single title of *The Workers Monthly*, the influence of Eastman and Dell upon the radical literary movement has waned. Even before that, to be precise, Eastman had deserted the American scene and gone to Soviet Russia; when he returned to America it was as a disillusioned Trotskyist, isolated from the left-wing group as a whole. In later years that isolation has deepened instead of disappeared. At the present time, his contact with revolutionary writers has entirely evaporated. Dell's fate has been similar. Although he never went to Soviet Russia, and never allied himself with any hostile factions, he early incurred the enmity of the radical group by continuing to write sentimental novels about modern sophisticates instead of devoting his attention to more serious and significant things. While *Moon Calf*, his first novel, was greeted with enthusiasm by many of the old *Masses* group and *The Liberator* following, his recent novels have been attacked either with determined vigor or contemptuously ignored by radical critics here and abroad.[97]

The organization of *The New Masses* in 1926 signified the next development in the proletarian tradition.[98] Although

[97] In a letter which the author of this book received from Floyd Dell, anent the general criticism of the latter's work by various radical critics, Mr. Dell endeavored to explain the contradiction between his earlier attitude and the nature of his present novels as due to a conflict within himself between his "narcistic impulses and the sexual-social impulses." The letter, which appeared in *The Modern Quarterly* under the title of "A Literary Self-Analysis" (Vol. IV, No. 2, pp. 148–152: June–September, 1927), is important in revealing, in admirably honest fashion, something of the conflict which has not only affected Mr. Dell's work but also that of many other radicals of the old days—and the present day too.

[98] In the critical field, the organization of *The Modern Quarterly*, in

Joseph Freeman, James Rorty, and Edmont Arens were on the staff along with Michael Gold, it was Gold who soon came to dominate the spirit of the magazine. Before Rorty's resignation not long after the magazine had begun, Gold's influence had been limited by the conflicting ideas which existed as to precisely what the policy of the magazine should be. After the resignation of Rorty, however, and the departure of Arens, Gold became the moving force in the new organization. In the last few years, indeed, it was Gold who, aided by the indefatigable labors of Walt Carmon, kept *The New Masses* alive. Until recently, when a new editorial board was chosen for the magazine, Gold acted as its sole editor. While it cannot be claimed that *The New Masses* made marked headway under Gold's editorship, it can certainly be said that Gold's editorials which for several years appeared regularly each month were frequently among the best pieces of left-wing writing that America has seen in the last decade. In addition to Gold's contributions, important work has appeared in *The New Masses* from the pens of Joseph Freeman, Whittaker Chambers, Paul Peters, Langston Hughes, A. McGill, Joshua Kunitz, and Herman Spector.

The New Masses, notwithstanding its title, began as an extension of *The Liberator* rather than of the old *Masses,* for what had been so vigorous about the latter magazine, its critical articles and editorials, found little place in the new magazine, whereas what had become artiness with a clever, radical twist in *The Liberator* became equally suitable food for *The New Masses.* Once the editorial conflicts were ironed out, however, resulting in the resignation of the thwarting presences of several of the obdurate editors, and Michael Gold acquired comparatively full charge of the policy of the

1923, had marked another extension of the same tradition. *The Modern Quarterly* has featured above everything else criticism of the arts and of society from a Marxian point of view. Among the numerous proletarian critics whose work has appeared in its pages are Joseph Freeman, Michael Gold, Joshua Kunitz, Bernard Smith, Max Eastman, Walter Long, Joseph Vanzler, Huntley Carter, and others.

magazine, the whole project assumed a different character. It then became an exclusively proletarian magazine, which unlike both *The Masses* and *The Liberator,* aimed to make its main appeal direct to the workers instead of to the intelligentzia. If the magazine so far has not succeeded in achieving that aim it certainly has not been due to lack of zeal on the part of the editor—or the present editorial board.

At the present time, with the exception of *Left,*[99] which has had only two issues, *The New Masses* is the only proletarian magazine in America which is functioning in the field of creative literature. In its way, with an enthusiasm that is altogether laudable, it is trying to encourage workers as well as writers to express themselves in its pages, and if it has not yet succeeded in discovering any great abundance of rich talent, it unquestionably has provided a stirring medium for the communication of social protest of a proletarian cast. Unfortunately, in its zeal for things proletarian, it too often fails to realize that proletarian art as well as bourgeois art has to be art if it is to be significant. The proletariat as well as the bourgeoisie and the aristocracy deserves good art for its inspiration. If a painter sets out to make a portrait or a mass drawing it is important that he possess the technical knowledge and skill which are necessary to make it effective as well as the proletarian ideology which should give it direction. Just as in Soviet Russia the importance of the expert is continuously emphasized, and special training is being constantly provided for the workers in order to make them into experts, so in America in whatever field we turn, to that of painting and sculpture, or that of literature and engineering, the proletariat needs men and women who are trained and equipped to master whatever materials it is their function to work with and mould. In providing such a training-ground for young proletarian writ-

[99]There is also a small magazine, appearing in mimeographed form, entitled *Left Writers,* which has appeared within the last year. *Left Writers,* however, is more critical than creative in vein, and so far has not won a very wide reading public.

ers, *The New Masses* is serving an excellent purpose; when
it tends to exalt their work as proletarian art, however, it
falls into error—and an error which is thwarting to the
development of the proletarian tradition.

In *Literature and Revolution,* Trotsky deals with that
problem in illuminating detail. "Weak poems do not make
up proletarian poetry," he contended, "because they do not
make up poetry at all. . . . It would be monstrous to con-
clude that the technique of bourgeois art is not necessary to
the workers. Yet there are many who fall into this error.
'Give us,' they say, 'something even pock-marked, but our
own!' This is false and untrue. A pock-marked art is no art
and is therefore not necessary to the working masses. Those
who believe in a 'pock-marked' art are imbued to a considerable extent with contempt for the masses."[100] It is that
lesson which our proletarianists must learn or proletarian
art in this country will be hindered instead of accelerated in
its growth.

Genuine proletarian criticism has seldom sought to deny
the importance of literary values because of its desire for
social significances. On the contrary, except in the United
States, revolutionary critics have often been harder task-
masters from the point of literary quality than æsthetic
critics. Scarcely any critic, for instance, has emphasized the
importance of the formal element in art any more than the
Russian Marxist, Plechanov. Plechanov always insisted upon
the importance of the formal element in art as well as the
social. Mehring, the leading Marxian critic of literature in
Germany during the last century, was no less exacting in his
demand for formal excellence as well as social significance.
Trotsky, as we have noted, was even more severe in his stress
upon formal value as well as social. Friche, in Soviet Russia,
was equally strict in his formalistic emphasis. Even such
American Marxians as Joshua Kunitz and Sidney Hook—
although Hook has done little literary criticism, his Marxian

[100] Leon Trotsky: *Literature and Revolution:* New York, 1925: pp. 202,
204.

position in reference to literature is in keeping with this tradition—maintain the same position.

The revolutionary critic should demand as much of the art he endorses as the reactionary. No revolutionary critic, for example, should deny that art in itself, in whatever form, is a trade just as pottery-making is, and as a trade it has its technique which has to be mastered if that which is produced is to be worthwhile. *Revolutionary art has to be good art first before it can have deep meaning,* just as apples in a revolutionary country as well as in a reactionary country have to be good apples before they can be eaten with enjoyment. The fact that the pottery or the apples are the products of a revolutionary culture—that is, made or grown by revolutionists—does not of itself, or by any kind of special magic, make them good. It simply gives them a new form of ideological identification. Eisenstein's and Pudowkin's films are great not because they are communist—there are many communist films that are not great—but because they are *great* first in their formal organization, and then greater still because of the social purpose which they serve.

The revolutionary proletarian critic does not aim to underestimate literary craftsmanship. What he contends is simply that literary craftsmanship is not enough. The craftsmanship must be utilized to create objects of revolutionary meaning. Only through this synthesis does the revolutionary critic believe that art can serve its most important purpose to-day. Revolutionary meanings without literary craftsmanship constitute as hopeless a combination from the point of view of the radical critic as literary craftsmanship without revolutionary purpose. If proletarian literature fails in so many instances in America, it is not because it is propagandistic—most of the literature of the world has been propagandistic in one way or another, including even that of William Shakespeare and George Bernard Shaw—but because it is lacking in qualities of craftsmanship.

In a word, the revolutionary critic does not believe that we can have art without craftsmanship; what he does believe is that, granted the craftsmanship, our aim should be to make art serve man as a thing of action and not man serve art as a thing of escape.

Before turning to the leading proletarian writers in America to-day let us venture a few definitions in order to avoid unnecessary confusion on the part of the reader. Proletarian writers are not necessarily proletarians, any more than Marx or Lenin were proletarians, but they are writers who are imbued with a proletarian ideology instead of a bourgeois one. They are writers who have adopted the revolutionary point of view of the proletarian ideology, and who try to express that ideology in their work. That often they fail in such expression is inevitable in a transitional stage of society such as we are living in to-day. This much should be clear, however, and that is that proletarian writers are not to be confused with literary rebels. Literary rebels believe in revolt in literature; left-wing, that is proletarian, writers believe in revolt in life. The literary rebels, for example, who became the advocates of free verse as opposed to conventional verse must not be associated with proletarian writers, who are opposed to the society in which we live and aim to devote their literature to its transformation.

Proletarian writers, then, are more interested in social revolt than in literary revolt. As a group they are convinced that present-day industrial society is based upon exploitation and injustice; that it creates distress and misery for the many and brings happiness only to the few; that its dedication to the ideal of profit instead of use is destructive of everything fine and inspiring in life; and that until its private-property basis is destroyed and replaced by the social control of all property, the human race will never be able to escape the horrors of unemployment, poverty, and war.

More than that, proletarian writers believe that their literature can serve a great purpose only when it contributes, first, toward the destruction of present-day society, and, second, toward the creation of a new society which will embody, like Soviet Russia to-day, a social, instead of an individualistic, ideal. Unlike Ibsen, they do not ask questions and then refuse to answer them. Unlike the iconoclasts, they are not content to tear down the idols and stop there. Their aim is to answer questions as well as ask them, and to provide a new order to replace an old one. Their attitude, therefore, is a positive instead of a negative one.

In the mainstream of the proletarian tradition to-day are to be found a fresh group of authors who have supplanted the earlier dominancy of Eastman and Dell. In creative field this leadership has been seized by such novelists as John Dos Passos, Michael Gold, and Charles Yale Harrison; in the critical field this leadership has already begun to fall upon such men as Sidney Hook, Joseph Freeman, Bernard Smith, and Joshua Kunitz. In the pages of the two leading radical magazines in America at the present time, *The New Masses* and *The Modern Quarterly*, the former devoted mainly to the creative field and the latter chiefly to the critical, most of these authors have found literary expression.

The success of John Dos Passos has been the most important event in the history of the American left-wing movement in literature. Adopted as one of its leading authors by a long-established, significant publishing house, Harper and Brothers—within the last few months Dos Passos has left Harper and Brothers and joined the list of Harcourt, Brace —Dos Passos has had the advantage of being brought before a larger reading public than any radical writer in recent years save Upton Sinclair. Ever since the appearance of his war novel *Three Soldiers,* Dos Passos has moved steadily toward the left. In *Manhattan Transfer* this leftness was already apparent although not yet formulated. In his present trilogy, which is still unfinished, and of which *42nd Parallel* was the first part, and *1919* is the second, his left-wing outlook has already crystallized into a challenge. Convinced that American society cannot continue in its present capitalistic form, Dos Passos believes that the only way out is through a social revolution which will emancipate the workers from their present state of subjection to the industrialists. In his articles as well as in his novels, in prose that is perhaps richer and more rhythmic and varied than that of any other American writer to-day, he has communicated the spirit of his philosophy with an impact which has overwhelmed even the more conservative critics. No other left-wing writer in America at this time has won such sweeping approval from the public and the press. *Manhattan Transfer* and *42nd Parallel* not only were best-sellers for a considerable period, but stirred the American reading public as well as the critics from a state of moral lethargy into one of new realization. Here was an American author writing novels in a new style, with fresh impulse and progressive vision, who had something to say and knew how to say it. Whatever he touched he made into art—an art which lingered and lasted long after first glimpse and appreciation. It was this first-rate artistry of conception and execution which early gave John Dos Passos the most significant position in the radical literary movement in America to-day.

Michael Gold, whose *Jews Without Money* was one of the most popular novels—or shall we call it autobiography?—in 1930, is the second most important revolutionary writer in this country. Michael Gold has been in the left-wing literary movement much longer than John Dos Passos and for that reason he has exerted, no doubt, greater influence over young revolutionary writers than his literary compatriot. In his younger days, Michael Gold was one of Max Eastman's protégés. It was under Eastman's influence that Gold grew up in the radical literary movement. Later on, when Eastman went to Europe, Gold played a more important part on the editorial staff of *The Liberator*, and as we have seen, when *The New Masses* was begun in the middle of the twenties, Gold became the leading power in the organization. Gold is not a logical, dialectical thinker. A poet by nature, his conclusions spring from him with a fury that often seems more instinctive than rational, and yet there is in this very fury, susceptible as it is to sentimentalism at times, a kind of literary beauty born of biblical simplicity and candor. This forthright power of style which characterizes Gold's writing to-day is a recent acquisition. Present in *Jews Without Money* and in his editorials and reviews which have been written in the last two years, it was absent from most of his earlier work. Gold's first book, *120 Million,* was lacking in that stylistic power. Even his plays, *Hoboken Blues* and *Fiesta,* were crude efforts in comparison with his later work. It is very likely that in the book he is now writing, a life of John Reed, his growing literary powers will attain full focus.

Charles Yale Harrison, another radical writer, who won distinction with the publication of his novel *Generals Die in Bed* is a direct product of the influence of Michael Gold and *The New Masses* school. While Harrison has not advanced as far as Dos Passos or Gold, his work gives greater evidence of growth than that of any other left-wing fictionist except the aforementioned pair. If his second novel, *A Child Is Born,* was lacking in certain of the literary excellences characteristic of the best work of Dos Passos and Gold, it was really more "left" in spirit than the work of either of those writers.

The manner in which these men have attacked our industrial society differs very sharply from the method employed by Upton Sinclair. Upton Sinclair's method of attack was, and still is, an oversimplified one. What Sinclair has always done has been to flay an evil with mannikins instead of men; he has visualized a situation, conceived of its totality in terms of his theme, and then made his characters fit into that situation in order to illustrate its logic. As a result his characters have become the appendages of action instead of the creators of action, and have been no more real than puppets on parade. For that very reason many of Sinclair's most vigorous attacks upon the capitalist system have failed of their purpose. John Dos Passos, Michael Gold, and Charles Yale Harrison have escaped that fallacy. They do not start out with a specific situation and then harness their characters to it with artificial reins. They fuse character and situation in such a subtle way that what they attack becomes all the more tragic.

In *Jews Without Money* Michael Gold does not erect his characters on stilts, and then, by means of a highly synthetic plot, try to force them to walk like natural men. On the contrary, he makes his characters walk on their own legs and in their own environment. The Jews he describes come to life in the pages of his novel because he is more interested in communicating the horrible tragedy of their lives by means of their personal suffering and deprivation than by means of a carefully contrived plot which aims, in its ramifications, to communicate the same tragedy. In the case of Gold the approach is more emotional than intellectual, which is the necessary approach for the creation of that emotional reaction which is the aim of art; in the case of Sinclair the approach is more intellectual than emotional, which is the approach that is better adapted to critical literature than to creative.

The approach of John Dos Passos is more in line with Gold's than with Sinclair's. Dos Passos, like Gold, makes his characters live by virtue of their own flesh and blood rather than by virtue of the ideas which they are supposed to convey. They are, therefore, emotional creations rather than conceptual ones. *Manhattan Transfer*, *42nd Parallel*, and *Jews Without Money*, as a consequence, are better indictments of present-day society than *Mountain City*, *Roman Holiday*, or *The Wet Parade*.

Proletarian criticism has been strengthened in the last decade by the appearance of a number of vigorous critics. The four who stand out most conspicuously are Sidney Hook, Joshua Kunitz, Bernard Smith, and Joseph Freeman. Hook's criticism has been confined mainly to philosophy, and thus has had little effect upon the literary direction of left-wing writers, however much of an influence it has had upon other sections of the left-wing movement. Without doubt, Hook, who is associated with the department of philosophy at New York University, is one of the most important critical thinkers produced by the radical movement in America in the last decade. Joshua Kunitz in *The Jew in Russian Literature* contributed a most important addition to Marxian criticism in America. Kunitz's work received as high praise in the liberal and radical press in England as in this country. Bernard Smith, formerly associate editor of *The New Masses,* in divers articles and reviews has applied the left-wing method in a more specific sense than any of these other writers. At the present time he is writing a left-wing *History of American Criticism* which will embody his critical approach in more conclusive form. Joseph Freeman, perhaps the most brilliant of these critics, with the exception of his contribution to the trifold critical volume, *Voices of October,* and his collaboration with Scott Nearing in the composition of *Dollar Diplomacy,* has confined his radical criticism to the magazines. If his work has had less influence than some of the others, it has been only because it has appeared with less frequency and less consecutiveness.

By way of conclusion, it is worth while to note the presence of certain other writers whose work deserves mention as close to, if not an intrinsic part of, the proletarian tradition. In this connection the work of Edwin Seaver at once suggests itself. While Seaver has hovered about the skirts of the left-wing movement for many years he has never become a part of it in an intimate sense of the word. Eight years ago when he founded his modernistic magazine, *1924,* which is now effete, he was much farther removed from the left-wing tradition than he is to-day. In his first novel, *The Company,* which was published in 1930, there were new signs of his movement toward the left. In more recent days he has begun to swing still more to the left, as his work in *The New Masses* attests. Samuel D. Schmalhausen, whose interests have been more psychological than literary, has made, nevertheless, striking psychoanalytic contributions to left-wing criticism. Agreeing with Radek that criticism should effect a fusion of Marx and Freud, Schmalhausen has pursued a somewhat different path from that followed by other revolutionary critics in America. Nor should Em Jo Basshe be forgotten. Although Basshe has been silent for the past few years, it was he, along with Michael Gold, who dominated the experimental left-wing theatre, The New Playwrights Theatre, in which such left-wing plays as Gold's *Hoboken Blues*, John Dos Passos' *Airways Inc.*, John Howard Lawson's *The Loudspeaker*, Paul Sifton's *The Belt*, and his own plays, *The Centuries* and *Earth*, were produced. Gifted with a greater genius for the theatre than any of his other left-wing associates, Basshe soon came to exercise a marked influence over young left-minded dramatists. At the present time, as winner of a Guggenheim fellowship, Basshe is in Europe studying radical drama there. Harry A. Potamkin, quondam editor of *The Guardian*, has deserted literary criticism at the present moment for cinema criticism. In this latter field, he is unquestionably the only proletarian critic of established position.

In the light of the changes which are already in the process of transforming our society in a most drastic way, there is little hazard in the statement that within the next five years we shall witness a rapid growth in the proletarian tradition in American literature.[101]

[101] There is an abundance of literature about the workers that has begun to spring up in America in recent years, and while much of it has not been proletarian in ideology, it has marked a change in outlook on the part of American writers who in the past have tended to eschew the proletariat as fictional material. Among the more interesting expressions of this tendency have been such novels as Agnes Smedley's *Daughter of Earth*, Louis Colman's *Lumber*, and such plays as Paul Sifton's *The Belt*, and *1931*, Hallie Flanagan and Margaret Ellen Clifford's *Can You Hear Their Voices?* and Paul Peters's *Wharf Nigger*. The Flanagan and Clifford play, it is interesting to note, was produced as one of the Vassar Experimental Theatre Plays. In addition, *The New Masses* has printed some striking work by H. H. Lewis and Jack Conroy which possesses a proletarian emphasis. Lewis's new volume of poetry, *Thinking of Russia*, marks a definite growth in his talent.

Chapter VII

LIBERATION

IN the previous chapters we have endeavored to trace the social changes which have occurred in American life and shown their reflection in the literature of the nation. It should not be thought, however, that the relationship between social life and literature is one in which the latter is an inevitable reflex of the former. On the contrary, they are both part of the same phenomenon, and interact upon each other in the process of change. The literary artist is not, therefore, as many people think, a hopeless victim of his environment, but is a creative part of it, able to help shape and rebuild it. Although he derives his ideas and direction from the social environment, he in turn, by virtue of those same ideas and direction, is able to assist in the transformation of that environment.

At the present time, for example, the artist is faced with an environment which is in a stage of dissolution, an environment in which the tentacles of the past have lost their grip, in which old traditions have broken down and new ones, in America at least, have scarcely been able to more than begin to form. An old America—an old world in fact—is in the process of dying, and a new one, still in the chrysalis stage, is struggling to be born. The artist can ally himself with that old world, either by accepting it tough-mindedly, as do Henry L. Mencken and Joseph Hergesheimer, as the best that we can expect, or, as does Joseph Wood Krutch, by tender-mindedly despairing of the possibility of a new world creating anything but a fresh reign of barbarism. The attempt to make the romantic escape to a world of fantasy, as does Cabell,[1] or the religious escape, as does T. S. Eliot, are but other forms of the tender-minded acceptance. On the other hand, the artist can reject the old world by subscribing to the possibilities of the new, believing, as do the proletarian artists of to-day, that it can create a superior sense of values and a loftier literary vision. There is no in-between path which can be pursued. The artist can no more escape the contradictions in contemporary life, the maladjustment of man and mass, the fusion of steam and steel with mind and soul, than can the educator, the physician, or the nameless man in the street.

Within the last few years, especially since the Wall Street crash in 1929, America has entered a new and more critical stage in its history. While the struggle between the big bourgeoisie and the petty bourgeoisie had been settled insofar as fighting was concerned even before the decade of the twenties, it was the developments of industrial enterprise in the twenties which put the final quietus on the struggle, leaving the petty bourgeoisie in a state of blind and helpless retreat. The Democratic party, which in 1912 had still represented the interests of the petty bourgeoisie, had already begun to ally itself with the interests of big business by the turn of the twenties. The twenties furthered that alliance. A number of the small industries, headed by individuals who were members of the Democratic party, were transformed into large industries during that decade, and it was those individuals whose interests had become identified with those of big business who secured control of the party. At the present time, for instance, the dominant controls in the Democratic party, represented by such big business men as Raskob, DuPont, and others, are more definitely allied to big business than to small business. This change, reflecting the surrender of the petty bourgeoisie on the political field as well

[1]Cabell's recent change of name, from James Branch Cabell to Branch Cabell, signifying as he states his reversion from romanticism to realism, from Poictesme to reality, promises little that is significant in this new vein, that is if his new book is indicative of the nature of the change that has come over him.

as on the economic, predicates the beginning of a new epoch in the political as well as economic life of the nation. The petty bourgeoisie, becoming more and more absorbed into the maw of the industrial structure and shot off into the proletariat, can no longer function as a decisive force in the country. Even in 1924, when LaFollette arose as the political and economic defender of the petty bourgeoisie, declaring himself in favor of a return of the days of 1776 and an opponent of all forms of trusts and monopolies, the petty bourgeois challenge had lost its sting. If the boom years which preceded the crash of 1929 saved the petty bourgeoisie for a time from appreciating the real nature of its status, the panic years which followed taught it the truth about its situation. At this very moment the remaining strength of the petty bourgeoisie is being sapped at the root by the economic crisis which is upon us. Although when this panic is over and the wheels of industry begin to run once more, the petty bourgeoisie will not vanish as a class, it will never be able to regain even the waning vigor which it possessed before the crisis. The entire direction of our economic life will prevent it.

It is this collapse of the petty bourgeoisie which is helping to prepare the way for the rise of the proletariat. Along with the breakdown of the petty bourgeois ideology will disappear, slowly perhaps but steadily, the petty-bourgois-minded outlook of the American proletariat. As the conditions of economic life make it impossible for the petty bourgeois philosophy to inveigle the masses any longer with its promise of individual opportunity and advance, the American working class, in line with the European working classes, will adopt a proletarian ideology in keeping with the realization of its new status. The very structure of industrial enterprise in America at the present time is inevitably bound to increase the strength of the proletariat at the same time that it weakens the position of the petty bourgeoisie.

Nothing has revealed so well what has happened to the tradition of the petty bourgeoisie as the change which has

come over American literature in the last thirty years. In the
nineteenth century, before the Civil War, when the frontier
was in full swing and the petty bourgeois ideology filled the
minds of the lower classes with faith in the future, the
dominant note in American literature was optimistic. Emerson and Whitman, as we have shown, adopted that faith as
a living thing. Thoreau, Alcott, and even Melville shared
something of that faith. Twain translated it into humor and
satire. The humorists of the period turned it into a comic
tradition. Not even Longfellow, despite the coming of tragedy into his life, and notwithstanding the fact that the West,
except in terms of the Indian, meant little to him, seldom
surrendered to the pessimistic strain. Whittier did not even
allow his anti-slavery tirades to destroy the essential optimism
of his spirit. Holmes and Lowell were convinced optimists to
the end. And Howells, the last of the nineteenth-century optimists, epitomized the philosophy of them all when he declared that "the more smiling aspects of life are the more
American." These men, except for an occasional contradiction
here and there, believed in individualism, in democracy, and
most of them in equality. They envisioned the future in
terms of the fulfillment of those traditions. Progress for them
meant the advance of those ideas and principles. Then came
the close of the century and the inauguration of the next,
and darkness came upon the land of their faith. The petty
bourgeois principles they had believed in were sacrificed to
the industrial machine; individualism began to lose its pertinence in the new scene; democracy faded as a political
panacea; and equality lost its meaning as industry began to
divide the nation off into more and more widely separated
classes. Toward the close of the century, the realization of
this change had already begun to penetrate into literature
through the works of Hamlin Garland and Frank Norris.
Since that time the dominant note in American literature has
become overwhelmingly pessimistic. From the time that
realism advanced beyond the reticent radius of Howells,
American literature has steadily become more and more

minor in its key. Twain, as we have seen, witnessed the death of his democratic faith, and became more pessimistic in his philosophy than Schopenhauer. Dreiser arose as a titan among twentieth-century pessimists. In fact, with but few exceptions, American literature throughout the century, extending through Dreiser, Anderson, Lewis, O'Neill, and Hemingway, has been impregnated with the spirit of despair.

This change in American literature, from a literature of hope to one of despair, signifies the rise and fall of the petty bourgeois tradition. With the passing of that tradition, in city and country, the future could no longer hold out hope for the individual or for democracy.

In many cases as the individual writer has lost his faith in social reality, he has become increasingly more detached from the group, and been forced to turn inward instead of outward for his materials as well as his inspiration. The chaos which has resulted from his loss of faith has left him bewildered and desolate. The sickness of the ego to-day, tortured as it is by its disalliance with the group, has found many of its most striking manifestations in the work of men who have striven in most desperate earnest to discover something of clarity in the present chaos. The breakdown of consciousness and the rapid deterioration of rationality and normality which have sprung out of this sickness of the ego have attained amazing and arresting expression in the works of Eugene O'Neill and Robinson Jeffers. Overwhelmed by the age that is upon him, and driven within himself for a solution of the contradictions which that age represents, O'Neill has fumbled and floundered in every direction in an attempt to find truth and free it from its fetters. Mentally bandaged as he is by a world which has provided no faith for him to live by or accept, his excursions into the psychic frontiers of personality have resulted only in a kind of magnificent confusion. In play after play he has endeavored to escape that confusion—but the confusion only mounts and multiplies. Brilliant with insights into individual personalities as his

plays always are, nowhere do they catch up with those personalities in terms of those deeper values, which reveal the
relationship between personality and civilization. In Soph-
ocles, Shakespeare, Racine, Moliere, that relationship is clear
and unmistakable. In fact, it was the certainty of that relationship which gave such admirable clarity and strength to
their dramas. It is the pathology of our age, the hospital-
like atmosphere in which our civilization has its being, which
prevents O'Neill's mind from attaining such clarity and his
dramas from achieving such strength. If we consider for a
minute such a play as *Dynamo,* which is one of O'Neill's
most realistic dramas, we shall see at once wherein that lack
of clarity and conviction exists. *Dynamo* is a play of the
machine age. In it the machine becomes a mystic force, a
monster, a god. Everything in the drama is subservient to
the machine, reflecting its dooming magic. The awe-inspiring
whirl of dynamos runs like mysterious undertone throughout every act. But, when all is said, only a sick malaise of
spirit emerges from its climax. It is not the fact of defeat
which evokes that sickness. After all, the Greek tragedies
ended in defeat also, but it was heroic defeat. In *Dynamo,*
it is a defeat that does not even satisfy or convince. The
dedication of Ralph to the dynamo, even his sexual consecration to it, failed to convince the spectator. The climax is
too direct a plunge into madness to move an audience with
its horror. The catastrophe is a sick catastrophe instead of a
great tragic one.

In Robinson Jeffers another aspect of literary pathology
emerges into the foreground. Jeffers envisions the world as
a monstrous miscarriage of fate. Believing that we are much
closer to the animals than to the angels, he is much more
fascinated by instinctive man than by intellectual man. In
Tamar the incest motif blazes into the poem like a challenging meteor. It is not the incest of Jean Cocteau's *Les Enfants
Terribles* or Gunther's *Room in Berlin,* but a potent, world-
defying incest which is as furious as it is unashamed. More
than that, this incest of Jeffers is not the incest of *Œdipus*

Rex. In the Greek tragedy incest is the great crime to eschew; with Jeffers there is the exultant sense of victory, the victory of the instinctive over the intellectual. Jeffers is more than il-logical; he is a-logical in his whole approach to life. Only God remains for him, with whom by subduing ourselves we may finally become one—if we have the courage to face our doom. Never has such desperately dooming poetry been written in this century, never such mad, chaotic, crucifying verse which overwhelms by a power that is more thunderous than tragic. The tragedies of Æschylus are not pathologic; the tragedies of Jeffers are pathologic. Æschylean tragedies are a direct reflection of a sturdy civilization; Jeffers' tragedies are a reflection of the violent toppling-ruins of a dying civilization. Like tortured introverts, contemporary writers have turned in every direction in an endeavor to discover new reservoirs of impulse within themselves, explored every emotion in an attempt to find new strength, exploited every idea in a desperate hope of creating a new ideal. Lost in the pathologic loneliness of individuality detached from the social strength of the group, they have battered against the walls of personality, bludgeoned their way into the catacombs of the unconscious, and with maniacal determination released the instinctual energies of primeval man which still live within the human frame. Aided by psychoanalysis, which gave them new weapons, many of the poets and novelists and dramatists of our day have dug into the most perverse of human complexes, exposing them with the scalpel of a surgeon rather than that of a philosopher. Incest, homosexuality and all the madnesses which go with minds perverted out of normal function, make up their repertoire of revelation.

II

While American literature, then, has been plunged from optimism into pessimism and from order into chaos, it has at the same time liberated itself from two handicaps, namely, the colonial complex and the petty bourgeois censor, which combined weighed down upon it so heavily in the past that it was almost impossible for it to soar. Its pessimism and its chaos are the products of the passing of an old tradition, and old faith, and the failure on the part of its writers to discover a new tradition and a new faith. The liberation from that pessimism and chaos can only follow when that new tradition and faith are found.

But it is not only the decay of the petty bourgeois ideology which has driven literature to such confusion and despair. It is the decay of the whole middle class way of existence, that of the upper bourgeoisie as well as the petty bourgeoisie, which has robbed the contemporary writer in Europe as well as in America of his faith in life, and left him without beliefs or convictions. The sickness and sham which underlay the nature of middle-class life is no longer concealed from him. He can see through it as easily as he can see through a sophomoric literary conceit. It is the whole middle class, he realizes, that has broken down, the middle class with its ogle-eyed morality, penetrating into every corner and crevice of life; the middle class with its hypocrisies and deceptions, justifying slavery as an aid to Christian conversion and defending democracy as a means of mass coercion. Aristocracies, whatever else may be said in attack upon them, seldom needed such deception. The Divine Right of Kings was the only deception they employed. Aristocracies were based upon force and they openly made that manifest. Aristocracies were built upon the stratification of classes, the lower classes supporting the upper, and no attempt was made to hide that fact from commoner or lord. The power of the aristocracy was flaunted rather than concealed. Aristocratic society, thus, living though it did upon the masses as has every ruling class, was more forthright and infinitely less deceptive than middle-class society, which has maintained itself by virtue of the most vicious technique ever employed by any ruling class in historic times. Aided by the printing-press and the development of literacy which was necessary to its own rise, the middle class had managed to construct such a civilization of lies, warping, distorting, and throttling the very attempt of the mind to face reality itself, that only to-day, with the breakdown of that class, are we able to appreciate the catastrophic extent to which human thought and impulse were sold out to the burgher. Thus putatively the most moral of all ruling classes was fundamentally the most immoral. Having built its civilization upon a most flagrant lie, it is no wonder that it was this class which, as a defense mechanism, had to advertise truth as a holy ideal. The most dishonest of all classes in practice, it had to be this class which exalted "honesty as the best policy," and sanctioned the theft of wealth in Wall Street but threw up its hands in righteous horror at its occurrence in the corner grocery store. More than that, it was this class whose power was as obviously based upon force as that of any previous ruling class, which managed to sell the idea to the people—and to the intelligentzia—that its rule was dependent upon choice rather than compulsion. Utilizing the democratic idea, it succeeded in making the masses believe that they had as much to say in the choice of government as the financier and industrialist. But not only the masses were deceived by it; the whole mentality of the period was poisoned by it.

It will only be generations later, in the light of a more remote perspective, that we shall completely realize the full extent to which middle-class rule closed and corrupted the better possibilities of the human mind. The mind, despite all that middle-class pundits have contended to the contrary, is a social product, and its operation is contingent upon the culture which nurtures it. Middle-class culture driven to a deception in its economic defense, justifying exploitation as a virtue and competition as a sign of progress, translated the contradiction of its economic life into every form of human endeavor. The myth of the free worker, free to work for an exploiting employer when his work was a source of profit and free to starve when his work was not, found its parallel in politics with the myth of equal suffrage, in education with the myth of equal opportunity, and in religion with the myth of equal salvation. The contradiction inherent in each of these myths invaded and debauched economic, political, educational, and religious thought, made philosophy into an intellectual mausoleum for escape and converted the so-called social sciences into mental laboratories for the distillation of ruling-class dogmas. Nothing was unaffected by this process of intellectual prostitution which it set into motion and perpetuated by its subsidized universities, its privately controlled newspapers and magazines, and its endowed Sunday-schools and churches with its lickspittle parsons and priests.

It would be absurd to think that the literature produced by such a culture could do anything more than reflect its deceptions. And that is exactly what its literature did. The fighting spirit which characterized the middle class and electrified it with creative energy in its early struggles against the aristocracy expired with the generation that followed the French Revolution. At the height of its conflict with the aristocracy the middle class was candidly and creatively revolutionary, and in England that revolutionary spirit took fire in the minds and hearts of the young Wordsworth, Coleridge, Shelley, and Byron, and even set Burns aflame with its fervor and moved the mystical Blake to outbursts of romantic enthusiasm. With the passing of that generation that enthusiasm and fervor ended. As soon as the middle class got into power its revolutionary spirit decayed, and it became as reactionary as the aristocracy which it had displaced. It was from that point on that the middle-class ideology established its hegemony of deception.

Although nineteenth-century civilization was built upon those contradictions and deceptions, nineteenth-century authors believed that those deceptions were truths, and, therefore, had a working faith from which to draw their inspiration. Twentieth-century authors, cognizant at last that those deceptions were lies and not truths, have no such faith from which to derive their strength. At best they can but break down further the barriers of personality, and, verging still deeper into the pathologic, attempt to dig closer into the roots of the subjective—or, to pursue an easier course, launder their art with the literary starch of sophisticated futility. If they turn to the outside world, they can only be reporters, like the "hard-boiled" school of American fiction to-day, and not interpreters. Interpretation, which is one of the most significant functions of art, is beyond them. Having no chart of values, interpretation is impossible. Products themselves of middle-class culture, they can no longer find meaning in so-called middle-class idealism.

Caught in such a contradiction, American writers of to-day, although liberated from the affliction of the colonial complex and the petty bourgeois moral code, are liable to plunge into an even deeper chaos and despair, unless they can succeed in allying themselves with the growing proletarian tradition. The only writers of importance in America to-day who have not surrendered to the pessimism and pathology which are predominant in American literature are those who are exponents of the proletarian outlook: John Dos Passos, Michael Gold, and Charles Yale Harrison. As the petty bourgeois ideology continues to wither at the root, more and more of the literati tend to swing over to the ideology of the proletariat. Theodore Dreiser's recent adoption of the proletarian point of view is only one of many such conversions. Edmund Wilson, perhaps the best literary critic from an æsthetic point of view that this country possesses, startled the liberal reading world some months ago with an article in *The New Republic,* in which he asserted his belief that the capitalist world was nearing its end and that a communist world would arise in its place. In a more recent article which appeared in the "What I Believe" series in *The Nation,*[2] he elaborated still further upon his point of view, declaring that he had "a special interest in the success of the 'intellectual' kind of brains as opposed to the acquisitive kind," and urging artists to ally themselves not with the capitalists but with the proletarians who "will remodel society by the power of imagination and thought." Newton

[2]*The Nation,* January 27, 1932: Vol. 134, No. 3473, pp. 95–98.

Arvin, the author of an authoritative biography of Hawthorne and a well-known critic, was scarcely less explicit in
his declaration in favor of the proletarian viewpoint. In an
article entitled *Individualism and American Writers,* which
also appeared in *The Nation*,[3] he stated that "now that American writers, consciously or unconsciously, have made their
final break with the middle class, it should be obvious
that, unless they prefer a bleak or an elegant futility, they
can turn in but one direction, to the proletariat." Waldo
Frank in his new book on Soviet Russia, which is soon to
be published, has moved far closer to the left than he has
ever done in the past. Other American writers who have
allied themselves more definitely with the proletarian position are Sam Ornitz, Lester Cohen, and Granville Hicks.[4]

What is needed in America to-day is a renewed faith in
the masses. American literature has to find something of that
faith in the potentialities of the proletariat which Emerson
and Whitman possessed in the nineteenth century. It was
Emerson, we should remember, who was so enthusiastic about
the civilization which was being created in the West by men
in shirt sleeves, men of unexalted station and plebeian origin,
and who looked to that civilization with its democratic spirit
to transform the country. It was Whitman who was ecstatic
about the fact that it was democratic America which had
elevated the poor man into the lord of creation, and had
made the world recognize "the dignity of the common people." The car-conductors, the steeple-jacks, the bridge-builders, the boiler-makers, the sailors, the firemen, and all the
other members of the working class, Whitman exalted as
representative of the finest essence of humanity. "They begin at the roots of things—at first principles—" he maintained, "and scorn the doctrines founded on mere precedent
and imitation." But the faith in the common man which

[3]Ibid., October 14, 1931: Vol. 133, No. 3458, p. 392.
[4]While a number of these men who have recently moved toward the
left might not be classified as ideologically left by many bonafide left-
wingers, the importance of their swing as an index to social change cannot thereby be denied.

Emerson and Whitman entertained was faith in him as an individual and not as a mass. It was faith in him as an individualist and not as a collectivist. In that sense, their faith was founded upon a false premise; fitting and persuasive enough in their generation it led only to disaster in the next. What we need to-day is a return of that faith in the common man, in the mass, but a faith founded upon a collective instead of an individualistic premise. The faith of Emerson and Whitman belongs to the past, and not to the future. Their belief in the common man was a belief in him as a petty bourgeois individualist; our belief must be in him as proletarian collectivist. In that belief lies the ultimate liberation of American literature—and American life. More, the literature and life of the world, for so long as the vast masses of the population are suppressed by the few, the colossal energy of the race can never be released for creative fulfillment. Just as in its struggle against the feudal aristocracy the middle class with its fresh vigor let loose upon the earth a flood of energy which did not spend itself until it had remade civilization, so the proletariat in the twentieth century with its new impulse can remake the modern world.

Index